Jerusalem Curiosities

Nov. 1, 1993

To my friend
Shoshanah,
With cordial regards.
and best wishes.

Abraham E. Millgram

Jerusalem
CURIOSITIES

ABRAHAM E. MILLGRAM

An Edward E. Elson Book
The Jewish Publication Society

PHILADELPHIA • NEW YORK   5750 • 1990

The publication of this book was made
possible by a gift in honor of
Esther Elson.

© 1990 by Abraham E. Millgram
Printed in the United States of America

Library of Congress Cataloging-in-Publication Data
Millgram, Abraham Ezra, 1901–Jerusalem curiosities / Abraham E.
    Millgram. p.   cm.
    ISBN 0-8276-0358-4
    1. Jerusalem—History—Anecdotes.   2. Jerusalem—
        Description—1981-   3. Shrines—Jerusalem.
        4. Curiosities and wonders—Jerusalem.   I. Title
    DS109.9.M55   1990
    956.94'42—dc20   90-33896
                                                                CIP

Design: ADRIANNE ONDERDONK DUDDEN

To the blessed memory of my lifelong friend
AZRIEL EISENBERG
with every sentiment of love and esteem

Contents

ONE *Curiosities of Former Times* 13

Jerusalem A Buried City • The Empty Jewish Tombs • The Discovery of the Siloam Inscription • The Crucified Jew • The "Roman" Cardo in the Jewish Quarter • Why Jerusalem Did Not Become the Center of Christendom and Islam • The Crusaders' Conquest of the Holy City • King Solomon's Stables • A Church with Blasphemous Inscriptions • The Legacy of the Hospitallers • The King Who Willed His Heart to Jerusalem • Under the Turks, Bakshish Lubricated the Wheels of Life • Napolean's Proclamation "From Jerusalem" • The Colorful Body Guards of Foreign Dignitaries • The Filth That Used to Pervade the Streets of Jerusalem

TWO *Jerusalem the Blessed* 49

"A Spectacle One Might Gaze on Forever" • The Center of the World • "All Roads Lead to Jerusalem" • A City of Many Names • One of the Most Cosmopolitan Cities in the World • The Temple Mount in the Jewish, Christian, and Moslem Traditions • The Would-Be Destroyers of Jerusalem's Walls • Did King David Erect the Tower of David? • Two Mysterious Pools • Water—"Jerusalem's Eternal Problem" • Tomb Dwellers • Beggars • The Curious Architecture of Jerusalem's Old Houses • Old Jerusalem—A City of Alleys and Staircases • Avenue of the Righteous Gentiles • Sharp Bargaining • The Old City at Night • A Revolution in Jerusalem's Architecture

Foreword

A City That Is Lifted Up

Jerusalem is not situated on a picturesque river or a seashore; nor is it surrounded by a countryside with pastoral scenes; nor can it boast of the regularity and harmony of Paris or the massive populations of New York or Tokyo. Yet it transcends them all by its unique charm, its holy shrines, its ancient monuments, and the moving associations that it evokes in the hearts of visitors, be they pilgrims or tourists. Jerusalem is a city that is lifted up. Henry Van Dyke remarks that "twenty-five hundred feet above the level of the sea is not a great height, but," says he, "I can think of no other ancient and world-famous city that stands as high."[1]

Jerusalem is a subject of which the mind of man has never tired. It has been and still is a place of wonder and awe and everlasting interest to people from all over the world. It has been the theater of events that have revolutionized our views and convictions. While other cities boast of their industry and commerce, Jerusalem is proud of its prophets and psalmists, its saints and scholars. The word of God issued forth from Jerusalem and conquered hearts and minds the world over. Jerusalem's "beauty, her majesty, her utter fascination" inspired the psalmist to utter that memorable paean to the Holy City:

Great is the Lord and highly to be praised,
In the city of our God, His holy mountain,
Fair in situation, the joy of the whole earth;
Mount Zion . . . the city of the great King (Ps. 48:2,3).

Visitors in Jerusalem invariably write about the city with fascination and praise. The epic story of Jerusalem, the lyric poetry of its prophets and psalmists, and the hopeful message of its God-inspired teachers still uplift and soothe the soul. No wonder that every shout of jubilation and every cry of anguish that issue forth from Jerusalem are heard throughout the world. No wonder that the hearts of men and women everywhere respond with quickened beats of joy or sorrow, with sympathy and concern to Jerusalem's cry of merriment or affliction. "The very name of Jerusalem on a title page," said Ronald Storrs, "conjures up an image and an emotion which . . . arrests and holds the heart."[2] And Saul Bellow, in his book *To Jerusalem and Back* quotes a story by Isaac Bashevis Singer in which a person looks at the sky in Jerusalem and says: "No, this isn't just an ordinary *khamsin* [heat wave], but a flame from Sinai. The sky above is not just atmosphere, but a heaven with angels, seraphim, God." Bellow resists this type of imagination. "Yet," he states, "I, too, feel that the light of Jerusalem has purifying powers and filters the blood and thoughts: I don't forbid myself the reflection that light may be the outer garment of God."[3]

There isn't a city on earth where so many memories crowd upon a visitor's mind as in Jerusalem. No single foot of ground here seems to be without its stirring history. "The extraordinary fact about Jerusalem is that it has not crumbled under the weight of its own history; it goes on living with a vitality felt in few modern cities."[4] To record the memories that crowd upon one's mind as he enters Jerusalem is a task that has occupied the talents of many writers and continues to do so. The record of these memories begins with the biblical account of David's conquest of the town of Jebus and the transformation of this town into the national and religious center of the tribes of Israel. During the three thousand years that have passed, the city has been beseiged by foreign armies almost fifty times. Israelite, Egyptian, Assyrian, Babylonian, Persian, Greek, Roman, Arab, Crusader, Mongolian, Mameluke, Turkish, British, and Israeli armies have successively entered the city as conquerors and rulers. With the arrival of each conqueror the spoken and written word of Jerusalem was displaced by a new tongue. Hebrew, Aramaic, Greek, and Arabic have dominated the city's life. And today the language of the psalmists and prophets is once more the dominant tongue of Jerusalem.

More than 1,800 years ago the Roman Emperor Hadrian thoroughly destroyed the city and ran a plow over its ruins to signify its death. He built on the city's wreckage a pagan city and named it Aelia Capitolina.

Hadrian thus hoped to erase Jerusalem's name from the map and from the memory of man. But the Holy City rose from its ashes, and pilgrims resumed their journeys to worship at their holy shrines.

It was Jerusalem's ill fortune to have been for centuries a mere provincial town within powerful and ruthless empires. It suffered from corrupt and unscrupulous governments, from extortionate rulers, and from official neglect. By the beginning of the nineteenth century, Jerusalem's population was a mere 15,000 poverty-stricken and disease-ridden inhabitants. During the nineteenth century, however, Jerusalem gradually emerged from its long torpor and started on its path to modernity. Early in that century the Great Powers launched their competitive schemes aimed at inheriting the empire of the Sick Man of Europe whose demise they expected momentarily. Under the respectable cloaks of religion and philanthropy, they established their colonial presences in the Holy City. France, England, Germany, Austria, Italy, and other states built institutions in Jerusalem, looking forward to taking possession of her presumably to safeguard their precious, holy investments. Jerusalem was thus enriched with a multitude of magnificent shrines, ecclesiastical hierarchies, missionary societies, benevolent institutions, and meddling consulates. The city expanded, and large suburbs sprang up outside its fortifications. To the west of the city walls, grew up a large, modern city inhabited almost exclusively by Jews. And to the north, a large Arab suburb arose. Commerce and industry, modern housing, and public facilities were introduced. Some Christian pilgrims deplored the arrival of modernity. Their concept of the Holy City was that of a museum of shrines and holy sites within a medieval setting. Narrow alleys with exotic bazaars, donkeys, camels, and open sewers were the distinguishing characteristics of the Jerusalem of their dreams. They resented the encroachments of such modern facilities as electricity, telephones, and paved streets. Jerusalem's mayor, Teddy Kollek, was once criticized by some pilgrims for modernizing the city. He is reported to have answered them by saying: "You ride to your office in Buicks, but you expect me to ride to my office on a donkey!"

Notwithstanding the city's modernization, the Old City has retained its historic medieval appearance, and it has also remained a biblical city. Where else does one find pools named Hezekiah's Pool, Siloam Pool, and Bethesda Pool? Where else does one hear of springs named Gihon Spring, the Virgin's Fount, En Rogel, and the Fullers' Fountain? And where else does one climb hills named Mount Moriah, Mount Zion, Mount of

Olives, and Mount of Offence? Only in Jerusalem does one meet with biblical hills, valleys, fountains, and pools. In modern Jerusalem the shrines and holy places have been protected and preserved. The winding alleys and narrow bazaars are still teeming with their cosmopolitan throngs. But the sewers are now underground; the alleys are paved; the streets are lighted at night; and running water and electricity have been brought into the dwellings.

These changes have changed little. The visitor still feels the presence of the ancient Holy City, the city where the great monotheistic religions had their birth. For the Jew Jerusalem is still the *Ir Hakodesh,* the City of Holiness; for the Christian the city is still *Terra Sancta,* the Holy Land; and for the Moslem it is still *El Kuds,* the Holy [City]. The three celebrated shrines — the Western (Wailing) Wall, the Holy Sepulchre, and the Dome of the Rock — stand within yards of each other and their proximity bears witness to their close spiritual relationship. And they likewise bear witness to Jerusalem's destiny which inheres to its name, the "City of Peace."

Jerusalem is surrounded by scattered olive trees, entitling the city to claim the olive branch for its emblem. But peace has eluded Jerusalem throughout her three millennia of recorded history, and peace is still not in sight. Indeed some scholars have ventured to forecast Jerusalem's future as dismal and foredoomed. Among these scholars was Arnold Toynbee who stated in his introduction to *Cities of Destiny:*

> If any Jerusalem survives, this will be the Jerusalem of the Wailing Wall and the Holy Sepulchre and the Dome of the Rock, not the Jerusalem that has been David's and Godfrey's and Ben Gurion's secular capital city. [5]

Notwithstanding these gloomy prophesies, Jerusalem is today the capital of an earthly kingdom and is at the same time the Holy City of Judaism, Christianity, and Islam. Jerusalem began its recorded history as the temporal and spiritual center of the Jewish people, and in our day it has resumed its ancient role. Life is not departmentalized into secular and holy spheres any more than human beings are divided into bodies and souls. Nor can Jerusalem thrive as a disembodied holy city. Its destiny is to become a living, earthly city with a divine message for mankind. Jerusalem has already returned to its historic beginnings and is the Holy City and the established capital of the State of Israel. It is hoped that in time it will become "a crown of beauty in the hand of the Lord, and a royal diadem in the open hand of God" (Isa. 62:3).

Preface

That Jerusalem is a holy city for Jews, Christians, and Mohammedans is common knowledge. But not many people are aware that Jerusalem is also a city of strange contradictions and astonishing curiosities. In Jerusalem the sacred and the profane mingle and produce startling results. Elizabeth Anne Finn states in the preface to her novel *Home in the Holy Land:*

> Life in the Holy Land is singular in many respects, but in none more than in the strange mixture of circumstances and events. Associations, sacred and profane, sober and ridiculous, civilized and barbarous, sorrowful and merry, jostle each other in a manner which is hardly to be conceived by those who have not experienced it.[1]

And Charles Warren, whose pioneering archeological work in Jerusalem has gained him world-wide fame, claimed that Jerusalem was "a city of contradictions." "In her," said Warren, "all nature is in disorder; all order would be unnatural."[2] No wonder that Jerusalem has been a happy hunting ground for people with an eye for the odd, the strange, and the curious. Yet no one has ever published a book on the curiosities of Jerusalem. This book, it is hoped, will partially fill this lacuna.

Curiosities have often been confused with trivia, and books dealing with curiosities have been regarded as mere "browsing" matter. They are said to require no intellectual sophistication on the part of the reader, for curiosities are expected to provide only amusement. This characterization can not apply to this volume which not only seeks to provide pleasurable reading but also enables the reader to grasp Jerusalem's unique role in the history of mankind. Too many visitors in Jerusalem see only the surface, leaving virtually untouched by the city's unique charm, its matchless shrines, and its historic monuments. The writer is confident that those who read this book will encounter Jerusalem with eyes that see and hearts that understand. Even the tourist who "does" the city in a couple of days, hurrying from one site to another, will be better equipped to comprehend the wonders of Jerusalem's spiritual and historical phenomena.

The curiosities chosen for this book are the result of much exploration. They were selected with utmost care and arranged in a logical context. The writer hopes that they will delight and inform the readers as much as they have fascinated and enlightened him.

The writer is indebted to a number of friends who helped him in the preparation of the manuscript, among them his friend Howard Schwartz, without whose help this book would have remained unpublished. He read the manuscript, did much editing, and made all arrangements with the publisher. The writer is also grateful to his young colleague, David Geffen, who read the manuscript and encouraged the writer to see it through to publication. Most of all, he is grateful to his son, Hillel, a fellow lover of Jerusalem, who read the material and counseled him on the selection of the curiosities. The writer is also indebted to Hannah Gromi, who prepared the manuscript for printing with dedication and intelligence, and to the staff of the National and University Library in Jerusalem, whose courteous help at all times made his work a blessed adventure.

Finally, the author hopes that those who will do him the honor of perusing these pages will not take the curiosities for more than what they are—a faithful record of impressions and incidents which the writer thought would be read with interest and, he hopes, for intellectual and spiritual enlightenment.

Acknowledgments

Jerusalem Curiosities contains many quotations from books and periodicals. The source of each quotation is provided in the notes section at the end of the book. Each note specifies the author, title of the book or periodical, place and date of publication, and the pages where the excerpt is found.

The author expresses his profound thanks to the publishers and authors who graciously granted permission to include excerpts from their works in this book.

A. P. Watt, Ltd, London, for excerpt from *The New Jerusalem* by G. K. Chesterton.

Mrs. Buchanan-Smith, Alick, M. P., for excerpts from *Historical Geography of the Holy Land* and *Jerusalem* by George Adam Smith.

The Community Church of New York for excerpts from *Palestine Today and Tomorrow* by John Haines Holmes.

The Christian Century (Apr. 12, 1978) for excerpt from "Jerusalem the Blessed: The Shrine of Three Faiths" by Thomas A. Andinapolus.

Church's Ministry Among the Jews, London, for excerpts from *Walks In and Around Jerusalem* by J. E. Hanauer.

Curtis Brown, London, for excerpt from *Modern Sons of Pharaoh* by S. H. Leeder.

Franciscan Printing Press, Custodia Terra Sancta, Jerusalem, for page from their Daily Calendar.

George Allen and Unwin, Ltd., for excerpt from *Napoleon and Palestine* by Philip Guedalla.

G.P. Putnam's Sons, New York, for excerpts from *The Memoirs of Sir Ronald Storrs* by Ronald Storrs.

Harold Matson Company, Inc., New York, for excerpts from *Our Jerusalem* by Bertha Spafford Vester.

Harper and Row Publishers, New York, for excerpts from *Jerusalem* by John M. Oesterreicher and Anne Sinai.

Harvard University Press, Cambridge, Massachusetts, for excerpt from *Pausanius: Description of Greece* in Loeb Classics.

Her Majesty's Stationery Office for excerpt from *Jerusalem: The City Plan, 1918–1948* by Charles Robert Ashbee.

Herzl Press, New York, for excerpts from *The Complete Diaries of Theodor Herzl* by Raphael Patai.

Houghton Mifflin Co., New York, for excerpt from *The Holy Land under Mandate* by Fannie Fern Andrews.

The Jerusalem Post, Jerusalem, for excerpts from articles by Malka Raymist (Aug. 3, 1984) and Mordecai Gur (April 19, 1974).

John Murray, Inc., London, for excerpts from *When We Lived in Jerusalem* by Estelle Blyth.

Marshall, Morgan and Scott, London, for excerpts from *Reminiscences* by Elizabeth Anne Finn.

Mazar, Benjamin, Jerusalem, Israel, for excerpt from *The Mountain of the Lord.*

The Methodist Publishing House, London, for excerpts from *We Saw the Holy City* by Leslie Farmer.

Ministry of Religious Affairs, Jerusalem, for excerpts from *Christian News From Israel.*

Oliver and Boyd, Edinburgh, for excerpt from *Robert Bruce, King of Scots* by Agnes Mure Mackenzie.

Princeton University Press, Princeton, N.J., for excerpt from *Journal of a Visit to Europe and the Levant* by Herman Melville.

Robert Hale, Ltd., London, for excerpt from *A History of Jerusalem* by John Gray.

Routledge and Kegan Paul, Ltd., London, for excerpts from *Jewish Travellers* by Elkan N. Adler and *From Vine Street to Jerusalem* by Joseph F. Broadhurst.

St. John, Robert, Waldorf, N.J., for excerpt from *Shalom Means Peace.*

Shocken Books, Inc., New York, for excerpts from *From Berlin to Jerusalem* by Gershom Scholem and from *Road to Zion* by Kurt Wilhelm.

Viking Penguin, Inc., New York, for excerpts from *To Jerusalem and Back* by Saul Bellow.

William Heinemann, Ltd., London, for excerpts from *Days of Our Years* by Pierre van Paassen and from *A Palestine Notebook 1918– 1923* by Charles Robert Ashbee.

Jerusalem Curiosities

Introduction

"Jerusalem, the Joy of the Whole Earth"

From ancient times, Jerusalem has been a magnet which drew to itself many of the peerless and the precious of mankind as well as many of the world's cranks and freaks. It attracted hermits and mystics, kabbalists and those who merely sought burial in Jerusalem's holy soil. The city has also attracted fanatics and eccentrics of various degrees of mental derangement, especially men and women who thought themselves to be the reincarnation of phophets, priests, messiahs, and kings. More important has been Jerusalem's attraction for a multitude of ordinary pilgrims and tourists for whom the city's monuments and shrines are invested with sanctity and charm. The pilgrims came with a deep reverence for "the city our God . . . the city of the great King"; the tourists came with a keen desire to see the city that is "fair in situation, the joy of the whole earth" (Ps. 48:2–3).

Until not very long ago, the Old City was the only Jerusalem that existed. Surrounding it there were only bare, rocky hills. When the nineteenth-century visitor arrived in Jerusalem, he usually entered from the east and immediately caught sight of the city's towers and pinnacles. Standing on the Mount of Olives early in the morning, he saw the golden dome of the Mosque of Omar, or, more correctly, the Dome of the Rock, and the silver dome of the El Aksa Mosque shining in the sunlight. Behind these he saw the Old City with its many cupolas, minarets, and steeples. Standing out among these contours of Jerusalem, he saw the large domes of the Church of the Holy Sepulchre and, prior to the war of 1948–1949, the prominent domes of the Hurvah and the Nissan Bak synagogues. Framing them all were the majestic walls and towers of the city. What a memorable sight! What a moving vision! No wonder people saw Jerusalem as "the perfection of beauty!" (Ps. 50:2).

When the nineteenth-century visitor entered the city and observed it at close range, what he saw depended largely on the sentiments and expectations that he brought with him. Thus, the famous traveler, Edward D. Clarke, who visited Jerusalem early in the century, reported:

> We had not been prepared for the grandeur of the spectacle which the city alone exhibited. Instead of a wretched and ruined town, by some described as the desolate remnant of Jerusalem, we beheld . . . a magnificent assemblage of domes, towers, palaces, churches, and monasteries; all of which, glittering in the sun's rays, shone with inconceivable splendor.[1]

But another traveler, Laurence Hutton, who came in 1893, rendered quite a different report:

> Its houses are small, irregular in shape, squalid, and mean. Its streets, if streets they can be called, are not named nor numbered; they are steep, crooked, narrow, roughly paved, never cleaned, and in many instances they are vaulted over by the buildings on each side of them. Never a pair of wheels traverse them, and rarely is a horse or a donkey seen within the walls. The halt, the maimed, and the blind, the leprous and the wretchedly poor, form the great bulk of the population of Jerusalem, and with the single exception of the Hebrews, they are persistent and clamorous beggars. Trade and commerce seem to be confined to the bare necessities of life, and to dealers in beads and crucifixes. . . .
>
> Jerusalem is unique as a city in which everything is serious and solemn and severe. It has no clubs, no bar-rooms, no beer-gardens, no concert-halls, no theatres, no lecture-rooms, no places of amusement of any kind, no street bands, no wandering minstrels, no wealthy or upper classes, no mayor, no aldermen, no elections, no newspapers, no printing-presses, no book stores, except one outside the walls, for the sale of Bibles, no cheerfulness, no life. No one sings, no one dances, no one laughs in Jerusalem; even the children do not play.[2]

Strange to say, both reports are true. They represent the proverbial two sides of the same coin. Some approach Jerusalem with a "quivering sensitiveness," with an awareness of the city's history and sanctity, while others visit it as just another Levantine city. Some seek Jerusalem and find it; others seek nothing anf find nothing. They "do" the city, see everything, and feel nothing. Then they leave, untouched by Jerusalem's inimitable grace and grandeur. It never even occurs to them that they have been witnessing not only the cradle of three great religions, but the very foundation of Western civilization.

A City of Many Misfortunes

That Jerusalem, up to recent times, did contain many sickly, festering sores, one cannot deny. Their source is to be found in the city's misfortunes throughout its long history. Natural disasters such as droughts and plagues, earthquakes and famines often brought grim suffering and bitter affliction. Even more distressing has been the scourge of armed forces bent on conquest. Unfortunately, Jerusalem has always been regarded as a grand prize by empire builders and religious adventurers. It has been besieged almost fifty times and was repeatedly destroyed. Hebrews, Assyrians, Babylonians, Egyptians, Greeks, Romans, Persians, Saracens, Crusaders, Mongols, Ottoman Turks, and, in our century, British, Arabs, and Jews have fought for it.

No greater fame could attach itself to a warrior than to become the conquerer of Jerusalem. Titus, Omar, Saladin, and Allenby captured it. Their fame reached every corner of the world, not so much because of their victories, though some of these were, indeed, notable, mainly because of the magnitude of the prize. But after each of these calamities, Jerusalem rose from its ashes and regained its spiritual role as the misress of great religions.

Jerusalem's greatest affliction, however, has been the neglect, misrule, and shameless despoliation by ruling officials. The systematic plunder and unending neglect made the city a wretched place to live in or even to visit. Eighteenth- and nineteenth-century travelers vividly describe the open sewers, the pestilential stench, the decrepit hovels, the wretched poverty, the pervading filth, and the pitiful disease-ridden population that one found there. One writer says that many visitors remembered it with their nostrils and carried away the memory of their discomforts. Many of the very same travelers, however, blessed their good fortune for the privilege of visiting the Holy City and worshiping at the shrines and holy places of their respective religions.

One of the remarkable facts about Jerusalem is that despite its many destructions it was never moved from its desolate foundations, as has been the fate of most other demolished cities. Only once did Jerusalem change its location and that was from the Ophel which is south of the Temple Mount to the Upper City which is immediately west of the Temple Mount. But the Temple Mount itself has remained inviolate for the Jews these 3,000 years, and for the Moslems these 1,300 years. Similarly, the spots of the crucifixion and resurrection of Jesus have remained fixed for the Christians these 2,000 years.

Jerusalem has seen many wars and was more than once soaked in rivers of blood, but its glory is to be found in the peaceful words of prophets, psalmists, saints, and scholars. Jerusalem's essential role in history has been performed not by soldiers but by teachers, and its future glory will emanate from its spiritual institutions.

A Holy City

An aura of sanctity has always hung over Jerusalem, and it has cast a spell over many a saint and mystic, as well as ordinary men who not infrequently became its willing captives. Throughout the centuries people have been coming the Jerusalem, each with his own peculiar piety, and all have helped to create the city's baffling and inscrutable mystery. For them, it has been first and foremost a holy city. Jews have called it *Ir Ha-Kodesh,* the Holy City; Moslems have called it *El Kuds,* an expression that is identical with the Hebrew appelation; and Christians have known it as *Terra Sancta,* the Holy Land where Jesus' sepulchre is located.

Because Jerusalem is the Holy City for hundreds of millions, it is difficult to see it with absolute clarity, or to describe it with thorough accuracy. It demands a vision that penetrates the reality of ordinary substance and transcends the dimensions of precise measurement. This is what has made it the queen of holy cities, the mother of great religions.

In our secular age this may seem irrelevant. However, this is not actually so. Many modern people, having lost much of their traditional commitments to things sacred, have been burdened by a spiritual emptiness. Among them, there are not a few who are in search of something sacred to fill this void. They want their secular lives to be sanctified notwithstanding the obvious contradiction. In their search they respond, willy nilly, to Jerusalem, at times only nostalgically, just because it is the Holy City.

The secret of Jerusalem's greatness is a baffling mystery only for those who measure greatness in terms of size and material assets. By these criteria Jerusalem would be just another city of small promise, for it is not located strategically. It is not a port city, it does not lie astride a navigable river or a caravan route, it has no rich natural resources, and it has been plagued by perennial water shortages. However, it has been blessed with intangibles of spiritual significance and sacred associations. As George Adam Smith said, "Nowhere else has the universal struggle (between the spirit of God and the spirit of man) been waged so consciously, so articulately as in Jerusalem."[3] This intense struggle was waged by the inspired teachers and sublime religious institutions to which Jerusalem gave birth. And it is this struggle that has endowed Jerusalem with an irresistible power to move the hearts of men, to excite their enthusiasm, and to rouse them to righteous action. These spiritual assets have enabled Jerusalem to speak to man's conscience; they have made Jerusalem great; these fragile attributes have endowed even Jerusalem's ruins with spiritual meaning and its desolation with everlasting significance.

The Center of the World

Judaism, Christianity, Islam agree that Jerusalem is the center of the world. While Jews and Moslems put that center on the Temple Mount, Christians put it in the Church of the Holy Sepulchre, both in the Old City. No doubt the Christian and Islamic designations derive from the earlier Jewish tradition which is recorded in the Bible, the Apocrypha, and the rabbinic literature. Thus we read:

> The world may be compared to the eye of man. The white of the eye is the ocean which surrounds the whole world; the iris is the inhabited land; the pupil is Jerusalem; the face in the pupil is the Temple, may it soon be rebuilt.[4]

From rabbinic literature this idea passed to Christianity. Jerome speaks of Jerusalem as the "navel of the earth," a phrase derived from his Jewish teachers. And the Moslems took the idea from both the Jews and the Christians. These poetic expressions were literalized, so that we find a sixteenth-century map in the form of a three-leaved clover representing the three continents of Europe, Asia, and Africa. The center out of which the leaves grow is a circle with the name of Jerusalem inscribed in it.

In Jerusalem the visitor is shown the exact spot in the Church of the Holy Sepulchre where the center of the world is located. Some skeptics mock at the ignorance and credulity of the simple folk who point to a specific spot and say, "This is the center of the world." But neither the rabbis of the Talmud, nor the anonymous authors of the Apocrypha, nor "the credulous monks" fancied that Jerusalem was geographically in the center of the world. What they did know was the singularity of Jerusalem as a spiritual force of central and worldwide potency. The prophet Isaiah concisely expressed this idea: "Out of Zion shall go forth the devine teaching, and the word of the Lord from Jerusalem" (Isa. 2:3). From Zion God's teaching has gone forth and has affirmed man's striving for salvation. From Jerusalem has gone forth the word of the Lord with the comforting promise that the bleak history of mankind will yet turn into the brighter world to come. From this life-giving source Western civilization has derived its vitality.

Jerusalem the Eternal

When a Jew is called up to the reading of the Torah at a synagogue service he pronounces a benediction in which he thanks God for "planting eternal life in our midst." He attributes Israel's eternity to the divine teachings of the Holy Scriptures which God has transmitted to the Jewish people through His prophets. Jerusalem shares this eternity for exactly the same reason. A mere glimpse at the city's career reveals that its survival, against enormous odds, is as baffling a mystery as the survival of the Jewish people. It also reveals that the secret of its eternity can be understood only in terms of its spiritual assets.

Jerusalem has had a most inauspicious political history. It began its existence as a small mountain town in a small Middle Eastern country. Three thousand years ago it became the capital city of a small people and its political fortunes were anything but promising. Nonetheless, during the three millennia of its recorded history, mighty empires and their proud capital cities have vanished, while Jerusalem has not only survived but has manifested remarkable powers of resilience and renewal.

This miracle of survival in the face of overwhelming political and military disasters and destructions has been explained in terms of its spiritual career, which began three thousand years ago when King David moved his capital from Herbon to Jerusalem. He built an altar on Mount Moriah, which came to be known as the Temple Mount, and brought there the tablets of the Ten Commandments. His son, King Solomon, then erected the Temple on the site of his father's altar. Equally if not more decisive was the fact that Jerusalem heard the voice of the prophets who brought God's message to Israel. It also heard the voice of the psalmists who sang of God's compassion and mercy. The role of the prophets and the psalmists was later taken up by the rabbis of the Talmud who applied the prophetic message to the daily experience of the people. They also founded a new religious institution, the synagogue, and formulated its liturgy.

At the end of the first millennium of Jerusalem's sacred history, a Jewish teacher named Jesus gathered a handful of disciples and followers who carried his teachings far beyond the geographical borders and won over multitudes of adherents. The city thus became holy not only for the Jews but also for millions of Christians. Six hundred years later, a religious teacher arose in the Arabian Peninsula who heard from Jews and Christians about their respective traditions. He adopted some parts of them, often in a garbled form, and incorporated them into the new religion which he founded. In the new faith, called Islam, Jerusalem occupied a place of sanctity for millions of Moslems.

The sanctity is the secret of Jerusalem's survival. It is holiness that has endowed it with everlasting life. It has survived because it transcends the ordinary earth-bound and time-bound realities; it is a city that awakens yearnings for the immutable and the timeless. In Jerusalem, current history seems irrelevant, because the remote past and the ultimate future press on one's consciousness. Eternity is the hallmark of Jerusalem.

The Perfection of Beauty

Visitors find Jerusalem a city of surprises. Apart from its monuments, shrines, holy places, and sacred associations, it is invested with novelty and beauty. The Talmud states that ten measures of beauty descended to the world; nine were taken by Jerusalem, and one by the rest of the world (*Kid.* 49b). No wonder that many have fallen in love with it. "How the poetry of the place gets hold of you!" says C. R. Ashbee.[5] Indeed, many have claimed that Jerusalem has gotten into their blood, and they have become its lifelong, dedicated lovers, among them, unabashedly, this writer.

But not everyone has this reaction. Only those who bring with them a sympathy for Jerusalem's unique essence can see it with their hearts and their imaginations. Yet even those who see it only with their eyes are not altogether immune to its charm. Hardened globetrotters and sightseers who are sated with the attractions of London, Paris, Rome, Athens, and Cairo find Jerusalem absorbing, especially because it is so cosmopolitan and exotic. In its streets the visitor meets not only the ubiquitous, camera-laden tourists and the earnest, sad-looking pilgrims from all over the world, but also a vast variety of people of diverse nationalities, languages, dress, and manners who live apart yet mingle freely in the bazaars and side streets. One meets Christians, both Occidentals and Orientals, adherents of more than thirty churches and sects, each with its own ritual, who are regarded by all the other sects as in deadly error. Then one meets an amazing diversity of clerics — priests, monks, and nuns — a variety of not to be matched in any other place in the world. And not to be overlooked are the missionaries and men possessed by strange visions, all proclaiming their panaceas for the world's ills.

One finds a similar variety among the Jews and Moslems. There is the Orthodox Jew with his long, curled earlocks, wearing his long gabardine coat and white stockings and, on Sabbaths and festivals, a heavy fur-trimmed headgear. Alongside this replica of seventeenth-century Polish fashion, walks a *halutz* (pioneer) from a *kibbutz* in his short-sleeved shirt and short trunks and sandals. This scene is in sharp contrast to the Arab with his flowing *khafiah,* long coat and skirt, walking with his fellow Moslem dressed in the latest Western outfit. Add to these the variety of rabbis, dervishes, and imams, each with his own distinctive vestments. What a medley of God's creatures! What a cosmopolitan throng! And, as happens occasionally in the spring of the year, Jerusalem is overflowing with a multitude of humanity in an indescribable variety of dress participating in diverse rituals and ceremonies, the like of which no city can match.

The Joy of All Earth

To write about Jerusalem is often frustrating, because it is a unique and compounded enigma. G. K. Chesterton aptly said that "Jerusalem is a small town of big things; and the average modern city is a big town of small things."[6] A modern poet writes in ecstasy:

> Jerusalem has many faces,
> Expressions that vary with the seasons and with the centuries,
> But its granite heart beats once in a thousand years,
> And resumes the inscrutability of stone.[7]

How really can one capture this unique city in mere words? How can one adequately describe Jerusalem's beauty, her halo of holiness, her sacred history? How can one fathom her soul, her charm, her meaning? What a powerful magnet is built into her very structure! What bewitching charm inhabits her very essence! The lover of Jerusalem is forever shackled to her, yet, serving beloved Jerusalem is a joyous and lifelong task, for Jerusalem is, indeed, "the joy of all the earth" (Ps. 48:3).

ONE

Curiosities of Former Times

Jerusalem — A Buried City

Jerusalem—both the Old and the New City—is vibrant, bustling. Yet, Jerusalem is often called a buried city. This truth undermines the validiy of several traditional beliefs, especially beliefs regarding some of the holy places. And the traditional concept of Jerusalem's topography has undergone some radical changes.

It may surprise some people to learn that the ancient city of Jerusalem is buried as much as forty feet below the modern City. The houses of the Old City stand on the ruins of ancient aqueducts, pillars, and palaces. Even a superficial glance at the history of the Holy City reveals that the City of Peace has repeatedly been turned into a desolation, and its surface has gradually risen so that the ancient city has become an underground heap of ruins, waiting for archaeologists to explore and decipher their hidden secrets.

Today pilgrims of all nations, kindreds, and tongues crowd the streets of the Old City. When they walk in the Via Dolorosa they imagine themselves treading the very street that Jesus trod on his way to the crucifixion. However, Charles Wilson states in his *Jerusalem the Holy City* that "the Via Dolorosa is forty to fifty feet above the level of the ancient roadway."[1] And when the pilgrims are shown a dent in a wall as the very spot against which Jesus fell while carrying the cross, the implication is that Jesus was an inordinately tall person. In fact, more than forty feet tall!

Jerusalem in the mid-nineteenth century. (From J. Boudet, Jerusalem: A History. *New York, G.P. Putnam's Sons, 1967, p. 251.)*

To see how deeply the ancient city of Jerusalem is buried beneath the rubble of the centuries, go to the Damascus Gate and walk up to the end of the ramp that leads to the gate. Before entering the gate, gaze over the left side of the ramp and see a Roman gate, the top of which is below the present street level. A Roman entering Jerusalem from the north could not use the Damascus Gate since it did not exist in those days. Our hypohetical Roman entered through the gate below the ramp. Looking down at that ancient gate, recalls the biblical words: "Her gates are sunk into the ground" (Lam. 2:9).

One can also see the ground level of ancient Jerusalem in the center of the Old City. At the Muristan, near the Church of the Holy Sepulchre, the Church of John the Forerunner may be found at the corner of Christian and David Streets. Beneath this church, about twenty feet below street level, is a crypt. This is a Byzantine church which in its day stood on the street level.

A third place to view the depth of the accumulated debris on which the modern city stands is at the Western (Wailing) Wall. At the northern end of the Wall, a tunnel entrance leads to an extension of the Wall where many Jews pray. A shaft sunk near the Wall reaches down to the street level of ancient times. The depth of that shaft gives one an idea of how deeply the ancient city of Jerusalem is buried beneath the alleys of the modern city.

From the arched gate below the Damascus Gate and the underground Byzantine church in the Muristan, and from the writings of competent archaeologists, one can say with certainty that the Old City of today is not the Jerusalem of ancient days. The Old City stands on the accumulated deris and rubbish of many centuries. To know ancient Jerusalem one must study the city which lies buried beneath. Some of today's holy places are no longer the exact spots where sacred events once took place; they have become only proximate sites. This detracts less from their sanctity than from the credibility of guides who persist in pointing out "the very spot" where a sacred event took place.

The Empty Jewish Tombs

Jerusalem is girdled with tombs dating back two and three thousand years. Most are concentrated in the Valley of Hinnom. This valley starts its course near the Jaffa Gate, proceeds southward, and then turns eastward where it becomes deep and narrow. In the rugged cliffs rising out of this section of the valley are numerous man-made caves which are the ancient Jewish tombs. Among the more famous are those attributed to the kings of Judah, the biblical Judges, and the Prophets. There is no evidence that any biblical king, judge, or prophet was actually laid in any of these tombs. But these traditions are firmly established in the area and only scholars and skeptics dare question them.

Burial in ancient Jerusalem did not consist of lowering the dead into the ground and covering the corpse with earth. In those days the Jews buried their dead in artificial caves cut into the rock of the hillsides. These tombs were entered by a door which led in turn to a number of rock-hewn chambers. In these chambers the dead were deposited in hewn niches in the walls.

Since the ancient rock-cut tombs which encircle Jerusalem are now empty, the question arises, Where are the corpses that were deposited in them to "sleep with their fathers?" The natural process of decomposition offers a partial explanation. A fuller explanation concerns the activity of grave robbers who ransacked the graves in search of treasure. Among these grave robbers were the Mongolian hordes, known as the Hwarizmanians, who captured Jerusalem in 1244. They plundered the holy places, looted the monumental tombs, and scattered the bones of the dead. A third explanation has to do with people who moved into these sepulchres. The new occupants of the tombs removed the bones to make the caves habitable. Thus the village of Siloam or Silwan came into being.

Sheer vandalism is the most recent cause of desecrated tombs. When Jerusalem was reunited after the Six-Day War, countless human bones were found scattered in the Jewish cemetery on the Mount of Olives. The Jordanians who ruled the Old City for nineteen years (1948–1967) not only removed many of the tombstones for building material, but also removed the bones from many of the graves and scattered them abroad. Seeing this, Saul Bellow was moved to say: "[Jerusalem] acts queerly on my nerves . . . because I feel that a good part of this dust must be ground out of human bone."[2] When the Old City was recaptured by Israel in the Six-Day War, the bones were gathered and reinterred in a common grave.

Jerusalem is girdled with tombs, but they are untenanted.

The Kidron Valley at the foot of the Mount of Olives, with Absalom's "tomb" on the left, the Tomb of Zachariah on the right, and the Jewish family tomb of Bnai Hezir (St. James's Tomb) in the center. (Courtesy of the Israel Government Press Office.)

The Siloam inscription, which commemorates the meeting of the two groups of workmen who built the tunnel during the reign of King Hezekiah (c. 700 B.C.E.). (Courtesy of Central Zionist Archives, Jerusalem.)

The Discovery of the Siloam Inscription

One of the most exciting archaeological discoveries in Jerusalem was that of the Siloam inscription. Curiously, this major discovery was made not by trained archaeologists but by a sixteen-year-old boy, intrigued by the biblical account of King Hezekiah's preparations for Sennacherib's siege of Jerusalem. The story of that remarkable find is told by Mrs. Bertha Spafford Vester, who was the guiding spirit of the American Colony in Jerusalem.

The Bible tells how King Hezekiah dug a tunnel from the Gihon Spring, which was outside the city walls, to the Siloam Pool within the city's fortifications (2 Kings 20:20). Mrs. Vester's account relates the rest of this exciting story:

> . . . Jacob determined to explore the tunnel.
>
> Because of its reputation for being haunted he had some trouble persuading his friend Sampson, a boy about his own age, to explore it with him, but at last he was persuaded. The boys kept their plan a profound secret.
>
> They had no idea of the height or width or length of the tunnel, nor how deep the water. They prepared floats with candle and matches attached, and tied these around their necks with strings. Jacob started from the Pool of Siloam side while Sampson entered from the Virgin's Fount [Gihon Spring]. Their plan was to meet in the middle.

Jacob found himself in total darkness and muddy water up to his chin. It was cold and draughty in the tunnel, his candle blew out, his float with the matches submerged in the water, and he could not relight the candle. But he kept on, guiding his way by keeping his hand on the damp stone wall and feeling under his fingertips the marks of ancient chisels going forward, from right to left.

The tunnel he followed forms an enormous and irregular S, a fact that has puzzled archaeologists. . . .

Jacob, feeling his way, suddenly was conscious that the chisel marks had changed and were now going from left to right. He realized he must be in the exact place where the King's workmen had met under the city. Carefully he felt all around the walls, and was certain that his fingers detected an inscription chiseled in the stone.

He hurried through the watery tunnel to tell Sampson. A point of light shone ahead and he knew that he must have reached the other end and was coming out at the Virgin's Fount where he was certain Sampson would be waiting. He did not know Sampson had long since abandoned his friend and gone back to school.

Jacob rose out of the pool dripping muddy water and half blind from the dark tunnel, and dimly perceived many figures about. Among them was a lad about Sampson's size. Jacob clutched him, crying: "Sampson, I have succeeded!"

It was not Sampson but a peasant boy, who thought the genie of the tunnel had captured him, and collapsed into the water in a dead faint.

The women about the pool, filling their jars with water and doing their washing, nearly tore Jacob to pieces. He ran for his life, followed by their screamed curses.

When he reached school, he confessed the escapade to the head master. He expected punishment. Instead, his report of an inscription in the Siloam tunnel caused a sensation in the school and throughout Jerusalem. Plans were soon afoot to investigate, but before they were completed a Greek with an eye to financial gain entered the tunnel by night and blasted the inscription out of the solid rock, breaking it in the process. Before he was able to spirit it away the Turkish authorities captured him. He paid for the theft, and the inscription is now in the museum at Istanbul, with the crack plainly across it.[3]

The inscription is not on a separate piece of stone but crudely cut in the wall, very likely by one of the workmen. Its translation was published by the Palestine Exploration Fund Quarterly Statement for July 1881:

Behold the excavation. Now this has been the history of the excavation.

Arab boy taking a dip in the water of the Siloam tunnel (September 1967). (Courtesy of Israel Government Press Office.)

While the workmen were still lifting up the pick, each towards his neighbour, and while three cubits still remained to be cut through, each heard the voice of the other who called to his neighbour since there was an excess of rock on the right hand and on the left. And on the day of the excavation the workmen struck each to meet his neighbour pick against pick and there flowed the waters from the spring to the pool for a thousand two hundred cubits and a hundred cubits was the height of the rock over the head of the workmen.

Professor Sayce, the great archaeological authority, described the Siloam Inscription as the oldest record of Biblical Hebrew yet discovered.[3] Laurence Oliphant, in his letters published under the title *Haifa or Life in Modern Palestine,* mentions this remarkable discovery. After a description of Charles Warren's exciting and dangerous exploration of the tunnel, Oliphant writes:

> The honor of finding the [Siloam] inscription was reserved for a naked urchin of the town, who . . . announced he had seen writing on the wall. Whereupon Professor Sayce and Herr Schick and Doctor Guthe plunged naked into the muddy tunnel with acid solutions and blotting paper and everything necessary to make squeezes, and emerged shivering and triumphant with the most interesting Hebrew inscription that has ever been found in Palestine.[4]

Regrettably, visitors in Jerusalem can not see this remarkable relic of close to three thousand years ago. The Siloam inscription is one of many historic monuments that have been pilfered or "legally" removed. To see this ancient memorial of biblical history one must go to Istanbul and visit the Imperial Museum.

The Crucified Jew

In June 1968 the Government Antiquities Department was notified that bulldozers digging in the Giv'at ha-Mivtar area for construction of new houses had unearthed some ancient tombs. The area is located in a section of the city which used to be no-man's land, separating the Jordanian and Israeli sectors prior to the Six-Day War. The sepulchres uncovered were the usual ancient burial chambers with niches in the walls into which the corpses were laid. Some of these niches still contained skeletons. Most of the bones, however, were gathered up in ossuaries to make room for new corpses. The time of these burials was established to have been about two thousand years ago.

In one of the ossuaries the archaeologists found a bone pierced by a rusty nail to which adhered a piece of wood. This bone was obviously part of a crucified man's leg with the nail and a piece of the cross. This was a unique find. Since the nails were usually extracted before the corpses were buried, no remains of such a crucified person had ever before been found.

The bone, the rusty nail, and the piece of wood that adhered to it were examined by scholars and the story of that crucifixion was reconstructed.[5] It was assumed that the nail transfixed both heels and that the victim's knees were laid sideways, one on top of the other. It was also

Schematic drawing of the proposed position in which the first-century C.E. *Jew was crucified. (From Benjamin Mazar,* The Mountain of the Lord. *New York, 1975, pp. 228–229.)*

conjectured that the victim was provided witn a small crossbar, called a *sedecula*, upon which the crucified person rested his buttocks. This was not unusual in Roman crucifixions and was not meant to be an act of kindness. On the contrary, it was an act of additional cruelty. This contraption prolonged the victim's life and thus protracted his agony. It was also conjectured that the hands were nailed to the cross.

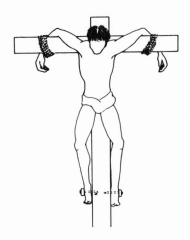

New schematic drawing of the proposed position of crucifixion. (From Joseph Ziaz and Eliezer Sekeles, "The Crucified Man from Giv'at ha-Mivtar: A Reappraisal," in Israel Exploration Journal, *Vol. 35 (1985), Nos. 2–3, pp. 22–27).*

A careful re-examination of the above conclusions revealed a number of misjudgments which were due largely to the pressure of the religious authorities for the release of the bones for reburial. The archaeologists worked hurriedly and reached their conclusions under stress. More careful examination of the available data led to revised conclusions. It was demonstrated that the nail was not eighteen centimeters long but only eleven and a half centimeters. The nail was not long enough to penetrate the heels of both legs. Anatomical evidence revealed that the nail was driven through the victim's leg to the upright shaft of the cross, and that the hands were not pierced by nails, but were evidently tied to the crossbar. This procedure was not unusual in Roman crucifixions. It was also established that the victim was a young man of about twenty-five years.

On the ossuary was inscribed the crucified man's name — Yehohanan. Since Yehohanan's crucifixion was approximately contemporaneous with that of Jesus and his burial place was only about three kilometers from Calvary, the discovery aroused great interest throughout the world, especially among Christians. It also raised some irksome questions. People have wondered who was that unfortunate young Jew, Yehohanan, the victim of Roman rule in Judea? Since crucifixion was applied in Roman law only to crimes against the state or the Emperor, what was Yehohanan's political offense? Were his subversive activities peaceful like those of Jesus or were they rebellious like those of Bar Kokhba? Judging by his elegant tomb, Yehohanan was evidently a man of means, capable of living a life of ease. Yet, what a miserable end!

The "Roman" Cardo in the Jewish Quarter

In 1884 a mosaic map was discovered in the floor of a Greek Orthodox church in the Jordanian town of Madeba. The map was of Byzantine origin and it depicted the various towns in the Holy Land and Trans-Jordan. Most of the fourteen-hundred-year-old mosaic map had deteriorated, but the section depicting Jerusalem was well preserved. The map clearly shows the general outline of the city during the Byzantine period. The most prominent feature of the map is a broad street, lined by columns on either side, stretching from what is now the Damascus Gate in the northern wall all the way to the southern wall. Such a north-south, wide public boulevard was typical of Roman cities, and was known as the Cardo. The map also indicated the location of some of the historic

Romans carrying the spoils from the Jerusalem Temple, sculpted on the Rock of Titus in Rome. (From Israel Abrahams, ed., Legacy of Israel. *Oxford, England, Oxford University Press, 1927; facing p. 28.)*

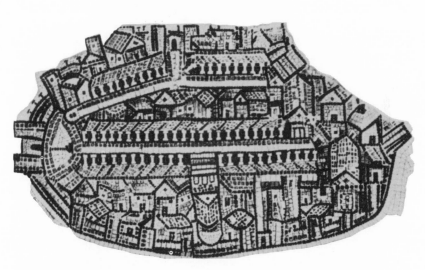

Jerusalem of the sixth century, as depicted on the Mosaic map discovered at Madeba. (Courtesy of Central Zionist Archives, Jerusalem.)

religious buildings in the city. The discovery of the Madeba map is regarded as one of the most important finds of its kind.

In 1975 excavations in the Jewish Quarter of the Old City discovered a broad street, thirteen meters wide, flanked on either side by a portico, three and a half meters wide. The porticos were separated from the wide central road by rows of columns which supported the roofs of the porticos. The central, open section was reserved for vehicular traffic while the porticos sheltered the pedestrians from sun and rain. This discovery confirmed what historians had known, and people quickly arrived at the conclusion that the discovery was the ancient Roman Cardo of the pagan city Aelia Capitolina that the Romans built on the ruins of Jerusalem after the Bar Kokhba rebellion in the second century. In that war the Romans had suffered enormous casualties. When they finally succeeded in subduing the Jewish rebels they avenged their losses by thoroughly destroying Jerusalem. They ran a plow over the devastated and depopulated city as a symbol of Jerusalem's death. The Romans then built on the ruins of Jerusalem a pagan city and called it Aelia Capitolina in honor of the Roman Capitoline god (Jupiter) and in honor of Emperor Hadrian whose family name was Aelius. The new pagan city was built in typical Roman style, including the broad central avenue which they called the Cardo.

When the archaeologists discovered in the Jewish Quarter a section of a broad street with a central open section, paved with large flagstones and draining channels, and lined on either side by columns which evidently supported porticos, it was concluded that it was part of the Roman Cardo which Hadrian built in the second century. This assumption was immediately publicized by the journalists and was accepted by the general public as gospel truth. However, the assumption was false. All the archaeological finds in the area, such as pottery and coins, were exclusively of the Byzantine period. Absolutely nothing of the Roman period was found in the area of the discovered broad, colonnaded thoroughfare. Archaeologists have concluded that the Roman Cardo of Hadrian's time ran from today's Damascus Gate only up to the David Street Bazaar. Beyond that street the city was practically uninhabited. The Bar Kokhba war had so depopulated the city that hardly anyone lived south of what is now David Street. But in the Byzantine period, especially during the reign of Emperor Justinian in the sixth century, the city flourished and its population increased. The section of the city south of David Street was inhabited, and Justinian erected there the large Nea Church. The emperor saw fit to extend the Roman Cardo southward toward the Nea Church. It was this Byzantine section of Jerusalem's Cardo that was unearthed. It should be noted that when the archaeologist, Nahman Avigad, presented his official report on his discovery he pointed out that the Cardo is Byzantine in origin, and that no evidence supported the general claim that it is of Roman origin. But the press had already published the exciting news of the discovery of the "Roman" Cardo of Aelia Capitolina, and the public had already accepted the report as an established fact. The "Roman" Cardo became part of local folklore, and folklore, like tradition, dies hard. So it is that Jerusalemites continue to tell their friends from abroad about the marvelous discovery of Jerusalem's "Roman" Cardo.

The discovered Cardo runs from the David Street Bazaar southward into the Jewish Quarter. It has been restored and promises to become one of the exciting sights to which visitors will flock in large numbers. A section of the Cardo has been developed as a commercial area as it had been in the Crusader period. The Southern section of the Cardo will serve as a "living museum." Shafts have also been sunk in several sections of the Cardo where visitors can see relics of the ancient Jerusalem wall of the Hasmonean period, erected about 2,200 years ago, and a segment of Jerusalem's fortifications that existed at the time when the Babylonians besieged Jerusalem about 2,600 years ago. Visitors to the Holy City are advised not to miss this historic site, irrespective of its being Roman, Byzantine, or even Crusader in origin.

Why Jerusalem Did Not Become the Center of Christendom and Islam

Jerusalem is the mother city of Christendom. Estelle Blyth states that her father, Bishop Blyth of the Anglican Cathedral in Jerusalem, "always called Jerusalem the Mother City of the Faith." There is no disagreement among quarreling Christian sects on the fact that Jesus taught, died, and was resurrected in Jerusalem. The holiest Christian relics and memorials are in Jerusalem. The first Christian church was established in Jerusalem, and the apostles went forth on their respective missions from Jerusalem. John Finley who claims to have been "the first of pilgrims . . . to walk the breadth and the length of the Holy Land after its deliverance" [from the Turks], speaks of the Holy Land as the "religious homeland of Christian and Jew, of Catholic and Protestant alike."[6] Yet the seat of the Latin Church is in Rome and the center of the Greek Church is in Istanbul.

This strange set of circumstances can be understood by a glimpse at the growth and development of early Christianity. As the new religion gained adherents among the pagans, it drifted from the "Mother City" to

Rome and Constantinople where the pagan shrines were Christianized and the cities were made into Christian Mother Churches. Theology, being "the handmaiden of conscience," found good explanations for abandoning Jerusalem for the more convenient and more expedient religious centers. The Christian Bible speaks of the heavenly Jerusalem (Rev. 21). This spiritual Jerusalem, say the Christian theologians, need not be identical with terrestrial Jerusalem, where the Christian faith was born. Any place where Christianity is practiced is the heavenly Jerusalem. Christianity thus broke its ties with the Holy City. Only the holy places remained and to these shrines pilgrims flock, especially during the Easter season.

The Moslems, too, at first turned to Jerusalem in prayer. So they were instructed by their prophet. But the prophet changed his mind when the Jews of the Arabian Peninsula refused to recongnize him as a true prophet. He fought the Jews, defeated them, and ordered his faithful to turn in prayer to Mecca. To be sure, Jerusalem remained a holy city for the Moslems, but only of third rank, after Mecca where Mohamed was born and Medina where he was buried.

The Christian and Moslem connection with Jerusalem was aptly described by a fifteenth-century Dominican monk, Brother Felix Fabri, who noted in his *Book of Wanderings:*

> At this present day the Christians would care little about the Saracens' bearing rule in Jerusalem, provided only that we were allowed freedom to pass in and out of our temple of the Lord's sepulchre without fear, and without vexations and extortionate payments. Neither would the Saracens mind if the Christians were lords of the Holy City if we would render up the temple to them.[7]

Only the Jews have maintained their ties with Jerusalem as their religious and national "homeland." This relationship began three thousand years ago in the days of King David and it has continued throughout the centuries. And as long as Judaism and the Jewish people are in existence they will implore the All-Merciful three times daily—"May our eyes behold Thy return in mercy to Zion."

The Crusaders' Conquest of the Holy City

"The Crusades were like fevers that calm down after a few deliriums." This characterization is illustrated by Thackeray's account of the Crusaders' conquest of the Holy City in 1099. Thackeray, who is, according to many, the greatest English historical novelist, visited Jerusalem in 1845, and then published his *Notes of a Journey From Cornhill to Grand Cairo*. In this work, he writes:

> When the Crusaders entered the mosque [of Omar], they rode knee-deep in the blood of its defenders, and of the women and children who had fled thither for refuge: . . . Then after three days of butchery, they purified the desecrated mosque and went to prayer.[8]

Thackeray's brief statement on the Crusaders' butchery of the Holy City's inhabitants is not original. It is based on accounts by contemporary chroniclers who recorded the gory tale in all its gruesome details. Walter Besant and E. H. Palmer in their history of Jerusalem give an account of the Crusaders' conquest of Jerusalem and the "delirium" that characterized that victory:

> The city was taken, and the massacre of its defenders began. The Christians ran through the streets, slaughtering as they went. At first they spared none, neither man, woman, nor child, putting all alike to the sword; but when resistance had ceased, and rage was partly appeased, they began to bethink them of pillage, and tortured those who remained alive to make them discover their gold. As for the Jews within the city, they had fled to their synagogue, which the Christians set on fire, and so burned them all. The chroniclers relate with savage joy how the streets were encumbered with heads and mangled bodies, and how in the Haram Area, the sacred enclosure of the Temple, the knights rode in blood up to the knees of their horses. . . .

> Evening fell, and the clamour ceased, for there were no more enemies to kill, save a few whose lives had been promised by Tancred. . . . They remembered that the city they had taken was the city of the Lord, and this impulsive soldiery, sheathing swords reeking with blood, followed Godfrey to the Church of the Holy Sepulchre, where they passed the night in tears, and prayers, and services.

> In the morning the carnage began again. Those who had escaped the first fury were the women and children. It was now resolved to spare none. Even the three hundred to whom Tancred had promised life were slaughtered in spite of him. Raymond alone managed to save the lives of those who capitulated to him from the Tower of David. It took a week to kill the Saracens, and to take away their dead bodies. Every Crusader had a right to the first house he took possession of, and the city found itself absolutely cleared of its old inhabitants, and in the hands of a new population. The True Cross, which had been hidden by the Christians during the siege, was brought forth again, and carried in joyful procession round the city, and for ten days the soldiers gave themselves up to murder, plunder and prayers!

> And the First Crusade was finished.[9]

King Solomon's Stables

Who has not heard of Solomon's Temple, Solomon's Quarries, and Solomon's Stables? The attribution of the ancient Jewish Temple and Jerusalem's vast quarries to King Solomon has a historic basis. But his stables are absolutely fictitious. To be sure, King Solomon had many horses, as we are told in the Bible: "Solomon had forty thousand stalls of horses for his chariots" (1 Kings 4:26). And his stables were obviously near the royal palace which stood on the Temple Mount where the El Aksa Mosque is now located. It is logical to assume that the subterranean vaults under the southeastern section of the Temple Mount where King Solomon's palace stood served as stables for his horses. What is more, there are holes in the piers indicating that horses were actually tethered to these massive pillars. It has therefore been generally accepted that these subterranean quarters were stables for Solomon's horses.

Historians, however, say that this widely accepted belief is only a legend. These subterranean structures were erected by King Herod who lived a thousand years after King Solomon's time. Herod wanted to enlarge the area of the Temple Mount. His architects built retaining walls around the expanded area. But instead of filling the space between the southern wall of the Temple Mount and the slope of the hill with dirt, they built strong pillars with vaults over them to support the platform. Thus the earlier area of the Temple Mount was enlarged to meet the architectural concept of the new Temple area.

Herbert Rix, who visited Jerusalem in 1906, tells the story of these stables and of their origin:

> We proceed to the southeast corner [of the Temple Mount]. Here we descend by a flight of steps. . . . Thence more steps led us down to Solomon's Stables, vast vaults supported by no fewer than eighty-eight columns. Solomon's Palace undoubtedly lay to the south of the Temple, and he is declared in Scripture to have had forty thousand stalls of horses for his chariots; moreover, the Knights Templars actually found these underground avenues convenient as stables for their own steeds, so those who like can put these facts together and call the place Solomon's Stables. But a soberer view recognises in them . . . [the] substructures which Herod built to support his cloisters, when he extended the area of the Temple Courts. Some remains indeed of Herod's original work, and a good deal of the original material, may still be seen. Perhaps the most interesting historical association of the place is that on the dread day when the city was stormed by Rome, hundreds of poor panic-stricken Jews crowded these hidden spaces for refuge from inevitable death. [10]

The holes in the pillars indicate that horses were tethered to them. But these horses were not King Solomon's; nor were they King Herod's. These subterranean vaults became stables more than a thousand years after they were built. In the year 1099 the Crusaders captured Jerusalem. The Knights Templars established their headquarters on the Temple Mount, right over these underground vaults. The Templars found these vaults suitable for their horses. In order to provide access for their horses they opened a gate in the wall. This gate, which is now walled up, is known as the Single Gate, to distinguish it from the other walled-up gates known as the Double Gate and the Triple Gate. The Crusaders also found the columns supporting the Temple platform convenient for tethering their horses. So they pierced the corners of the columns for the ropes used to fasten the horses.

Notwithstanding the available evidence which confirms that Solomon neither built these subterranean quarters nor had stables in this location, these vaults continue to be called Solomon's Stables. The visitor in Jerusalem who wishes to be directed to this "interminable vista of underground arches" is advised to ask for Solomon's Stables and not for the Crusaders' or Templars' Stables.

A Church with Blasphemous Inscriptions

When the Crusaders captured Jerusalem, the Templars established their headquarters on the Temple Mount. In their ignorance they concluded that the El Aksa Mosque was the original palace of King Solomon, and the Dome of the Rock was Solomon's Temple. They named the El Aksa Mosque the Temple of Solomon and the Dome of the Rock the Temple of God.

For almost a century the Templars worshiped blissfully in their *Templum Domini.* Little did they suspect that they were surrounded by blasphemous inscriptions. The reason for these anti-Christian inscriptions is that the Caliph al-Malik had erected this shrine in order to counter the Christian pride of their beautiful churches in Jerusalem, especially the Church of the Holy Sepulchre. In choosing verses from the Koran for the dome's decorative inscriptions, he selected pointedly anti-Christian ones such as:

> "He [God] taketh not unto Himself a son, and none can be a partner to His kingdom."

"Believe then in God and His prophets and do not say that there are three gods."

"It is not for God to take unto Himself a son, far be it from Him."

The Crusaders were not only unable to read the anti-Christian inscriptions that fill the building, but they did not even suspect that these beautiful decorations were inscriptions. Had they suspected them to have meaning, they would have found someone to decipher them. In their ignorance the Crusaders continued to worship amid these blasphemies, proud of their privilege to offer prayers in their *Templum Domini.*

The Legacy of the Hospitallers

In a small garden in the Muristan, next to the Lutheran Church of the Redeemer, there is a memorial inscription marking the spot where the headquarters of the Order of the Knights of St. John of Jerusalem was located during the Crusader period. The inscription reads:

> Here in the Muristan was situated the first hospital of the Knights of St. John of Jerusalem during the twelfth and thirteenth centuries. In 1882 the Grand Priory in the British realm of the Most Venerable Order of the Hospital of St. John of Jerusalem established an ophthalmic hospital in the Holy City in emulation of the humanitarian and charitable efforts of its medieval predecessors. For the eleven years from 1949 to 1960 this work was centered in the adjacent properties known as Watson House and Strathearn House. To commemorate these events the Most Venerable Order, owner of this site, constructed this garden and inscribed this stone in 1972.
> *Pro Utilitate Hominem*

At the bottom of "this stone" there is a postscript which reads: "In 1960 the work was moved to a new hospital in the Sheikh Jarrah Quarter of Jerusalem."

The history of the Knights of St. John of Jerusalem, usually called the Knights Hospitallers, is one of the strangest stories in the annals of Jerusalem. The Knights Hospitallers were monks. As such one would expect them to have been gentle and peaceful men, dedicated to the service of the Church and engaged in humanitarian activities, all the more so because their headquarters were located in the City of Peace. However, the story of the Hospitallers does not conform to our anticipations. This religious brotherhood distinguished itself mainly on the battlefield and its fame derives from glorious victories achieved on the ground of battle. To be sure, the members of the order were monks and as such were sworn to poverty, celibacy, and obedience, but their primary occupation was the waging of unceasing war against the Moslem infidels. They were actually a professional army in the service of the Christian states in their wars against the Moslem advance into Europe. The order's unceasing battles against the infidels justified the rich endowments and the privileges which the order acquired in all the Catholic states. The order waxed rich and powerful and held extensive properties throughout Europe. The order's chapters or priories in Western Europe provided the income it needed to sustain its military and charitable activities.

The order's origin predates the arrival of the Crusaders in Jerusalem. It was in 1050 that a hospital which had been destroyed by the mad Khaliph Hakkim was restored by merchants from Amalfi. But this hospital, located in the Muristan, really came to life in 1108, shortly after the conquest of Jerusalem by the Crusaders. It was then that the order, commonly called the Hospitallers, was established to provide care and healing for the sick among the Christian pilgrims who came annually to the Holy City. The central role of the Hospitallers, however, soon changed. The Hospitallers noted the fame and fortune of a neighboring brotherhood in Jerusalem known as the Templars and decided to emulate them. The Templars were a religious order which was established for the purpose of protecting the Christian pilgrims from the ravages of the Arab robber bands. The Templars expanded their military functions and became the defenders of the Latin Kingdom of Jerusalem. Their victories on the battlefield gained them fame and wealth. The Hospitallers followed the example of the Templars and added the defense of the Christian Kingdom of Jerusalem to their original purpose of healing the sick among the pilgrims. The Hospitallers soon became predominantly a military order and their name was changed to the Order of the Knights of St. John of Jerusalem. Henceforth the Hospitallers provided the four Crusader States in the Holy Land, especially the Kingdom of Jerusalem, with a permanent, reliable, experienced, and disciplined military force. And when the Crusader kingdoms ceased to exist, the order served Western Christendom as a bulwark against the Moslem advance into Europe. The order engaged in battles against the Moslems as far west as Spain. In addition to the unceasing wars between the Christian and Moslem states, the order also engaged in wars of its own and not infrequently quarreled with the Templars. They always acknowledged their subordination to the papacy. On occasion, however, they adopted policies not to the liking of the reigning pope, and they were frequently party to political intrigues among the European monarchs.

When Saladin drove the Crusaders out of Jerusalem in 1187, the Knights of St. John of Jerusalem took up residence in Acre, and they held their stronghold for over a century. In 1291 they lost Acre in a ferocious battle. The Mamelukes of Egypt, who conquered the city, massacred the Christian and Jewish inhabitants and only a small remnant of the Hospitallers managed to escape. They established their convent and hospital in Cyprus but their fortunes there declined. In 1310, however, they succeeded in driving the pirates out of the Greek island of Rhodes. They settled there, fortified the island, and thereafter provided the crusading expeditions with a safe harbor as well as an experienced body of warriors. Since the struggle for the defense of the Christian East was an unceasing one, the military role of the Hospitallers was an unending battle on land and sea.

At Rhodes the Hospitallers enjoyed many attributes of independence. They passed laws, coined money, issued passports, and sent ambassadors to the European seats of government. But their sovereignty was restricted by the popes who exerted authority over the masters and brethren, and often caused them to digress from or totally change their political directions. Despite their European involvements the Hospitallers never abandoned their hope of recapturing Jerusalem and reestablishing their hospital in the Holy City.

The Turks repeatedly laid siege to the island of Rhodes, but they could not subdue the Hospitallers. Only in 1522 did the powerful Turkish armies of Suleiman the Magnificent succeed in defeating the Hospitallers. Suleiman granted the Hospitallers honorable terms of surrender which enabled them to withdraw and settle permanently on the island of Malta. In 1530, Emperor Charles V transferred the island to the Hospitallers who became the island's sovereign rulers.

In Malta the order reached the height of its power. Its navy became the most powerful in the Mediterranean and it waged incessant war on the Ottomans and the Barbary pirates. For over two hundred years the Knights of Malta, as the Hospitallers came to be called, patrolled the Mediterranean and blocked the advance of the Moslems toward the heart of Christendom. Galleys of the Order also took part in the battle of Lepanto in 1571 which broke the Ottoman tide.

But the decline of the order was inevitable. The Crusading spirit waned; the Reformation deprived the order of its possessions in England

and in some of the German states; and the growing nationalism of that era clashed with the order's supranational character. Disputes with the popes and the reigning monarchs intensified; inner decay manifested itself in many ways. For example, membership in the order became increasingly a perquisite of exalted families who sought to establish their younger sons in the order's priories as benefices. Discipline became lax, and internal dissension increased. Then came the French Revolution which despoiled the order of its holding in France. Finally, Napoleon, on his way to Egypt, seized the island in 1798, and the Knights of Malta scattered in search of new homes. Some of them found a resting place in Russia where Tsar Paul I welcomed them. The Knights of Malta elected the Tsar as their Grand Master, this despite his being a non-Catholic. But this grasping of the proverbial straw did not save the order from drowning. For all practical purposes the Knights of Malta ceased to exist in 1801.

Thirty-three years later the order was reestablished in Rome with papal sanctions. It was renamed The Sovereign and Military Order of the Knights Hospitallers. The order's activities were now limited to its original humanitarian purpose. The sovereign character of the order has been recognized by many Catholic states to which the order accredits ministers.

In England the order of the Knights of St. John of Jerusalem ceased to exist in 1540 when Henry VIII confiscated the order's properties. The order remained dormant for almost three centuries until it was revived in 1831 as a Protestant order. In 1888 Queen Victoria made it into a British chivalrous order, named the Most Venerable Order of the Hospital of St. John of Jerusalem. The British reigning monarch is its sovereign head and its grand priors are members of the British royal house. Like chivalry itself, the order is an institution of the nobility, but it also includes members chosen on the basis of merit. There are now about twenty thousand members in the order of whom about seven hundred are knights.

The order maintains liaison with the Sovereign Military Order in Rome and thus bears a distant but unofficial relationship to the original Hospitallers of Jerusalem. The Most Venerable Order has distinguished itself for its relief and hospital work and for the creation of the St. John's Ambulance Association during World War I.

Among the Most Venerable Order's benevolent activities is the maintenance of the St. John Ophthalmic Hospital in Jerusalem which is located in the Sheikh Jarrah quarter on the Nablus Road. At the entrance to the hospital there is an inscription which reads:

The Order of St. John
The Ophthalmic Hospital in Jerusalem

This corner stone was laid by the Chancellor of the Order, Sir Henry Pownall K.C.B. etc., and the Hospitaller of the Order, Sir Stewart Duke-Elder G.C.V.O. on the 5th March, 1959.

This hospital is built in the service of the people of the Middle East and has been provided by donations collected for this purpose by members of the Order of St. John.

Within the entrance there is another plaque with an inscription that reads:

The Order of St. John
The Ophthalmic Hospital in Jerusalem

To commemorate the visit of His Royal Highness, the Duke of Cloucester, K.G.

Grand Prior
of the Order of St. John of Jerusalem
March 19th 1963

and to record the opening of the hospital on October 11th 1960 in the presence of the Lord Wakehurst K.G., Lord Prior of St. John and Sir Stewart Duke-Elder, G.C.V.O.

Hospitaller of St. John

It is thus that the fighting monks of crusader days who were driven out of Jerusalem almost eight centuries ago are remembered today in the Holy City of their origin by an impressive memorial inscription in the Muristan and by a hospital for the treatment of eye diseases. After all their glories on the battlefield and their worldwide fame the Knights Hospitallers have left in Jerusalem a rather meager legacy. But their memory will, in all probability, endure. Jerusalem does not forget those who made history within its gates.

An American chapter of the Hospitallers was organized in 1926, known as the Association of Master-Knights of the Sovereign Military Order of Malta in the United States of America. Like its model in Rome, it has dedicated itself to religious and benevolent activities. In 1960 a chapter of the British Most Venerable Order of the Hospital of St. John of Jerusalem was established in America. The American chapter, too, is dedicated to the performance of humanitarian work.

The King Who Willed His Heart to Jerusalem

Judah Halevi, who is regarded as the greatest of medieval Hebrew poets, lived in Spain from 1086 to 1142. His celebrated poem, "Ode to Zion," opens with the oft-quoted words: "My heart is in the east and I am in the uttermost west." A celebrated European king, who lived about two centuries after Judah Halevi, also had his heart in the east. Robert Bruce, king of Scotland, had vowed to join in a Crusade to rescue the Holy City from the Saracens. But he was preoccupied with the incessant wars for the freedom of Scotland and could not fulfill his vow. On his deathbed he instructed that his heart be removed, embalmed, and taken to Jerusalem for burial.

Robert Bruce was crowned king of Scotland in 1306, but it was only in 1314 that the English recognized him as ruler of the Scots. He was prevented from fulfilling his vow due to a serious illness, possibly leprosy. Before his death in 1329 he made known his wish and entrusted the mission into the hands of his friend, Sir James Douglas. A vivid account of Robert Bruce's death and Sir James Douglas's ill-fated journey to Jerusalem was recorded by a contemporary writer. An excerpt of that anonymous account (as published, in modernized spelling) follows:

> It fortuned that King Robert of Scotland was right sore aged and feeble: for he was greatly charged with the great sickness, so that there was no way for him but death. . . . He called to him the gentle knight Sir James Douglas, and said before all the lords: "Sir James, my dear friend, ye know well that I have had much ado in my day to uphold and sustain the right of this realm, and when I had most ado I made a solemn vow [to go on a Crusade to rescue the Holy Sepulchre from the infidels], which as yet I have not accomplished, whereat I am right sorry. . . . And sith it is so that my body cannot go nor achieve that my heart desireth, I will send the heart instead of the body to accomplish mine avow instead of myself: and by cause I know not in all my realm a knight more valiant than ye be, nor of body so well furnished to accomplish mine avow instead of myself, therefore I require you, mine own dear and special friend, that ye will take on you this voyage for the love of me, and to acquit my soul against my Lord God. . . . I will that as soon as I am trespassed out of this world that ye take the heart out of my body and embalm it, and take of my treasure, as ye shall think sufficient for that enterprise, both for yourself and such company as ye will take with you, and present my heart to the Holy Sepulchre where Our Lord lay, seeing my body cannot come there. . . . "

> Then all the lords that heard these words wept for pity. And when this

knight Sir James Douglas might speak for weeping he said; "Ah, gentle and noble king, a hundred times I thank your grace of the great honour that ye do to me, sith of so noble and great treasure ye give me in charge. And, sir, I shall do with a glad heart all that ye have commanded me to the best of my true power, howbeit I am not worthy nor sufficient to achieve such a noble enterprise. . . . "

And then soon after this the noble Robert de Brus King of Scotland trespassed out of this uncertain world and his heart taken out of his body and embalmed, and honourably he was interred in the Abbey of Dumfermline, in the year of our Lord God 1329, the 7th day of the month of November.[11]

Sir James Douglas set out on his mission and digressed to join the king of Spain in a war against the Moors. In one of the battles he lost his life. But his precious treasure, the embalmed heart of Robert Bruce, was saved and brought back to Scotland where it was buried.

On one of Jerusalem's hills overlooking the Valley of Hinnom and facing the western wall of the city's fortifications stands the Church and Hospice of St. Andrews, "The Scots Kirk in the Holy City." The foundation of the church was laid on May 7, 1927, by General Allenby in whose army were many "Scots laddies kilted and braw" who fought for the Holy City. The dedication took place on St. Andrew's Day (Nov. 30), 1930. Prior to the dedication, in 1929, on the six hundredth anniversary of Robert Bruce's death, the people of Dumfermline, where the king's body was buried and the people of Melrose, where the king's heart was interred joined in memorializing their hero's wish. They presented St. Andrews in Jerusalem with a brass plaque which lies in the floor of the church in front of the Communion Table. The inscription reads: "In remembrance of the pious wish of King Robert Bruce that his heart should be buried in Jerusalem." In the margin of the plaque one reads: "In celebration of the sixth century of his death — 1329, 7th June, 1929. Given by citizens of Dumfermline and Melrose."

Three decades prior to the installation of the plaque in St. Andrew's Church, Robert Bruce's pious wish was redeemed by a descendant of his. This event was recorded in *The Innis Review* of 1904:

In 1865, shortly before [John Patrick Crichton Stuart, third Marquess of Bute] was received into the Catholic Church, he made his first pilgrimage to Jerusalem and ever after treasured the testimonial given him by the Father Guardian of the Franciscan Convent of Mount Sion, stating that from his arrival in Jerusalem on 10th May, 1865, until the issue of the document on 29th May, 1865, Bute had piously visited all the traditional sanctuaries of

Interior of the Scots Church of St. Andrew (1951). (Courtesy of Israel Government Press Office.)

the Holy City. Bute made several pilgrimages to Jerusalem. . . . At the end of his days, this historically minded nobleman, re-enacting the desire of his fourteenth-century ancestor, King Robert Bruce, instructed that his heart should be carried to Jerusalem, where it was laid to rest by his wife and children in the garden of the little chapel, called *Dominus Flevit,* on the slope of Mount Olivet and a tablet set up at the entrance to the garden. [12]

A. Martens, D.F.M., in his work, *Who Was a Christian in the Holy Land,* notes that "since the family Stuart are of royal descent, the burying of the heart [in the Holy City] was considered as fulfilling by proxy the wish of Robert Bruce, whose heart never reached Jerusalem." [13]

Under the Turks, Bakshish Lubricated the Wheels of Life

In Jerusalem everyone knew that bakshish lubricated the wheels of government. From the highest to the lowest, from the pasha to the judge to the policeman, everyone asked for bakshish. It was said that the Turkish officials were underpaid because they were expected to augment their incomes as best they could, which is—bakshish.

Pilgrims usually assumed that bakshish was undercover graft. But they soon discovered to their amazement that bakshish was a way of life. It removed all obstacles and opened all doors. It was the foundation of "justice" and made the governor accessible and the judge sympathetic. It closed the policeman's eyes to open transgressions and rendered the streetcleaner attentive to his duties near your place of business. Bakshish was not accepted as a gift; it was demanded as an obligation.

The plague of bakshish was not limited to government officials. Everyone demanded bakshish. John Finley tells of his pilgrimage in the Holy Land during the First World War, and a real pilgrimage it was, for he *walked* the length and breadth of the land. He writes:

> I travelled alone through the night without serious molestation. I was stopped by a group of men at dusk and asked rather savagely for cigarettes and "backsheesh," both of which requests I had to refuse after some parleying, because I had no cigarettes, and I was not disposed to give "backsheesh." [14]

There were also occasions where bakshish was extorted at the point of a deadly weapon, as examplified by an incident recorded by a pilgrim in the mid-nineteenth century:

Having waded down one day in the [Siloam Pool] to show it to the Rev. Mr Sampson, a rector of the Irish church near Londonderry, an Arab from the village of Selwan watched us enter the little chamber above the pool, and then stopped up the egress, demanding backshish. *Mafeesh backshish* was the immediate reply, whereupon he raised above his head a short axe he carried, and threatened to make a cut at us, still demanding backshish. We were both unarmed. I raised my umbrella, prepared to strike in return; Mr Sampson put his hand into his breast, as if he had a pistol there, and thus we stood for about a couple of minutes facing one another, while the demands for backshish become more fierce. At last, finding that we were not to be intimidated, and judging probably that with two against him he would have the worst of it if we came to blows, he slunk off very sheepishly, and we went our way without further molestation.[15]

The corruption of the pashas also affected the administration of justice by the kadis who were the religious judges. They were just as susceptible to bakshish as the pashas. James Finn, the British consul in Jerusalem during the mid-nineteenth century, describes the administration of justice by the kadis:

> Every town has its judge, a native of the country (except at Jerusalem), who decides causes on the principles of the Korah and its Commentaries, as far as he is acquainted with them. These minor judges are appointed by the Kadi of the next capital city, who is himself commissioned by purchase from Constantinople for a term of three years, the scale of purchase rising from that of the lowest appointment up to the highest, which is Baghdad, and Jerusalem stands rather high upon the ladder.
>
> The Kadi's court is called the *Makhkameh,* and the judge receives a fee of three per cent upon the value of suits decided, to be paid by the gainer in the cause. . . .
>
> The Kadis and their courts are notorious, and always have been so (see 'Arabian Nights' *passim,* and elsewhere), for the prevalence of bribery, jealousy, favouritism, interested intercession, etc.
>
> The suborning of false testimony from men waiting at the door for employment in perjury, for even a trifling pay, is a matter of frequent occurrence; and the failings of the Kadi give a zest to social conversation, or to poems or narrations at the coffee-houses: so much so that among Christians who occasionally get pork to eat, the pig's head, when brought to table, is in mockery designated the 'Kadi's head.'[16]

An example of how bakshish lubricated the wheels of government is related by H. Rider Haggard who was in Jerusalem at the turn of the century. He relates in his book, *A Winter Pilgrimage:*

Some years ago the Baroness Burdett-Coutts offered to restore the broken aqueduct [from Solomon's Pools to Jerusalem] at a cost of £20,000. Thereupon the Turkish authorities, wishing to profit by this strange folly of a Frank, asked for another £3000 *baksheesh* in return for the honour that must accrue to a stranger who, at her own expense, proposed to provide their city with a supply of pure water. I am glad to say that, according to the story, the Baroness refused to submit to this imposition. Subsequently, after the pause common in the East, it was intimated to her that her original offer would be accepted. To this she is reported to have replied that she had now spent the money in building or endowing a church in England. As a result, Jerusalem remains, and is likely to remain, without any constant supply of drinking water. [17]

The Pasha always concentrated on the fiscal matters of government. He had paid an exorbitant amount for his post and his main concern was to recoup his "investment" and to make as much profit as he could. In addition to the heavy taxes that he imposed, he also resorted to extortion and torture as means of extracting as much bakshish as possible. William Jowett reports one such incident which was not an exception:

Rabbi Mendel was suffering from terror, the impression of which was not yet effaced from his mind; he having been, about a week before, forcibly seized in the night, and carried off to prison by order of the new Governor. The pretext alleged that his street-door had been left open in the night; for this he was compelled to pay a heavy fine of three purses; about £37 sterling. The officer, who apprehended him, burst with violence into his inner chamber — waked him — spurned all his protestations of his having European protection — he having an Austrian Firman; and forthwith took him, his disciple Rabbi Isaac, and two others, to the prison, from which after twenty-four-hours' confinement, and the payment of the fine, they were set at liberty. . . . The money was, clearly, the sole motive for this proceeding — a new Governor, in this devoted city, generally making his advances, by rapid steps, first to the Jews, next to the Greeks and Armenians, and finally to the Latins. [18]

How was one to handle the situation? When bakhshish was demanded by government officials, foreign nationals could appeal to their consuls. The native population, however, was helpless. In dealing with all others, Ermete Pierotti, in his *Customs and Traditions of Palestine,* offers practical advice on how to deal with it:

What traveller in the East, especially in Syria, does not know the word Bakhshish? So many thousand times has it been dinned into his ears that he uses it at home, and it has thus become almost naturalized in Europe. I cannot here enumerate all the occasions on which bakhshish is demanded, for they are numberless. Sleeping or waking, dressing or undressing, working or idling, still the same cry is heard, hateful as the fly's buzz, the gnat's trumpet, or the flea's bite to the weary traveller. In a word, in Palestine men are born, live, and die, to the one tune "bakhshish, bakhshish." I will relate a few anecdotes to show some of the cases in which it is demanded by the Arabs, remarking that the Christians are as bad as the Mohammedans, and that the nomad tribes alone have sufficient self-respect to ask for it only on reasonable grounds.

Once, in 1857, a missionary of the Latin rite was entreated by some Arabs to visit their district and preach to them. Their protestations of respect and their supplications were such that the good man had not the heart to refuse, and on a fixed day he went. A large number of Arabs attended and listened to his words. Much pleased with the attention of his hearers, and trusting that they had received some spiritual benefit, the preacher prepared to depart, when the whole congregation crowded around him demanding bakhshish, "for," said they, "we have come hither and listened to you." He threw some small coins to those who brought his horse and helped him into the saddle, and then rode away among the yells and curses of his disappointed flock.

I have frequently come upon men or women quarreling in a village or in the open country, grasping each other by the dress or the hair, and scolding vehemently at the top of their voices. Sometimes I have interfered to prevent a fatal termination to the strife and separated the combatants, after protecting the weaker party. As soon as tranquility has been restored, both have pronounced the mighty word; and when I asked on what pretext they claimed it, was generally informed, "Because I had interrupted their business," or "because they had left off to please me." I need not say that they forthwith received bakhshish from my horsewhip or stick, as a lesson for the future. In fact, the Arabs sometimes get up a quarrel when they see a European coming, in hopes that they may be parted and so get an excuse for asking a gift.

One day, I was returning from inspecting the repairs of the road between Jaffa and Jerusalem (which were executed by order of Surraya pasha in 1859), and, about two hours' journey from the latter place, found a labourer lying by the way side, who had been badly hurt in exploding a mine. I stopped, washed and bound up his wounds as well as I could, and then placing him on my horse, walked slowly by his side, accompanied by his brother, to the Latin Hospital in the town, and placed him in bed. It would naturally be supposed that the patient thanked me for my care. Not a word, he only asked for a bakhshish; and as he was so badly hurt, I had not the heart to refuse it. This, however, was not all; on quitting the hospital I was met by the brother, who made the same demand. Out of patience, I asked "Why?" He replied, "Because I have accompanied you hither." "But you have accompanied your brother." "No, sir," he answered, "you told me to come, otherwise I should not have stirred!" He will not quickly forget the "bakhshish" that I administered.

As I was going to Bethlehem, one Monday morning (the day on which labourers employed on buildings come to Jerusalem), I found a small bag containing a stonemason's tools; I returned and after some trouble found the owner, who, instead of thanking me, asked for a "bakhshish," which was given heartily in the same coin as in the last case.[19]

With the arrival of the British, bakshish ceased to lubricate the wheels of government. And now, under Israeli rule, bakshish has practically disappeared. If one encounters an incident of bakshish, it is one of the last gasps of a dying institution.

Napoleon's Proclamation "From Jerusalem"

Napoleon was never in Jerusalem. Yet there is ostensibly a document, dated April 20, 1799, which Napoleon issued in Jerusalem, offering Palestine to the Jews as a national homeland. To be sure, no such document actually exists. But historians believe that the document was composed by Napoleon in anticipation of his conquest of Jerusalem. When he failed to capture the Holy City, he suppressed his offer to the Jews.

On April 20, 1799, Napoleon's army was besieging Acre and he was sure of the city's fall. After the capture of Acre he planned to take Jerusalem. Napoleon's intentions were foreseen by the inhabitants of the Holy City who hastily improvised defenses around the city. Napoleon expected to capture the Holy City without difficulty, and he figured that his victorious entry into Jerusalem would make his proclamation credible. It would also have the impact of a messianic call to the Jews. The historian, Salo W. Baron, says that Napoleon's proclamation "symbolized Europe's acknowledgement of Jewish rights in Palestine."[20] This proclamation was a sort of forerunner of the Balfour Declaration.

Philip Guedalla in his published lecture, *Napoleon and Palestine*, states that among the thousands of papers on Napoleon's correspondence which relate to his Egyptian expedition there is one proclamation to the Arabs of Palestine. "But there is no trace of a proclamation to the Jewish people." The only contemporary evidence of such a proclamation consists of two news items in a French periodical, *Moniteur*, published in Constantinople, in which it was reported that Napoleon issued such a proclamation and appealed to the Jews of Asia and Africa to join his army for the restoration of Jerusalem. Philip Guedalla concludes that—

> the report in the *Moniteur* cannot have been a canard issued on his [Napoleon's] instructions. One possibility alone remains: that . . . the strange story which it told was true. Bonaparte had called the Jews to arms *pour rétablir l'ancienne Jérusalem,* and for a few weeks in the spring of 1799 he was a momentary Zionist.[21]

Napoleon did not succeed in capturing Acre. On May 20 the siege was raised and Bonaparte was in full retreat. Napoleon's proclamation "from Jerusalem" was at best an empty gesture.

The Colorful Bodyguards of Foreign Dignitaries

Turkish law required consuls, bishops, and patriarchs to engage official bodyguards known as kavasses, who were responsible for the safety of their masters. In time this function became purely ceremonial. The kavasses wore lavish uniforms with a silken sash around their waist, baggy, bright colored pants, and a jacket embroidered in gold braid. The kavasses also wore long, curved scimitars. When walking before their masters or anyone of the masters' households, the kavasses held in their right hands long, silver-headed staffs and they struck the ground at each step, thus warning people to make way for the dignitaries behind them. The rhythmic, clicking sound of the kavasses' staffs worked magic. Man and beast made way for the dignitaries. Some foreign notables had two or more kavasses. In that case, the kavasses struck the pavement in concert and their authority was that much the greater.

Mrs. Elizabeth Anne Finn, wife of James Finn, the British Consul in Jerusalem, describes this strange institution which she experienced at the consulate:

> We found that the consuls always had military attendants called Kawasses (bowmen), who now carry sword and pistols. Their duty is to act in case of any riot or disturbance. Christians would be of no use in such a case, as they could not have raised a hand against a Mohammedan. The Kawasses were, in fact, soldier servants, and were furnished with silver-headed staves of office shod with iron, with which they marched before the consul when he went out. I was not allowed to go out without the attendance of one or more of these men, of whom we usually had two, but sometimes eight on duty. One could tell the approach of a consul by the rhythmic clicking of these staves on the pavement as the men marched, and their

appearance was imposing when on horseback, for then they also carried these staves resting in the shovel stirrup. All this was sometimes tiresome, but very necessary in order to maintain order amongst the Oriental population and the dignity of the office. We clad our men in scarlet and gold-embroidered jackets, these being given to them on the Queen's birthday.[22]

Henry Gilman, American Consul in Jerusalem from 1881 to 1891, describes his kavasses in his novel, *Hassan: A Fellah:*

And just now there is an unusual stir at the gate, for the American consul is entering, on his return from the official function, which he has attended. . . . He is preceded by his cavasses or guards, resplendent objects, in their gold-embroidered jackets, and with enormous much-curved sabres in solid silver scabbards by their sides. They carry, also,

Bodyguards (kavasses).
(Courtesy of the National and
University Library, Jerusalem.)

long staves, heavily mounted and knobbed in silver, with which, as they advance, they smite the pavement, till it resounds again and again. This is an old custom, observed with dignitaries, to give notice of their approach, and to clear the way.[23]

Foreign consuls and church dignitaries were required by Turkish law to provide themselves with kavasses not as a matter of proper protocol, but in order to relieve the pasha of the responsibility of providing protection for these foreigners. Why should the pasha squander his precious bakshish merely to protect the population? If Turkish subjects were plundered or murdered no one cared. But if foreign dignitaries of state or church were injured, the pasha might be called upon to answer for these crimes. Hence the Turkish law required that every foreign dignitary have his own guards.

Lord Nugent, in the account of his travels, provides another compelling reason for the strange institution of kavasses. He writes in his itinerary:

> Not much above three years ago, one of the first fruits of the restoration of what was called the lawful authority of the Porte in the East was this—A gentleman officially connected with one of the Christian governments of Europe was walking, with his niece, in the open street. They were met by a band of these drunken Arnaouts [Turkish soldiers], one of whom having offered some outrage to the girl, and being struck by the uncle, drew a loaded pistol and instantly shot—not him who had stepped in to protect the girl from brutal insult, but the poor girl against whom the insult had been directed. The uncle bore his dying niece to his house. He applied to the Turkish authorities to prevent, by punishing the murderer, a like calamity being inflicted on other victims. He was told, with many expressions of regret, that his testimony to the fact could not be taken; that the religion of Mahomet was the law of the Mohammedan courts, and that, conformably with it, no oath of Christian or Jew could be taken against a true believer. In vain was other evidence sought. Mohammedans had seen the murder, but not one of them could be brought to give true evidence in the case, and the crime has to this day been followed by no legal consequences. Only this was done: the Arnaout was removed by the arbitrary order of the Governor, who was convinced in his own private judgment that the accusation was true. Accordingly you are always advised to take with you a Cavash, or some other Musulman, not as a guard, but as a witness to any dispute which may occur. Even this is a very imperfect security; for, in such a case, it is very unlikely that your Musulman will tell the truth to convict a co-religionist; but perchance his presence may act upon the fears, however groundless, of some ruffian who might otherwise assail you.[24]

Today the rhythmic clicking of the kavasses' staffs is no longer heard in Jerusalem, and the kavasses are no longer seen in Jerusalem's streets. A colorful institution has disappeared, an institution that is missed by no one.

The Filth That Used to Pervade the Streets of Jerusalem

The travel literature dealing with Jerusalem during the nineteenth century is replete with descriptions of Turkish neglect and misgovernment. Nowhere was this negligence as evident as in the filth that used to pervade every lane and alley of the Old City. Street cleaning or any other aspect of sanitation was of no concern to the pasha. His primary responsibility was to keep order, to collect taxes, and gather as much bakshish as possible. In wintertime the rains served as streetcleaners. In summertime the rubbish and garbage kept piling up during the day, and at night the half-starved dogs roamed freely in the alleys and devoured the carcasses of dead animals and other edible garbage. Were it not for these scavengers life would have been impossible. As it was, the stench from the rotting filth and the open sewers made sightseeing in the Old City unpleasant. Many a visitor during the summer months remembered the city mainly by his nostrils.

The Reverend J. A. Spencer, who visited Jerusalem in the mid-nineteenth century (April 1849), noted in his travelogue:

> To a European or American accustomed to the broad avenues and clean, paved and well-lighted streets of most of our cities and towns Jerusalem, like all oriental cities, must, at first, appear unpleasant and disagreeably dirty. . . . The traveller has to make his way as best he can amid loose stones, dirt and nastiness, and fill his mind with sadness and regret that the Holy City should be thus degraded and brought low.[25]

And the American, Bayard Taylor, who visited Jerusalem at about the same time, noted in his itinerary:

> Jerusalem, internally, gives no impression but that of filth, ruin, poverty, and degradation. . . . All the [streets], to the very gates of the Holy Sepulchre, are channels of pestilence.[26]

A half a century later, the famous landscape artist, Henry A. Harper, visited Jerusalem. In his book, *An Artist's Walks in Bible Lands,* he writes about the filth in Jerusalem's streets:

> There are in some places gutters to carry off surface water, but these gutters soon become open sewers, receptacles for every kind of filth in which offal of every kind festers in the sun. It is difficult enough to walk through David Street in the daytime, jostled as you are at every step by camels, horses, and donkeys; but still more difficult is it to walk through at night, when the flickering lantern of your attendant fails to reveal the numerous pitfalls of stinking mud into which your uncertain steps plunge.[27]

Theodor Herzl, the "founder" of modern Zionism, also took cognizance of the filth that pervaded the Old City during the Turkish rule. In his diaries he noted that in rebuilding Jerusalem, he would, first of all, "empty the nests of filth and tear them down."[28]

The British, during their thirty years of rule in Jerusalem, tried to improve the situation but with only partial success. Thus Pierre van Paassen describes the filthiness of the bazaar as he witnessed it in 1939:

> Of cleanliness there is not a trace: the blood of slaughtered animals gushes into the streets; a million flies zoom over the heaps of refuse and offal into which little brown children dig for overripe figs or cucumbers. Here is a donkey taking advantage of a traffic jam to relieve itself. The urine spatters over a row of crackling flat loaves of bread that a baker's assistant has spread out on the edge of the roadway to cool off. The baker, viewing the scene from his cellar through an opening just level with the street, emits a stream of vile names addressed at the mother of the donkey's owner. This gentleman, until then calmly sucking a pomegranate, suddenly purses his lips, spits out the pips, and hits the baker smack in the eye. A gale of laughter greets this performance. Business is suspended. There are explanations to passers-by who have missed the show. A policeman elbows his way through the crowd and traffic begins to move again.[29]

It is only after the Six-Day War that reasonable cleanliness arrived in the Old City. A modern sewage system was installed and street cleaning was instituted. Butchers were made to install refrigerators in their shops, and dogs ceased to wander about in search of carcasses and other edible garbage. Today, visitors in Jerusalem need not hold their nostrils as they wander about and enjoy the marvelous sights, religious and historic.

TWO

Jerusalem the Blessed

"A Spectacle One Might Gaze on Forever"

The modern traveler usually approaches Jerusalem from the west. He thus misses the most glorious and unforgettable view of the city, a view that pilgrims and tourists used to speak of with rapture. In former years visitors planned their entry into the Holy City so as to approach it from the east, over the Mount of Olives. When the visitor reached the crest of the mount, a grand vision burst into view. Standing on the crest or the declivity of the Mount of Olives, the visitor saw the Holy City spread out before him as a huge, living map with every street and shrine clearly marked. He saw the prominent Dome of the Rock (Mosque of Omar) and the dome of the El Aksa Mosque, the dark domes of the Church of the Holy Sepulchre, and the less prominent but notable domes of the Hurvah and the Nissim Bak synagogues.[1] He saw the many minarets and steeples, the Via Dolorosa, and the Armenian and Greek convents, the bazaars and the multitude of pilgrims and tourists slowly moving in opposite directions or standing and haggling over the "bargains" offered for sale. Jerusalem seen from the Mount of Olives was truly a city that is "beautiful for situation, the joy of the whole earth . . . the city of the Great King" (Ps. 42:2). The visitor irresistibly blessed the Holy City in the words of the psalmist: "Peace be within thy walls, and prosperity within thy palaces" (Ps. 122:7).

Many of the visitors who saw Jerusalem from the Mount of Olives testified in glowing words to the glorious view. Among these was the noted French scholar, F. de Saulcy, who said:

> I doubt if the world can produce a panorama to be compared with it. . . . This is a spectacle one might gaze on for ever with the deepest emotion, and which cannot be left without regret, often turning back to enjoy the sensation it gives birth to, as long as possible.[2]

Another visitor, Dr. Philip Schaff, who was Professor of Sacred Literature at the Union Theological Seminary of New York, spoke of Jerusalem, seen from the Mount of Olives, with equal emotion:

> The best place from which to study the panorama for orientation is Mount Olivet, with the Bible in the right hand and Josephus in the left. There you see the holy city in her lonely melancholy grandeur, with her walls and towers, her churches, mosques, and dome-roofed houses. It is the saddest, and yet the most impressive view in the world.[3]

Let the visitor go to the top of the Mount of Olives and he will recapture some of that thrilling experience. Let him ascend that hill, preferably early in the morning, immediately after sunrise, or shortly before sunset. Any time, however, will prove rewarding.

The Center of the World

In the ruins of the Roman Forum one can see a spot which was known as *Umbilicus Urbis,* the navel or the center of Rome. But in Jerusalem one can see not just the center of Jerusalem, but the center of the world. What is more surprising is that there are in Jerusalem two centers of the world. Jews and Moslems are agreed that the Holy Rock on Mount Moriah is the authentic center of the world. The Sages of the Talmud say:

> The Land of Israel is in the center of the world; Jerusalem is in the center of the Land of Israel; the Holy Temple is in the center of Jerusalem; the Holy of Holies is in the center of the Holy Temple; the Holy Ark is in the center of the Holy of Holies; and the Foundation Stone (the holy Rock) from which the world was established is before the Holy Ark.[4]

But the Christians claim that the navel or center of the world is in the Greek Cathedral within the Church of the Holy Sepulchre. To prove their geographical doctrine, they quote the psalmist, who said, "God is my King of old, working salvation in the midst of the earth" (Ps. 74:12). The

*The Greek Cathedral in the Church of the Holy Sepulchre. The chalice in the
foreground indicates the traditional center of the earth (1970). (Courtesy of Israel
Government Press Office.)*

midst or center of the earth is where God works salvation, that is,
obviously, the Church of the Holy Sepulchre where salvation was achieved
for all believers. In the Greek Cathedral, within the Church of the Holy
Sepulchre, there is a short marble pillar fixed in the pavement which
marks the precise navel of the earth.

There is a famous sixteenth-century map which represents the world
as a three-leafed clover. Each leaf represents one of the main continents—
Europe, Asia, and Africa, and the center where the three leaves are joined
is marked "Jerusalem."

Sophisticated visitors in Jerusalem smile when they are told that
Jerusalem is the center of the world. They know better. The world is
round and every city can claim this distinction. Geographically, Jerusalem
is no more the center of the world than Boston, San Francisco, or Tokyo.
Spiritually, however, Jerusalem has really been the center of the world.
The prophet Isaiah affirmed this truth when he said: "Out of Zion will
come forth the Teaching (Torah) and the word of the Lord from Jerusalem"

Jerusalem as the "center of the world," in a sixteenth-century map.

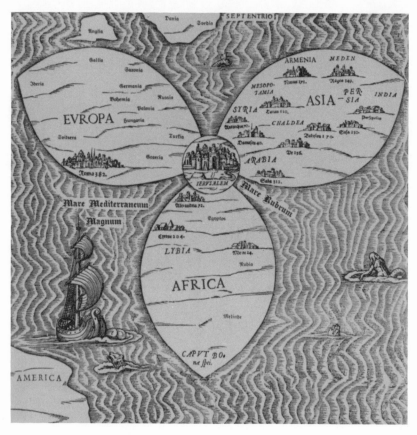

(Isa. 2:3). The alleys of Jerusalem have been trodden by prophets, psalmists, saints, and other spiritual giants. Jerusalem has been the mother of great religions, and it continues to inspire spiritual greatness. Jerusalem is indeed the spiritual center of the world.

J. E. Hanauer, former honorary canon of St. George's Cathedral in Jerusalem, says that "the idea of a centre of the world in the Holy City, though a quaint one, is not actually absurd." He quotes "a remarkable address, delivered in Jerusalem in 1904 by the Rev. Dr. Munro Gibson:

> Palestine, though small, was in no corner of the earth. South of it was Egypt; east, Babylon; north-east, Assyria; north, Tyre, Sidon and Syria; and west, Greece and Rome. If you take Jerusalem as the centre of a radius of twelve degrees of latitude, and describe a circle you will include the capitals of all the countries which figured in the world's history up to the time of Alexander the Great. There is no other capital of which this can be said. . . . The world was not nearly so large in ancient times as it is now, but such as it was, the Holy Land was in the centre of it. Think of it and you will see that it would have been impossible to have chosen a better position. This rocky ridge — lifted up above the great river plains around where grew and flourished the empires of antiquity — was a magnificent rostrum from which to reach the nations with the Word of God. Well might the Hebrew prophets lift up their voices to the nations far and near, with a cry like this: 'O earth, earth, earth, hear the word of the Lord.' Or, this: 'Hear, ye people, all of you; hearken, O earth, and all that therein is.'[5]

It is fitting to conclude this brief account of Jerusalem's spiritual centrality with the inspired statement by George Adam Smith in his work, *The Historical Geography of the Holy Land:*

> [Jerusalem has] no harbors; no river, no trunk-road, no convenient market for the nations on either side. In their commerce with each other these pass by Judea, finding their emporiums in the cities of Philistia, or, as of old, at Petra and Bosra on the east of the Jordan. Gaza has outdone Hebron as the port of the desert. Jerusalem is no match for Shechem [Nablus] in fertility or convenience or site. The whole plateau stands aloof, waterless, on the road to nowhere. There are none of the natural conditions of a great city.

> And yet it was here that She arose who, more than Athens and more than Rome, taught the nations civic justice, and gave her name to the ideal city men are ever striving to build on earth, to the City of God that shall one day descend from heaven — the New Jerusalem. For her builder was not Nature nor the wisdom of men, but on that secluded and barren site the Word of God, by her prophets, laid her eternal foundations in righteousness, and reared her walls in her people's faith in God.[6]

Jerusalem has indeed been a spiritual center of the three great monotheistic religions, and may yet again resume her mission to be a light to the nations. But Jerusalem cannot possibly resume her blessed role without first achieving the blessing of peace. Regrettably, peace is still far from her grasp.

"All Roads Lead to Jerusalem"

In the Holy Land all roads should lead to the Holy City. But, as we shall see, there was a time not so long ago when the case was vastly different. By the middle of the nineteenth century, no wheeled vehicle could reach Jerusalem, because there were *no* roads to the Holy City. Jaffa has always been Jerusalem's port city. But when pilgrims or tourists arrived in Jaffa they were surprised to discover that all travel to and from Jerusalem was by horse, camel, and donkey. The trip from Jaffa to Jerusalem, a distance of about forty miles, took two days. Thus the first Anglican Bishop, Reverend M. S. Alexander, who arrived in Jerusalem in 1842, remarked in a letter he wrote describing his entry into the Holy City: "[The road] is nothing but one continuation of awful ascents and precipices over most strangely rugged paths, which no English horse or other animal could encounter."[7]

And the noted American author, orator, and traveler, George William Curtis, reported in one of his letters first published in *The New York Tribune* and then in his book, *The Howadji in Syria:*

> There are no roads about the city. It is not accessible for carriages, nor would its narrow streets permit them to pass. This profound silence characterizes all the Eastern cities, in which wheels do not roar, nor steam shriek, and invests them, by contrast, with a wonderful charm. The ways that lead to the gates of Jerusalem, are horse-paths, like dry water-courses.[8]

It was only in 1869 that the first wheeled vehicle entered Jerusalem. In that year the Suez Canal was officially opened. One of the dignitaries who participated in the ceremony was the Austrian Emperor Francis Joseph. The emperor decided to include in his itinerary a pilgrimage to the Holy City. The Sublime Porte decided to construct a road from Jaffa to Jerusalem to enable the royal guest to travel in his carriage rather than on a donkey or on horseback. The Emperor was thus the first to arrive in Jerusalem in a wheeled vehicle. Roads to Jerusalem's neighboring cities of Jericho and Hebron were not opened until 1890. It should be noted, however, that notwithstanding the fact that the road from Jaffa was built in honor of a royal guest, it was not paved. The road was dusty in summer and "rivers of mud" in winter. This was equally true of all the roads to Jerusalem.

In 1892 the narrow gauge railway between Jerusalem and Jaffa was completed. The trip from Jaffa to Jerusalem then took only five hours. Of course, today one travels from Tel Aviv or Jaffa to Jerusalem in less than one hour.

A City of Many Names

Jerusalem is a city of many names. It has been called Jebus, Zion, Shalem, Urushalem, the City of David, Yerushalayim, Ariel, Aelia Capitolina, God's City, the Holy City, the Faithful City, the City of Peace, the Beautiful City, the Blessed City, and a number of other names. A rabbinic tradition has it that "Jerusalem has seventy names."[9] However, the name that stuck is Yerushalayim or, in its Latinized form, Jerusalem. How did Jerusalem come to have so many names? A glimpse at the city's long political and spiritual history will provide the answer.

About three thousand years ago, there stood a small fortified town to the south of the present city of Jerusalem. It was inhabited by a people called Jebusites, and the name of the town was Jebus. The town was also a religious center where the local deity, called Shalem, was worshiped. Hence the town was also known as Urushalem (the city of the deity Shalem) or just Shalem. The town also had a castle which the inhabitants regarded as impregnable. They called their castle Zion. When King David captured the town of Jebus or Urushalem, he made it his capital and renamed it the City of David. The name Jebus was forgotten and never used again. But the alternate name, Urushalem, was retained. The Hebrews confused the component "Shalem" with the Hebrew word "Shalom," which means "peace." Thus the ancient name of the town Urushalem became the "City of Peace."

To the north of the town there was a hill, Mount Moriah, which was an ancient place of sacrifice. On this sacred hill King David built an altar and his son, King Solomon, raised a Temple to the God of Israel. The city and the Temple rapidly won the hearts of the people and it became the everlasting religious and political center of the Jewish people. The prophets and the psalmists of Israel glorified the city and lovingly called it the Holy City, the City of God, the Faithful City, the Eternal City, the City of

The citadel, with the minaret popularly called the Tower of David. (Courtesy of Israel Government Press Office.)

the Great King, and other endearing and reverential names. When King David died, the secondary name, City of David, was abandoned. Only Yerushalayim (Jerusalem) and occasionally Zion continued to be used.

In the second century, the Romans attempted to erase the city and its name from the map and from the memory of mankind. They thoroughly destroyed the city and ran a plow over it. This act symbolized a city's death. On the ruins of Jerusalem the Romans built a new, pagan city which they named Aelia Capitolina—"Aelia" in honor of the Emperor Hadrian whose full name was Aelius Hadrianus, and "Capitolina" in honor of the god Jupiter Capitolinus. The new name endured for two centuries. In the fourth century C.E., the Emperor Constantine embraced Christianity, and he restored the name Jerusalem. But the name Aelia continued to be used among many Christians for at least two centuries. The name Jerusalem was used concurrently. The Jews never used the Roman name. For them the city, although it had been paganized, continued to be, both in prayer and in ordinary usage, the city of Jerusalem. They also called it *Ir Ha-Kodesh*—the City of Holiness. Christians have called it *Terra Sancta,* and the Moslems still call Jerusalem *El Kuds,* the Holy (City).

One of the Most Cosmopolitan Cities in the World

One is not surprised to hear it said that New York, London, or Paris are cosmopolitan cities. Their large populations, wealth, and culture have attracted immigrants and visitors from all over the world. Foreign colonies have been established and cosmopolitanism thus became a manifest feature of life. To say, however, that a backward, poverty-stricken town is one of the most cosmopolitan cities in the world is hard to believe. Yet, Jerusalem—which till recent times had a population of less than fifty thousand—has been repeatedly described by travelers and historians as one of the most cosmopolitan towns in the world. Even when the city's population was only fifteen thousand, pilgrims and tourists noted the cosmopolitan nature of the city. Thus we read in William Hepworth Dixon's account of his pilgrimage in Jerusalem in 1863:

> All centuries, all nations, seem to hustle each other in this open court under David's tower. In pushing through the crowd of men, you may chance to run against a turbaned Turk, a belted Salhaan, a gaudy Cavash, a naked Nubian, a shaven Carmelite, a bearded papa, a robed Armenian, an English sailor, a Circassian chief, a Bashi Bazouk, and a converted Jew. In crossing from the gateway to the convent, you may stumble on a dancing dervish; you may catch the glance of a veiled beauty; you may break a procession of Arab school-girls, headed by a British female; you may touch the finger of a leper held out to you for alms.[10]

When one leaves the square near David's Tower and enters the bazaar on David Street one meets an endless procession of men and women of numerous cultures, arrayed in every style of Eastern and Western garb. Bedouin and their tattooed wives, Franciscan friars (in brown robes, rope girdles, and tonsured heads), Greek priests (in flowing black frocks and tall cylindrical hats) and Armenian priests (in similar frocks but a pointed hood for a hat), modern Arabs (in red fezzes and Western clothing), townswomen (in long white sheets reaching from head to foot), fellahin (their heads covered with the keffiah), ecclesiastics (in black, brown, and white robes), bearded Jews (in long kaftans and black, round hats), blacks, Hindus, Orientals—all meet and jostle each other as they make their way through the narrow bazaar. As Mark Twain observed: "It seems to me that all the races and colors and tongues of the earth must be represented among the fourteen thousand souls that dwell in Jerusalem."[11]

Estelle Blyth stated that "over forty languages and dialects are spoken every day within these walls [of Jerusalem]."[12]

Water carrier (1935). (Courtesy of Israel Government Press Office.)

The noted archaeologist, Charles Warren, in his *Underground Jerusalem*, marks the city's cosmopolitanism by its profusion of hats:

> Here is the most perfect study of hats to be met with, and by-the-bye all unsightly. The American has a chimney-pot hat, with the brim at the bottom; the Greek priest appears to have the same hat, only he has put his head in through the wrong end, and the brim stands out at top; the Persian hat rakes backwards, the Druse is worn forward; the Armenian priest has a hood like an extinguisher; the mountaineers and northmen of Asia wear caps of fur: all are ugly and unsuitable. The turban is the only dress suited to the head of man, it gives him a good presence; while on the other hand the fez is the most degrading in its effects on the features.[13]

A further testament to the cosmopolitan character of Jerusalem is found in this observation by John Haynes Holmes, distinguished minister of the Labor Temple in New York:

> What peoples—all the tribes of earth! Bedouins wrapped warm in their abundant and picturesque robes of varied colors; Arabs distinguished in

bearing, some of them cultured scholars, others wild barbarians from the desert; Jews with their long beards, hanging curls, and queer hats and gabardines; veiled ladies, from the Moslem homes; superb women, young and old, bearing with noble carriage their baskets or jars or bundles upon their heads. . . . A water carrier with his goatskin water bag across his back; a letter writer squatting on the pavement with ink, pen and paper; a Nubian peddler blacker than any Negro; a blind beggar whining for alms; an alert native boy eager to serve as interpreter with either Arab or Jew; little children playing about the stalls and gutters; a donkey boy leading his patient beast; a camel driver guiding one, two, three lordly camels with packs so bulky that they threaten to crush the passer-by against the unyielding wall; a rabbi, an Abyssinian priest, a Moslem effendi. There is no end to the variety and picturesqueness of this spectacle. "Stand at the Jaffa Gate," said a Palestinian friend to me, and in fifteen minutes you will see as many different kinds of Jews—Jews from Arabia, from Syria, from Afghanistan, from Persia, from Russia, from Morocco, from South Africa, from America." They are all distinctive in dress, in language, in type, in character. For the dispersion was wide, and it lasted long. But here is the homeland, and the tribes are gathering.[14]

And another pilgrim of the late nineteenth century concludes her description of Jerusalem at Easter time by saying:

It would be difficult to find a more heterogeneous multitude in any other part of the world, and the confusion, jostling, haggling, dirt, and Babel-like mixture of tongues, baffle description.[15]

The Temple Mount in the Jewish, Christian, and Moslem Traditions

The sanctity of the Temple Mount rests on both historical and theological foundations, rooted in the national and religious consciousness of Jews, Christians, and Moslems. For the Jews the Temple Mount is the site where Abraham, the "father of multitudes," built his altar, intending to offer up his beloved son, Isaac, as proof of his boundless faith in God. On this hill King David set up an altar to God, and his son, King Solomon, erected the Temple which became the center of worship for the Children of Israel. The Temple Mount became "the place on which God has chosen to rest His name" (Deut. 14:24). On this hill both the First and Second Temples stood. And when the Romans destroyed the Second Temple and the Jews were scattered to "the four corners of the earth," they continued to pray daily for the rebuilding of the Temple on the holy mountain. To this day the Temple Mount remains, for the Jews, the holiest spot on earth—so holy that many Jews do not enter its precincts lest they defile its sanctity by not being in a perfect state of ritual purity. It is reported that Sir Moses Montefiore was granted permission by the Moslem custodians to visit the Temple Mount. At that time, Jews and Christians were strictly forbidden entry to the sacred compound. In order to circumvent the rabbinic prohibition against entering the holy place, he resorted to a legal fiction. He had himself carried by several Moslems. Similarly it is reported that—

> when Rothschild visited Jerusalem many years ago now, he was carried over the ground of the Temple Area, lest his feet should desecrate holy things. [16]

In the Christian tradition, too, the Temple Mount is a sacred place, since Jesus taught and worshiped there. But the sanctity of the Temple Mount was not always critical in the Christian tradition. In the Byzantine era the Christians dumped their garbage on the Temple Mount to demonstrate their contempt for the Jews. In the days of the Crusaders, however, the Templars established their headquarters on the Temple Mount and turned the Dome of the Rock into a church. Since that time, the Temple Mount has been treated with respect and has been regarded as a Christian holy place, but only of secondary rank. The central Christian holy places are in the Church of the Holy Sepulchre. While the custodians of the Christian holy places in Jerusalem would rather suffer martyrdom than abandon the Holy Sepulchre, they have left the Temple Mount in Moslem hands with relative equanimity. No Christian sect would do battle for the possession of the Temple Mount as they would surely do for the Holy Sepulchre.

As to the Moslems, their connection with the Temple Mount is relatively of a late date. Islam was born in the far away Arabian Peninsula in the seventh century. Jerusalem was conquered by Omar in 638. Moslem tradition has it that Mohammed ascended to heaven from the holy Rock on the Temple Mount over which Abd al-Malik built the exquisite dome in 691. Although Jerusalem is not as holy as Mecca and Medina, and the Rock on the Temple Mount is not as holy as the Black Rock in Mecca, the Moslems would surely go to battle were anyone to try to dispossess them of the *Haram* as they call the Temple Mount.

For centuries the Moslems did not permit Jews and Christians to enter the *Haram* lest the infidels defile the sacred compound. When it was necessary to repair the clock in the El Aksa Mosque and only a Christian was sufficiently skilled to do so, the Moslems resorted to a legal fiction, similar to the one utilized by the Jews. Dr. J. T. Barclay, a mid-nineteenth century American medical missionary, relates:

> When the clock of the Mosk needs repairing they are compelled, however reluctantly, to employ a Frank. But in order to have a clean conscience in the commission of such *an abominable piece of sacrilege* as the admission of an *infidel* upon the sacred premises, they adopt the following expedient. The mechanic selected being thoroughly purged from his uncleanness by ablution *a la Turc,* a certain formula of prayer and incantation is sung over him at the gate. This being satisfactorily concluded, he is considered as exorcised, not only of Christianity [or Judaism, as the case may be], but of humanity also; and is declared to be no longer a man but a donkey. He is then mounted upon the shoulders of the *faithful,* lest, notwithstanding his depuration, the ground should be polluted by his footsteps; and being carried to the spot where his labors are required, he is set down upon matting within certain prescribed limits; and the operation being performed, he is carried back to the gate, and there, by certain other ceremonies, he is duly *undonkeyfied and transmuted into a man again!*[17]

The Moslem exclusion of all infidels from the Temple Mount was lifted after the Crimean War when the Sultan realized that he sat on his throne only by the grace of the European Powers. The gates to the Temple Mount were opened to all and have remained open to this day. Only on Friday mornings and on other occasions when there are Moslem services in the El Aksa Mosque are the gates to the Temple Mount closed to non-Moslems.

The Temple Mount is still the most sacred spot on earth for the Jews. It is also a holy place, of secondary importance, for the Christians; and a very holy site for the Moslems, next in importance only to Mecca and Medina. The Moslems worship within the precincts of the Temple Mount, the Jews worship at the foot of one of the Temple Mount's sustaining walls, known as the Western (Wailing) Wall, and the Christians visit the Temple Mount to admire the Dome of the Rock and the other Moslem shrines in that enclave. Tourists of all nationalities and faiths visit the Temple Mount to marvel at the elegance and charm of the Moslem shrines and wonder how strange it is that a mere hilltop should rouse in the hearts of so many such deep emotions of reverence which at times turn into violence. Who really can fathom the soul of man?

The Would-Be Destroyers of Jerusalem's Walls

Jerusalem has been a fortified city for more than three thousand years. More than once were the city's walls destroyed by foreign armies. However, they were always rebuilt. It was only in the twentieth century that Jerusalem's walls were threatened with permanent demolition not by invading armies, but by local rulers. One of the would-be destroyers was Djemal Pasha, the Turkish military governor during the First World War. His plan is described in Bertha Spafford Vester's oft-quoted book, *Our Jerusalem.*

> Few cities can claim rampart walls of such perfect preservation. These picturesque battlements narrowly escaped demolition by Djemal Pasha, who was Turkish Generalissimo of the campaign against the British in 1914–1917. *Demolire* was one of his favourite words. I heard him say that he intended to give Jerusalem fresh air by demolishing the city walls and make it more modern by hacking a boulevard, which would of course bear his name, from the Jaffa Gate to the Temple area.[18]

More surprising it is that such a thought also occurred to David Ben-Gurion, the renowned first prime minister of Israel. Saul Bellow reports in his book, *To Jerusalem and Back:*

> Teddy Kollek has told me that after 1967 Ben Gurion was all for tearing down the walls of the Old City. "Let it all be open. Make one city, no walls," he argued. "No sense of beauty," says Kollek.[19]

While some people talked of pulling down the walls of Jerusalem, Theodor Herzl, the "founder" of modern Zionism, dreamed of preserving the walls while pulling down the slums within the walls, as he termed them, "the nests of filth." In his diaries, he notes:

> I would isolate the old city with its relics and pull out all the regular traffic; only houses of worship and philanthropic institutions would be allowed to remain inside the old walls. . . . Tender care can turn Jerusalem into a jewel. Include everything sacred within the old walls, spread everything new round about it.[20]

Happily the stately, castellated walls of Jerusalem have not been razed. Actually a National Park is in the process of development around the walls. The park will set off the walls of the Old City from the modern suburbs which have grown up during the past century. The official City Plan also calls for the restoration of the gaping breach in the wall next to the Jaffa Gate. When the National Park and the restoration work will be finished, the majestic walls of Jerusalem will stand out, as of old, in all their grandeur and glory.

Did King David Erect the Tower of David?

The Tower of David has stirred the imagination of all lovers of Jerusalem. The eastern walls of many Jewish homes were once adorned by stylized pictures of either the Western (Wailing) Wall or the Tower of David— signs of attachment to the Holy City and hope for its restoration. These two ancient relics were regarded as the most genuine symbols of Jerusalem. Christians, too, gazed at the Tower of David with intense interest, because King David was, according to the Christian tradition, the ancestor of Jesus. Prior to modern times, neither Jews nor Christians questioned the authenticity of the tradition that the tower was erected by King David. But modern research uncovered a different origin.

The Tower of David, adjacent to the Jaffa Gate, is part of Jerusalem's Citadel. This "massive fortress of five mighty towers" occupies the area where once stood the palace of King Herod. In its present configuration the Citadel dates back to the early fourteenth century with some sixteenth-century additions. In recent years the Citadel has been intensively excavated and restored and made into a museum of the history of Jerusalem.

The Tower of David is the northeast tower of the Citadel. It is a relic of three towers which King Herod erected and named in honor of his three favorites: his brother Phasael, his friend Hippicus, and his wife Mariamne. These towers were spared demolition when Jerusalem was destroyed by the Romans in the year 70. Josephus, in his classic work, *The Jewish War,* writes:

> When the [Roman] soldiers found no more persons to kill, Caesar ordered his legions to raze the city and the Temple to their foundations, but to respect the towers that surpassed all the others in height, such as Phasael, Hippicus, and Mariamne. . . . The towers were preserved merely as memorials to future generations of the flourishing and powerful city which Roman valour had succeeded in subduing.[21]

These three towers were finally demolished by the Moslems in 1219. Only a part of the Tower of Phasael was spared.

When this relic first came to be called the Tower of David is not known. Historians of the Crusading period already called it the Tower or the Citadel of David. The association of the tower with the ancient Jewish monarch was generally accepted and was adorned with imaginative details. The most intriguing of these is one that tourist guides used to tell pilgrims and other "innocents"—that it was from this tower that King David gazed at beautiful Bathsheba as she was taking her bath, whereupon he fell deeply in love with her. Pilgrims were shown the exact spot where the king stood, the "window" through which he gazed, and the spot where Bathsheba was taking her bath. "It was from a window in this castle," writes Thomas Whaley early in our century, "that King David first saw fair Bathsheba, as she was bathing in a fountain which is overlooked by the tower."[22] The fact that the most ancient section of the tower was erected a thousand years after King David's reign made no dent in this romantic story. Pilgrims loved to hear of the royal romance and guides enjoyed telling it.

The lower section of the so-called Tower of David is easily identified as one of the famous constructions of King Herod. The massive stones resemble those of the Western (Wailing) Wall. They are inferior in size, but they bear the same distinctive marks of that architectural era. Each stone is of prodigious magnitude, and is exactly fitted, the joints being perfectly true. Their definitive earmark is the beveling around the edges of each stone. The Herodian section of the tower rises about thirty or forty feet. The rest of the tower is a Turkish addition. The contrast between the massive grandeur of the Herodian workmanship and the relative frailty of the more recent section is striking.

There are still many people who do not question the Davidic origin of the tower. They marvel at this "three-thousand-year-old fortress" still standing near one of the city's main gates. Others know the history of the tower as one of King Herod's constructions. They, too, marvel at this two-thousand-year-old fortress. Among the uninformed traditionalists and the informed modernists, few are aware that the tower is utterly futile as a barrier to an attacking army. Yet, in all who see it, the tower awakens historic associations and stimulates reflection on the vanity of royal grandeur.

Two Mysterious Pools

Jerusalem's pools are dilapidated open tanks of large dimensions and high antiquity. Most of these pools were utilized to store water for use during the dry summer months. Two of the pools are regarded as holy and reputedly possess miraculous healing powers. They attract pilgrims by their presumed therapeutic attributes. And some pilgrims claim that one or another of the holy pools cured them of their ailments.

The first of these reservoirs is the Siloam Pool which derives its water from the nearby Gihon Spring. The tunnel connecting the spring with the pool was dug by King Hezekiah in the seventh century B.C.E., when he anticipated an invasion by the Assyrians. By means of this tunnel he brought the water of the Gihon Spring, which was outside the city's fortifications, into the Siloam Pool, which was within the city walls.

The Gihon Spring and the Siloam Pool are located in the Kidron Valley near its junction with the Valley of Hinnom. To reach the spring one descends a steep flight of thirty slippery steps cut in the rock and worn smooth like marble. Water from the spring starts on its course through the subterranean tunnel and winds its way slowly till it reaches the Siloam Pool. It flows so gently that it seems to be standing still. The pool is a relatively small, shallow, oblong reservoir into which flows the ankle-deep brook from the tunnel.[23]

The sanctity of the spring and the pool derives from their biblical associations. The construction of the tunnel is described in Second Kings (20:20) and Second Chronicles (32:30), and the prophet Isaiah speaks of "the waters of Shilo'ah that flow gently" (Isa. 8:5). In ancient times there used to be an elaborate ritual in the Temple service on the Festival of Tabernacles in which the drawing of water from the Gihon Spring was a central feature.

In the Christian tradition, too, this spring is sacred. Christians call it the Virgin's Fount because it is believed that the Virgin Mary washed the child Jesus' linens in the water of this spring. More important is the reference to the Siloam Pool in the Christian Bible in which it is told that Jesus healed a blind man who then told his neighbors: "the man called Jesus . . . said to me: 'Go to Siloam and wash;' so I went and washed and received my sight" (John 9:11).

In addition to its biblical fame the water of the Gihon Spring suddenly becomes agitated several times daily; its level rises considerably; and it flows in copious quantities. Then the water subsides to its normal gentle flow. Edward Robinson and E. Smith in their *Biblical Researches* describe this mysterious phenomenon:

As we were preparing to measure the basin of the upper fountain . . . and explore the passage leading from it, my companion was standing on the lower step near the water, with one foot on the step and the other on a loose stone lying in the basin. All at once he perceived the water coming into his shoe; and supposing the stone had rolled, he withdrew his foot to the step; which however was also now covered with water. This instantly excited our curiosity; and we now perceived the water rapidly bubbling up from under the lower step. In less than five minutes it had risen in the basin nearly or quite a foot; and we could hear it gurgling off through the interior passage. In ten minutes more it had ceased to flow; and the water in the basin was again reduced to its former level. . . . The flowing of the water occurs at irregular intervals; sometimes two or three times a day, and sometimes in summer once in two or three days.[24]

The strange behavior of the Gihon Spring has enhanced its sanctity and its presumed therapeutic properties. One can still see Christian pilgrims washing their eyes at the Gihon Spring or the Siloam Pool in the belief that the water possesses healing powers. If Jesus restored the blind man's sight by washing in this water, perhaps all eye ailments can be cured by washing with this holy water. Some pilgrims drink the water reasoning that since the water can heal eye ailments why should it not heal other ailments as well?

The archaeologist, Sir Charles Wilson, reported that "the modern Jews believe the waters of this pool to be a sure cure for rheumatic complaints. They often go in numbers, men and women together, and stand in their clothes in the pool, waiting for the water to rise."[25]

Where does the water of the spring come from? There is a tradition that the water emanates from the spot where once stood Solomon's Temple, where now stands the Dome of the Rock (the Mosque of Omar). According to this tradition, the water flows underground from the heart of Mount Moriah and is therefore sacred. As to the mystery of the water's periodic rise, scientists have explained this strange occurrence on the principle of the syphon. But the traditional explanation is simpler. A dragon lives in that spring, and every time he stirs the water is agitated and it rises. It is an explanation which still persists among many of the old-timers.

When the British captured Jerusalem in December 1917, they were faced with a pressing problem. There was not enough water in the cisterns and pools for both the civilian population and the military personnel. They thought that the Gihon Spring would solve their problem. "For eight days and nights," writes Fannie Fern Andrews,

> they had engineers pumping up the water for the purpose of ascertaining how much water there was, and also what were the periods of irruption. It was found that the flow varies considerably in quantity and that the number of its irruptions varied in the twenty-four hours. The experiment showed that there was not sufficient water to supply the need. It was also found that the water itself was not perfectly pure. So the project was dropped.[26]

Jerusalem's other miraculous reservoir is the Bethesda Pool. The name derives from the Aramaic, Beth Hisda, House of Mercy. The water of this pool is also said to have stirred, but this peculiar characteristic is no longer in evidence. And the pool is no longer functioning as a reservoir. A fifteenth-century pilgrim, Pietro Casola, described this sacred pool in terms of the Christian tradition:

> This was a pool which had the virtue that an angel descended from heaven into the said pool and moved the water, and the first sick person who entered the pool after the moving of the water was cured of all his infirmities. Therefore, under those porches, there used to lie a great multitude of sick persons in order to be ready to enter the water quickly; and Christ with a word only healed one who had been there eighteen years.[27]

The traditional Bethesda Pool is actually a twin pool. It is located on the west side of St. Anne's Church on the Via Dolorosa, near the St. Stephen's Gate. The pool is cut out of the rock on at least two sides. No spring or aqueduct has been discovered. The pool's fame rests on the miracle referred to above and recorded in the Christian Bible (John 5:2–9).

The traditional Bethesda Pool has been excavated, but not restored.[28] Because of its neglected condition, few pilgrims visit this Christian holy place. One day, perhaps, the Church will see fit to restore the pool. Its religious distinction merits not only its maintenance but its full restoration and renovation.

The waters of Shiloah still flow softly as they have done for thousands of years, and the Gihon Spring is still as mysterious as ever. And the Bethesda Pool is still cherished in the Christian tradition. Its fame is attested by the residential suburb of the American capital which bears its name. The two mysterious pools will undoubtedly continue to stir the imagination of thousands of people, and visitors in the Holy City will continue to regard them as places to be visited and revered.

Water—"Jerusalem's Eternal Problem"

Most people take water for granted. It is almost as free as air, except that air is distributed more or less equally over the face of the earth while water is plentiful in some areas and scarce in others. In some regions there are rivers and springs aplenty; in others the people "drink water by measure."

In Jerusalem water is deficient despite the biblical description of the Promised Land as "a land of brooks of water, of fountains and springs flowing forth in valleys and hills" (Deut. 8:7). Actually the deficiency of water was one of the prime considerations for locating Jerusalem at this site. A village, which in time became the city of Jerusalem, was established near the only fair-sized living fountain in the region. This spring was known in biblical times as the Gihon or Siloam fountain. As Jerusalem grew and eventually became the capital of King David's empire, the Gihon spring could no longer provide the inhabitants with enough water for their needs. The water problem became acute, plaguing the inhabitants. Water thus became Jerusalem's "eternal problem." So crucial a role did it play in the life of the people that the Prophet Isaiah described God's bountiful blessings for Israel in terms of water:

> Thus says the Lord: "Behold, I will extend prosperity to Jerusalem like a river,
> And the wealth of nations like an overflowing stream" (Isa. 66:12).

And when John Finley wanted to describe the vital role of water in this region he wrote: "The one characteristic universal figure in Palestine is the erect woman with the water-jar upon her head . . . or the bent man with the goatskin [full of water] upon his back."[29]

At the end of the winter the hills and valleys are abloom with myriads of flowers. The blessings of the winter rain are felt everywhere. Gradually the flowers and the grass begin to wither, and the hillsides become barren. The thirsty land begins its long wait for the rains in the fall and winter ahead. But the inhabitants of Jerusalem can not wait for the rains. They must have water all year round. They learned to store the rainwater of the winter months for use during the dry season. The government built several large pools, and the people built cisterns in the basements or courtyards of their houses. Every drop of rain that fell on the roofs was channeled into the cisterns, and the rainwater of the gutters was not allowed to run off into the wadis. It was channeled, along with the dirt of the alleys, into the cisterns. By the end of the rainy season the cisterns were full. The water was used sparingly so as to last to the next winter.

But there were years when the rains were not plentiful so that at winter's end the cisterns were only half full. Then the inhabitants of Jerusalem did not rejoice when the balmy spring days arrived. Fear and gloom could be felt everywhere. By mid-summer many of the cisterns were nearly empty; the people began to suffer great hardships. They drained their cisterns to the last drops, including the stagnant, evil-smelling liquid of the gutter filth that had settled to the bottom of the cisterns. Afterward, people resorted to purchasing water from Arabs who brought their precious merchandise in goatskins from the Gihon Spring. Lucky were those who could afford to buy water. The others suffered. The biblical malediction, "water you shall drink by measure," afflicted the Jerusalemites. In *The Jewish Chronicle* of July 26, 1901, there appeared a letter, signed by Elkan Nathan Adler and Herbert M. Adler. They wrote:

> We were in Jerusalem a few weeks back and can corroborate the story of the misery which this year's drought has caused. Provisions and especially water are at famine prices. . . .

Toward the end of the dry summer months the so-called "summer fever" would spread. Still worse, a plague would occasionally break out. The poor were the ones who suffered most. The plague took its greatest toll in the Jewish Quarter where the poorest people lived and where the cisterns were most polluted. Infants were the most frequent victims. It was estimated that seventy per cent of the babies born in Jerusalem died, most of them during the periodic plagues.

When the summer months came to an end, the people's eyes were raised in prayer for a good rainy season. The harvest of the following year and their daily supply of water during the coming summer depended on the rains. During the Feast of Tabernacles which usually falls early in October the Jews recited (as they still do) special prayers for rain. And if the rains did not come by a certain date, a general fast was proclaimed.

The prospect of a drought was a matter of anxiety for everyone. Mrs. A. Goodrich-Freer, in her book, *Inner Jerusalem,* reports on such a situation and the prayers which it sparked among Jerusalemites of all faiths:

> This important year [1882], threatened to end disastrously with a drought, and the anxiety felt upon the subject of rain can scarcely be comprehended except by those who have lived where there are no rivers, lakes, nor even springs, and where the water supply is dependent upon the rain caught in the domestic cistern. The Moslems inaugurated a procession of penitence: the chief men of the city, with the Pasha, walking barefoot around the sacred Haram enclosure. . . . The Jews, too, fasted and prayed—let us hope the Christians followed suit. Finally, in despair, the Moslem authorities, who seem to preserve a certain intermittent regard for the Hebrew faith, appealed to their fellow-sufferers and offered to the Jews free entrance into the Sacred Courts [the Temple Mount] if they would assemble there and beseech the mercy of Heaven.

This they declined, but asked permission to pray at the Tomb of David, a jealously guarded sanctuary of Moslem fanaticism, and receiving permission, assembled there on December 17. Before evening the rain fell in torrents, and a glorious rainbow spanned the Holy City.[30]

When the rains were plentiful there was great rejoicing. Andrew Thomson visited Jerusalem in 1869 and witnessed a rare scene. The Kidron flowed, indicating the rain had been plentiful. He heard the cry, "The Kidron flows!" and he described the happy event:

> When the cry is carried through Jerusalem in a morning, "The Kidron flows!" it is heard with universal welcome, for it is a sure sign that the hidden fountains beneath are filled, and that there will be no scarcity of water during all the summer months. The Kidron water is then sold in the city like milk, and thousands come crowding out from its various gates to keep holiday upon its banks. Turbaned men sit under the olive-trees and smoke their long tchibouks or gurgling nerghiles; white-robed women regale themselves with fruits and sweetmeats; children of both sexes gather flowers from the torrent's side, and splash in it merrily with hands and feet at the point where it seems to leap into life; even the Pasha with his suite rides along the margin of the sparkling brook as if to inaugurate its new birth.[31]

Jerusalem's "eternal problem" was partially solved when the British conquered the city in December 1917. They immediately recognized that the 5,300 cisterns and the several reservoirs were inadequate for both the civilian population and the Army of Occupation. The Royal Engineers made a thorough study of the water resources in the area and discovered an ancient system of aqueducts, built during the days of Herod. These aqueducts had been allowed to deteriorate and their water to go to waste. The system was located in Wadi Arrub, about thirteen miles south of Jerusalem on the Hebron road. The Royal Engineers repaired the aqueducts and on June 18, 1918, fresh water began to flow into Jerusalem's reservoirs. This was the first step in the creation of Jerusalem's modern water supply system. Jerusalem's cisterns were no longer needed. So the people thought. But their judgment was hasty. The cisterns had not yet become obsolete. During the Arab-Israeli war of 1948–1949 Jerusalem was again faced with its "eternal problem," and turned to its abandoned cisterns for relief. In 1947, a year before the outbreak of the war, the Jewish National Council instructed the Jewish inhabitants to clean their old, unused cisterns and to let the winter rains fill them. The leadership of the Jewish community realized that, in case of war, the Arabs would cut off the water supply and force the Jews to surrender. For no city can hold out without water for more than several days. The people obeyed. They filled the cisterns and sealed them. Neither the British nor the Arabs were aware of this stratagem. When war broke out in 1948, the Arabs immediately cut off the water supply and waited for the surrender of Jerusalem's Jewish community. To their great surprise, the Jews held out. The cisterns were opened and the Jewish community had water. To be sure, the water was rationed and it was not as clean as the spring water they had been getting from their taps. But it sufficed for the duration of the war.

The year 1926 was a year of suffering for the inhabitants of Jerusalem. During the previous winter the rainfall was only twelve inches, about half the average. The shortage of water caused the government to act, and it was then that the much talked-of plans to bring water to Jerusalem from Ein Farrah, a copious spring, northeast of the city were implemented. The spring is 1400 feet below Jerusalem. Three relays of pumps were necessary to bring the water up to the city.

But the city grew rapidly and more water was needed. In 1935 a new source of water was tapped at Ras-el-Ain, forty miles from Jerusalem, not far from Lydda. The water was brought up to the city, 2,700 feet, through a series of pumping stations. With this achievement, Jerusalem never again experienced a shortage of water, nor have any epidemics arisen from the periodic droughts and filthy cisterns.

Tomb Dwellers

To the southeast of Jerusalem's walls, overlooking the Siloam Pool, there is a quaint suburb, the village of Silwan, a corruption of Siloam. From a distance it appears like a cluster of stone houses scrambling up the southern slope of the Mount of Offence. One traveler described the village as "hanging on the hillside." The houses are hardly distinguishable from the limestones to which they adhere.

The history of the village is stranger than the proverbial fiction. The ancestors of the current inhabitants were poor Arabs in search of homes. They found outside the city walls ancient Jewish tombs dug into the mountainside. Some of these tombs had been occupied by Christian hermits who left their imprints in the form of crosses marked on the walls of their lonely abodes. Why not move into these empty caves? The bones of the dead, if there were any, were swept out; the new tenants moved in. The caves provided adequate shelter from the sun in summer and from the rain in winter. A settlement of living tomb dwellers was thus established.

As the families increased and more dwelling space was needed rooms were built at the openings of the caves. The village of Silwan grew and took form. The houses stand at the openings of caverns which had been tombs, and the caverns now serve as additional subterranean rooms. The village is quaint and attractive from afar, and has often been painted by local and visiting artists. At close quarters, however, the village is not so pretty. It is definitely not a tourist attraction. One visitor, a mid-nineteenth-century artist, choosing to take a close look at the village, left a graphic portrayal in his itinerary:

> I had often been struck with the quaint and picturesque appearance of the little hamlet of *Silwan,* whose houses seem to cling like swallows' nests to the gray cliffs of Olivet. It takes its name from the fountain on the opposite side of the Kidron, at the base of Moriah; and it alone brings down to modern times the sacred name of "the waters of *Siloah* that flow softly" (Isa. 8:6), and of that "pool of *Siloam"* in which our Lord commanded the blind man to wash (John 9:7). Its inhabitants have a bad name, and are known to be lawless, fanatical vagabonds. I resolved, however, to explore their den, and I succeeded, notwithstanding repeated volleys of threats and curses, intermixed now and again with a stone or two. I was well repaid.

Silwan Village (1967). (Courtesy of Israel Government Press Office.)

The village stands on a necropolis; and the habitations are all half caves, half buildings,—a single room, or rude porch, being attached to the front of a rock tomb. It is a strange wild place. On every side I heard children's prattle issuing from the gloomy chambers of ancient sepulchres. Looking into one I saw an infant cradled in an old sarcophagus. The larger tombs, where the ashes of Israel's nobles once reposed, were now filled with sheep and goats, and lambs and kids gambolled merrily among the loculi.[32]

The early tomb dwellers of Silwan were known not only for their poverty, but also for their thieving and robbing, in which they engaged professionally. J. T. Barclay in his *The City of the Great King* says of the residents of Silwan:

a more corrupt, offensive, and scandalous set of scamps is nowhere to be found! They are, with few exceptions, real troglodytes—dwelling not only in natural caves, but in the tenements of the dead, with which that cliff abounds.[33]

After World War I, when the British established law and order in Jerusalem, the inhabitants of Silwan turned to honorable labor. They are now part of Jerusalem's industrious and reliable working population.

Beggars

During the nineteenth century travelers invariably reported the depressing sight of Jerusalem's beggars. The city was infested with them. Mark Twain noted in his *Innocents Abroad:*

Rags, wretchedness, poverty, and dirt, those signs and symbols that indicate the presence of Moslem rule more surely than the crescent flag itself, abound. Lepers, cripples, the blind, and the idiotic, assail you on every hand, and they know but one word of but one language apparently—the eternal "bucksheesh." To see the numbers of maimed, malformed, and diseased humanity that throng the holy places and obstruct the gates, one might suppose that the ancient days had come again, and that the angel of the Lord was expected to descend at any moment to stir the waters of Bethesda.[34]

Another American traveler, reputedly the greatest orator of his generation, described his experiences with Jerusalem's beggars in his travelogue, *The Howadji in Syria:*

There are no rich men in Jerusalem. Every one has the air of a citizen of ruins, and begs like a Belisarius.

The oriental genius applied to begging is delightful. It has the same sententious gravity that marks it in every development, and the same poetic phrase. I was constantly sure that I saw the Mecca beggar of whom Bruck-hardt tells a characteristic story.

Upon his first visit to Mecca, that traveller had employed a Delyl, or Guide, who was useful to him. But when he came again he had no use for him. He told him so. But the undaunted Delyl came regularly to Burckhardt's dinner, and, after satisfying his present hunger, he produced a small basket which he ordered his host's slave to fill with biscuits, meat, vegetables, or fruit, which he carried away with him. Every three or four days he asked for money — saying loftily, "It is not you who give it; it is God who sends it to me."

Burckhardt soon wearied of this arrangement, and told the Delyl, with great emphasis, that he could endure it no longer.

In three days the Delyl returned and begged a dollar.

—"God does not move me to give you anything," replied Burckhardt gravely, "if he judged it right he would soften my soul, and cause me to give you my whole purse."

"Pull my beard," said the Delyl, "if God does not send you ten times more hereafter than I beg at present."

"Pull out every hair of mine," replied Burckhardt, "if I give you one para until I am convinced that God will regard it as a meritorious act."

Upon hearing which the Delyl arose suddenly and walked away, saying sublimely, "We fly for refuge to God, from the hearts of the proud, and the hands of the avaricious."[35]

There were three distinct types of beggars: the professionals, the Arab children, and the lepers. All were experts in their lucrative trade. They pestered the pilgrims and tourists to such a degree that even a kindly cleric, Rev. J. E. Hanauer of St. George's Cathedral, advised visitors to harden their hearts and refrain from dispensing alms, notwithstanding that "many of the beggars are blind and crippled." He writes:

I cannot recommend the visitor to give any alms here, because that would be the signal for the whole swarm of beggars to beset and pester the good-natured philanthropist to such an extent that he will repent his ever having evinced a desire to be kind.[36]

Mr. W. F. Lynch, who led an American expedition to explore the Jordan River and the Dead Sea area, visited Jerusalem. In his report on his exploration he described his visit in the Church of the Holy Sepulchre. He relates what happened when he entered the court in front of the entrance to the church:

> The appearance of a poor cripple excited my compassion, and I gave him a piastre; but the consequences were fearful. The war-cry of the Syrian pauper, "backshish! backshish!" instantly resounded from all quarters, and we were hemmed in, pressed, and swayed to and fro by the rabble. Our cicerone plied his stick vigorously in our defense, and it truly seemed to be gifted with miraculous powers, for the blind saw, and the lame walked, and amid their imprecations upon our Christian heads we entered the church.[37]

Among the most persistent beggars were the Arab children. Were a tourist to yield to the pleas of a child and give him a coin, all the children in the area would immediately descend upon him like a pack of famished wolves. The swarm of little beggars would surround the soft-hearted tourist and physically molest him. The helpless stranger would be forced to distribute alms in order to extricate himself from the mob of little beggars. But the voracious appetite of these pests was insatiable. The tourist would then throw a handful of coins as far as possible. While the children scrambled for the coins, the tourist would make his get-away. This explains the Rev. J. A. Wylie's comment:

> When a village occurs, lying near the highway, it is an unwelcome apparition. The traveller prepares himself for a half-hour's torment. A swarthy troop of half-naked youth of both sexes are sure to let themselves loose upon him, and dog him for a mile on end, whining all the way for backsheesh.[38]

The most successful of Jerusalem's beggars were the lepers. They used to waylay pilgrims and tourists, and extort their bakshish by exposing their loathsome deformities. Their begging was so profitable that they refused the care of a clean hospital, preferring to pursue their profitable trade. Estelle Blyth describes the beggar colony in Jerusalem:

> The Moravians had a Leper Hospital at Jerusalem, where lepers were most tenderly and patiently cared for, but the majority of the Palestinian lepers preferred to sit out by the roadsides, begging from the pilgrims, who never turned a deaf ear to such misery as theirs. They were terrible and loathsome objects, fearfully maimed and covered with large open sores under their rags, and there they would sit in little groups, holding out tins for the alms of the charitable, and chanting their plaint in dreary tones. . . . Undoubtedly, the Turkish Government should have insisted upon their being gathered away from public sight and touch; but the Turkish Government never did interfere

with the liberty of the unprofitable subject. It was said that the lepers made quite good incomes out of alms, and that one leper, who was less helpless than many of his fellows, though no less urgent in his begging, was the owner of a flourishing olive-grove. By day they hung upon the outskirts of the city, in the roads most often used by pilgrims and travellers, and by night they slept in the caves in which the hills and valleys about Jerusalem abound.[39]

It is only in recent years that the beggars have diminished, and the visitor can walk in the streets of Jerusalem without being molested by insistent demands for bakshish. Gone are the lepers and few are the Arab children who pester the visitors. The lepers, if any are still left, are in hospitals, and the economic condition of the Arabs in Jerusalem has greatly improved so that the children go to school instead of roaming the streets in search of tourists. To be sure, there are still some beggars in Jerusalem, but hardly like a half a century ago. The Israeli government has made several attempts to remove the remnant of the beggars from the streets. One such attempt involved legislation. Begging is unlawful. But the police are reluctant to perform their duty. Besides, the populace comes to the defense of the beggars so that no policeman dares arrest a beggar. The Jewish tradition of *Tsedakah* (the duty to help the poor) is stronger than the police.

It is said that the government had offered to reimburse the beggars and give them weekly stipends equivalent to their income from begging. The beggars, however, turned down the offer. "Why accept charity from the government when we can be respectable self-employed tradesmen?"

Begging is regarded by the professional beggar as a trade. As long as begging is profitable there will be beggars plying their trade. In former times begging was a social affliction of massive proportions. Now it is only a minor nuisance. In time it may totally disappear.

The Curious Architecture of Jerusalem's Old Houses

Visitors in Jerusalem are usually too busy to note the simple but significant things which characterize the city's life. One of these characteristics is the architectural style of Jerusalem's old buildings. Even before one enters an old Jerusalem house the observant visitor notes the domed roofs. Saul Bellow in his book *To Jerusalem and Back*[40] speaks of Jerusalem's "small houses with bulbous roofs." And Mark Twain in his *The Innocents Abroad* characterizes Jerusalem as the "knobbiest town in the world." He writes:

> The appearance of the city is peculiar. It is as knobby with countless little
> domes as a prison door is with bolt-heads. Every house has from one to half a
> dozen of these white plastered domes of stone, broad and low, sitting in the
> center of, or in a cluster upon, the flat roof. Wherefore, when one looks
> down from an eminence, upon the compact mass of houses (so closely
> crowded together, in fact, that there is no appearance of streets at all, and so
> the city looks solid) he sees the knobbiest town in the world. . . . It looks as
> if it might be roofed, from center to circumference, with inverted saucers.
> The monotony of the view is interrupted only by the great Mosque of Omar,
> the Tower of Hippicus [the Tower of David] and one or two other buildings
> that rise into commanding prominence.[41]

These small domes gave Jerusalem a most picturesque appearance,
and antiquarians bemoan the gradual disappearance of this quaint feature
of old Jerusalem.

On entering an old Jerusalem house one notes another peculiarity, the
unusually stout walls. The late Professor Gershom Scholem relates in his
autobiography: "Escha and I were married in November of 1923 and
moved into two rooms in an Arab house whose walls, believe it or not,
were four feet thick."[42]

Why, one wonders, did the Jerusalemites build such massive walls?
The usual answer given by tourist guides and other "knowledgeable"
people is that Jerusalem is located in the earthquake belt. The Bible
mentions the violent earthquake which took place in the days of the
Prophet Amos. This earthquake was so disastrous that people marked
time by that calamity, and Amos dated his initiation as a prophet as
having occurred "two years before the earthquake" (Amos 1:1). The
Prophet Zechariah describes this earthquake: "You shall flee as you fled
from the earthquake in the days of Uzziah, king of Judah" (Zech. 14:5).
Visitors in the Church of the Holy Sepulchre are shown a slit in the rock
under Calvary and are told that it was caused by the earthquake which
took place at the time of the Crucifixion.

In more recent times, too, a number of earthquakes have occurred in
Jerusalem. In 1927 an earthquake damaged the dome of the Church of the
Holy Sepulchre, and in 1937 an earthquake damaged the structures on the
Temple Mount. On the basis of these incidents many people have concluded that building thick walls in Jerusalem was intended to give the houses
added strength to resist the anticipated earthquakes. The thicker the
walls, they figured, the firmer and safer the houses. But experience has

shown that during earthquakes the thick walls cracked and some houses collapsed.

Alternative explanations have been offered. The stout walls, some have said, insulate the houses against the excessive heat in the summer and against the chill of the winter. But this is a post-factum effect of the thick stone wall not an initial reason for their construction. If this were the reason, one would find thick walls in other subtropical countries.

To explain the unique architecture of Jerusalem's old houses one must go back to the Arab conquest of the Holy Land. The Arab conquerors were nomads whose chief concern was the grazing of their flocks. And the Arab women were concerned with cooking and baking and in the winter months, with heating their damp stone houses. The black goats stripped the bark of the trees and the dead trees were cut down for fuel. The Arab culture did not provide for planting new trees to replace those that were cut down. Thus the forests disappeared and lumber became scarce. How was one to build a ceiling without wooden beams? The dome saved the situation. In the center of the ceiling the Arabs learned to build one or more small domes. This solved the problem created by the destruction of the forests. But these vaulted ceilings required massive walls to support the immense weight of the stone roofs.

The archaeologist, Charles Warren, sums up this strange architectural development in Jerusalem:

> In early days they built more suitably to the climate, but now that all the wood in the hill country is cut down, stone only is available; and to support a stone roof a wall is required thick enough for a dungeon.[43]

Still another characteristic of old houses in Jerusalem is a standard inscribed stone slab. The inscription includes the date the house was constructed, a verse from the Koran, and a picture of the Dome of the Rock. Frequently, the owner's name is also noted. Early in 1983 the municipality adopted a by-law requiring each new building to carry a "citation" giving the year of its construction and the names of the architect and builder. The by-law also stipulates that the "citation" be not merely a sign attached to the building, but must be imbedded in the structure and must be so placed as to be easily seen by pedestrians. The purpose of the by-law is not only to preserve an historic tradition but to stimulate the architects' and builders' professional pride and thus encourage creativity in the design and construction of new houses in Jerusalem.[44]

Old Jerusalem—A City of Alleys and Staircases

Old Jerusalem is a city of alleys and staircases. So it was in ancient times; so it is today; and so it will probably remain. In the New City streets are graded to enable vehicles to travel unhindered. Not so in the Old City. There one walks continually up or down ever-recurring stairs. While modern cities boast of their broad boulevards and spacious squares, the Old City of Jerusalem can hardly claim any streets to speak of. It has only narrow lanes and crooked alleys without sidewalks, and the ubiquitous staircases. Even in David Street, which is the city's main bazaar, the tourists and pilgrims push their way up and down the recurring stairs. Jerusalem is a city for nimble feet.

This characteristic of the city has not changed since antiquity. In his classic work, *Jerusalem,* George Adam Smith cites Josephus who lived almost two thousand years ago:

> There are no streets or squares, but only close and sombre lanes, climbing steeply from the Temple Court to the west, or, at right angles to these . . . Jospehus frequently mentions the "narrow streets," and the fighting from the

A street in the Old City of Jerusalem (1967). (Courtesy of Central Zionist Archives, Jerusalem.)

housetops [in the year 70 C.E.]. Through these lanes, ever close, steep and sombre as they are to-day, there beats the daily stir of the City's common life: the passage of her buzzing crowds, rumour and the exchange of news, the carriage of goods, trading and the smaller industries, the search for slaves and criminals, the bridal processions, the funerals, the tide of worshipers to the Temple, and occasionally the march of armed men. And through them also raged, as Josephus describes, the fighting, the sacking, the slaughter: all the fine-drawn pangs and anguish of the days of the City's overthrow.[45]

Mark Twain in his *Innocents Abroad* left an unforgettable description of the so-called streets of Old Jerusalem:

Projecting from the top of the lower story of many of the houses is a very narrow porch-roof or shed, without supports from below; and I have several times seen cats jump across the street from one shed to the other when they were out calling. The cats could have jumped double the distance without extraordinary exertion. I mention these things to give an idea of how narrow the streets are. Since a cat can jump across them without the least inconvenience, it is hardly necessary to state that such streets are too narrow for carriages.[46]

Many decades have passed since George Adam Smith and Mark Twain visited Jerusalem, but the Old City is still characterized by its narrow lanes, crooked alleys, and ubiquitous staircases. Visitors in the Old City must literally watch their step.

Avenue of the Righteous Gentiles

In Jerusalem there is a street which bears a most curious name. It is called Avenue of the Righteous Gentiles. The story of this street and its strange name is connected with the Nazi Holocaust.

The tragedy of the Holocaust is so staggering that it is beyond human comprehension. The death of a child or several children is heart-breaking, but the deliberate massacre of a million and a half children is so far beyond human imagination that it practically has no impact on one's emotions. When one hears it said that six million Jews, among them more than a million and a half children, were murdered in the Nazi death camps, no tears well up in the listener's eyes; no heart beat is skipped in his breast. The enormity of the crime is so baffling that its meaning does not penetrate the listener's mind and heart. It is only when one learns of the unspeakable cruelties suffered by individual victims that shock begins to have an impact on one's consciousness. The question then arises—how could the Nazis, who were born as human beings, presumably in the image of God, sink to such depths of bestiality? There is no satisfactory answer. But there is a measure of comfort to be found in one of the buildings erected as a memorial to the martyrs and heroes of the Holocaust. On one of Jerusalem's hills, now called the Mount of Remembrance, there is a building called the Hall of Names in which are registered the names of the victims of the Holocaust. As one enters this building, one notes an inscription on the wall that reads:

> The Jewish people will never forget the righteous among the nations who endangered their lives in order to save Jews from the Nazi murderers and their collaborators.
>
> In their praiseworthy deeds they saved the honour of mankind.

Who were these "righteous among the nations" who "saved the honor of mankind?" According to the Sages of the Talmud these righteous gentiles were assured "a share in the world to come."[47] Maimonides, too, states in his monumental work that "the righteous gentiles have a share in the world to come."[48] In 1953 the Knesset passed a resolution, known as the Martyrs' and Heroes' Remembrance Law, which stipulated that a memorial was to be established to commemorate "the Holocaust victims, their communities, organizations and institutions, the rebels and fighters who rose up against the enemy in defense of the people's honor." The memorial was named *Yad Vashem,* a biblical expression taken from Isaiah 56:5 which reads: "I will give (them) in my house and within my walls a monument and a name [*Yad Veshem*] better than sons and daughters."

Yad Vashem contains, in addition to several memorial sculptures, a number of monumental buildings, among them a museum, a synagogue, a Hall of Names, and a Hall of Remembrance. The last of these structures contains a mosaic floor on which are inscribed the names of the twenty-two Nazi death camps, a vault containing ashes of the martyrs, and an eternal light. Leading up to these memorial buildings and monuments is a tree-lined street, named Avenue of the Righteous Gentiles, a memorial to "the non-Jews who risked their lives in order to save victims of the Nazis." To determine who are the people deserving to be designated as "righteous gentiles" a committee was set up to hear testimony and examine documents. Only people who actually saved victims and, by doing so, endangered their own lives are designated as righteous gentiles and are honored by the planting of a tree along the Avenue of the Righteous Gentiles. They are also presented a suitable citation and a Yad Vashem medal.

Who are the righteous gentiles that are thus honored? It is difficult to characterize these rare men and women, each one of whom represents a heroic person with unique human qualities; each one a noble yet humble personality who by his or her courageous action "saved the honor of mankind." Thus we read of a righteous gentile named Oscar Schindler:

"He was a saint, a true saint in his lifetime." These words of deep-felt reverence were spoken by an Orthodox Jew, come, with his family, from Haifa to pay his last respects to Oscar Schindler, a German Catholic who saved him and over a thousand other Jews during the Second World War. Schindler was laid to rest on 28 October 1974 in the Latin cemetery on Mt. Zion. Among the multitude accompanying the coffin were three hundred and more of his former proteges now living securely in Israel. . . . During the Second World War Schindler had employed as many as twelve hundred Jews in his factory, all of whom he contrived to keep out of the clutches of the Nazis. As he told in Kurt Grossman's *The Unsung Heroes* (German), "In many cases I took the aged parents and other relatives on my payroll, although I had no real work for them. Refusal would have meant the concentration camp for them."[49]

Another news item in the same periodical reads:

Mother Claire Bernes, of the Daughters of Charity, who heads the St. Vincent de Paul Hospice for mentally-retarded children in Ain Karem, was honoured at "Yad Vashem" on 16 January for her humanitarian aid to Jews fleeing Nazi persecution during the Second World War. She planted a sapling along the "Avenue of the Righteous Gentiles" on the Mount of Remembrance in Jerusalem, and was presented with a medallion inscribed — "He who saves a single being saves a whole world."

At the ceremony . . . the Mayor of Jerusalem paid homage to this gracious nun, a long-time resident of the capital, who also bears the title of "Honoured Citizen of Jerusalem" for her dedicated service to the welfare and development of the city. There were also present members of the Finzi family of Haifa, who owed their lives to her. They had been sheltered by her with other Jewish families within the St. Joaquin Convent in Rome during 1943–44, all their needs provided by her and the means of practicing their religion ensured, mortal risk though she herself ran.[50]

A surprisingly large number of such heroes were identified and trees were planted in their honor on the Avenue of the Righteous Gentiles. When there was no more room on either side of the street, a section of the Mount of Remembrance was set aside for the additional planting of such trees. This section is called the Garden of the Righteous Gentiles. Thus far more than three thousand trees have been planted. Each tree bears a plaque with the name of the righteous gentile and his or her nationality.

Every city has streets which are named in honor of heroes, but nowhere is there a street named after so many noble souls whose heroism is of such moral stature as those honored in Jerusalem's Avenue of the Righteous Gentiles. When foreign dignitaries visit Jerusalem they usually go to Yad Vashem and lay a wreath in the Hall of Remembrance. As they proceed through the Avenue of the Righteous Gentiles, they note the memorial trees and, among the names of these mostly humble people, they search for their compatriots whose moral actions "saved the honor of mankind."

Sharp Bargaining

In former years, pilgrims and tourists went to Jerusalem's bazaars not only to purchase things but also to watch the haggling which characterized bazaar transactions. Haggling was an art that the Western visitor could rarely grasp, let alone master. But he always enjoyed watching the show as it developed from stage to stage till its happy consummation. Among the many who described these bouts, as seen at the turn of the century, was Edwin Sherman Wallace, American consul in Jerusalem from 1893 to 1898. In his *Jerusalem the Holy* he writes:

> But the great thing in the bazaars is to see the buyer and seller proceed to business. The former comes along as unconcernedly as possible, as though the intention to purchase anything was farthest from his thoughts. Coming to the bazaar he patronizes, the greeting is passed and some general conversation indulged in. Seeing what he wants he may pick it up, examine it indifferently and lay it down carelessly, all the time talking about something else. Finally he ventures to ask, as though the notion had just struck him, how much the desired article is worth. The dealer is just as sly and asks about three times what he is willing to take and expects to get, but he does it in such a way as to convey his belief that the one about to purchase has no intention of doing so. With the same indifference the purchaser replies offering about a third the amount mentioned. Then comes the battle, first quietly, then more emphatically, until finally their voices are being used under full pressure. You would imagine a real fight was imminent, but there is little danger. The bargain-driving may last half an hour or half a day. The buyer may go away without the article, but he is likely to return on the same or some succeeding day and renew the business. When he does secure his purchase it is at a price from a third to a half the amount first asked. I once

The Shuk *(Bazaar) in the Old City of Jerusalem (1972). (Courtesy of Israel Government Press Office.)*

purchased some rugs from one of these Turkish merchants. He came with his wares at a time when I was busy with other matters. He had three rugs of good quality which I wanted. I told him I had no time to bargain with him and therefore he must name me his last price. After pondering a moment he named it very solemnly, as though it were wrenching his soul to let them go so cheaply. I pursued the same tactics, thought a moment, then took another small rug and added it to the three already selected and offered him for the four just half the amount he had said was the last price for the three. He was shocked and insulted, to judge from the expression on his face, and said it was impossible to think of selling them at the price I had mentioned. I started to go and when he saw I meant it called me back and gave me the rugs at my price and was glad to do it. I have no doubt he made a fair profit on the sale.

This is the way of doing business at every place in the city except in one or two European stores. It is annoying and unsatisfactory, but objecting to it does no good. You are met with the assertion, "It is the custom of the country;" and that is final. He who attempts to reform the customs of the Oriental gets little sympathy and less success. He has always done a certain thing a certain way and will continue to do it just that way "even unto the end."[51]

About half a century later, in 1940, Pierre van Paassen, in his autobiography, *Days of Our Years,* also described the Jerusalem bazaar and the art of bargaining:

Every transaction before the vegetable stalls makes you think of preliminary sparring in a prize fight. Instead of the American rule that the customer is always right, the bazaars' fundamental principle seems to require a demonstration of blazing enmity towards a prospective client. During the first dickerings in a business transaction the parties involved eye each other through narrow slits of suspicion. Soon their voices rise to a crescendo, hands begin to fly out, and the faces of the customers and salesmen become red and swollen with the heat of an argument carried on in hoarse guttural expletives. The antagonists look each other straight in the eye, fists are clenched, the veins in their necks protrude, their bodies grow taut with the pent-up tension of boiling kettles. You pause in expectation of the first blow. They are almost spitting into each other's faces. Then with a roar both burst into laughter. Half a minute later the debate resumes.[52]

Lately some Arab merchants have reluctantly yielded to the persistent persuasions of the Israeli government to change the "custom of the country" and to establish a one-price policy. Government approval certificates are issued to merchants who adopt the one-price policy. But some of the merchants who display these certificates are guilty of occasional backsliding. Gullible tourists often ask for a sharp deal, and some of the reformed bazaar merchants find the opportunities irresistible.

The bazaar is no longer as exotic as it was in the nineteenth and early twentieth centuries. But it is still one of the most fascinating sights in Jerusalem. No visitor can afford to miss a stroll through the bazaars and an occasional transaction with or without a little bargaining.

The Old City at Night

Tourists do not venture forth in the alleys of the Old City after sunset, because there is nothing for them to do there at night. The bazaars are shut and bolted, and the so-called streets are empty. Yet to walk in the Old City at night is an unforgettable experience.

John Finley, formerly editor of *The New York Times*, was in Jerusalem in 1918. He described the Via Dolorosa at night:

> The Via Dolorosa [is] a dark, rough and sorrowful street by day, but a woeful one by night. There was but one lamp burning its entire length. . . . The arches, gates, and flying buttresses which give character to the street by day make it seem a way of sepulchres by night, and the few stray persons I met or passed as wanderers among the tombs. When I emerged at the lower gate (Lions or St. Stephen's Gate), called [by the Arabs] the "Lady Mary" Gate, I was actually among the graves outside the wall.[53]

A decade later another distinguished American came to Jerusalem as a pilgrim and left us a vivid description of the Old City at night. The city was then governed by the British, but its "streets" and bazaars were just as silent and haunting as they had been under the Turks. John Haynes Holmes, the eminent minister of New York's Labor Temple, recorded his impressions of a walk through the lanes of the Old City:

> Only once did I see this street quiet—in a late evening stroll when my son and I set out to see the Mosque of Omar by moonlight. We saw the Mosque for a fleeting moment bathed in luster and crowned with stars, but this was "snooping," and an alert guard soon put us to flight. So we plunged again into the darkness of David Street. The closed shops gave everywhere the appearance of a dead city. Shut out from the sky by the low archways overhead, we found no light to guide our stumbling steps save an occasional lantern which only increased the surrounding blackness. Now and again we saw a candle gleam behind a latticed window up above, and here and there were pools of light from open taverns. . . . David Street was as empty by

night as it was crowded by day. Its silence was almost uncanny—no baby's cry, no man's laugh, no woman's scream. Yet people were living in all these upper stories and hidden away in the walls in these side alleys. Jerusalem goes to bed early. By nine o'clock the city has fallen into slumber. As we walked along that night, we met a berobed old man thumping the pavement with his cane, a young man treading cat-like in the shadows, three or four officers on their beats, perhaps one or two others. But we saw no woman, and in block after block not a living soul. I envied the East its habit of living naturally and happily by the sun.[54]

When the sun sets, a deathlike silence fills the bazaar and alleys of the Old City. Every stall and store is barred and bolted. Not a sound is heard. Nothing stirs, except an occasional cat crossing over to another lane in search of scraps of food in the garbage left from the day's bustle.

Under the Turks, the streets in Jerusalem were not lighted at night. The pashas demanded that the inhabitants provide their own street lighting. Anyone who ventured forth at night had to carry a lantern. If he failed to carry a lantern, it was proof that he was an outlaw who sought the shelter of darkness. It was no valid excuse for anyone to claim that he had no lantern. The only reasonable explanation that brought release from the law was adequate bakshish, duly and proportionately distributed among the pasha and his subordinates.

Horatius Bonar, in his mid-nineteenth century itinerary, *Days and Nights in the East,* notes this aspect of Jerusalem's mode of life:

As there are no street-lamps in Jerusalem, one must have his lantern or *fanus* when needing to be in the streets after sunset; both because you would be laid hold of by the guard as a suspected person, if found without a light, and because the rough narrow streets really require it. Our Jerusalem waiter, Gabrael, considered it as regular a part of his duty to come for us with his lantern, as to wait at table. On he marched before us, up one narrow street and down another, always holding the light as near the ground as possible, to indicate the ruts and stones, for it was our feet that alone seemed to need the light. We thus found new meaning in the passage, "Thy word is a lamp unto my feet, and a light unto my path" (Ps. 119:105).[55]

Today the alleys of the Old City are no longer shrouded in darkness at night. Yet, to walk in them after sunset still gives one a weird and eerie feeling. The total emptiness and ghostly silence fill one with a ghastly feeling. It resembles more a cemetery than a living city.

A Revolution in Jerusalem's Architecture

The Holy Land has been afflicted with destructive earthquakes throughout the centuries. Although the area most vulnerable is near the Jordan rift, the tremors are usually felt in far-removed areas including Jerusalem. Josephus records a disastrous earthquake which occurred during King Herod's reign.

> And there was an earthquake in Judaea, such as had not been before, which caused great destruction of the cattle throughout the country. And about thirty thousand persons also perished in the ruins of their houses.[56]

In more recent times, too, several earthquakes have struck Jerusalem. In 1927 an earthquake whose epicenter was north of Jericho affected a vast area from Lebanon to the Negev; it did considerable damage in Jerusalem. It so damaged the Kaiserin Augusta Victoria Hospice on Mount Scopus that the British Mandatory government, which had its offices there, had to move out. The earthquake also damaged severely the Church of the Holy Sepulchre and the monastery of the Sisters of St. Claire as well as many private residences.

Jerusalem's houses, despite their four-foot-thick walls, are not immune to earthquake damage. They do not withstand the earth tremors. Their walls crack and the heavy stone cupolas collapse.

Toward the end of the nineteenth century a revolution in the architecture of Jerusalem's houses took place. The story of the drastic change in the style of building is related by Bertha Spafford Vester in her autobiographical work, *Our Jerusalem:*

> Dr. Bailey Willis, professor of geology at Stanford University, California, and famed as "Earthquake Willis," because he hunted earthquakes in every corner of the globe, had known Palestine was due for a quake and hastened to be in "on the kill." He missed our quake by a few hours. He had reached Cairo when the tremors shook Palestine.

> He stopped with us in Jerusalem. His stories of the earthquakes he had experienced were so instructive and interesting that we asked him to give a lecture on the subject in the American Colony hostel, and among others we invited the acting High Commissioner, Colonel, later Sir John Symes.

> Dr. Willis had been awarded many of the world's highest honours for his research in seismology, but his great interest was in building to resist earthquake damage, and many of his discoveries at Stanford University had been made requirements in California building codes.

His lecture at the American Colony revolutionized building in the Holy Land. He was requested to put it into writing by the Palestine Administration. From that time on the demand was for reinforced concrete with a facing of stone. The outside held the same appearance.[57]

Today the houses in Jerusalem are built of reinforced concrete. The thick walls and copulas are to be found only in the old houses, mostly within the walls of the Old City. The new houses appear to be built of the local stone as they had been in former times. But this feature of Jerusalem's building is due to the wisdom of Sir Ronald Storrs who was Governor of Jerusalem during the British mandatory government. Sir Ronald Storrs wanted to preserve Jerusalem's character and beauty. He therefore issued an ordinance that all buildings in Jerusalem be constructed or faced with local stones. When the British left in 1948, the Israeli government reconfirmed Ronald Storrs's ordinance. Hence all the newer buildings, though built of reinforced concrete, are faced with the local stone. Jerusalem has thus retained its traditional appearance and its buildings still shine in the sunlight with their characteristic rich, golden glow. But the little domes are disappearing, and with them much of the city's picturesque panorama. In place of the copulas there are now flat cement roofs. This is part of the price paid for the modernity which has at last arrived in Jerusalem.

THREE

The Jews and Their Holy Places

The Jews and Their Western (Wailing) Wall

Baedeker's classic *Handbook for Travellers* advises that "this spot (the Wailing Wall) should be visited repeatedly, especially on a Friday after 4 p.m., or on Jewish festivals, when a touching scene is presented by figures leaning against the weather-beaten wall, kissing the stones, and weeping."[1] For the Christian traveler this was indeed one of the most curious sights in Jerusalem.

The Western Wall, or, as Christians call it, the Wailing Wall, stands in the Tyropean Valley in the Old City. Its height is impressive—about seventy feet—but hardly as impressive as it was originally when it was erected by King Herod about two thousand years ago. At that time the wall was almost twice as high. The engineers of the Palestine Exploration Society sank shafts close to the Wall. The shafts reached down sixty feet before they touched the foundation rock. One can look down these shafts and see twenty-six courses of Herodian masonry below ground level. One can readily imagine how impressive the Wall was in ancient times and how awed a person would be if he stood at the original ground level and looked up to the wall's top.

To grasp the significance of this holy place to the Jews one must learn the history of the Wall and its unique role in the spiritual life of the Jewish people. The Christian traveler, not equipped with this specialized knowledge, is perplexed by the strange sight of people standing before a huge wall, "weeping for the glory of their nation that has departed two thousand years ago." One Christian pilgrim noted with astonishment: "They traverse broad continents and wide seas to visit and weep over the ruins of what was once the City of Solemnities, clinging with tenacious grasp to the fragments of their ancient temple."[2]

For the Jews the Western Wall is the relic of their ancient holy Temple, a most sacred place, next only to the spot on the Temple Mount where the sanctuary itself stood. Since observant Jews will not enter the precincts of the Temple on Mount Moriah, the place in front of the Wall has become their holiest place.

The Wall is more than a national memory of past glory; it is also the symbol of a great hope. It represents the Jewish commitment to a future when the messianic ideals will be fulfilled, when the land of their fathers will be restored, and the brotherhood of man will be realized.

Jewish tradition claims that when Israel went into exile, God accompanied them, but the *Shekhinah* (God's Presence) never departed from the Western (Wailing) Wall. Hence prayers offered at the Wall are especially efficacious, and God is especially attentive there to beseechments for Israel's deliverance. When the Messiah will come, the Holy Temple will again rise on Mount Moriah, above the Western Wall, and God will reign in Israel and in the whole world.

For centuries Jews have regularly gathered in what used to be a narrow alley in front of the Wall and prayed with tears and lamentations. The prayer area was cramped. It measured only ten feet in width. Jewish worshipers were never allowed to pray in peace. Not only did Christian travelers stand by and watch the strange spectacle, but Arabs who lived nearby saw fit to walk back and forth among the worshipers, occasionally leading their donkeys through the congregations. And the donkeys not infrequently saw fit to relieve themselves among the worshipers. If that was not enough, some Arab boys would amuse themselves by throwing dung from the top of the Wall upon the worshipers' heads.[3] In the midst of these humiliations, the helpless Jews continued to pray and bewail their lot.

The significance of the Jewish prayers at the Western Wall of the Temple Mount usually escapes the tourists who watch the strange spectacle of worship accompanied by weeping and "wailing." It is an amazing fact that only the Jews have wept for Jerusalem. On the anniversary of Jerusalem's fall to the Babylonians in 586 B.C.E. and to the Romans in 70 C.E. Jews everywhere fast and shed tears over the fate of their beloved city.

Worshippers at the Western (Wailing) Wall after the Moghrabi slum had been cleared away (1968). (Courtesy of Israel Government Press Office.)

Neither the Christians nor the Moslems have mourned, fasted, or shed tears when the city was conquered and overrun by their enemies. When the Christians lost the city to the Arabs in the seventh century and again in the twelfth century, they did not set aside a day for mourning and fasting. Nor did the Moslems establish an annual fast to commemorate the loss of Jerusalem to the Crusaders in 1099. Only the Jews have shed tears over Jerusalem's fate these two millennia and more. The reason is simple. The attachment of the Christians and Moslems to Jerusalem is based primarily on holy places which are memorials to events in the lives of Jesus and Mohammed. For the Jews, however, Jerusalem has been their religious and national center throughout the centuries. For the Jews no other city has ever fulfilled the role of Jerusalem. While the Christians moved their religious center from Jerusalem to Rome and Constantinople, the Jews, though scattered throughout the world, have clung to Jerusa-

Jews praying at the Western (Wailing) Wall (1967). (Courtesy of Israel Government Press Office.)

lem. When the Jews lost control of Jerusalem the tragedy was of incalculable dimensions; no city in the world could take its place. No wonder they continue to shed tears at the relic of their holiest shrine, especially on the Ninth of Av, the anniversary of the fall of Jerusalem.

In 1948 the prayers at the Wall ceased. In that year the new State of Israel fought its War of Independence against six invading Arab armies. The war was concluded with an armistice agreement in which Jerusalem was divided between Israel and the Hashemite Kingdom of Transjordan. The New City became Israel's capital and the Old City was annexed by Transjordan.[4]

The Armistice Agreement provided that Jews would have access to the Western (Wailing) Wall for prayer. But Transjordan reneged on its pledge, and for nineteen years no Jew prayed in the alley in front of the Western Wall.

In 1967, Israel captured the Old City and Jews immediately flocked to the Western Wall to resume their traditional prayers at their holy place. The Israeli army cleared away the slum in front of the Wall, and the North African Moslems who lived there were relocated. The area was made into a spacious plaza where many mass religious and national celebrations are held.

When the annual fast of the Ninth of Av was observed on August 14–15, 1967, 100,000 Jews gathered at the Western (Wailing) Wall. *The Christian News from Israel* reported:

> On the night of 14 August, coinciding this year with the eve of the Ninth of Ab (anniversary of the destruction of both First and Second Temples), some 30,000 Jewish pilgrims prayed at the Western (Wailing) Wall for the first time in twenty years. Among them was the President of Israel, Mr. Zalman Shazar. Since 1948, the Jordanian authorities had refused the Jews access to this, their holiest shrine, in violation of the Israel-Jordan Armistice Agreement.
>
> It was also the first time that Jews had come to the Wall as masters of Jerusalem since the city and the Second Temple fell to the Romans.
>
> The pilgrimage encompassed Jews from all parts of the world, men and women of every walk of life, who came to kiss the ancient stones and lament the calamity of long ago, their grief now mingled with joy at deliverance and with happiness in the reunification of Jerusalem. On the following day, 70,000 more persons made the pilgrimage.[5]

Ambitious plans were drawn up for the restoration of the area in front of the Wall. One of these plans calls for the removal of the two-thousand-year accumulation of rubbish and debris in the Tyropean Valley and to expose the buried section of the wall. What a magnificent shrine the Wall will then be! People standing at its original ground level will be bending their heads backward and straining their eyes to gaze at the Wall's height. What a majestic relic! Truly one of the world's wonders!

At the time of this writing the Arab nations are demanding that the Old City be returned to Arab control. Israel insists that the united city of Jerusalem remain its capital. Never again, says Israel, will Jerusalem be divided; nor will any part of it be bargained away. Jerusalem, says Israel, is not negotiable, and the Western (Wailing) Wall will never again be entrusted to the care of the Jordanians or of any other nation. Who will prevail? Future generations will know the answer.

"Letters to God"

In 1966, a charming book, entitled *Children's Letters to God,* was published in New York.[6] In their letters the children ask God for various favors, such as pets, toys, help for themselves and for others, and similar boons. In Jerusalem one can see thousands of "letters to God" written by adults and deposited where the correspondents believe their "letters" will reach God and that God will take note of them. These "letters" are in the form of crumpled pieces of paper on which the correspondents write their petitions. Then they squeeze their missives into the crevices between the Herodian stones of the Western (Wailing) Wall. No sensitive person would think of removing these humble petitions. Occasionally, however, a tourist will yield to temptation and remove some of these personal petitions to the deity as curiosities to be exhibited among their friends at home. Thus we read in one travel book:

> With much difficulty I extracted a scrap of paper, brown with age, written in Hebrew characters. Being translated, it was found to contain nine names of a Jewish family, probably brought by some pilgrim from a distant land, and with pious object laid in the crevices of the huge blocks.[7]

Similarly does Charles Warren, the British archaeologist report:

> On one occasion, I met a Frank diligently (when no Jews were by) collecting as many of these letters as he could, to send home as curiosities; such documents, I think, ought to have been looked upon as worthy of remaining in their places.[8]

In the course of things, these petitions do not remain in the crevices of the wall. In winter the winds blow many of them out of the fissures. Rains sometimes wash them from their tiny perches. But new "letters" are constantly added.

It was reported in the press that during the Six-Day War Mr. Moshe Dayan, Israel's Minister of Defense, arrived at the Wall immediately after it was captured from the Jordanians. He was seen writing on a piece of paper, folding it, and inserting it in one of the crevices of the Wall. Mr. Dayan was asked by a member of the press what boon he asked of God. He answered: "Just two words, the eternal prayer of the Jewish people, the word 'Shalom' [peace] and the word 'now.'"

A similar anecdote was told of the former American Vice-President Walter Mondale. When the Vice-President came to Jerusalem on June 30, 1978, on the occasion of Israel's thirtieth anniversary, he visited the Western (Wailing) Wall and he put a note into one of its crevices. His prayer was also just two words—"Peace—*Shalom.*"

One of the most moving notes placed between the ancient stones was inserted at a service held in front of the Wall by a number of Christians who gathered on the eve of Christmas "to express their solidarity with the Jewish people and to testify to the free exercise of religion in the State of Israel." The event was reported in the quarterly, *Christian News from Israel:*

> The Pilgrimage to the Wall was led by Father Malcolm Boyd, an American Episcopalian priest. . . . After recital of a psalm, a moment of silent meditation was observed. Then Father Boyd, with a Canadian student studying in Jerusalem, walked to the Wall where Jews were praying and placed in a crevice between the stones a slip of paper bearing the first line of Psalm 96: "Sing a new song unto the Lord," a psalm read on the Sabbath eve in synagogues. He declared: "Above the Western Wall stood the ancient Temple. Abraham was prepared to sacrifice Isaac on its great rock. Later Jesus preached here. Mohammed ascended to the heavens from there. We revere these faiths and their peoples."[9]

The number of petitionary notes stuffed yearly into the crevices between the mighty ashlars of the Wall is estimated in the thousands. Many people wonder about the ultimate fate of these humble entreaties of the divinity. Their fate is an honorable one. They are treated like all sacred texts, such as Hebrew Bibles, rabbinic texts, or prayer books that have been rendered useless due to wear and tear. To be sure, a few are blown or washed away by the winter winds and rains. But most are firmly wedged in the crevices. The scraps of paper that fall out of the crevices are gathered daily, while those that are firmly set are removed twice annually, before Passover and before the Day of Atonement. Men equipped with long sticks dig them out and gather them in large sacks. The sacks are taken to a cemetery where they are buried. There is no religious ritual. These scraps of paper are regarded as sacred texts by virtue of the fact that their contents are addressed to God.

Charles Warren Takes a Party of Jews to See His Excavations near the Wailing Wall

One of the curious incidents recorded by the archaeologist Charles Warren is a guided tour that he arranged for a group of rabbis from Jerusalem's Jewish Quarter. His lucid account follows:

> Now having roughly gone over the leading characteristics of these vaults, let me describe the visit paid to them by the party of learned Jews. They assembled together under the charge of their Chief Rabbi, assisted by Hersh Berlina, the son of the late Chief Rabbi of London. . . . Our Jews being assembled, the first check we met with was in going into the vault under the Hall of Justice, from the Wailing Place; the door was kept by a Moslem, and he objected to Jews coming in; this being got over, we climbed on the top of his little house, which is built under an arch, and then, keeping along some passages, we stood at the little opening down into Wilson's Arch. There, below, I had lighted up magnesium wire, and they could view its vast proportions, and see the mouths of the shafts sunk below the springing of the arch at each end. We now descended the ladder under the arch itself, into the void place which of late years has been above the rock, and thirty-two feet below the roadway leading to the Temple area.
>
> Before going down here, the rabbins [*sic*] asked me many questions. Was I quite sure we were not going under the Temple area? This was their great fear, for they have a tradition that the volume of the Sacred Law is buried somewhere within the enclosure. Having been reassured on this point, they trooped down after me, and I had them mustered, to make sure none were lost. Then I took them to see the spring of water we had found, fifty-two feet below our standpoint: drawing up a can of water, they drank, and pronounced it good; then I threw a stone down, to let them hear the splash, upon which they all took up stones and threw down. I lowered down a magnesium light, so that they might see the old wall, so splendidly cut, so many feet below us, and explained to them that this wall was once exposed to view. Only two cared to go down to examine it.

I took them to the shaft at the other side, showed them the pier of the arch, well cut to twenty-five feet, and after that rough; and explained the reason. By this time rabbins and all were becoming greatly excited, and I was obliged to call them to order.

We now went outside from under Wilson's Arch, and, traversing the recent Moslem substructures of the Justice Hall, got through the small hole I had made, and emerged upon the continuation of the arches of the causeway to the west. Here there was grand enthusiasm, and I was very much afraid I should lose a few rabbins; but fortune favoured us. Although we had several shafts open, they always fell just clear of them. These vaults were certainly curious places for visitors to examine, with the various arches upon arches, aqueducts and shafts. We now went into some peculiar water-courses with pointed arches, which have been substituted for those semicircular, since the Moslem conquest, and, turning up one of the little ducts, found ourselves overlooking the Masonic Hall.

Here was a chamber built of well-cut drafted stones, pilasters at each corner, and semicircular roof, once high above ground, now deep below it. Our troop came tumbling into this vault in the most intense excitement, to see this old chamber, with the broken column standing up in the centre. Beside this column we were now digging a deep shaft, and nearly had an accident with some of the party, for the vault was full of debris, which when we cleared from one side, we had to pile up on another; in their scramble, they brought much of it down on them; however, they had come for sight-seeing, and did not mind a few bruises. From hence we pressed on to see the remainder of the arches, and the vaulted secret passage, which I lighted up for them. This pleased them mightily, and they went away fully impressed with the magnitude of the works of their forefathers. It was not only one party I took round, but many, and they all conducted themselves well, were delighted with what they saw, and so impressed, that they had prayers in their synagogues for the welfare of our undertaking, and at last had a grand ceremony at the synagogue, to which I was invited, and in which they prayed for me, and the work in which I was engaged.[10]

Four Monumental Jewish Tombs

In the Valley of Jehoshaphat, at the foot of the Mount of Olives, there are four famous tombs. They have been visited by many antiquarians, travellers, and pilgrims, and have been described in hundreds of books. They still arouse the curiosity of visitors and hardly a tourist fails to stop at these monuments.

Of the four sepulchres the tomb attributed to Absalom and the one attributed to Zechariah are immense monuments, each hewn out of a single block of stone from the mountainside. Edward Clarke in his classic work, *Travels in Various Countries*, suggests that these tombs—

> being of one entire block of stone . . . may therefore be considered as belonging to sculpture rather than architecture; for, immense as are these stones, they are sculptured instead of being built. . . . In order to form the sepulchres of Absalom and of Zechariah, the solid substance of the mountain has itself been cut away: sufficient areas being thereby excavated, two monuments of prodigious size appear in the midst; each seeming to consist of a single stone, although standing as if erected by an architect, and adorned with columns appearing to support the edifice, whereof they are in fact themselves integral parts. [11]

More puzzling is the fact that no one has ever discovered an entrance to either of these sepulchres. In order to gain admittance to these tombs, holes were broken into them, through which people crept inside. But no bones or other evidence of human burial was found to suggest that a prince was buried in the one or a prophet in the other. The Tomb of Absalom, the rebellious son of King David, is well-known and needs no identification. [12] The Tomb of Zechariah is identified with the prophet by that name, the son of Jehoiada, who was stoned to death in the court of the Temple in the days of King Joash. Some Christians say that this tomb is the burial place of the father of John the Baptist whose name was Zechariah. The Moslems claim that the two Zechariahs are the same person. Indeed they also include another Zechariah, the son of Berechiah, whose prophecies are recorded in the Bible. Here we have a strange Moslem trinity—three Zechariahs who lived centuries apart merged into one person and commemorated by one tombstone. It seems that Mohammed was not well informed in matters of chronology because almost half a millennium separates the Zechariah who was murdered in the Temple Court and the Zechariah who was the father of John the Baptist.

Of the other two sepulchres one is traditionally ascribed to Jehoshaphat, a king of Judah, and the other was named after the apostle St. James, because it had served as a hiding place for him. These tombs are caves, in the ancient tradition of Jewish burial. They contain burial chambers and receptacles for the dead bodies, hewn out of the stone in the hillside.

The authenticity of the sepulchres of Jehoshaphat and St. James have been questioned. These two tombs have been found to be connected by tunnels with their neighboring monoliths. The tomb of Jehoshaphat is

Tomb of Hezir family in Kidron Valley (1916). (Courtesy of Zionist Archives, Jerusalem.)

connected by a tunnel with the Tomb of Absalom, and the Tomb of St. James is connected by a tunnel with the Tomb of Zechariah. More important is the discovery of a Hebrew inscription in the Tomb of St. James, listing the names of the people who were buried in this sepulchre. They were all, according to the inscription, members of a priestly family, known as Bnai Hezir, mentioned in the Bible (1 Chron. 1:15,24). The four tombs are in fact only two Jewish family underground sepulchres each with a noble mausoleum over it. The other family, too, must have been of noble rank and ample affluence to have been able to erect for themselves a tomb of such grandeur. Judging by the architectural characteristics of these mausoleums, they were erected during the the Second Temple period.

The Jackal in the Tomb

Absalom's Tomb is a prominent monument in the Kidron or Jehoshaphat Valley, southeast of Jerusalem. Tourists find the monument interesting because of its architecture and even more so because of its attribution to a colorful prince who lived three thousand years ago. To be sure, Absalom was not an edifying personality, but he was the son of King David with whom Jerusalem's sacred history began.

The most intriguing aspect of this monument is its role in local tradition. Felix Bovet, the French biblical scholar, was in Jerusalem in the mid-nineteenth century. His work, *Egypt, Palestine, and Phoenicia: A Visit to Sacred Lands,* has been translated into many languages and frequently republished. Bovet writes about his visit at Absalom's Tomb and his confrontation with the tomb's "modern tenant":

> The Tomb of Absalom is the largest and the most curious. It is surrounded with a heap of small stones which conceal its base from view; for still, to this day, every Jew and every Mahometan who passes by, throws a pebble at this monument, repeating the Biblical malediction, "Cursed is he that setteth light by his father or his mother!" (Deut. 27:16).

> So has Absalom, who so much feared lest his memory should perish with him, succeeded in keeping it alive, —a malediction ceaselessly repeated has preserved his name for this cenotaph; and this imperishable monument secures for its builder an immortality of anathema.

> By the help of breaches which have been made in its walls one manages, though with difficulty, to effect an entrance into the interior of the mausoleum; there also the ground is covered with stones thrown into it by passers by.

I have spoken before of the cone which crowns it; it is possible to climb into its interior, like a sweep into a chimney. While I am trying to do so, I hear a noise above me. I raise my eyes, and find myself face to face with a jackal. He looks at me with some terror, and wishes to get away. I have time to examine him leisurely; his head and his yellow coat make him very like the dogs of this part of the world, but he has a thicker neck: his tail is very fine, and like that of a fox. This is the animal so often mentioned in Scripture as the denizen of desolate places. But I should not have suspected that he would have chosen the very gates of Jerusalem for his dwelling. [13]

In Jerusalem jackals are not the only ones to occupy empty tombs, turning them into residences for the living. There is in Jerusalem an entire suburb of human tomb dwellers. [14]

Why Jews Are Forbidden to Enter the Precincts of the Temple Mount

At the southern end of the Western (Wailing) Wall there is a ramp which leads up to Mount Moriah. Near the ramp there is a sign which reads:

Notice and Warning! Entrance to the area of the Temple Mount is forbidden to everyone by Jewish law owing to the sacredness of the place.

(*Signed*) *The Chief Rabbinate of Israel.*

Visitors, including many Jews, disregard the warning and walk up the ramp. At the entrance to the Temple Mount an Israeli soldier makes sure that the visitors are peaceful folk. Some Jews, however, resist the temptation. They betake themselves to the Via Dolorosa, go up to the traditional First Station of the Cross, and from there they view the spacious grounds of the Temple Compound. They gaze at the Dome of the Rock and admire this architectural jewel from afar.

Why do Orthodox Jews refrain from entering the precincts of the Temple Mount? In the travel literature one reads that the Jews believe that the holy vessels of the Temple are buried somewhere in this area. Not knowing the place of their burial there is the danger of treading on that holy spot. Some travel books add that the Jews believe that a Jew who treads on the holy site where the Temple vessels are hidden incurs the wrath of the Almighty and is doomed to die within the year.

Another reason often given for the Jewish prohibition against entering the Temple Mount enclosure is that the gates of the Temple were not consumed when the Temple was burned. Nor were they carried into captivity as were some of the holy vessels of the Temple. The gates sank into the ground and they will rise when the Messiah comes. They will then be restored in the Temple that will be rebuilt. This tradition is based on a statement in the Midrash:

> All the vessels of the Sanctuary were carried into exile . . . but the gates of the Temple were hidden away in the place where they had stood; as is proven by the text: "Her gates are sunken into the ground" (Lam. 2:9).[15]

All this has been repeated innumerable times, each writer copying from his predecessor, until it has spread even among Jews who should know better. What then is the true reason for the Jewish prohibition? The answer is quite prosaic. It is a matter of ritual purity. Biblical and rabbinic law forbids entry within the compound of the Temple to anyone who is in a state of ritual impurity. Since no one can be absolutely sure that he is in a state of purity, it is best to be on the safe side and not enter at all. Observant Jews follow this rule; others disregard it. One of those who disregarded the ban and entered the precincts of the Temple Mount was Moses Montefiore. For his violation of the ban, he was excommunicated by the Orthodox community.

As to the holy vessels of the Temple, Jewish tradition confirms the belief that they are hidden away; their secret hiding place to be revealed when the Messiah will come. In that glorious day the Temple will be rebuilt, the vessels will be recovered, and they will again be used in the sacred ritual of the Temple service.[16]

The Cyclopean Stones of the Western (Wailing) Wall

One of Jerusalem's wonders is a cave of huge dimensions, generally known as Solomon's Quarry. That this enormous underground labyrinth is a quarry and not a natural cave is obvious not only from its artificial shape but also from the chisel marks which can be seen everywhere and from the chippings that are scattered throughout the cave.

Jews call this vast quarry the Cave of Zedekiah. According to Jewish tradition, it was through this cave that King Zedekiah escaped from his palace in Jerusalem when the city fell to the Babylonian army in 586 B.C.E. The Babylonians caught up with the king, killed his sons in his presence, and then blinded him so that he might live with the vivid memory of his sons' deaths. But no one has been able to discover a passage from the cave to the city above. Hence this traditional designation has been discounted. King Zedekiah managed his escape through some other means, probably a secret tunnel from his palace to a distant exit outside the city's fortifications.

In general, this subterranean labyrinth is called Solomon's Quarry. A quarry it surely was. But was it the quarry whence came the stones for the building of Solomon's Temple? Most historians agree that the stones quarried in this cave were used for the building of the Temple, but the Temple was Herod's not Solomon's, and Herod's Temple was erected a thousand years after Solomon's reign.

About a century after the erection of Herod's Temple, a tragic event occurred in the cave. The historian, Josephus Flavius, relates in his classic work *The Jewish War* (VII, 2,2) how Simon Bar Giora, one of the Jewish leaders of the First Revolt against Rome, tried to avoid falling into the hands of the victorious Roman legions by hiding here. He and his loyal followers tried to dig a tunnel from the cave to a safe exit. In the end, they failed and were forced to surrender to the Romans. In his triumphal parade in Rome, Titus led Simon Bar Giora in chains and then beheaded him.

Near the Damascus Gate there is a prominent precipice over which the city wall climbs up and then descends to the ground level. The cliff and the wall over it are part of the city's fortifications. They merge so naturally that they seem to be part of a unified design. The entrance to the quarry is located in the center of this precipice. The entrance is appropriately marked in English as Solomon's Quarry and in Hebrew as the Cave of Zedekiah. The National Park which surrounds most of the Old City is narrow on that side of the city wall, but at this point it is of sufficient width for an attractive garden which makes the entrance to the cave impressive and inviting.

In the early nineteenth century the cave had been forgotten and its existence was practically unknown. Local residents knew of the cave's existence but did not regard it of sufficient interest to mention it to any visitor. The cave's entrance in those days was only a hole in the high cliff. Blocked by an accumulation of rubbish, this hole went mainly unnoticed. But the cave was not empty. It was inhabited by jackals and thousands of bats—all living there undisturbed. In the mid-nineteenth century the cave was rediscovered and curious explorers began to visit it. The bats, frightened by the unwelcome visitors, would circle endlessly about the intruders, often close enough to frighten them. These explorers dared not venture into the quarry without an ample supply of candles. The interior was dark as midnight and there was the danger of losing one's way in the labyrinth. Unlike the catacombs of Rome which are a series of narrow galleries, Solomon's Quarry spreads out in all directions and the roof rises above one like a vast dome of overhanging limestone strata.

Entering the cave in those days meant lowering one's body carefully down through the hole till the feet touched ground. Once inside, the explorer dared not move in the total darkness till he lit one of his candles. To have been left in the cave without light was most dangerous, as we read in Sarah Barklay Johnson's description of the cave's exploration after her father took part in its rediscovery in 1852:

> In their wanderings through the dark cavern, the light of their torches fell upon a human skeleton. It lay in the bottom of a deep and precipitous pit, making more awful the stillness of the night, and adding tenfold to the fearfulness of the scene. This was, perhaps, the skeleton of an explorer, insufficiently supplied with light; and coming unconsciously upon the verge of the pit, was, without a moment's warning, precipitated headlong down the frightful chasm. Fortunately for our more provident explorers, they were well supplied with lights....

> Along the intricate passages, through the vast white halls, they roamed the greater part of the night—now seating themselves to rest in a sub-grotto, which, anywhere else, and at any other time, would be a most lovely little retreat; and now gazing with wonder at the colossal pillars; themselves and the flitting bats being the sole living intruders upon the solitude of this gloomy place.

> Besides the white pile of human bones, there were smaller heaps strewn about, which, upon examination, proved to be the skeletons of animals brought in by jackals—the real proprietors of the cave![17]

Another explorer of the mid-nineteenth century, W. M. Thomson, described his exploration of the cave with fascination and awe:

> Pausing to take breath and look about, I was surprised at the immense dimensions of the room. The roof of rock is about thirty feet high, even above the huge heaps of rubbish, and is sustained by large, shapeless columns of the original rock, left for that purpose by the quarriers, I suppose. On we went, down, down, from one depth to a lower, wandering now this, now that way, and ever in danger of getting lost, or of falling over some of the many precipices into the yawning darkness beneath. In some places we climbed with difficulty over large masses of rock, which appear to

have been shaken down from the roof, and suggest to the nervous the possibility of being ground to powder by similar masses which hang overhead.[18]

The quarry was rediscovered not by archaeologists, nor Dr. J. T. Barclay, as most people believe. Dr. Barclay's daughter credits the family's dog. "Let me give honor to whom honor is due. Our dog had first attracted our attention to the cavern by scenting a jackal at its mouth; and to this noblest of the canine race must really be awarded the palm of discovery."[19]

The cave was formed by quarrying stones for the building of the Temple on Mount Moriah. The Bible tells of the building of the First Temple by King Solomon, that the stones were quarried and fully fashioned in the cavern before they were brought to the site of construction:

> The house, when it was in building, was built of stone, made ready before it was brought thither, so that there was neither hammer, nor axe, nor any tool of iron heard in the house while it was in building (1 Kings 6:7).

This procedure was also followed in the building of Herod's Temple. The stone in the quarry is relatively soft. But it hardens when exposed to the sun and wind. This is no doubt the reason that the stones were shaped in the quarry and not at the site of the building operations.

The method of quarrying the huge blocks was ingenious. "By means of a pick," writes Edwin Sherman Wallace, "or similar tool, a deep groove was cut in the face of the rock to the width desired. This was followed by . . . driving in a wooden wedge and then pouring water on the wedge which, as the wood swelled, split the stone."[20]

While we are reasonably informed regarding the source of the huge limestones in the Western (Wailing) Wall, we are totally in the dark regarding the means of their transportation from the quarry to the building site. Some of these stones are said to weigh as much as a hundred tons. How did Herod's architects manage to remove these huge stones from the quarry and bring them to their designated places. Horatius Bonar relates that he spoke to an Arab who owned land near the Western (Wailing) Wall, and asked him, "How could such enormous stones be lifted?" He was told that "the 'Gins' (or genii) did it for Solomon." If this explanation does not satisfy the reader, we can only inform him that the Pharaohs of Egypt solved a similar problem when they built the pyramids. The ancients had their ways of building huge structures with the simple tools available in their days.

To enter this enormous cavern and to explore it today is a pleasant experience. Gone are the bats and jackals, and one need not go armed with candles or searchlight. After the Six-Day War, the Israeli government cleaned the cave of its accumulated rubbish and dispossessed its strange squatters—the jackals and the bats. Paths were laid out and electric lights were installed. Visitors now explore this strange labyrinth with ease and safety.

The One Hour When Jews Ruled Jerusalem

In the nineteenth-century travel books there is a recurring tale of sorrow which describes the Jews weeping at the Wailing Wall "for their ancient glory that is gone." The writers usually compare the days when Jewish kings reigned in Jerusalem with the remnant of miserable Jews who wept at the Wailing Wall. To relieve this tale of woe, some travel books describe a glorious hour when the Jews were symbolically the masters of Jerusalem. During that illustrious hour the Jews actually possessed the keys of Jerusalem. According to an old tradition this took place every time a new sultan ascended the throne. Ermete Pierotti in his *Customs and Traditions of Palestine* relates:

> On July 8, 1861, the day on which the news of the death of Abdul Megid and the accession of Abdul Azis arrived at Jerusalem, the Jews waited with all formalities on the governor Surraya pasha, and requested him to restore to them the keys of Jerusalem, according to a right which they claimed on the death of one sultan and the accession of another. At the same time they brought forward such proofs of the justice of their demand, that the pasha did not refuse it, but referred it to his ordinary council, consisting of the mufti or chief officer of religion, the khadi or chief judge, and other persons of distinction, natives of the country. Their decision was in favour of the Israelites, the whole council being aware that they were the ancient owners of the country. The ceremony was accordingly performed in the following manner. Said pasha, the general of the forces, accompanied by the officers of his staff, and some members of the council, and followed by a crowd of sight-seers, went to the Jews' quarter, where he was met by a deputation of that nation and conducted to the house of the chief rabbi, who received the pasha at the door, and there was publicly presented with the keys. The pasha was then entertained with the utmost respect at the divan of the rabbi; refreshments, coffee, and tobacco, were served, and then the rabbi (not having a garrison to defend the keys) restored them with many thanks to the general, who was escorted back by the chief men of the Jews to the governor of the city, Surraya pasha, to give an account of his mission, and shew him that none of the keys were missing. So, in 1861, the Jewish nation possessed for

one hour the keys of Jerusalem, which were delivered over to them by the Arabs in consequence of the unvarying tradition which they had preserved.[21]

This strange ceremony is also described by James Finn, the British consul in Jerusalem. In his memoirs, *Stirring Times,* he writes:

[One of the curious customs of the Jews] is that of getting possession of the great keys of the city gates on the decease of each Sultan of Constantinople, and after a religious service of prayer, and anointing them with a mysterious preparation of oil and spices, allowing them to be returned to the civic authorities on behalf of the new monarch. For the exercise of this traditional custom they make heavy presents to the local governors, who allow of a harmless practice that has prescription to show on its behalf. It is a matter of 'bakhsheesh' to them, and there is also a class of superstitious people to be found in Palestine who think that the benediction of the ancient 'children of Israel' is worth having; the Jewish feelings are gratified, their expectation of the future is refreshed, and the Jerusalem Rabbis are enabled to boast the world over among their people that they suffer the Sultan of Turkey to keep possession of the Holy City.[22]

As to the keys of Jerusalem, they were only "rusty representatives of the originals." So writes William Beaumont in his *Diary of a Journey to the East.* He records how he arrived in Jerusalem just as the guards were about to lock the gates.

The guards jingling the rusty representatives of those silver keys which locked and unlocked the city, while the Latin kingdom stood, and which on its fall were carried away by the Knights of St. John, and are now in their archives at Malta.[23]

It should be noted, however, that the gates of the nineteenth century were not the ones that existed during the Crusader Kingdom of Jerusalem. The gates of Beaumont's day were built in the sixteenth century by Suleiman the Magnificent. These "rusty keys" were, in all probability, the very keys that were fashioned when the sixteenth century walls and gates were erected.

The Strange History of a Synagogue Called "The Ruin"

Of all Jerusalem's synagogues none had a history as strange as that of the synagogue called The Hurvah (The Ruin). Its history began in 1700 when a group of mystics under the leadership of Rabbi Judah He-Hasid arrived

*Ruins of the Hurvah Synagogue in the Jewish Quarter of the Old City (1967).
(Courtesy of Israel Government Press Office.)*

in Jerusalem. These mystics were pledged to the messianic goal of bringing redemption to Israel through kabbalistic studies and ascetic living. Three days after their arrival, Rabbi Judah He-Hasid died and, without their leader, the group began to disintegrate.

Notwithstanding their diminished numbers, their poverty, and their lack of leadership, the new arrivals acquired a plot of land in the Jewish Quarter and commenced the building of a synagogue. One of these pietists, Gedaliah of Siemiatycze, wrote a small Hebrew book, entitled *Seek the Peace of Jerusalem,* in which he described how the remnant of Judah He-Hasid's disciples built their synagogue:

> A beginning was made at the building of the new synagogue and of forty dwellings for the poor. A magnificent House of Study containing many books was likewise built. . . .

These buildings consumed a great deal of money. The Turks in Jerusalem had to be heavily bribed before they permitted the building. Then the Jews of Jerusalem wished to construct the new synagogue on a larger scale than the old one, but the Turkish government permitted them to build it only as high as the previous building. So then they had to bribe the pashas heavily again, in order that they might approve a larger building.

Now there is a law in Jerusalem that while building is going on the pasha has to be paid five hundred lion thalers a year for three years. But as the synagogue had been built higher than the old one without the permission of the Sultan, another pasha came and wished to stop the building. So he also received five hundred lion thalers. Finally, a new pasha came from Constantinople to whom five hundred lion thalers had to be given. Thus the Jews were compelled to borrow money from the Turks at a high rate of interest. . . . [So] our debts press like a heavy yoke on our necks. We are continually taken into custody and before one debtor can be redeemed, another has already been detained. One scarcely dares to go out in the street, where, to cap it all, the tax collectors lie in wait like wolves and lions to devour us.[24]

In 1720 the Arab creditors demanded payment and the congregation could not meet the demand. A mob of Arabs burned down the synagogue

The dome of the Hurvah Synagogue, before it was destroyed in 1948. (Courtesy of Central Zionist Archives, Jerusalem.)

and drove Rabbi Judah He-Hasid's followers out of the city. The site of the synagogue came to be called Hurvat Rabbi Judah He-Hasid (The Ruin of Rabbi Judah He-Hasid) or, for short, The Hurvah (The Ruin).

For a hundred years The Hurvah remained an actual ruin, a heap of rubble. In 1812 an epidemic broke out in Safed, and twenty disciples of the Gaon of Vilna sought refuge in Jerusalem. At that time only Sephardi Jews were permitted to settle in Jerusalem. The refugees therefore adopted a subterfuge. They dressed in the distinctive garb of the Sephardi Jews and thus gained permission to settle in the Holy City. Ironically, the newcomers were firm opponents of the mystics. They were committed to strict scholarly study of the rabbinic texts. They were thus the opposite of the disciples of Rabbi Judah He-Hasid. Yet they were destined to carry on the tradition of the Hurvah Synagogue. In 1836, an enterprising member of the congregation, Abraham Shlomoh Zalman Zoref, succeeded in obtaining permission to build a synagogue on the site of The Ruin. This success led to his murder by the local Moslems. However, a modest synagogue was erected and was named Menahem Tziyon (The Comforter of Zion).

The following year an earthquake devastated the city of Safed, and many Ashkenazi Jews came to Jerusalem, swelling the ranks of the small congregation. Plans were therefore made for the building of a larger synagogue in the Hurvah courtyard. In 1854, Lord Napier, the British ambassador to the Sublime Porte, secured a firman, granting permission to build the synagogue. Three years later, in 1857, this firman was handed to Sir Moses Montefiore who was in Constantinople on his way to Jerusalem. Montefiore was making his fifth pilgrimage to the Holy City. A year later a cornerstone was laid by Baron Alphonse de Rothschild, head of the Paris branch of the Rothschild family. Funds were raised in far-flung Jewish communities. It is both interesting and noteworthy that the largest gift to the building fund of this Ashkenazi synagogue came from the Sephardi family of Yehezkel Reuben of Baghdad.

In 1864 the new synagogue was dedicated and named Beit Yaakov (House of Jacob). The British consul, James Finn, was one of the guests invited. In his two volume work, *Stirring Times,* James Finn describes the dedication ceremony:

> Many of this community [the Ashkenazi Jews] were British *protégés* and they invited us to be present at a religious thanksgiving service of prayers within the walls, in token of gratitude to the British government.

We were placed at a small table with a white cover, between the '*Al mem'r* (reading desk) and the Ark. The enclosure was fully crowded; but the women were all put into an adjoining house, from whence they could both see and hear the proceedings.

First came the prayer, "O Thou who givest Victory to Kings," which is the usual prayer throughout the world for the monarch of the country; but in this instance, I believe, the names which occurred were those of our own Sovereign and of her Royal family. Then followed a prayer for the British Consul, his wife, "the first-born son, and all their children"; followed by beautiful chants and anthems in Hebrew, not equal, in execution of the singing, to what may generally be heard in synagogues in Europe, but still far superior to that of the native Oriental Jews; and there was singing in parts, which was peculiar to themselves.

The walls were not yet built high enough for the domed roof to be thrown over them, but it was easy to see that the proportions would be excellent. After the religious ceremonial, lemonade and cakes were brought in, while a clarionet and a drum in a corner played various pieces of Russian and of Austrian music, particularly the Austrian coronation anthem, for the clario-net player had formerly served in an Austrian regimental band.

Some more Hebrew anthems were then sung, including several Psalms, and the "*Adon Olam*" . . .

Thus the Jews, as well as other communities, held a public religious service with rejoicings. It was, indeed, a new thing in Jerusalem for them to be able thus to lift up their heads, and erect a synagogue that should be visible all over the city and from the country round.[25]

The completed synagogue was a magnificent structure with a promi-nent dome. It became the central synagogue of the Ashkenazi Jews in Jerusalem. Still the Jews continued to call this synagogue The Hurvah. In this synagogue the Ashkenazi Chief Rabbis were installed, and prominent guests were officially received. "The Ruin" was the pride of Jerusalem's Jewry where important communal events took place. Thus *The Jewish Chronicle* of London reported on March 1, 1901:

On Sunday, February 3, 1901, at 3 o'clock in the afternoon an impressive Memorial Service for Queen Victoria was held in the Great Ashkenazim Synagogue presided over by Chief Rabbi Samuel Salant. This large place of worship was filled to its utmost capacity, and policemen had to keep off the crowds, who vainly sought admission by force.

And after the First World War, the Jewish Legion, which fought with General Allenby for the liberation of the Holy Land from the Turks, deposited its flags in The Hurvah. In 1920, Sir Herbert Samuel, the first

British High Commissioner in Palestine, came to The Hurvah to pray. He was called to the Torah, and he chanted The *Haftarah* (prophetic portion), which happened to be Isaiah 40—"Comfort ye, comfort ye, My people, saith your God"....

In 1948, the Old City was captured by the Jordanian army. The Jews were expelled from the Jewish Quarter, and almost all Jewish buildings and monuments were systematically destroyed, among them, The Hurvah. Plans for the restoration of the Hurvah have been drawn up though not officially adopted. The Ruin may yet rise again from its shambles and once more become the pride of the Holy City's Jewish community. But it will continue to be called The Hurvah.[26]

A Kabbalistic Synagogue

In the Jewish Quarter of the Old City there is a synagogue named Beth El. The name is not unusual. Many synagogues throughout the world are named Beth El, the House of God. The name derives from the biblical story in which Jacob dreamed of a ladder that reached up to heaven with angels ascending and descending upon it. In the dream, God blessed Jacob and promised him that the land of Canaan would be the land of his descendants. When Jacob woke up, he "called the name of that place Beth El" (Gen. 28:19).

The Beth El Synagogue of Jerusalem differed from all the synagogues in the Holy City in that it was the center of Jerusalem's mystics or Kabbalists.[27] In this small synagogue many a mystic spent days and nights contemplating the mysteries of life and death, the essence of the deity, the nature of creation, and the secrets hidden in the words of Holy Scripture. Some of the mystics also tried to control and utilize the mystery and the power of prayer, and how the words uttered by mere mortals can penetrate the seven heavens and affect the divine order.

The story of the mystics who founded the Beth El Synagogue is told with touching tenderness in a booklet by Shimon Ben-Eliezer, entitled *Destruction and Renewal*. The author meant his booklet to be a memorial to the synagogues of the Jewish Quarter which were destroyed by the Arabs in 1948. In his booklet Shimon Ben-Eliezer describes the founders of the Beth El Congregation:

> Its members formed a tightly knit group, known as the Lovers of Peace, all
> devoted to Cabbalistic studies, mystic meditation, pious living and good

deeds. Their founding covenant drawn up in 1757 by one of the first Yemenites to return to the Holy Land, Rabbi Shalom Shar'abi, enjoined upon them austere rules of saintliness.

The deed, affixed to the doors of the Holy Ark, and signed by all founding members, read *inter alia:* "With the help of God and His succour, as the Lord desires penitence and contrition, the spirit moved us, the youngest of His flock, to be like one man, brethren for the sanctification of His holy name, to gladden our Creator, upon which we have made this Covenant among us. . . , that we all be attached to one another, in great love of body and soul, to gladden our Creator. . . and if God forbid an affliction befall one of us to aid him in common . . . and we further undertake that every rule or restriction or good custom upon which the majority of the brethren will be of accord, shall be binding upon all and each of us to observe and live by it .. . . and we further undertake that none of us shall pride himself on his wisdom . . . and if one sins to his brother the latter shall forthwith forgive him with all his heart and soul . . ."[28]

In regard to the devotional practices of the Beth El mystics, Shimon Ben-Eliezer writes:

There were none of the elaborate poetical embellishments grafted on the original prayer texts since medieval times. Even so services would take long hours. In Cabbalistic tradition worshipers would immerse themselves in profound meditation on every holy word and letter. They would also seek spiritual uplift, following the example of Rabbi Shar'abi, by enhancing their devotions through mystical tunes . . . After days given up to study they would rise at midnight to lament the fall of the Holy Temple. At the break of dawn their beadle would, at the rabbi's bidding, climb up the roof, much like a muezzin, and call the faithful for morning devotions. They would also refrain from worldly talk and take upon themselves frequent fasts—all this to hasten the advent of Messiah.[29]

The Kabbalists of the Beth El Synagogue aimed especially at directing the worshipers' thoughts to the mystic connotations of each word of the traditional prayers, especially of the divine names, each letter of which was to be associated with special kabbalistic connotations. By means of these "concentrations" one could achieve many important goals, such as driving out an evil spirit from an afflicted person, the redemption of a poor soul from its suffering in the netherworld, and most important, the advancement of Israel's deliverance from its exile.

In the year 1916 a prayer book was published in Jerusalem by the leader of the Beth El mystics, Rabbi Shalom Sharabi. The prayer book, which is commonly known as the *Sharabi Siddur,* carried the idea of mystic

סידור תפלה להרש"ש

ואומר החזן חצי קדיש.

קדיש זה סוד דאתר נפ"א ודאתר קס"ת ודקודם עמידה ואחריה דמנחה וערבית :
יכוין באומרו שבח הקדום הזה בלשון תרגום להכניע הקלי' ולברר מחוכם את
י"א מיני קדושה שנשארו נכסס מז"מ זו"ן שהם ו"ה, ולחבדם לאותיות י"ה
שהם או"א :

ויתקדש   יתגדל

ויתקדש (טור שמאלי)

יבוין להמשיך ללם דנ"ר דנרנח"י דרום
דמומין דיניקה דאבא שהס ג'
אלהים מלובשים בנה"י. ויסוד הטודף
הוא שדי מלא ג"י יתקדם. לפרלוף נה"י
ותג"ת דמג"ס דו"א. (שהס א"א ונוק'
וישסו"ת הגק' ז"א) דהיכל ק"ק דבריאה
דז"א דאלי ודבריאה

כ"ר דנרנח"י דרום דאבא

אֶהְיֶה אֶהְיֶה
יְהֹוָה יְהֹוָה

אהיה אהיה
יהוה יהוה
אֶהְיֶה אֶהְיֶה
יְהֹוָה יְהֹוָה
אוהיונהו אוהיונהו
יונהוונהו יונהוונהו
אלהים אלהים

הוד   נלח

אלהים
שין דלת יוד

יסוד

לפרלוף נה"י ותג"ת דמג"ס דו"א
דהק"ק דבריאה דז"א דאלי ודבריאה
התחתונה.

שמיס

יתגדל (טור ימני)

יכוין להמשיך ללם דנ"ר דנרנח"י
דרום דמומין דיניקה דאימא
שהס ג' אלהים מלובשים בנה"י דאימא
שהס מילוי לבד דקס"א קמ"ג קנ"א עס
סורסס שהוא אהיה פשוט. לפרלו' נה"י
ותג"ת דמג"ס דו"ק (שהס יעקב ורחל
הגק' ו"ק) דז"א דבריאה. והאדם המו'
מלובשים במילוף אהיה לנוק'.

כ"ר דנרנח"י דרום דאימא

אֶהְיֶה אֶהְיֶה
יְהֹוָה יְהֹוָה

אהיה אהיה
יהוה יהוה
אֶהְיֶה אֶהְיֶה
יְהֹוָה יְהֹוָה
אוהיונהו אוהיונהו
יונהוונהו יונהוונהו
אלהים אלהים
אלף הי יוד הי אלף הא יוד הא

נלח   אלהים   סוד
אלף הה יוד הה

יסוד

אהיה
לפר' נה"י ותג"ת דמג"ס דו"ק דז"א.
ונס בובו עס האדם המו' לנוק'.

Page from the Sharabi Siddur.

"concentrations" to such an extreme that each word of the liturgy, especially the divine names, required extensive meditation. Each letter and the various combinations of the letters, required special concentration. The photostatic copy of a page from that prayer book, herewith reproduced, covers the first two words of the mourners' prayer—*Yitgadal, v'yitkadash* (Glorified and sanctified [be His Great Name]). These two pages are typical. Thus the six initial words of the benediction formula—*Barukh attah Adonai, Elohenu, Melekh Ha-Olam* (Praised art Thou, O Lord, our God, King of the Universe) cover five pages, and the first paragraph of the *Amidah* (the Eighteen Benedictions) covers no less than fifty-six pages of "concentrations."

The recitation of the morning, noon, and evening prayers required most of the day. However, the Kabbalists never spared time in matters of such importance. They spent their days and most of their nights trying to penetrate the mysteries that inhere in the words of the Torah and in the prescribed prayers of the synagogue ritual.

The Beth El Synagogue suffered the fate of all the synagogues in the Jewish Quarter. It was demolished by the Jordanians in 1948, and its members were driven out of the Old City along with all the Jewish inhabitants. The main legacy left us by these mystics is the *Sharabi Siddur,* an intriguing kabbalistic work, the contents of which are, not surprisingly, veiled in utter mystery.

Recently the Beth El Synagogue has been restored and a number of Kabbalists have made it their spiritual home. They study the kabbalistic literature and they hope to revive the tradition of the Beth El mystics. Since Jerusalem still attracts mystics and visionaries, the Beth El Synagogue may again become a center of kabbalistic studies.

The Synagogue That "Removed Its Hat" for an Emperor

If men remove their hats in honor of royalty, why really should not a domed structure remove its dome in honor of an emperor? This analogy may seem ridiculous. But it happened in Jerusalem, and the respectful synagogue was duly rewarded for thus honoring an emperor.

The synagogue that honored an emperor was officially named *Tiferet Israel* (The Glory of Israel), but it was popularly known as the Nissan Bak Synagogue, because Nissan Bak had been the prime mover of the building project. The synagogue's large dome shared the city's skyline with the

Ruins of the Nissan Bak Synagogue in the Jewish Quarter of Jerusalem, destroyed by the Arabs in 1948 (1969). (Courtesy of Israel Government Press Office.)

lofty domes of the so-called Mosque of Omar, the Church of the Holy Sepulchre, and the Hurvah Synagogue. It is reliably related that when the Austrian Emperor Francis Joseph visited Jerusalem in 1869, he asked to be shown the new synagogue, because many of its members were former Austrians. He was shown the new, unfinished building. The emperor turned to Nissan Bak and asked why the synagogue had no dome. Nissan Bak replied that the synagogue had removed its dome in honor of His Majesty. The emperor was pleased with his guide's wit and donated one thousand francs to complete the structure.

The Nissan Bak Synagogue and its lofty dome were destroyed by the Jordanians after 1948. As of this writing the Tiferet Israel Synagogue is still waiting for restoration.

The Synagogue on the Via Dolorosa

On Via Dolorosa, next to the Fourth Station of the Cross, there is a synagogue which bears the strange sign, *"Igud Lohamay Yerushalayim"* (Association of the Veterans of the Battle for Jerusalem). At its entrance there is a second tablet which reads: *"Yeshivat Torath Hayim,* founded 1886 by the Grand Rabbi Isaac Winograd." How does a synagogue come to be situated in the midst of the Christian holy places on Via Dolorosa? And why was this synagogue spared when all other synagogues and *yeshivot* (talmudic institutes) were destroyed by the Jordanians after they captured the Old City in Israel's War of Independence?

The story of this synagogue began in the 1880's when a young Russian rabbi, Isaac Winograd, became obsessed with the idea that the time had come for the realization of the prophecy that "out of Zion shall come forth the divine Teaching and the word of the Lord from Jerusalem" (Isa. 2:3). Why should the great *yeshivot* be located in Russia? It was his mission and destiny, he felt, to establish a great seat of rabbinic learning

Yeshivat Torat Hayim, *after the Arab disturbances of 1920. (Courtesy of Central Zionist Archives, Jerusalem.)*

in Jerusalem. This *yeshivah* would become the center of rabbinic scholarship for Jews everywhere. This was a cause that demanded his total dedication. No danger, suffering, or deprivation would deter the young scholar from pursuing his ideal.

Rabbi Isaac Winograd arrived in the Holy City in 1886 and launched his *yeshivah* in the Jewish Quarter. The new academy prospered and soon outgrew its quarters. Rabbi Winograd looked for a site on which to erect a suitable new building for his expanding academy. An unusual opportunity presented itself when a plot close to the Temple Mount became available. The Messiah, figured Rabbi Winograd, will surely announce his arrival by sounding "the great Shofar" on the Temple Mount. He will then go forth to redeem the Jews from their exile. The available plot was strategically located. It would provide the Messiah a first stopping place upon emerging from the Temple Mount on his way to the Jewish Quarter. What a providential opportunity! The fact that the plot was located on Via Dolorosa, in the midst of so many Christian churches, convents, and hospices did not deter Rabbi Winograd from purchasing the plot. Before long building operations were begun.

The Christian community of Jerusalem, especially the Latin Church, were alarmed. The prospect of having a Jewish institution right in the center of the Christian holy places was an embarrassing and provoking intrusion within the sacred domain of Christendom. To permit such a site to pass into the hands of the Jews was unthinkable. Strenuous efforts were made to purchase the plot from the Jews. Tempting sums were offered, but Rabbi Winograd would not sell. Indeed, how could he sell the plot which had become associated in his mind with the divine plan? When persuasion failed more drastic methods were employed. The laborers engaged in the construction of the building were waylaid and assaulted. In desperation Rabbi Winograd and his associates turned for protection to the Russian consul in Jerusalem on the grounds that they were subjects of the tsar. This was a curious expedient, for the relationship between the Russian government and its Jewish subjects was one of mutual contempt and hatred. Alexander III, the Russian tsar, was hardly known for his solicitude toward his Jewish subjects. It was during his reign that the most shocking government-inspired riots were launched against the Jews. More than one hundred and sixty pogroms took place during the reign of Alexander III. Yet Rabbi Winograd and his associates saw fit to claim their Russian birthright and to ask for Russian protection. More surprising, the Russian consul readily responded and provided armed cavasses who daily brought the Jewish workers to the building site, watched over them during the working hours, and then escorted them to their homes. This service was provided by the Russian consul not out of love of the Jews but out of hate of the Latins. In the late nineteenth century it was widely believed that the Sick Man of Europe would soon yield up the ghost, and the Great Powers were engaged in a race to establish footholds in the Holy City, which would enable them to lay claim to Jerusalem as their share of the divided Turkish empire. Jerusalem was regarded as a prize worthy of political intrigue and financial expenditure. Russia would rather have the Jews build their *yeshivah* and synagogue on the Via Dolorosa than let the Latin Church acquire another choice plot in the center of the Holy City.

The building was completed in 1894 and was dedicated with great rejoicing. It contained living quarters for the head of the *yeshivah* and for some of the instructors, administration offices, and a spacious study hall and synagogue on the top floor of the building. The *yeshivah* prospered. At its peak it boasted of three hundred students, among them several who became renowned personalities, such as Jerusalem's Chief Rabbi Zevi Pesah Frank, the saintly Rabbi Arye Levine, and the spiritual mentor of the *Gush Emunim,* Rabbi Zevi Yehudah Ha-Cohen Kook.

After the First World War, the *Yeshivat Torat Hayim* came upon evil days. In 1920 the first of the Arab nationalist disturbances took place. Arab mobs attacked the Jewish residents of the Old City. *Yeshivat Torat Hayim* was attacked and plundered, and the synagogue appurtenances and the institutional records were demolished. The residents in the building managed to save their lives by hiding in the cellar. When quiet was restored, the *yeshivah* resumed its functions and the synagogue resumed its regular services. Then came the Arab disturbances of 1921, 1929, and finally the Arab insurrection of 1936 which was directed against the British as well as the Jews. Life in the Moslem Quarter became too risky for the Jewish residents. The Jews were evacuated and the *yeshivah* building was abandoned. Twelve years later the 1948–1949 Jewish-Arab war broke out and the Old City was captured by the Jordanians. The Jewish inhabitants were expelled from the Jewish Quarter and the Old City.

In 1931, five years before the *Yeshivat Torat Hayim* building was abandoned, an Arab janitor was hired. In return for his services he was given living quarters in the building rent free. The Arab died shortly before the 1948–1949 war. Before his death, he gave the keys to the *yeshivah* building to his brother. When the Jordanians conquered the Old

City and the Jews were driven out the Arab janitor rented the apartments in the *yeshivah* building to Arab tenants. But the upper floor he regarded as a holy place. He locked it and permitted no one to enter. In 1967, when the Israeli forces captured the Old City, General Hayim Herzog heard that there was in the Moslem Quarter a synagogue which managed to survive the destruction of the Jewish institutions in the Old City. He hurried to the building and, to his great astonishment, discovered that the synagogue and its appurtenances, as well as the library with its three thousand volumes, were exactly as they had been left thirty-one years before. The Arab janitor was asked: "Weren't you afraid to watch over the synagogue when all the other synagogues in the Old City were demolished?" The Arab is reported to have answered, "The holy place watched over me more than I watched over it."

The survival of this synagogue made a deep impression on some of the soldiers who participated in the capture of the Old City. They saw in the survival of this synagogue in the heart of the Moslem Quarter an omen that Jewish life was destined to be revived in this area. They decided not to abandon this holy place until this area is once more populated by Jewish families. They pledged themselves to reconstitute the religious services in this synagogue notwithstanding that their homes were located at considerable distances from the Via Dolorosa. Since Jewish religious law prohibits riding on Sabbaths and religious festivals, these men walk on Sabbaths and festivals to the Old City to conduct services in the *Yeshivat Torat Hayim* building. They named their organization *Igud Lohamay Yerushalayim,* (Association of the Veterans of the Battle for Jerusalem). The time will surely come, they assert, when hundreds of Jewish families will again reside in that area and there will again be in that locality twenty-two synagogues and six *yeshivot,* as there were prior to the Arab disturbances of the 1920s and 1930s.

As of now these hopes have not materialized; to be sure, some Jews have moved into the area, but the neighborhood is predominantly Moslem. Recently a *yeshivah* specializing in the study of the ancient rites of the Temple service moved into the building, and the study hall once more resounds with the traditional sing-song of talmudic study. But the original *Yeshivat Torat Hayim* is no longer there.

What happened to the *Yeshivat Torat Hayim* after it abandoned its building in 1936? The academy has wandered from one temporary location in the New City to another. In 1978, an attempt was made to return to the old building but the time was not propitious. The Moslem neighbors are unfriendly. The worshipers who assemble there for services on Sabbath mornings are reputedly armed and unafraid. On one occasion they extricated themselves from a threatening Arab mob by firing into the air. But the teachers and students of the *yeshivah* are neither trained in the use of arms, nor are they content to visit weekly for a couple of hours. They lived at the *yeshivah* or commuted daily to their study hall. They found it too risky. There was also the problem of the Arab squatters who would evacuate their apartments peacefully only in return for exorbitant compensation. The attempt to resume studies at the *Yeshivat Torah Hayim* building was short-lived. As of this writing, the *Yeshivat Torah Hayim* has acquired a building at 48 David Yellin Street, near the Mahaneh Yehudah market. But here, too, the tenants will not move without "proper" compensation. Only the administrative office is located in the new quarters. The *yeshivah* itself carries on its teaching in a large rented hall a block away at 36 David Yellin Street. An American-born Talmud scholar, Rabbi Mosheh Rosmarin, is the *Rosh Yeshivah* (academic head). Rabbi Rosmarin and his students are looking forward to the time when their *yeshivah* can peacefully return to its home in the Old City on the Via Dolorosa, near the Temple Mount.

The Synagogue That Was Under a Curse

The Karaites are a Jewish sect that broke away from the mainstream of rabbinic Judaism in the eighth century. They rejected the rabbinic legislation and ordered their life almost entirely on the basis of biblical law. Thus they do not put on *tefillin* (phylacteries) at weekday morning services because the Bible does not specifically prescribe this ritual. However, they are careful to have a blue thread in their *tzitzit* (fringes) in accordance with the biblical specifications. Since the *tefillin* are not used, a boy, upon reaching the age of thirteen, becomes a Bar Mitzvah merely by declaring his acceptance of the commandments of the Torah. The Karaite calendar is not based on astronomical calculations, as is the rabbinic calendar, but on visual sighting of the new moon. Hence the Karaite holidays—derived from the same Torah—do not always coincide with those of the Jews. But one of the Karaite loyalties which they share with the Jews is their attachment to Jerusalem. Throughout the centuries there was a stream of Karaite pilgrims to the Holy City and they always tried to maintain a synagogue in Jerusalem. In 1099 when the Crusaders rounded up the Jews in their synagogue and burned them alive, the Karaites shared this fate and their community was totally destroyed. In time they returned and managed to restore their synagogue but it was only a small underground compartment which, according to Karaite tradition, was established by their founder, Anan ben David. At the height of their prosperity, the Karaites of Jerusalem are said to have numbered two hundred souls. The sad story of the community's decline as preserved in folklore is told by J. E. Hanauer in his book *Walks In and About Jerusalem:*

> In the year 1762 . . . the Turkish government demanded an exorbitant sum of money from the [Jewish] community. The Chief Rabbi therefore directed that a secret consultatory meeting should be held in the Karaite synagogue which, as we have seen, being subterraneous, was suitable for such a purpose. Whilst descending the stairs leading to it, the Chief Rabbi suddenly felt faint and he stumbled. This led the other Jews present to suspect that evil agencies were at work. They at once began to tear up the stones forming the staircase and discovered copies of the works of Maimonides which the Karaites had buried there in order to prove their contempt, by treading them underfoot. In order to punish them for this act of sacrilege the Chief Rabbi condemned the Karaites to pay the money demanded by the Government, and besides this, he pronounced as a curse upon them the wish that they should never be able to furnish a Minyan, the quorum of ten male adults needed to form a congregation for public worship. The curse still rests upon them.[30]

The small underground Karaite synagogue shared the fate of the Jewish institutions in the Old City after the Israeli War of Independence. It was destroyed by the Jordanians and it remained in a derelict state till 1979 when it was restored. The Karaites in Israel, who are said to number about twenty thousand, live in a number of settlements and towns, especially in the town of Ramle where they have an attractive synagogue. In recent years they succeeded in reconstituting their community in Jerusalem where about fifty Karaite families reside, and they restored their synagogue in the Jewish Quarter. Unlike the familiar furnishings of a Jewish place of worship, the Karaite synagogue is practically free of furniture. The floor is covered with rugs on which the worshipers prostrate themselves at specified parts of the services. Like the Moslems they remove their shoes before entering the synagogue. Their prayers are mostly biblical selections, especially the psalms. The synagogue building also serves as a communal center where lectures, study groups, and other educational and social activities are sponsored. Although the Karaite community is small, its members preserve a thousand-year-old culture, maintaining its customs with considerable success.

Royal Tombs

The most magnificent of the ancient underground labyrinths which housed the dead in ancient Jerusalem is the one called the Tomb of the Kings. Its elaborate decorations and its cunning protection against grave robbers suggest wealth, power, and royalty. Only kings could have devised such a sepulchre.

The Tomb of the Kings is very unlike the mausoleums one sees in modern cemeteries. Modern mausoleums are massive structures with bold inscriptions which are calculated to impress the living with the virtues of the dead or to publicize the importance of the people in whose honor the noble monuments were erected. Modern mausoleums compete for the onlooker's attention. They seem to announce that immortality is the lot of the residents of these mansions of the dead. The Pharaohs of old built their pyramids in preparation for the life that awaited them after death. But the builders of modern mausoleums erect their monumental tombs purely out of vanity and pride.

The Tomb of the Kings is, by comparison, very modest. The sepulchre is hidden underground and there is no inscription whatever. Yet this

Entrance to the Tombs of the Kings (1948). (Courtesy of Central Zionist Archives, Jerusalem.)

tomb has been praised as one of the most beautiful sepulchres in the world. Its fame reached ancient Greece and is mentioned by Pausanias in his classic *Description of Greece*. Pausanias writes:

> I know many wonderful graves, and will mention two of them, the one at Halicarnassus and one in the Land of the Hebrews. The one at Halicarnassus was made for Mausolus, king of the city, and it is of such vast size, and so notable for all its ornament, that the Romans in their great admiration of it call remarkable tombs in their country "Mausolea." The Hebrews have a grave, that of Helen, a native woman, in the city of Jerusalem, which the Roman Emperor razed to the ground. There is a contrivance in the grave whereby the door, which like all the grave is of stone, does not open until the year brings back the same day and the same hour. Then the mechanism, unaided, opens the door, which, after a short interval, shuts itself. This happens at that time, but should you at any other try to open the door you cannot do so; force will not open it, but only break it down.[31]

The tomb's beauty led people to believe it to be a royal tomb—the Tomb of the Kings. Who were those kings? No doubt, the kings of Judah who lived in Jerusalem. This attribution was widely accepted. It became a tradition and like most traditions it ceased to be questioned. For centuries the sepulchre was known as the Tomb of the Kings of Judah. Modern scholars, however, began to ask questions and to search for authentic answers. The most obvious of the questions was the contradiction between the biblical account which says that King David's descendants, the kings of Judah, were buried in the City of David which is south of Jerusalem's walls, while the Tomb of the Kings is north of the city's walls. Scholars also found references to this tomb in Josephus's *The Jewish War*. This royal tomb, Josephus informs us, was built by Helena, Queen of Adiabene, an independent state on the banks of the Tigris River. Queen Helena became a devout convert to Judaism and when her husband died in the year 48 c.e. she settled in Jerusalem and built a palace and a royal sepulchre for herself and her family. She died during a visit to her country, but her body was brought to Jerusalem and was buried in the royal tomb. Her sons fought along with the Jews against the Romans in defense of Jerusalem.

The Temple was burned; the kingdom of Adiabene is all but forgotten; but the queen's tomb has survived. To be sure, the subterranean chambers have been plundered by grave robbers, antiquarians, and certain scholars. Not only were all valuables, including sarcophagi, stolen and placed on view in distant museums, but even the bones of the queen and her family are gone. But the royal sepulchre is in Jerusalem where visitors wonder at its grandeur.

The Tomb of the Kings is located about half a mile directly north of the Damascus Gate. The entrance, which is on the south side of a large square excavation, is adorned with ornamental carvings of vines, fruit, and flowers. But no human or animal figures are to be found in this royal tomb. One enters a large anteroom, nine paces in length and four paces in width. Doors lead from this anteroom to other chambers, and doors from these chambers lead to additional underground chambers, all hewn out of the rock. This series of subterranean chambers extend in different directions and form a sort of labyrinth. In each of the interconnected chambers there are hewn in either side small recesses in the walls. These are receptacles for bodies. The number of receptacles in each chamber varies from seven to as many as forty. Each of the chambers was secured by massive doors, neatly cut from solid rock, with hinges of rock set in sockets in the rock.

In these chambers were a number of elegantly carved sarcophagi, only some fragments of which lie about. They are the evidence of the "ravages of those who defiled the graves in search of treasure" and of those who plundered the graves for the relics that were in them. Thus the French scholar, de Saulcey, spirited away several beautiful sarcophagi which are now on display in the Louvre.

For the tourist this tenantless labyrinth is a marvelous curiosity; for the historian it is a remarkable monument; and for the pilgrim, a soul-stirring site.

The Jewish Cemetery on the Mount of Olives

The Jewish cemetery on the Mount of Olives is the oldest cemetery in continuous use anywhere in the world. The vast cemetery has puzzled many people, for the Jewish population of Jerusalem used to be small. Yet the mountainside was literally paved with small, flat tombstones. This is only the upper layer of graves. When place for burials ran out, new graves were made on the top of the earlier ones. Thus there were more than one layer of burials.

The clue to the above-mentioned puzzle is the constant stream of Jews to Jerusalem, whose goal was to be interred on the Mount of Olives. The reason for this overwhelming desire was the conviction that "at the end of days" an eschatological drama would be enacted in the valley at the foot of the Mount of Olives. The Jews believed implicitly that the Messiah would come and the departed would rise from their graves and would gather in the Valley of Jehoshaphat for the Last Judgment. Men of faith and

A section of the ancient Jewish cemetery on the Mount of Olives before it was desecrated by the Arabs in 1948. (From Hanns Reich, Jerusalem. *Munich, Hanns Reich Verlag, 1968, plate 111: with permission.)*

foresight arranged to be buried right on the spot in order to be on hand when the Messiah arrived and to be among the first to rise from the grave to participate in the great messianic events.

The Jews who arrived in Jerusalem were generally old and the number of funerals was far above that of a normal population. The cemetery was therefore overpopulated in relation to the size of the Jewish community.

The cemetery on the Mount of Olives has been one of the holiest of Jewish holy places. Throughout their two thousand years of exile pious Jews have prayed for the redemption that would follow the coming of the Messiah. Although the Messiah has tarried, they have waited and their faith has never faltered. This faith is based on the prophecy: "I will gather all the nations and bring them down to the valley of Jehoshaphat, and I will enter into judgment with them there" (Joel 3:2). No wonder then that pious Jews strove to be buried in this sacred burial place, and that a vast city of the dead has arisen on the Mount of Olives.

The missionary Norman Macleod came as a pilgrim in 1864. He saw the extensive Jewish cemetery on the Mount of Olives and he described it in his book, *Eastward:*

> I never saw a graveyard to me so impressive. Scutari is far more extensive, and more terribly deathlike. But from its huddled monuments and crowded trees, it is impossible to penetrate its dark and complicated recesses. Here, there are no monuments, and no trees. Each grave is covered by a flat stone with Hebrew inscriptions, and has nothing between it and the open sky. These stones pave the whole eastern slope of the valley. Every inch of ground where a human body can lie is covered. Along the banks of the Kidron, up the side of Olivet, and across the road leading from Bethany to Jerusalem, stretches this vast city of the dead. As a place of burial it differs from almost every other on earth, in being, as no other is, a witness to a faith that is firm, decided, and uncompromising until death. It is not therefore merely the vast multitude who sleep here, but the faith which they held in regard to their Messiah, that makes this spectacle so impressive.[32]

The Turks were not known for their delicate handling of the holy places of the infidels. Yet the bones of the dead and their humble tombstones on the Mount of Olives were not molested. The deceased lay peacefully in their crowded graves and waited for the Messiah. They were waiting when the first signs of redemption appeared on the horizon as the Jews of Palestine fought their War of Independence in 1948–1949. Independence was won, but the Old City and the Mount of Olives were lost to the Hashemite Kingdom of Jordan. In the Armistice Treaty signed under the auspices of the United Nations, Jordan pledged not only to respect the Jewish holy places, but to permit the Jews to bury their dead in their ancient cemetery on the Mount of Olives. That pledge was not honored. Not only were no Jewish burials allowed there, but the cemetery was desecrated and vandalized; tombstones were removed for the paving of pathways in the nearby Jordanian military camp; and many of the bones were dug up and scattered. Msgr. John M. Oesterreicher describes the vandalism of the Jewish Cemetery on the Mount of Olives:

> Many thousand tombstones were taken from the ancient cemetery on the Mount of Olives to serve as building material or paving stones. A few were even used to surface the footpath leading to a latrine in a Jordanian army camp. With the financial assistance of Pan American Airlines, Jordan built the Hotel Intercontinental—a plush hotel on the hill of Jesus' agony! Obviously a road was needed, worthy of the triumphant showpiece. Of all the possible routes, the one chosen cut through hundreds of Jewish graves: They were torn open and the bones scattered. An Israeli collection of

photographs of the mutilated graveyard bears this lament: "Because of this is our heart made sick; for these things our eyes are dimmed" (Lam. 5:17).[33]

The cemetery has been partly restored: Some old tombstones were returned to their former places; some of the missing tombstones have been replaced with new ones; and the scattered bones were buried in a common grave. The Jewish cemetery on the Mount of Olives is once more used as a burial place for Jews who are awaiting the arrival of the Messiah whose coming they believe to be imminent.

Jewish Hajis

A Haji is a Moslem who has made the pilgrimage to Mecca. Since only Moslems are permitted to make the pilgrimage it is most astonishing that there are Jewish Hajis in Jerusalem. The story of these Hajis is strange but not unusual in the singular history of the Jewish people.

In northeastern Iran there is a city named Meshed. The city is holy for the Shi'ite sect of Islam who are the majority of the population of Iran. In Meshed Ali Reza is buried, one of the most revered leaders of the Shi'ite sect. Ever since Ali Reza's death in the ninth century, the Shi'ite Moslems have been making pilgrimages to the shrine in Meshed. In 1726 Meshed was conquered by Nadir Shah. When the conqueror ascended the Persian throne in 1736, he made Meshed his capital and invited merchants and artisans to settle in the city. Forty Jewish families responded to the Shah's invitation. The Jewish community of Meshed grew numerically and flourished culturally.

In 1839 a blood libel initiated a series of events which led to the liquidation of the Jewish community of Meshed. According to one of the several versions extant, a Jewish boy was stricken with a skin disease which was believed to be leprosy. After the usual cures proved ineffective, it was decided to try a highly recommended "cure" which required the killing of a dog and bathing the affected areas of the patient's body with the dog's blood. A Moslem happened to pass by when the dog was being slaughtered. On hearing the dog's loud barking, the Moslem peeped into the backyard from where the noise issued, and then reported to his neighbors and friends that he witnessed a strange ritual in which the Jews killed a dog and called the victim by the holy name of Husain, son of Ali, the grandson of Mohammed. The mob fell upon the Jews, murdered and plundered, and then confronted the Jews with the choice between "Mohammed and the sword." The outcome of that incident was that thirty-five Jews were slain, their synagogues were burned, much of their property was looted, and the rest of the Jews saved their lives by apostasy. Since a new convert to Islam is known as a *Jadid al-Islam,* the newly converted Jews came to be known in Hebrew as *Jadidim* or *Gedidim.*

The Gedidim did not become true adherents of Islam, but remained loyal to their Jewish heritage. They lived a double life. Openly they meticulously observed the Moslem holy days, prayed to Allah five times daily, and attended mosque services on Fridays. Secretly, however, they met for Jewish prayers during which they faced toward Jerusalem. One of them stood guard and signaled at the approach of a Moslem. When the worshipers received a warning signal, they hid the Torah scroll and the prayer books, and scattered through the rear alleys and over the rooftops of the adjacent buildings. To be sure, the Gedidim were suspected of backsliding and were spied upon. They continued to adhere to the heritage of their fathers at great peril. One of these Gedidim related:

> I was born in the Persian city of Meshed, where our brothers, the children of Israel, live as secret Jews. In public they are Moslems and perform the religious practices of Islam, and in secret they are Jews, faithful to the laws of Moses and Israel. They have double names—a Hebrew name and a Persian name. My Hebrew name was Shalom ben Yehezkel, but in Persian my name was Shekharallah ben Abdul Samad. When I was young I did not know for sure who I was, a Jew or a Moslem. But when I grew up I was informed secretly that I was a Jew. . . . My good father brought me into a secret room and said to me: "Know, my son, that your name is not Shekharallah but Shalom and that my name is Yehezkel and not Abdul Samad. We are Jews and we serve the God of Israel. Now watch yourself and do not reveal our secret to any Moslem, for if it ever becomes known to them that we are observing the laws of our religion they will kill us. . . ." From then on my father used to take me into the secret room where he taught me the laws of our Torah.

The Gedidim observed the dietary laws at great risk and married only among themselves. A Moslem ceremony was performed publicly and at night they performed, in great secrecy, the Jewish marriage ritual.

Like all Moslems a member of the Gedidim was obliged to make at least one pilgrimage to Mecca during his life. Whenever one of the Gedidim made a pilgrimage to Mecca he made sure to perform the secondary pilgrimage to Jerusalem. At Mecca he acquired the title Haj, and when he arrived in Jerusalem, the erstwhile Jadid al-Islam, now a

Haji, openly returned to Judaism. Thus we find on display in the Israel Museum in Jerusalem a pair of miniature *tefillin* (phylactories), each of which is about half an inch cube. The annotation next to the tiny *tefillin* reads:

> Pair of miniature *tefillin*, Meshed, Iran mid nineteenth century....
>
> According to the late Mr. Aharanov, the *tefillin* belonged to his father, Matityahu ben Aharon Ha-Cohen of the Marranos of Meshed. When he went on a pilgrimage to Mecca, he hid his *tefillin* under his fez. His return journey led him to Jerusalem where his encounters with fellow Jews convinced him to make *Aliyah*[34] with a group of other Marranos from Meshed.

In due time there were in Jerusalem enough of these Hajis to form two congregations with spacious synagogues located in the Bukharian neighborhood of the New City. They also acquired a cemetery plot on the Mount of Olives. Their synagogues are named "Haji Adoniyah Ha-Kohen" and "Haji Yehezkel Levi" in honor of two prominent Gedidim who came to Jerusalem via Mecca.

By the 1950s most of the Gedidim had reached Jerusalem. Some had made their way to other countries where they likewise joined their fellow Jews. The descendants of these secret Jews of Meshed are fully integrated in the Israeli Jewish population, and some of them have achieved prominent places in the social and political life of the country.

When did Hebrew Become the Spoken Language of the Jews?

It is stated in many popular works dealing with the revival of the Hebrew language that when the Jews were exiled from the Holy Land and were scattered throughout the world the Hebrew tongue ceased to be a living language. Hebrew became exclusively a holy tongue limited in its usage to prayer and holy books. This view is partially confirmed in a publication of the London Society for Promoting Christianity Amongst the Jews issued in 1911. The writer discusses the difficulties encountered by the missionaries in Jerusalem. One of their problems was the difficulty of communication, because the Jews of Jerusalem spoke so many languages.

> It will be noticed that the Jews of Jerusalem speak many languages and dialects. Judaeo-German ("Yiddish"), Judaeo-Spanish (Ladino), and Arabic (in the three quite distinct dialects—Syrian, Mughrabi, and Yemen) are the

common ones, and in these the work of our medical mission is daily conducted. But English, French, German, Russian, Roumanian, Italian, Greek, Turkish, Persian, Georgian, as well as languages used in Central Asia and India, are in common use in the homes of the Jews.

It will be noticed that Hebrew is not even mentioned as one of the spoken languages among the Jews of Jerusalem.

James Finn, however, states in his work, *Stirring Times,* that Hebrew was actually the spoken language of the Jews in Jerusalem in his day, a century before the birth of the State of Israel and more than a half century before Ben-Yehudah began his intensive pioneering activities on behalf of the Hebrew language. James Finn relates an incident which occurred during Sir Moses Montefiore's visit in Jerusalem in 1855. This incident, says James Finn, proves that the Hebrew language was a living tongue in Jerusalem during the mid-nineteenth century. James Finn relates:

> It was with no slight interest that on one of my visits to the Montefiore tents, I observed a deputation of the Perushim [Ashkenazi] Jews come up, and having to be presented by Dr. Loewe, one of the Rabbis enquired of the Doctor, "Are we to speak in a language of the Gentiles?" to which he replied, "No, but in our own language." This was done, and he interpreted [in English]. Thus, I had one more of the many opportunities of observing in Jerusalem and throughout Palestine how much Hebrew is employed as a living language in conversation among themselves, in synagogues, in cities, in my office in Jerusalem when Jews met Jews from distant lands—from India, from California, or elsewhere.[35]

It should be added, however, that in Mr. Finn's day Hebrew was used only to bridge the communication gap between Jews of different cultural backgrounds. Today Hebrew is used in Israel by everyone, everywhere—in the household, in the street, in the school, and in business transactions. It is now the common language of all the Jews in Jerusalem and the State of Israel. It is the language of the vulgarian and the poet, the street hawker and the banker. It is indeed one of the miracles of the national revival of the Jewish people. And Eliezer Ben-Yehudah may rightly be credited with a considerable part of this miracle.

Jewish Burial at Night

Stephen Olin, a Methodist clergyman who later became president of Weslyan University in Middletown, Connecticut, made a pilgrimage to the Holy Land in 1839 and recorded his impressions of Jerusalem. Among them he noted that the Jews "bury their dead in the night."[36] He does not give the reason, but the assumption is that fear of molestation by the Arabs or by government officials is the cause of this strange custom.

This practice is repeatedly reported in the travel literature of the nineteenth century. Châteaubriand, who made his pilgrimage in 1806, states in his classic travel account that "On the death of any member of this proscribed community, his companion goes at night and inters him by stealth in the valley of Jehoshaphat, in the shadow of Solomon's Temple."[37] It seems that each of the writers saw a Jewish night burial and concluded that all Jewish burials were performed at night. The fact is that some burials did take place at night, because of the local tradition that no corpse was to remain in the Holy City overnight. This prohibition was probably due to the excessive heat in summertime which causes rapid disintegration of corpses. On Sabbath and holidays burial was prohibited by Jewish religious law. On those days burials were delayed till after sunset. And when a person died late on a weekday afternoon the funeral took place in the evening. Thus it came about that Jewish burials in Jerusalem frequently occurred at night.

These night burials were weird spectacles. In those days there was no street lighting in Jerusalem. On a moonless night one would see a procession with torches winding its way through the narrow alleys of the Old City. The dark figures were headed by a simple, open bier, which resembled a cradle. The procession halted on the slope of the Mount of Olives where the burial took place. The corpse, wrapped in a white shroud, without a coffin, was laid in the freshly dug grave; stones were wedged in firmly on all sides of the corpse; and larger stones were placed above. The grave was then filled up and the appropriate prayers were recited. The procession with the torches returned to the Jewish Quarter and the people returned to the hovels they called homes. Darkness and silence again reigned in the Old City.

Things have changed. Street lighting has been introduced, and the Jewish cemetery on the Mount of Olives is no longer the only Jewish burial place. One may still witness a night burial, but the torch-light procession has been replaced by a line of automobiles led by a hearse. These night funerals are no longer the weird rituals they were in the nineteenth century.

FOUR

The Christians and
Their Holy Places

The Church of the Holy Sepulchre:
An Oriental Institution

Pilgrims and tourists from the West are usually shocked to find that the Church of the Holy Sepulchre is not what they expected. They are surprised to discover that the Protestants have practically no presence in the church.[1] And the Roman Catholics possess only a minor chapel, known as the Chapel of the Apparition. To be sure, the Roman Catholics are proud of their small chapel because it is located on the spot where Jesus is believed to have appeared to his mother after his resurrection. The chapel also houses several precious relics among which are part of the Column of Flagellation and the sword and spurs of Godfrey of Bouillon, the first Crusader, who ruled in Jerusalem. But the Greek Orthodox Church owns the main cathedral in the Church of the Holy Sepulchre. And on Calvary the Greeks possess the chapel which stands on the place of the Crucifixion, while the Latins—as the Roman Catholics are called— possess the lesser chapel which stands on the place where Jesus was nailed to the Cross. The Greek chapel is actually on the top of the hill and it stands on solid rock. The Latin chapel is only an upper room beneath which are chambers where the Greeks store some of their relics. And, most important, the Greeks are the custodians of the Holy Sepulchre itself.

What shocks the visitor even more is the absence of the aura of sanctity which Westerners anticipate in a place of worship, especially one

The Edicule, containing the Chapel of the Angels and the Tomb of Jesus (1972). (Courtesy of Israel Government Press Office.)

that houses the Holy Sepulchre. The Western visitor expects to find in this holiest of Christian shrines perfect decorum, harmonious music, and earnest devotion. What the visitor often finds is pandemonium. Charles Robert Ashbee, in his *A Palestine Notebooks*, recorded his impression:

> When I went into the Church of the Holy Sepulchre . . . I tried hard to be by myself alone. I . . . sat down to think under the great dome, but I was pestered with beggars, cats, fleas, and horrible chantings. There were monks singing in some side chapel—atrociously; then a cat screamed for milk outside the tomb of Christ, and then a beggar, one of the tribe of wealthy professionals, caught me by the coat, and whined in language he thought becoming to my costume, "Please—will—you—give—mister—Jesus—mister—blood."

> I've never felt so pagan and repelled in my life. To come back to this medievalism after the quiet reverence and sanity of Islam, as one has observed it in Egypt, is something like a shock.[2]

Ashbee could have compared the Oriental atmosphere in the Church of the Holy Sepulchre with the Occidental decorum in a British church. He chose, instead, to compare it with the quiet and dignity of the mosque which is also an Oriental institution. The atmosphere in the Church of the Holy Sepulchre is characteristic only of Oriental Christianity.

Another Western visitor in Jerusalem, R. R. Madden, a devout Irish Catholic physician, expressed his shock at the Oriental Christian mode of worship. His experience was at the Sepulchre of the Virgin Mary. He writes in his two-volume work, *Travels in Turkey, Egypt, and Palestine:*

> In the valley between the Mount of Olives and the walls of Jerusalem, on the eastern side of the Brook Cedron, which is now without water, I visited "the Sepulchre of the Virgin." The Greeks were celebrating the festival of the Madonna, firing pistols before the altar, at which half a dozen priests were officiating, and squabbling in the most indecent manner on the very steps of the altar.

> The grotto was crowded with Greek and Turkish [Arab] women; and the husbands of the latter were amusing themselves by firing pistols close to my ear, and pulling off the turbans of their neighbours. But what most astonished me, was to hear the Greeks, on coming out, boasting of what a good festival they had, of the great many shots that had been fired, as if they literally hoped to make sure of heaven by a "holy violence."[3]

Still another nineteenth-century traveler, Thomas Skinner, described a scene in the Church of the Holy Sepulchre, which shocked him as it would have scandalized any Western visitor in this Christian holiest of holy places. He reported that—

> The devout mothers had brought their infants with them; and, as it became necessary to satisfy their appetites, the women drew away from the crowd, and, ranged in a line to the east of the sepulchre, gave their children the breast. It was too hot to cover the heads of the babes; the more, therefore, the mothers exposed their bosoms. More than a hundred were engaged in this interesting duty.[4]

The Greek Orthodox tradition predominates in the Christian shrines of Jerusalem, and the Oriental tradition does not regard indecorous worship as inappropriate. The Oriental worshiper is no less reverential or less pious than the Western Christian. He feels at home in his church and acts as he does as home. Western standards are different, but not necessarily superior in piety and devotion. Armed with this awareness, the Western visitor will not be shocked at the disorder which may otherwise be disturbing in the Church of the Holy Sepulchre and in some of the other holy places in Jerusalem.

The Moslem Custodians of the Church of the Holy Sepulchre

During the four hundred years of Turkish rule in the Holy City, the Moslems have employed several crude expedients to exalt Islam and to humiliate the infidels. Thus they entrusted the keys to the Church of the Holy Sepulchre to a certain Arab family who open and close the church in accordance with an established schedule—and at unscheduled times for an appropriate bakshish. This hereditary privilege has continued to this day.

Another expedient for humiliating the Christians consisted of placing Arab custodians within the church during the hours of Christian worship. The custodians sat on an elevated stand inside the church entrance and whiled away the hours sipping Turkish coffee or smoking nargillahs. Every time a Christian entered or left the church he was reminded that he worshiped in the Church of the Holy Sepulchre by the grace of the Moslem custodians. And up to the middle of the nineteenth century a small tribute in the form of an entrance fee was exacted from all Christians entering the church. This humiliating practice was abolished by Mohammed Ali when the Egyptians conquered the Holy City. When the city was returned to the Turks this fee was not reimposed.

Still another humiliating practice was the stationing of soldiers within the church to maintain order, especially during Holy Week. To be sure, there was always the danger of disorder due to the rivalries between the Christian sects. The pasha was responsible for the orderly conduct within the church and he could not afford to take chances. But the Turkish soldiers were coarse and often brutal in the performance of their duty. When the British mandatory government ruled in Palestine, they managed to keep the peace in the church without offending Christian sensibilities. Their soldiers were stationed at a discreet distance. The Israeli government, too, has been tactful in keeping the peace at the Holy Sepulchre.

Today the Christian visitor is no longer shocked by the presence of soldiers within their holiest shrine. The platform with the Arabs smoking their nargillahs or sipping their coffee is gone. More important, the violent historic rivalries between the Christian sects have subsided. There is even active cooperation among the sects in the current restoration of the church. The enlightened rule of the British between 1918 and 1948 and that of the Israeli government since 1967 have had their salutary effects on the age-old enmities between the Christian sects. An era of peace and cooperation is clearly in sight. But the keys to the Church of the Holy Sepulchre are still held by the Arab custodians. Neither the British nor the Israeli government has dared to alter the sacrosanct law of the *Status Quo.*

An Eyewitness Report of the Holy Fire Ceremony and the Panic of 1834

On the day before the Greek Easter, the most exciting ceremony of Eastern Christianity is enacted in the Church of the Holy Sepulchre. The ceremony, known as the Holy Fire, is the climax of the Holy Week observances; and the emotional outpouring on that occasion is so intense that Western observers have found it incomprehensible. The numerous published reports are generally pejorative. They describe the ceremony as "mummery," "palpable fraud," "gross imposture," and "superstitious jugglery." Seldom does a Western writer see in this ceremony the distinctive features and the rich symbolism perceived by the Eastern Church.

One of the many descriptions stands out as unique, because it records not only the Holy Fire ceremony, but also the tragedy of 1834 when a panic spread through the multitude and the people rushed to the door of the church to escape from they knew not what. Many perished from suffocation; others were trampled to death. More than three hundred dead bodies were counted after the panic.

Robert Curzon, a noted British antiquarian, was on his way to a monastery where he hoped to find and purchase some rare manuscripts. He stopped in Jerusalem for the Easter week and went to the Church of the Holy Sepulchre to witness the spectacle of the Holy Fire ceremony. As a guest of the British consul, he was seated on the balcony, near the governor, Ibrahim Pasha. He was thus in a position to see the ceremony from a safe place reserved for important guests. His sober and accurate account will be quoted in full. The only extant eyewitness report, vividly describes the ceremony and the tragedy:

> The behaviour of the pilgrims was riotous in the extreme; the crowd was so great that many persons actually crawled over the heads of others, and some made pyramids of men by standing on each others' shoulders, as I have seen them do at Astley's. At one time, before the church was so full, they made a race-course round the sepulchre; and some, almost in a state of nudity, danced about with frantic gestures, yelling and screaming as if they were possessed.
>
> Altogether it was a scene of disorder and profanation which it is impossible to describe. In consequence of the multitude of people and the quantities of lamps, the heat was excessive, and a steam arose which prevented your seeing clearly across the church. But every window and cornice, and every place where a man's foot could rest, excepting the gallery—which was reserved for Ibrahim Pasha and ourselves—appeared to be crammed with people, for 17,000 pilgrims were said to be in Jerusalem, almost the whole of whom had come to the Holy City for no other reason than to see the sacred fire. . . .
>
> A way was made through the crowd for Ibrahim Pasha, by the soldiers with the butt-ends of their muskets, and by the Janissaries with their kourbatches and whips made of a quantity of small rope. The Pasha sat in the gallery, on a divan which the monks had made for him between the two columns nearest to the Greek chapel. They had got up a sort of procession to do him honour, the appearance of which did not add to the solemnity of the scene: three monks playing crazy fiddles led the way, then came the choristers with lighted candles, next two Nizam soldiers with muskets and fixed bayonets; a number of doctors, instructors, and officers tumbling over each other's heels, brought up the rear: he was received by the women, of whom there were thousands in the church, with a very peculiar shrill cry, which had a strange unearthly effect. It was the monosyllable la, la, la, uttered in a shrill trembling tone, which I thought much more like pain than rejoicing. The Pasha was dressed in full trousers of dark cloth, a light lilac-coloured jacket, and a red cap without a turban. When he was seated, the monks brought us

some sherbet, which was excellently made; and as our seats were very near the great man, we saw everything in an easy and luxurious way; and it being announced that the Mahomedan pasha was ready, the Christian miracle, which had been waiting for some time, was now on the point of being displayed.

The people were by this time becoming furious; they were worn out with standing in such a crowd all night, and as the time approached for the exhibition of the holy fire they could not contain themselves for joy. Their excitement increased as the time for the miracle in which all believed drew near. At about one o'clock the Patriarch went into the ante-chapel of the sepulchre, and soon after a magnificent procession moved out of the Greek chapel. It conducted the Patriarch three times round the tomb; after which he took off his outer robes of cloth of silver, and went into the sepulchre, the door of which was then closed. The agitation of the pilgrims was now extreme: they screamed aloud; and the dense mass of people shook to and fro, like a field of corn in the wind.

There is a round hole in one part of the chapel over the sepulchre, out of which the holy fire is given, and up to this the man who had agreed to pay the highest sum for this honour was conducted by a strong guard of soldiers. There was silence for a minute; and then a light appeared out of the tomb, and the happy pilgrim received the holy fire from the Patriarch within. It consisted of a bundle of thin wax-candles, lit, and enclosed in an iron frame to prevent their being torn asunder and put out in the crowd: for a furious battle commenced immediately; every one being so eager to obtain the holy light, that one man put out the candle of his neighbour in trying to light his own. It is said that as much as ten thousand piasters has been paid for the privilege of first receiving the holy fire, which is believed to ensure eternal salvation. The Copts got eight purses this year for the first candle they gave to a pilgrim of their own persuasion.

This was the whole of the ceremony; there was no sermon or prayers, except a little chanting during the processions, and nothing that could tend to remind you of the awful event which this feast was designed to commemorate.

Soon you saw the lights increasing in all directions, everyone having lit his candle from the holy flame: the chapels, the galleries, and every corner where a candle could possibly be displayed, immediately appeared to be in a blaze. The people, in their frenzy, put the bunches of lighted tapers to their faces, hands, and breasts, to purify themselves from their sins. The Patriarch was carried out of the sepulchre in triumph, on the shoulders of the people he had deceived, amid the cries and exclamations of joy which resounded from every nook of the immense pile of buildings. As he appeared in a fainting state, I supposed that he was ill; but I found that it is the uniform custom on these occasions to feign insensibility, that the pilgrims may imagine he is overcome with the glory of the Almighty, from whose immediate presence they believe him to have returned.

In a short time the smoke of the candles obscured everything in the place, and I could see it rolling in great volumes out at the aperture at the top of the dome. The smell was terrible; and three unhappy wretches, overcome by heat and bad air, fell from the upper range of galleries, and were dashed to pieces on the heads of the people below. One poor Armenian lady, seventeen years of age, died where she sat, of heat, thirst, and fatigue.

Mass of celebrants of the Holy Fire ceremony in front of the entrance to the Church of the Holy Sepulchre (c. 1900). (Courtesy of Central Zionist Archives, Jerusalem.)

After a while, when he had seen all that was to be seen, Ibrahim Pasha got up and went away, his numerous guards making a line for him by main force through the dense mass of people which filled the body of the church. As the crowd was so immense, we waited for a little while, and then set out all together to return to our convent. I went first and my friends followed me, the soldiers making way for us across the church. I got as far as the place where the Virgin is said to have stood during the crucifixion, when I saw a number of people lying one on another all about this part of the church, and as far as I could see towards the door. I made my way between them as well as I could, till they were so thick that there was actually a great heap of bodies on which I trod. It then suddenly struck me they were all dead! I had not perceived this at first, for I thought they were only very much fatigued with the ceremonies and had lain down to rest themselves there; but when I came to so great a heap of bodies I looked down at them, and saw that sharp, hard appearance of the face which is never to be mistaken. Many of them were quite black with suffocation, and farther on were others all bloody and covered with the brains and entrails of those who had been trodden to pieces by the crowd.

At this time there was no crowd in this part of the church; but a little farther on, round the corner towards the great door, the people, who were quite panic-struck, continued to press forward, and every one was doing his utmost to escape. The guards outside, frightened at the rush from within, thought that the Christians wished to attack them, and the confusion soon grew into a battle. The soldiers with their bayonets killed numbers of fainting wretches, and the walls were spattered with blood and brains of men who had been felled, like oxen, with the butt-ends of the soldiers' muskets. Every one struggled to defend himself or to get away, and in the melee all who fell were immediately trampled to death by the rest. So desperate and savage did the fight become, that even the panic-struck and frightened pilgrims appear at last to have been more intent upon the destruction of each other than desirous to save themselves.

For my part, as soon as I perceived the danger I had cried out to my companions to turn back, which they had done; but I myself was carried on by the press till I came near the door, where all were fighting for their lives. Here, seeing certain destruction before me, I made every endeavour to get back. An officer of the Pasha's, who by his star was a colonel or bin bashee, equally alarmed with myself, was also trying to return: he caught hold of my cloak, or bournouse, and pulled me down on the body of an old man who was breathing out his last sigh. As the officer was pressing me to the ground we wrestled together among the dying and the dead with the energy of despair. I struggled with this man till I pulled him down, and happily got again upon my legs—(I afterwards found that he never rose again)—and scrambling over a pile of corpses, I made my way back into the body of the church, where I found my friends, and we succeeded in reaching the sacristy of the Catholics, and thence the room which had been assigned to us by the monks. The dead were lying in heaps, even upon the stone of unction; and I saw full four hundred wretched people, dead and living, heaped promiscuously one upon another, in some places above five feet high. Ibrahim Pasha had left the church only a few minutes before me, and very narrowly escaped with his life; he was so pressed upon by the crowd on all sides, and it was said attacked by several of them, that it was only by the greatest exertions of his suite, several of whom were killed, that he gained the outer court. He fainted more than once in the struggle, and I was told that some of his attendants at last had to cut a way for him with their swords through the dense ranks of the frantic pilgrims. He remained outside, giving orders for the removal of the corpses, and making his men drag out the bodies of those who appeared to be still alive from the heaps of the dead. He sent word to us to remain in the convent till all the dead bodies had been removed, and that when we could come out in safety he would again send to us.

We stayed in our room two hours before we ventured to make another attempt to escape from this scene of horror; and then walking close together, with all our servants round us, we made a bold push and got out of the door of the church. By this time most of the bodies were removed; but twenty or thirty were still lying in distorted attitudes at the foot of Mount Calvary; and fragments of clothes, turbans, shoes, and handkerchiefs, clotted with blood and dirt, were strewed all over the pavement.

In the court in the front of the church, the sight was pitiable: mothers weeping over their children—the sons bending over the dead bodies of their fathers—and one poor woman was clinging to the hand of her husband, whose body was fearfully mangled. Most of the sufferers were pilgrims and strangers. The Pasha was greatly moved by this scene of woe; and he again and again commanded his officers to give the poor people every assistance in their power, and very many by his humane efforts were rescued from death.

I was much struck by the sight of two old men with white beards, who had been seeking for each other among the dead; they met as I was passing by, and it was affecting to see them kiss and shake hands, and congratulate each other on having escaped from death.

When the bodies were removed many were discovered standing upright, quite dead; and near the church door one of the soldiers was found thus standing, with his musket shouldered, among the bodies which reached nearly as high as his head; this was in a corner near the great door on the right side as you come in. It seems that this door had been shut, so that many who stood near it were suffocated in the crowd; and when it was opened, the rush was so great that numbers were thrown down and never rose again, being trampled to death by the press behind them. The whole court before the entrance of the church was covered with bodies laid in rows, by the Pasha's orders, so that their friends might find them and carry them away. As we walked home we saw numbers of people carried out, some dead, some horribly wounded and in a dying state, for they had fought with their heavy silver inkstands and daggers.

In the evening I was not sorry to retire early to rest in the low vaulted room in the strangers' house attached to the monastery of St. Salvador. I was weary and depressed after the agitating scenes of the morning, and my lodging was not rendered more cheerful by there being a number of corpses laid out in their shrouds in the stone court beneath its window.

In the morning I awoke at a late hour and looked out into the court; the muleteer and most of the other bodies were removed, and people were going about their business as if nothing had occurred, excepting that every now and then I heard the wail of women lamenting for the dead. Three hundred was the number reported to have been carried out of the gates to their burial-places that morning; two hundred more were badly wounded, many of whom probably died, for there were no physicians or surgeons to attend them, and it was supposed that others were buried in the courts and gardens of the city by their surviving friends; so that the precise number of those who perished was not known.[5]

W. R. Wilde, a pilgrim who was in Jerusalem four years after the panic, describes the Holy Fire ceremony as all pilgrims do in their itineraries. He concludes his account with these words:

Since the occurrence of the catastrophe I have mentioned, there has been an open space left in the fan-light of the dome, and the doors of the church are not now closed as they were before.[6]

The Ubiquitous Franciscans

In Jerusalem one sees innumerable monks, priests, nuns, and many ecclesiastics of other sects and religions. Each of these devout functionaries is arrayed in his or her distinctive garb. Among this multitude of clerics the Franciscans are the most conspicuous. Wherever one goes, especially in the Old City, one meets them. They are attired in their characteristic brown frocks with long hoods and white knotted rope girdles. The girdles are especially striking. Hence they have often been called the Brotherhood of the Cord. One wonders why are there so many Franciscans in Jerusalem and what is their special role. The tour guides readily answer these questions. The Franciscans, say the guides, are the custodians of the Catholic holy places. The guides then list the most important of these holy places—Gethsemane, the Coenaculum, the Chapel of the Apparition, the section of Calvary where Jesus was nailed to the cross, and so on. The list of holy places is impressive and many tourists are content. Some visitors, however, ask additional questions, such as, why were the Franciscans chosen to be the custodians of the holy places? Are they especially worthy of the honor, or are they more reliable than the other Catholic brother-

Franciscans in the Via Dolorosa (1970). (Courtesy of Israel Government Press Office.)

hoods? And how have the Franciscans fulfilled their responsibilities?

The answers to these questions can be found not by examining the credentials of the various Catholic Orders and Congregations, but by a glance at the history of the Franciscan friars insofar as it is connected with their presence in Jerusalem.

The Franciscan presence in Jerusalem goes back more than 750 years, when their founder, Francis of Assissi, arrived in the Holy Land in 1219. During the fifth Crusade a small band of barefooted friars led by Francis of Assissi arrived in Egypt along with the Crusader army. They had joined the Crusade not as soldiers but as "peace-makers." Francis of Assissi hoped to convert the Sultan of Egypt and thus make an end of the Crusader wars which had been going on for over a century. He failed to convert the Sultan, but he obtained from him a letter addressed to the Sultan of Syria. The latter befriended the band of friars and their leader and gàve them a firman authorizing them to visit the holy places without payment of the usual fees.

Francis and his band landed in Acre in 1219, but he soon left for Italy, leaving some of his followers behind. When the Crusaders were finally expelled from the Holy Land in 1291, the Franciscans also left. In 1335 King Robert of Naples obtained for the Franciscans rights in the Chapel of the Holy Sepulchre and a clear title of ownership of the Coenaculum on Mount Zion. For these privileges King Robert paid a royal sum. The Franciscans settled down on Mount Zion and built themselves a friary near the Coenaculum. Henceforth their superior became known as the Guardian of Mount Zion. In 1342 Pope Clement VI issued a bull, declaring the Franciscans the official guardians of the Catholic holy places in the Holy Land. For over six hundred years thereafter the Franciscans have kept this custody with great dedication. They have suffered persecution at the hands of the Moslems—and at times even martyrdom—but they never abandoned their trust. When the Crusaders were expelled from the Holy Land, the Roman Catholic Patriarchate in Jerusalem was suspended and the Franciscans assumed the prerogatives of the Patriarchate and became the representatives of the Vatican in the Holy Land. They extended their activities to include such religious functions as preaching, teaching, pastoral care, and charity. They also built hospitals for the sick and hospices for pilgrims. No wonder the Franciscan Custody in the Holy Land has been called the "pearl of the Franciscan missions."

When the Turks captured the Holy Land in 1517 the Franciscans' troubles increased. The Greek Orthodox clergy were recognized as the official representatives of Christendom, and the status of the Franciscans was relegated to that of European foreigners. Every time there was a war, and the wars were almost incessant, it was an opportune time to oust the Franciscans from their holy places and to install the Greek Orthodox clergy in their place. The only appeal to justice was bribery. But money was not always available.

Soon after the Turks captured Jerusalem they expelled the Franciscans from the Coenaculum. The friars moved to a nearby place, but in 1552 they were driven out "for good," and the Coenaculum was converted into a mosque. In 1560 the Franciscans purchased a Georgian monastery, St. Savior, which is located in the Christian Quarter of the Old City. The Custos took up residence there and the Franciscan headquarters have been there ever since.

On October 12, 1808, a disastrous fire broke out in the Church of the Holy Sepulchre. The fire wrought tremendous havoc to the buildings, necessitating extensive restoration. With the lavish support of the Russian government, the Greeks outbid the Latins and were granted the privilege of rebuilding the Church. The Greek Orthodox Church thus gained many advantages, among which was the full custody of the Chapel of the Holy Sepulchre. The Franciscans, however, were permitted to celebrate Mass in the chapel.

In the nineteenth century, Jerusalem assumed an important role in the power politics of the European nations. The weakness of the Turkish Empire became evident and its fall was anticipated. The European empire-builders began to stake out their claims to the predicted division of the Turkish Empire. Jerusalem was regarded as the most precious of the Turkish provinces. The European Powers therefore established consulates in the Holy City and in 1847 the Vatican reestablished its Patriarchate which had been suspended ever since the Crusaders were expelled from the Holy Land. With the arrival of the Latin Patriarch many church orders and congregations began to rush into the Holy Land. By 1950, forty-three different orders and congregations had established themselves in the Holy Land, most of them in Jerusalem. Although the Franciscans ceased to be the official representatives of the Vatican they continued to be the custodians of most of the Catholic holy places and continued to maintain the many religious, charitable, and educational institutions which they developed in the course of the centuries. The Order is international but their Superior, the Custode, is, by tradition, always Italian, and a substantial number of the Brothers have been Spanish. "The Spaniards have been for centuries large benefactors of Jerusalem, it may be, to atone by money gifts for the fact that they alone of all the European nations took no part in the Crusades."[7]

The mid-nineteenth century witnessed another change affecting the religious institutions in Jerusalem. In 1852 the Turks decreed that henceforth the rights of the religious communities would remain unchanged and the status of the holy places would hereafter remain permanently fixed. This regulation, which came to be known as the *Status Quo*, was forced on the Sublime Porte by the European Powers. It has brought stability in the unending competition between the religious sects. To this day no government, Turkish, British, or Israeli, has dared to tamper with the *Status Quo*. Everyone has realized that the least modification would open a Pandora's box. But a new kind of competition for holy places supplanted that of the religious sects. The European Powers began to compete for so-called presences in the Holy City. By the ownership of religious shrines and holy places the European Powers hoped to establish themselves as protectors of the faith.

When a European Power acquired a shrine, it made sure that it remained under its control. Thus it came about that the custody of newly acquired Catholic shrines was not necessarily entrusted into the hands of the Franciscans. When the French received St. Anne's Church as a gift from the Sultan, it was turned over to a French African Order, generally known as the White Fathers. And when the German Emperor built the Dormition Abbey on Mount Zion he entrusted its custody to a German branch of the Dominican Order. Thus it came about that there are now in Jerusalem custodians of Catholic holy places who are not Franciscans. But these exceptions in no way deprive the Franciscans of their time-honored title of custodians of the Latin holy places.

When visitors in Jerusalem see the Franciscans in the alleys of the Old City or the streets of the New City, they should see in them members of an honorable brotherhood who have performed their duties in the Holy Land with singular distinction ever since the fourteenth century. The sacrifices attendant on their faithful service began early in their history when on November 14, 1391, four friars were beheaded and burned near the Jaffa Gate. These friars were canonized in Rome on June 21, 1970, as martyrs to the faith.

Today there are over 330 Franciscan priests and lay brothers as well as 130 Franciscan sisters in the Holy Land Custody, presided over by the Custos or Chief Custodian. They represent twenty-two nations and are responsible directly to the Pope in all matters pertaining to the custody of the holy places.

On October 4, 1976, the Franciscans celebrated in Jerusalem the 750th anniversary of the death of their founder with a series of lectures and an exposition of art work dealing with the major events of St. Francis's life. It was an impressive and fitting celebration of over seven centuries of uninterrupted service to the religious interests of the Catholic Church and its votaries.

The Treasures in the Latin Convent of Terra Santa

Many people are convinced that the Roman Catholic Church is rich. This conviction derives from rumor and may be bolstered by a visit to St. Peter's Basilica in Rome. No one, however, has ever suspected that the poor Franciscans in Jerusalem were custodians of great wealth. A visit to the Latin chapel in the Church of the Holy Sepulchre will convince anyone that poverty prevails in the Franciscan Order. Indeed, how can anyone accumulate wealth in poor Jerusalem? The pasha would have discovered it long ago and would have found ways of extracting it. And the pasha, as is well known, has many ways of finding out where hidden treasure is located and he has many ways of extracting it. To be sure, Elizabeth Anne Finn says in her *Reminiscences* that the Latins in Jerusalem "were extremely wealthy. In these convents were vast stores of wheat, oil and rice, also great cisterns of water, from which could be provisioned all the Christians in case of fighting, and in ordinary times the convents also paid house rent and other things for their people."[8] But this was not wealth. It was enlightened philanthropy. Yet the poor Latin Church of Jerusalem does have treasures. So says a mid-nineteenth century eyewitness, no less a personality than William C. Prime, who was professor of the history of art at Princeton University and vice president of the Metropolitan Museum of Art. He visited Jerusalem in 1855 and then published his excellent book, *Tent Life in the Holy Land*. He tells of an enlightening visit in the Convent of Terra Santa in Jerusalem:

> We were led into a remote room where was nothing to attract attention, nor would a stranger have supposed that it contained such treasures as we found in drawers, and cases, and closets. In the drawers were the robes of the Patriarch, gorgeous with jewels and gold. I had no means of estimating their value, except by comparing them with some which I had seen in the Crystal Palace at Paris during the previous summer, and in comparison with these I

had no difficulty in believing the monks, who stated the several costs of each dress as it was produced.

"This was a present from the King of Spain. It cost a hundred thousand francs of France. This was given by Napoleon the Great. It was worth a half million. This was from the Emperor of Austria, this from the King of Naples;" and thus they continued until they had shown us something like twenty of those splendid gifts of royalty to the service of the Church of the Sepulchre.

These robes were accompanied, each by its own proper suites of other articles of dress, which I am not able to name technically, nor the general reader to understand any better if I were. In a closet, fitted up expressly for it, were hung, pendent from the top, a number of lamps, of superbly-chased gold and silver, with which in former times it was customary to replace the brazen lamps of Calvary and the Tomb on important occasions. In drawers below these, were the jewels of the patriarchate, diamonds, emeralds, and rubies, flashing on superb croziers and heavy rings.

The Patriarch has obtained possession of the most valuable crozier, but the two which I saw here were estimated at thousands of dollars, how many I have quite forgotten. Indeed, I became puzzled with the splendor that surrounded me, and after coming away, found it difficult to recall the different articles I had seen, so many and similar in value were they.

In one corner of a large room, lay a huge pile, which appeared like the corner of a tinman's shop, and had not my attention been especially directed to it, I should have thought it a collection of old tinware, pans and water-leaders, gutters, spouts, and such chandeliers as I remember to have seen in old times in the church at Liberty, in Sullivan county, when I was taking trout on the Willoweemock.

This proved to be a heap of solid silver, more in weight we believed than a half ton, consisting of various church ornaments, and especially of huge candelabra, standing over seven feet high from the floor, wrought in beautiful shapes of the solid metal, and heavier than one man could well lift. Near this, some rough doors, on a temporary closet being opened, disclosed an altar, or a shrine, of the same white metal, pure, rich, and elegant, more than six feet high and four in breadth, wrought in gothic and other forms, beautifully chased and finished. It was a present from some crowned head in years long past, and it has been treasured in a garret chamber of the convent from the day it was received. Whether it will ever see the light is a question I can not answer. It may lie there a hundred years, to be seen only by such chance travelers as father Stephano shall be induced to guide to the treasure room.

The wealth contained in this chamber I have no means of estimating. Taking the value of the articles at their original cost, I have no doubt there were many hundred thousand dollars' worth; but in the present state of the faded robes, of which the value of many consists only in the jewels with which the cloth of gold is studded, and the massive silver candelabra, and shrines, and altar furniture, which are to be estimated only by weight, I am totally without the means of giving even an approximate guess at the wealth of the Convent of the Terra Santa. I should not call it theirs, for they regard it strictly as the Lord's property, and the evidence of this is, that for years these heaps of gold, and silver, and jewels have lain untouched in the custody of the Franciscan brothers.[9]

The Franciscans in Jerusalem are committed to poverty, but they have proved themselves through the centuries to be trustworthy custodians, not only of the Catholic holy places but also of the church's treasures of worldly goods.

Gordon's Calvary

Throughout the nineteenth and most of the twentieth centuries the controversy over the authenticity of the traditional holy places has persisted relentlessly. The controversy between the traditionalists and the skeptics was heated and often acrimonious. The skeptics argued their case logically but not always soberly. Some of them were vehement in their denunciations of the traditionalists, especially the priests and monks who were the custodians of the holy places. Thus we read in Dr. Edward Robinson's classic work *Biblical Researches in Palestine, Mount Sinai and Arabia Petraea:*

> In every view which I have been able to take of the question, both topographical and historical, whether on the spot or in the closet, and in spite of all my previous prepossessions, I am led irresistibly to the conclusion that the Golgotha and the tomb now shown in the Church of the Holy Sepulchre, are not upon the real places of the crucifixion and resurrection of our Lord. The alleged discovery of them by the aged and credulous Helena, like her discovery of the cross, may not improbably have been the work of pious fraud. . . . We know nothing more from the Scriptures, than that they were near each other, without the gate and nigh to the city, in a frequented spot (John 19:20). This would favour the conclusion, that the place was probably upon a great road leading from one of the gates; and such a spot would only be found upon the western or northern sides of the city, on the roads leading towards Joppa or Damascus.[10]

Similarly did Dr. Robinson's colleague on the faculty of the Union Theological Seminary in New York, Dr. Philip Schaff, write in his book, *Through Bible Lands:*

Were I to look for the site of the true Calvary in the present Jerusalem untrammeled by ecclesiastical tradition and controversy, I would find it on a skull-shaped rocky, isolated elevation, a few minutes' walk north of the Damascus Gate, not far from the Grotto of Jeremiah, where the prophet, according to tradition, is said to have written his Lamentations. This elevation is about half a mile from the site of the fortress Antonia (Pilate's judgment hall), and the same distance from Mount Zion (Herod's palace). It is on the highway to Damascus; it is encircled by rock caverns and tombs. It thus answers all the requirements of the gospel narrative better than any other locality I have seen around the city.[11]

An example of the unrestrained nature of the attacks on the tradition-al Church of the Holy Sepulchre is the following quotation from an otherwise balanced and reverent account of a pilgrimage to the Holy Land by a pious Scottish minister, the Reverend Horatius Bonar:

> I may mention here, that more than once I visited the Church of the Holy Sepulchre, going through all its parts, and witnessing some of its proces-sions. But there is nothing *true* in it; all is fiction, got up for show and gain. . . .

> As a coral reef is the product of innumerable insects, each one building his own cell and dying, yet in his death adding another atom to the mass; so is this Church; every stone, arch, pillar, altar, statue, image, picture, lamp, being a falsehood; the whole, from floor to dome, one gorgeous imposture. There is here nothing real, nothing genuine. It is out and out an ecclesiasti-cal hoax.[12]

Scholars knew that the modern city walls were erected in the sixteenth century and do not necessarily follow the contours of the ancient walls. According to Josephus, in the first century there were three walls on the northern side of the city. The third wall was built by King Agrippa after the Crucifixion. It was therefore the second wall that the New Testament speaks of. The question of authenticity therefore revolves around the exact location of the second wall. If that wall was north of the Church of the Holy Sepulchre, then the traditional Calvary and Holy Sepulchre are evidently fictitious, for they are situated within the second wall. If, however, archaeological evidence were to locate the foundations of the second wall south of the Church of the Holy Sepulchre, then the holy places within the church could be authentic. It happens that archaeologi-cal excavations have established that in the days of Jesus the traditional Calvary and Holy Sepulchre were outside the second wall. A section of that wall was found inside the Russian hospice on Palmers Street near the

Church of the Holy Sepulchre. Kathleen M. Kenyon, who did extensive excavations in the area, discusses the problem of the authenticity of the Christian shrines in her book *Jerusalem: Excavating 3000 Years of History,* and, after a lengthy presentation of her findings, concludes that "the evidence is thus clear that the traditional sites of Golgotha and the Holy Sepulchre *can* be authentic."[13]

Notwithstanding the archaeological evidence in support of the traditional Calvary and Holy Sepulchre, some Protestants still deny their authenticity. Asked for an alternative location of these holy places, they indicate a hill outside the northern wall, near the Damascus Gate. This hill fulfills two requirements mentioned in the Gospels. It is outside the wall and it is near a highway, the road that leads to Damascus. On this hill a tomb of the Herodian period was discovered in 1881. It is a rock-hewn sepulchre with an open door approximately four feet square. The rock-hewn ante-chamber is about ten feet square.

While the controversy over the authenticity of these holy places was going on, a colorful pilgrim came to Jerusalem. His name was General Charles George Gordon, but he was better known as "Chinese Gordon." His fame rested on his victories in China and the Sudan. He came to Jerusalem on a year's furlough. He spent his stay in Jerusalem studying biblical history. What intrigued him was the question of the authenticity of the Holy Sepulchre. He spent hours examining the hill across from the north wall of the city upon which the rock-hewn tomb had been discovered. After gazing at the hill day after day, he discovered on the hill the likeness of a skull. That discovery provided General Gordon with the reason why the hill of the Crucifixion was called Golgotha, which means "Skull." Gordon became convinced that the tomb on that hill was the authentic Holy Sepulchre, and he began his successful campaign in behalf of the Tomb in the Garden. His fame as a military hero gained much publicity and many followers for the idea. To this day many people call the hill on which the Tomb in the Garden is located "Gordon's Calvary," and the likeness of the skull on the rocky face of that hill is still pointed to as evidence that this is the actual Golgotha mentioned in the New Testament.

Archaeologists, however, deny the authenticity of the Garden Tomb. While Gordon's Calvary still has its devoted believers who come there to worship especially during Holy Week, the traditional site is now generally accepted as the authentic burial place of Jesus.

The Garden Tomb is maintained with appropriate reverence, and on

The surface of the cliff resembling a human skull.

Easter Sunday Protestant services are conducted there in several languages. Leslie Farmer, a British Second World War army chaplain stationed in Jerusalem, wrote in his book, *We Saw the Holy City:*

> Of all the popular fallacies that die hard, the identification of Calvary that is associated with the name of Gordon is the most persistent. He had far less claim to scientific knowledge than most of his contemporaries, but he was a famous soldier, the idol of the Victorian public, and the more dogmatic his statements upon subjects of which he knew little, the more were they popularly received. He was a fundamentalist, with mystical theories tainted with rabbinicism, and like-minded people to-day still regard him as one of their prophets. He had a strong personality, the enthusiasm of a neophyte being combined with the decision of a strategist; and he left his mark upon the topography of the Holy City. A hill outside the northern wall is known as "Gordon's Calvary.". . . I visited the Garden Tomb, of course, one Sunday afternoon, in company with the members of the Wednesday Fellowship, and we were impressed with the quietness and order of the place. We were shown an old wine-press, to demonstrate that it had been a garden in early times, and a rock-cut tomb containing three low trough-shaped graves. A hole to form a window had been cut in its wall, which we were told was part of its original form, enabling the disciples on the first Easter Day to see the interior without actually entering it. The doorstep was very worn, the result of visits of early pilgrims, our guide told us, and several rough crosses in red had been painted on the walls. There was a kind of ante-chamber which would permit the entrance of all the people mentioned as visiting the tomb of Jesus when His Resurrection became known. [14]

It is thus that Jerusalem has two Calvaries and two Holy Sepulchres. And this adds to the confusion of pilgrims and tourists who are not acquainted with the contending traditions and the sectarian rivalries in the Holy City.

Church Bells in the Holy City

When Jerusalem was captured by the Arabs under the leadership of the Caliph Omar in 638, the Moslem conquerors decreed that church bells were not to ring in the Holy City. It thus came about that in the city where Christianity was born and where the first Christian church was established no church bells were heard for almost 500 years. In 1099 the Crusaders captured the city and church bells rang loud and clear in all the churches of Jerusalem. But this lasted a relatively short time. In 1187 Saladin recaptured the Holy City. He smashed to pieces the bells in the bell tower of the Church of the Holy Sepulchre, but he left the tower intact. For over six hundred years, no church bells were heard in Jerusalem. The Moslem overlords decreed that the infidels were to be tolerated, but they were not to be the equals of the faithful. Jewish and Christian religious observances were to be permitted on condition that they were not obnoxious to the Moslems. Church bells were deemed offensive to the ears of the faithful, and they were an affront to Islam.

To summon their adherents to worship, the Christians were permitted to use gongs. Colonel C. R. Conder, in the introductory chapter to his book, *The City of Jerusalem,* describes the city in the early morning hours. Among the noises one heard in the marketplace was "the jangling of the metal plates that serve for bells in churches."[15] That was in the first decade of the twentieth century. One can still see relics of these gongs in the porch of the Armenian Church of St. James near the Jaffa Gate. A wooden plank is suspended by stout ropes, and a long plate of iron is suspended by chains. The Arabs permitted these noisy instruments because there is a Moslem tradition that Noah used such gongs to summon the workmen to the building of the ark.

In the nineteenth century, when the sultan became dependent on the Christian Powers of Europe, the anti-Christian laws were gradually relaxed and church bells began to summon Christians to worship. It is claimed that the first church bells that rang in Jerusalem were those of the Protestant Christ Church near the Jaffa Gate.

The reintroduction of church bells in Jerusalem is marked by a measure of intrigue as well as open defiance of the Sublime Porte. When Kaiser Wilhelm II made his pompous "pilgrimage" to the Holy City in 1898, he received a gift from the sultan—a precious plot on Mount Zion near the traditional Tomb of David. The Kaiser erected on that plot the Church of the Dormition. No sooner was the church completed than an "offer of large bells was made by a number of prominent Germans." An Imperial request was made to the Sublime Porte for permission to accept this gift. Indeed it would embarrass the Imperial Government to refuse this generous gift by such prominent donors. Of course, it was merely a courtesy, since these bells would never be rung. The sultan could not refuse so harmless a request. So the bells were brought to Jerusalem and duly installed. On the day the church was consecrated the bells were mysteriously rung. The Moslems were outraged, but the bells have been rung ever since.

The story of the arrival of another church bell in Jerusalem is worth telling. In the early 1880s the tsar of Russia sent a huge bronze bell weighing about eight tons as a gift to the Tur Malka Church on the crest of the Mount of Olives. The huge bell was shipped to the Holy City to be installed in the new church belfry. When the bell arrived at the Jaffa port, it was discovered that there was no way of transporting what Laurence Oliphant called the "bronze monster" to Jerusalem. There was no adequate road between Jerusalem and its port city of Jaffa. After the bell lay in Jaffa for more than six months the problem was solved by the Russian pilgrims who used to come to Jerusalem by the thousands. The pilgrims undertook to drag the "monster" to the Holy City. And so they did. They harnessed themselves to the bell and slowly dragged it over the mountainous terrain. Day and night they kept pulling the huge bell. They dragged it over mountains and across wadis. They pulled incessantly and sang sweetly as they labored for the glory of the Deity.

Laurence Oliphant tells of the arrival of the "bronze monster" in Jerusalem and its installation in the belfry of the church:

> One day while I was in Jerusalem the huge bell which I had seen dragged by Russian pilgrims along the road from Jaffa arrived. It was destined for a new Russian church which had lately been built upon the Mount of Olives. Anxious to witness the ceremony of its reception, I set out for the Mount and reached the summit just in time to see the bronze monster, which I calculated weighed about eight tons, arrive at its destination. A large crowd of Russian men and women, headed by two priests of the Greek Church in full canonicals, and chanting sacred songs, were dragging it to the platform from which it was to be finally elevated into the belfry prepared for it. When, after much pulling and hauling, it was at last placed upon the platform, a solemn religious service took place. Every individual man and woman in the crowd pressed forward to kiss the uplifted crucifix which the priest presented for their adoration, crossing and prostrating themselves, and crowding also around the bell to kiss the various sacred groups of figures represented upon it in basso-rilievo. At last, after a final melodious chant in which all joined with great earnestness, the officiating priest gave the signal for three cheers, which was responded to with heartiness, and the ceremony was over. [16]

The Christian Rivalries Within the Church of the Holy Sepulchre

Modernity, it is claimed, has brought the blessing of broadmindedness. People no longer do battle over religious differences; people are tolerant. It is to be wondered, however, whether the tolerance in Western society is not due, at least in part, to indifference. If their religious convictions were firm, would they be as tolerant? Whatever the answer, the religious communities in Jerusalem have not been tolerant. The Moslems look down with contempt upon the Christians; the Christians maintain an air of superiority and try to convert Moslems, Jews, and each other; and the Jews, God's chosen people, know that both Moslems and Christians are in error. They wait for the Messiah to open the eyes of the Gentiles to the truth, which, of course, is to be found in Judaism alone.

All the churches of Christendom are represented in Jerusalem. In no other city are there so many cleric and lay church representatives. Instead of living in harmony and mutual love, these church representatives have engaged in keen rivalries for the privilege of caring for the holy places. They cling tenaciously to their chapels in the Church of the Holy Sepulchre and are preoccupied with "hating one another for the love of God."

The Christian sects, especially their clerics, are inordinately jealous of their privileges and rights in the Church of the Holy Sepulchre. For them the holy places and the religious rituals in the church are of no less concern than are provinces to the rulers of empires. Kings do battle when their territories are threatened; so do the priests and monks and their co-religionists take up arms in defense of their holy places and their privileges in the Church of the Holy Sepulchre.

Mr. C. R. Ashbee, who was civic advisor and secretary to the Pro-Jerusalem Society during the British Mandatory Government, was scandalized by the Christian rivalries. In his *A Palestine Notebook,* he severely denounced them, saying:

> The theoretical agreement of all Christendom to keep holy and peaceful a spot common to all has in effect resulted in a condition of chronic feud and hatred between all the rival sects, Greek, Latin, Maronite, Copt, Armenian, Protestant—Lord knows! And this has been going on for centuries! . . .

> The Sabbath in Jerusalem is multiplied by three. The Moslems celebrate it on Fridays, the Jews on Saturdays, the Christians on Sundays. At first sight this appears reasonable, but it is really religious cussedness, and each group hates the other for profaning the Lord's day. The principal hatreds, however, are reserved for the Christians toward one another—how to fit all the services in as between all the fighting sects, how to satisfy all the little ritual squabbles as between all the contending priests, monks, and parsons, has been the problem of the ages. Every conceivable type of ecclesiastic is to be seen in the Holy City. What are they all there for? Do you burn a candle or don't you? I hate you. Do you celebrate Easter as I do or not? I hate you. Does the Holy Ghost proceed or doesn't it? I hate you. Was Christ crucified or not? I hate you. It is the perpetual Litany of Jerusalem.[17]

To sort out the tangled suspicions and to comprehend the bitterness that has characterized the relationships between the Christian sects is not easy. What is especially incomprehensible is that seemingly trivial incidents have led to bloody fights in the Church of the Holy Sepulchre. Harry Emerson Fosdick, the noted preacher of the Riverside Church in New York, wrote in his *A Pilgrimage to Palestine:*

> Typical alike of the bad temper and triviality of these Christian fanatics is the affair of the three nails. A pillar divides the Greek portion from the Latin in the Church of the Nativity and in the pillar are three nails. On one the Greeks may hang the end of their tapestry; on another the Latins may hang theirs; but the central nail is neutral, from which is supposed to depend a candlestick. One day the Latins in intense excitement complained to the government that the Greeks had hung their tapestry upon the central nail. This intolerable invasion of sacred rights became a matter of serious governmental investigation. Witnesses were sworn; the traditional use of the nails was traced and verified; and at last, under compulsion, pledges for the future were legally drawn up and signed. [18]

The Latin section of Calvary (the Chapel of the Nailing to the Cross) in the Church of the Holy Sepulchre (1970). (Courtesy of Israel Government Press Office.)

The Greek Orthodox section of Calvary in the Church of the Holy Sepulchre (1970). (Courtesy of Israel Government Press Office.)

And James Finn, the British consul in Jerusalem in the mid-nineteenth century, writes in his work, *Stirring Times:*

> The quarrel this time lay between the Greeks and Armenians for first possession of the Holy Fire. (The Latins were out of the fray; their Easter had been over a month.)

> Immediately on the appearance of the flame a disturbance broke out between the Greeks and Armenians, but both sides had evidently been prepared beforehand for a conflict. Pilgrims were provided with stones and cudgels, which had been previously concealed (it was believed by the Armenians) behind the columns and in dark corners, and our Vice-Consul, who had accompanied some English travellers into the gallery to witness the ceremony, saw a further supply of this sort of ammunition being thrown down into the body of the church from a window in the circular gallery which communicated with the Greek convent. A dreadful conflict ensued.

The Pasha left his seat in the nether gallery and ran down to direct his attendants, civil and military, in separating the combatants, and only succeeded in dividing them after he had himself received several severe blows on the head, and his secretary got a cut on the hand from a knife. The colonel in command of the troops and many of his soldiers got wounded and bruised. Some twenty-five Greeks and Armenians were severely wounded, and great numbers received heavy blows.[19]

A similar seemingly trivial matter led to a grave dispute and a bloody battle between the Greeks and Latins. *The Jewish Chronicle* of London, dated November 29, 1901, published a report from its Jerusalem correspondent under the heading "A Battle About Sweeping":

Who is to have the privilege of sweeping the courtyard of the Church of the Holy Sepulchre? This was the point of dispute between the Latins and Greeks during the last week, and was the cause of great excitement not to be forgotten soon. The Latins insisted upon their right of sweeping that part of the courtyard which faces their special chapel, on the ground that they had done so for the last forty years. The Greeks, however, claimed the same right for themselves.

The new Governor did not at first realise the gravity of the matter. He asked, why should not the Latin priests sweep as they had done so for years? But as he did not give a formal verdict, the Greeks thought they would prevent the Latins from sweeping, and were it even by force of arms. For a long while the Latins stood with their brooms and the Greeks with pistols hidden in their priestly robes. At last the Latins began sweeping and a serious fight ensued. Twenty-one priests were wounded, sixteen of the Latins and five Greeks, some of them seriously. Turkish police and soldiers interfered, and some of them also received wounds. The Turkish officer in charge had his eye blown out, and it has not yet been ascertained whether it is the Latin or Greek Church which will have to pay the injured officer damages.

The Governor is now convinced that a sweeping dispute is a serious matter. He has referred the dispute to Constantinople, and has given decisive orders that no one should meanwhile dare to sweep the courtyard.

The pasha always sent in his troops to quell the outbreaks in the church. As usual, he made sure to benefit from these Christian rivalries, because the representatives of the squabbling sects had to resort to the pasha to settle their disputes. And the pasha always settled the disputes profitably. Dr. R. R. Madden, a missionary physician who was in Jerusalem in 1827, attended to the pasha's health and reveals how the Turks exploited the rivalries between the Christian sects:

It is lamentable to observe the dissensions which exist in this city, between the various sects of Christians; the Turk, the common enemy of each, profits by their feuds, and literally enriches himself on the rancour of conflicting creeds.

There was lately a notable instance of Christian animosity and of Turkish interference, within the walls of the Church of the Sepulchre, in which it was my fortune to assist in the adjustment of the quarrel. . . .

During my visit to Jerusalem, the [Armenians] took possession, *vi et armis,* of the altar on Mount Calvary, which belonged to the Catholics, and which stands within the walls of the Church of the Sepulchre. The Catholics ejected them from the spot a few days after their usurpation; but the Armenian ecclesiastics rallied in a body round the altar next day, and a scene ensued which ill suited the sanctity of the place.

The Turks looked on with no small pleasure; the quarrel insured an *avanic* on either party; and the Governor finally interfered to decide on the validity of the title to Mount Calvary. He gave three days to both parties to adduce the necessary arguments; or, in plain English, to bring the bribes! Both parties awaited the result with anxiety, for neither of them knew how much the other gave.

At this juncture I was attending the Governor, who laboured under inflammation of the liver, brought on, I had reason to believe, from the immoderate use of ardent spirits. He had recently arrived from Damascus, and was in much need of money. I endeavoured to ascertain from him in whose favour he intended to decide; and which party had given in the most substantial arguments. I found the scale of *justice* weighed in favour of the Armenians, and that they had given eight thousand piastres while the Catholics had only offered six. This important information I lost no time in conveying to one of the fathers, who waited on me in the Convent, and the result was, that three thousand additional arguments were adduced in favour of the ancient title to Mount Calvary, and the Catholics continue the exclusive possessors of the altar in question.[20]

The only reasonable attitude one can assume toward these Christian rivalries is that of John Finley, who was in Palestine during the First World War as head of the Red Cross mission. He related in his book, *A Pilgrim in Palestine,* that he once stood near the entrance of the Russian Church of the Ascension on the Mount of Olives during a service within the church:

A woman of sharp, eager face, as of a zealot, with a gray shawl over her head, seeing me standing near the door, approached me and said in rather sharp voice, (speaking in French) *"Quelle croix?"* (What cross?) I did not at first understand the import of her inquiry, though I realized that she was putting to me an all-important question: *"Quelle croix? —grecque ou latine?"* ("What cross do you make, that of the Greek church or of the Latin Church?") My answer was, *"La Croix Rouge"* (the Red Cross), the sign of mercy universal, the symbol not of a creed, nor even of a Christian faith, but of human kinship and brotherhood.[21]

A hopeful sign of John Finley's spirit is to be seen in the current cooperation of the Christian sects in the extensive repairs and restorations taking place in the Church of the Holy Sepulchre. Does this cooperation mark the resurgence of goodwill and tolerance? Or is it a sign of the dilution of the faith? It is hoped it is the former.

Duplicate and Competing Holy Places

No one is surprised to learn that there are many holy places in Jerusalem. What else is one to find in a holy city? But people are baffled and confounded when they discover rival holy places, each claiming to be the authentic sacred site of biblical fame. The competition between the rival holy places often persuades people to question the authenticity of all the holy places. For example, the visitor is shown two centers of the world within a short distance from each other. Jews, Christians, and Moslems agree that Jerusalem is the center of the world. But when it comes to identifying the exact spot, their disagreement begins. The Christians point to a spot in the Church of the Holy Sepulchre, but the Jews point to an outcropping on Mount Moriah, where in ancient times stood Solomon's Temple. The Moslems did not create holy places. Since the Moslems deny the Crucifixion of Jesus, they reject the holy places associated with the Holy Sepulchre. They therefore accepted the Jewish center of the world on the Temple Mount. We thus have in Jerusalem two "authentic" centers of the world.

The existence of rival holy places has bothered even the credulous among the faithful. Sophisticated Christians simply ask, "How can two rival holy places be authentic?" Thus did W. M. Thomson, a noted American missionary, react in 1857 when he visited Ain Karem, where John the Baptist is said to have been born. The Reverend Thomson could not grasp how John the Baptist could have been born in two places. He writes sarcastically in his *The Land and the Book:*

Our padre labours hard to explain how it could possibly come to pass that the

Baptist should be born *in two places*—beneath the rich altar within the convent, and in the grotto at least a quarter of a mile from it, where a convent was also erected, over the house of Elisabeth. It is not very important how we dispose of this difficulty. Elisabeth may possibly have divided the time of that important occasion between the two, in order to multiply the number of sacred places, and thereby increase the piety of future generations.[22]

More confusing is the presence of several Gardens of Gethsemane on the Mount of Olives. John Finley, the famous American scholar and editor of *The New York Times,* writes in his book, *A Pilgrim in Palestine:*

I took the narrow way between the several Gethsemane Gardens, each of which wished to keep exclusively the memory of his sacred presence, but wishing myself that all these walls were razed and that all, Armenians, Greeks, and Latins alike, would merge their gardens into one garden that would beautify the whole hillside, instead of fencing each their little tract and leaving the greater part of the hillside as bare and broken and desolate as a bit of "No Man's Land."[23]

In the duplication of the Gardens of Gethsemane, the Latins have an obvious advantage. Their garden has eight ancient olive trees, which, they claim, are the very trees that witnessed the tragedy of that fateful night. The olive trees in the other Gardens of Gethsemane are relatively young and can not possibly claim to be two thousand years old.

Nevertheless, in the multiplicity of the Gardens of Gethsemane, one really has a wide choice. One can choose between the Latin, Greek Orthodox, and Armenian Gardens of Gethsemane. This hardly makes it easier for the visitor.

The most difficult choices are those connected with the sepulchres of Jesus and the Virgin Mary. The Sepulchre of Jesus, as everyone knows, is in the Church of the Holy Sepulchre. However, as we have seen, the authenticity of this sepulchre is vehemently denied by some Protestants who point to another tomb, called the Garden Tomb, which is on a hill outside the city's northern wall. This tomb, they say, is the authentic Holy Sepulchre. The traditional one, they say, is a fraud.

A similar controversy concerns the authenticity of Mary's tomb. This controversy is unique, because it is between two Catholic brotherhoods. The Franciscans support the authenticity of the tomb in the underground church in the Kidron Valley. This holy place is venerated by Christians and Moslems. But the Dominicans assert that the authentic tomb of Mary is at Ephesus. This claim is sustained by a tradition dating back to the fifth century. The ruin of a monastery in Ephesus is avowed to be the site of Mary's assumption.

Again, the visitor in Jerusalem has a choice, and the choice does not tend to confirm his faith in the holy places.

Strangest of all the competing holy places is the original bush in which a ram got himself entangled four thousand years ago. That was the ram that became the vicarious victim for Isaac. This holy bush is walled up in a Greek chapel. But the Ethiopians deny this Greek "bush," claiming they have the authentic one in their convent. They point to it in their quarters and expect the visitor to choose their olive tree as against the other one, which, they say, is false. Needless to add that the biblical account implies that the bush was on Mount Moriah. But the Bible does not say so specifically. So one can take the liberty of locating the bush a little farther away.

There are several other duplicate holy places. Among them are the two houses of Caiaphus, the two palaces of the rich man, two chapels of the catacombs, two rooms of the Last Supper, and others.

In addition to the double holy places, there are in Jerusalem dual holy days, and Christian pilgrims are shocked when they confront two Easters and three Christmases, each of which is observed with colorful ceremonies and intense devotion. Recently, the Latins and Protestants observed Holy Week in Jerusalem March 19–26, while the Orthodox Greeks, Armenians, and several other Christian sects observed it April 23–30. That same year, the Latins and Protestants observed Christmas on December 25, the Orthodox Greeks celebrated it on January 7, and the Armenians observed it on January 18. These duplicate (and triplicate) observances are known to everyone in Jerusalem because each Christian community marks its Easter week and its Christmas Day with public processions. Pilgrims, however, are obviously confused and tend to question the authenticity of all the rival dates, as they do of all the rival holy sites. It takes deep conviction to confirm one date and reject the others or to accept one holy place as authentic and reject the other as a fraud.

How Old Are the Olive Trees in the Garden of Gethsemane?

When people speak of the Garden of Gethsemane, they usually refer to the Gethsemane cared for by the Franciscan Friars. This small plot of land on

One of the ancient olive trees in the Garden of Gethsemane (1967). (Courtesy of Israel Government Press Office.)

the Mount of Olives is one of the most precious shrines in Christendom. It lies near the foot of the Mount of Olives, opposite the eastern wall of the Temple enclosure. The most impressive feature of the holy place is the eight ancient olive trees of tremendous girth. The Franciscan Friars claim that these very trees witnessed the agony that Jesus suffered the night before the Crucifixion. The Franciscan caretakers have planted flower beds which, by their artificial layout, do not add to the ancient appearance of the shrine. Henry Van Dyke visited the Garden of Gethsemane in 1908. In his itinerary he describes the holy place:

> The eight aged trees that still cling to life in Gethsemane have been inclosed with a low wall and an iron railing, and the little garden that blooms around them is cared for by Franciscan monks from Italy. . . . The boles of the olive trees hardly seem to be of wood; so dark, so twisted, so furrowed are they, of an aspect so enduring that they appear to be cast in bronze or carved out of black granite. Above each of them spreads a crown of fresh foliage, delicate, abundant, shimmering softly in the sunlight and the breeze, with silken turnings of the under side of the innumerable leaves.[24]

How old are the olive trees? The faithful believe them sufficiently ancient to be the trees among which Jesus spent the night before the Crucifixion. Skeptics, however, have questioned this belief. According to Josephus, Titus cut down all the trees around Jerusalem prior to his assault on the city. He surely did not spare a cluster of trees on the Mount of Olives close to the eastern wall of the city just to please the sensitivities of a few Christians, who, from his pagan view, were only cultists.

To counter this argument, the faithful have produced a logical explanation. Olive trees, they say, have the capacity of surviving the axe. When olive trees are cut down their roots sprout new shoots that grow into olive trees. Hence, they say, the trees that are now in the Garden of Gethsemane grew out of the roots of the original trees among which Jesus spent that fateful night. These trees can therefore be identified as the original trees without contradicting Josephus.

But the doubters had another argument. They claimed that the roots of the trees in the Garden of Gethsemane, though aged, are far from being almost two thousand years old.

In recent years, science came to the aid of the faithful. In March 1977, the Franciscans turned to the municipality of Jerusalem for help, because the trees began to show signs of sickness. They were shedding their leaves, and some branches were withering. The municipality called in Professor Shimon Lavi of the Volcani Institute. He advised some careful pruning and spreading of manure around the trees, but not close to the gnarled trunks. His advice was followed, and the trees began to show improvement. Professor Lavi was asked for his opinion regarding the trees' age. He responded that he would estimate their age to be 1,600 to 1,800 years, but they could be older. To know for sure, one would have to send some of the roots to the University of California to be subjected to a carbon 14 dating test. This was done, and the verdict was that the roots are old enough to have been here at the time of the Crucifixion. Thus ended the controversy regarding the age of the olive trees in the Garden of Gethsemane.

The Hole in Which Grew the Holy Tree

In Jerusalem one is never shown an approximate site where a sacred event took place. Every holy site is identified as the exact spot where the sacred incident occurred. Thus one is shown the exact spot where grew the tree from which the Romans made the cross for the Crucifixion of Jesus. Indeed, one is shown the very hole in which the tree trunk grew. And if one is an important personage, he or she may even be shown the crevice in the rock into which the main root of the tree extended. This intriguing holy place is located in a massive, irregular square building with high buttresses supporting the walls. The building is called the Monastery of the Cross. It is situated in the Valley of the Cross, which lies between the Israel Museum and the residential area known as Rehaviah. Prior to the invention of cannon, this monastery must have been one of Jerusalem's strongest fortifications. Albert Rhodes, who was the American consul in Jerusalem during the 1860s, was shown not only the hole in which the tree grew, but also the crevice into which the root of the tree had entered. In his book, *Jerusalem as It Is,* Rhodes relates:

> It is a massive building, with some pretensions to architectural finish, as well as strength. The entrance is by a low doorway, guarded by a heavy iron door, which is opened to the visitor with precaution. We were met here by my friend, Father Gregorius, who first took us to the old church, which is enclosed within the convent walls. . . .

> The centre of attraction to the faithful here is a little round hole, rimmed with silver, which Father Gregorius showed us in the sanctum, behind the altar-screen. According to the Greek tradition, here grew the tree from which the cross was made upon which the Saviour was crucified. . . .

> The Greek father afterwards conducted us behind the sanctum by a subterranean passage to a vault, where he showed us a large crevice in the rock, through which the main root of the tree extended! As the priest (who is an intelligent man) pointed to it he shrugged his shoulders and said, "It's a tradition, you know," in a deprecating manner.

After we had thus gotten to the root of the matter, we ascended to another church, or rather chapel, of recent construction, within the walls of the convent. . . . Here a book was produced, in which the autographs of distinguished visitors were kept, as the Greek father informed me. He was polite enough to ask me for mine. In turning over the leaves, I saw a star of the first magnitude which shone in this autographic horizon, beside which lesser lights paled their ineffectual fire—the Prince of Wales. My interpreter observed that it was a very small signature for the future king of a great power—that the Sultan required a space six inches square, at least, on which to write his.[25]

W. M. Thomson, a noted American missionary, came to Jerusalem as a pilgrim in 1857. In his itinerary, *The Land and the Book,* he tells of his visit at the Monastery of the Cross and remarks:

The monks were very polite, and one of them showed us the place where the tree grew from which the cross was made! Whether true or not, let others discuss; but one thing is certain,—this great convent, with all its revenues, has grown up out of that hole in the ground in which the tree is said to have stood.[26]

The Monastery of the Cross, seen from the rear (1972). (Courtesy of Israel Government Press Office.)

Thomson concludes with an irreverent statement by Henry Maundrell, who was in Jerusalem in 1697:

> Maundrell sums up its title to our reverence somewhat after the manner of the famous house that Jack built: "it is because here is the earth that nourished the root, that bore the tree, that yielded the timber, that made the cross;" and he adds, rather profanely, "Under the high altar you are shown a hole in the ground where the stump of the tree stood, and it meets with not a few visitants, so much verier stocks than itself as to fall down and worship it."[27]

Notably, the tree that grew in the hole that is venerated in the Monastery of the Cross did not just grow there accidentally. According to tradition, the tree was planted as an act of penitence by the biblical personage Lot. When Lot awoke after his daughters had seduced him, he was full of remorse. He wept bitterly and prayed for forgiveness:

> One day, whilst employed, an angel of God appeared to him, and gave him three cuttings of cypress trees, saying, "Plant and water these cuttings with water from the Jordan, where thou wilt go and draw every day. If they strike root, it is a sign that thou art forgiven, but if they die, it is a sign of thy condemnation." He obeyed, full of hope, and watched his cuttings. The distance to the Jordan and back would occupy a whole day, and be very hard work, especially for one carrying water.[28]

The saplings took root and became trees, and one of them grew in the hole over which the monastery was erected. This history of the tree is represented in curious pictures in the monastery and is part of the Greek Orthodox Church tradition.

The International Christian Embassy in the Holy City

In 1979 several Christian residents of Jerusalem concluded that the rebirth of the State of Israel was a sign of universal import. Is there another people that has been exiled and scattered to the four corners of the world for two thousand years and then restored to its homeland? In 1897 Theodor Herzl, the founder of modern Zionism, stated that within fifty years the Jewish state would become a reality, and fifty years later, in 1947, the United Nations General Assembly acknowledged the right of the Jewish people to a sovereign state. Was this a mere coincidence or the hand of

God? In 1917 General Allenby captured Jerusalem, and fifty years later, in 1967, the Old City was captured by the Israel Defense Forces. Fifty years are not an arbitrary number. Fifty years are the biblical Jubilee when alienated possessions were to be restored to their original owners. Again, is this a mere coincidence or the hand of God? These Christians were convinced that "Israel is inextricably bound up with God's purposes." Israel should therefore receive Christian prayer and support. To implement this resolve, these Christians founded an organization which they called The Almond Branch Association, an allusion to the vision recorded in the first chapter of the Book of Jeremiah.

Out of this desire to come to Israel's aid arose the idea of an international gathering of Christians to be held in Jerusalem during the Feast of Tabernacles in the fall of 1980. In *Christian News from Israel* this event was reported thus:

> It was to demonstrate this support [for Israel] that one thousand Bible-believing Christians from over twenty different countries—including Taiwan, Japan, Egypt, Finland and Nigeria in addition to those of Europe and of North America—made the journey to Jerusalem to take part in a Christian celebration of *Sukkoth,* the Feast of Tabernacles. The organizers, a group of Christian clergymen and laymen living in Israel, chose the *Sukkoth* festival because, according to the prophet, "it shall come to pass, that every one that is left of all the nations that come against Jerusalem shall go up from year to year to worship the King, the Lord of Hosts, and to keep the Feast of Tabernacles" (Zech. 14:16). [29]

These Christians came with enthusiasm and love for Israel and a desire to act in behalf of Israel's welfare.

The fall of 1980 was a critical time for Israel, and the arrival of these Christian pilgrims and their demonstration of friendship was especially meaningful. Those were the days when thirteen embassies left Jerusalem in protest against a resolution passed in the Knesset declaring that united Jerusalem was the eternal capital of Israel. To be sure, that resolution was a mere gesture, because united Jerusalem had already been officially declared the capital of Israel. But this reaffirmation of Jerusalem's status angered the Arab states that pressured the countries whose embassies were in Jerusalem to leave the city. It was during that time of Israel's isolation on the international political front that these Christians happened to be in the Holy City. To quote once more the report in *Christian News from Israel:*

> In the wake of the exodus of thirteen foreign embassied from Jerusalem for

reasons of political expediency, another embassy was demonstratively inaugurated in the capital city with the watchword, "Israel is not alone." Banners inscribed with this affirmation of solidarity were borne aloft at the festive opening of the "International Christian Embassy" in Jerusalem on 30 September. The event marked the climax of a ten-day international Christian congress to celebrate the Feast of Tabernacles in Israel's capital.[30]

These "Bible-believing Christians" also participated in the annual Jerusalem March, carrying their national flags and conspicuous banners proclaiming that "Israel is not alone." They touched the hearts of the Israeli spectators, many of whom were moved to tears. It was during that celebration of the Feast of Tabernacles that the International Christian Embassy in Jerusalem was born. It was then the only foreign embassy in Jerusalem. In one of the official statements issued at that time the Christian Embassy declared:

> The Embassy does not represent any government, denomination, church organization, Christian businessmen, group or political party. It does represent the concern of millions of Bible-believing Christians who love and honor the Jewish people and who wish to obey the will of God concerning them.

And one of the leaders of the Embassy, Jay Rawlings, a Canadian, summed up the embassy's objectives:

> This will not be an embassy in the political sense of the word, but an embassy in the biblical sense, in that we will be ambassadors for Israel and for the principles of God that Israel represents. This embassy will be a focal point for Christians all over the world, a place they can relate to in Israel.

The International Christian Embassy in Jerusalem was officially opened on September 30, 1980. Its offices were located at 10 Brenner Street in the New City. "Consulates" were set up in many cities in Europe and the Americas to stimulate participation in its program, which aims not merely to awaken sympathy for Israel, but to promote practical assistance to the beleaguered state. It asks its adherents to contribute generously to Israel's financial needs and to fight the Arab boycott. "Many people," says the Embassy, "do not want to buy Israeli products and others refuse to do business with Israel because they are afraid of losing Arab clients." Hence the Embassy asks Christian consumers to buy Israeli-made products, and it asks Christian retail businessmen to give Israeli products priority in their marketing efforts. In addition, the Embassy promotes tourism to Israel. The Embassy also asks its supporters to speak up in defense of Israel and of united Jerusalem under Israeli rule by writing letters to government leaders and the press. "Had the Christians spoken out in defense of the Jews in the 1930's," states one of the Embassy's official communications, "Hitler's lust for conquest would have been exposed and the world would have been saved from the horrors of the war and the Holocaust."

The Embassy promotes vigorously the annual mass pilgrimage to Jerusalem during the Feast of Tabernacles "to sing the high praises of the Lord" (Ps. 150) and to "comfort Zion" (Isa. 40). In 1980 over a thousand Christians came; in 1981 almost four thousand came. The Embassy's call is directed to that considerable section of the Christian world which is committed to the Bible. There are millions of these fundamentalists who have been waiting for an agency to harness and coordinate their sympathies for Israel and to direct these sympathies into practical channels.

Almost all the political embassies left Jerusalem.[31] One embassy has replaced them, an embassy which represents the spirit of millions of believing Christians. This embassy may yet prove that nations prevail "not by might, nor by power, but by My spirit, says the Lord of hosts" (Zech. 4:6).

The Monastery on the Roof

People associate a monastery with a large building, an inner court, and a sheltered path where the monks contemplate the mysteries of their faith. It is difficult to imagine a monastery situated on the roof of a building. In Jerusalem there is such a monastery.

The monastery on the roof is called Deir al-Sultan, and it belongs to the Ethiopians. Its location is on the roof of the Church of the Holy Sepulchre, immediately above the Chapel of St. Helena. The monastery's name, Deir al-Sultan, say the Ethiopians, derives from the fact that the Sultan (King) Solomon presented it to the Queen of Sheba to serve as a pilgrims' hospice. However, the Copts, who are the Ethiopians' perennial rivals, claim that the sultan who bestowed his title on the monastery was an Egyptian monarch of the Middle Ages. Be that as it may, the monastery Deir al-Sultan is only a group of white-washed mud huts, currently inhabited by fifteen monks, two nuns, and a young Ethiopian who prepares their food and performs other chores. The huts of the monastery are dank, and the walls are peeling. The ceilings are cracked, and the rain seeps into the small rooms. When winter comes, the monks and nuns suffer immensely.[32]

The Ethiopians were not always so destitute and lowly in the hierarchy of Christian sects in Jerusalem. There was a time when they were counted among the honored sects in the Holy City. During the Middle Ages they occupied several important shrines in the Church of the Holy Sepulchre. Among these was the Chapel of St. Helena. But in the course of time misfortunes befell the community, and the Ethiopians lost their prerogatives mostly to the Armenians. It was during the disastrous plague of 1838 when all the Ethiopian monks died that the Ethiopians lost their most precious possession, the Chapel of St. Helena, to the Armenians, who seized it and have held on to it ever since. Under the rule of the *Status Quo* this possession has achieved legality. Today the Ethiopians maintain their shabby foothold on the roof of the Church of the Holy Sepulchre, and even this sorry possession is contested by their perennial opponents, the Copts, whose monastery of St. Anthony occupies a neighboring section of the roof.

In more recent times the controversy between the Copts and the Ethiopians has focused on a passageway which leads down from the roof, passing the Chapel of St. Michael and the Chapel of the Four Creatures,[33] and ending up in the courtyard of the Church of the Holy Sepulchre. Whoever possesses the keys to the locks at either entrance to the passageway controls access not only to the passage from the roof to the entrance of the Church of the Holy Sepulchre but also to the two chapels. Up to 1838 the Ethiopians possessed the keys and were the masters of this strategic passageway. During the 1838 plague when all the Ethiopian monks died, the Copts appropriated the keys to the passageway and thus gained possession of the stairway from the roof to the Church of the Holy Sepulchre, wherein they possess a small chapel. This enabled the Copts to hold their processions on Easter and Christmas directly from the roof to their chapel unhindered. When new Ethiopian monks arrived in Jerusalem and resettled the huts on the roof, they found the way to their chapels closed. A sharp dispute over the passageway began and has continued to this day.

In 1948 the Old City was occupied by the Jordanians. The Ethiopians appealed to the government in Amman to recognize their rights to the two chapels and to the passageway leading to them. On February 27, 1961, the Coptic and Ethiopian communities were informed that a Jordanian ministerial committee had decided that the Ethiopians were the legitimate owners of the passageway. But a month later, on April 2, 1961, King Hussein made public a decision to suspend the former judgment and to restore the *Status Quo Ante.* The reversal came as a result of a protest lodged by the Coptic Patriarch of Alexandria and supported by the Egyptian government. The Jordanian decision was obviously based on political expediency. Accordingly, the Copts regained the keys to the passageway and refused the Ethiopians passage to the chapels.

In 1967, as a result of the Six-Day War, the Old City came under the jurisdiction of Israel. Shortly thereafter, the conflict between the Copts and the Ethiopians became explosive. The Ethiopians expected distinguished guests for the Easter services of 1969 and decided to install electricity in their Deir al-Sultan monastery. The Copts disputed the right of the Ethiopians to install electricity on the grounds because it was contrary to the *Status Quo*. On Easter, when the Ethiopians were performing their traditional rites on their newly illuminated roof, the Copts threw stones at the Ethiopians and their guests. The Ethiopians were now determined to settle matters without recourse to the law courts.

The following year, on Easter eve at midnight, the Copts made their traditional procession through the disputed passageway to their chapel in the Church of the Holy Sepulchre. While the Copts were at prayer, the Ethiopians changed the locks at both ends of the passageway. The Copts were outraged and appealed to the Israeli courts. The latter rendered a unanimous opinion that no one may take the law into his or her own hands and take property from persons in actual possession thereof. The keys to the passageway should by right be returned to the Copts. But the essential issue was not the possession (of the keys) but the actual ownership of the passageway. The court therefore asked that the return of the keys be deferred in order to allow the government to decide the basic issue. The government appointed a committee to hear evidence from both sides to the dispute and to make recommendations for solving the controversy.

As of now, decades after that court decision, the keys to the passageway are still with the Ethiopians, and the Copts are still waiting for a "just" solution of the controversy. Why has not the government-appointed committee made its recommendations, and why has not the Israeli government acted until now? The answer can easily be surmised.

The Greek Ritual of Washing the Feet

In ancient times many people walked about bare-footed. Washing the feet was then as normal a practice as washing the hands is today. We read in the Bible that Abraham saw three strangers and said to them: "If I have found favor in your sight, pass not away from your servant: Let now a little water be fetched, and wash your feet, and recline yourselves under the tree" (Gen. 18:3–4). When shoes came into common use, the washing of the feet ceased to be a general practice, and it persisted only in ritual. Thus one can see Arabs washing their feet before entering a mosque for prayer.

Among the Christians of Jerusalem, washing the feet is a ritual performed during the Holy Week of Easter. This ceremonial is one of the most spectacular of the Holy Week ceremonies. On the morning of Holy Thursday the Greek ceremony takes place in the courtyard of the Church of the Holy Sepulchre. The other Christian sects perform this ritual in their own churches. The twelve apostles are represented by twelve archimandrites. The patriarch, followed by a deacon who bears a golden basin and ewer, goes over to each representative of the apostles, kneels, washes the right foot, dries it, and kisses it. As the patriarch rises, the archimandrite kisses his hand. "St. Peter" properly protests, but submits.

The washing ceremony ended, the patriarch resumes his normal state. He puts on his crown and jewels and goes across the square to a platform on which a sort of miracle play is enacted. Three archimandrites assume the pose of sleep on the steps of the platform, and the story of the Agony in the Garden of Gethsemane is enacted. The crowd watches intently, and despite its annual repetition, the play moves them deeply. The sophisticated modern theater has not yet spoiled the dramaturgy of the local Christians or the Greek Orthodox pilgrims.

Knights of the Holy Sepulchre

From time immemorial princes of the realm rewarded their loyal and heroic warriors with gifts and honors, among them knighthoods. Why should not princes of the Church do likewise? And so they do. From time to time the Latin Guardian of the Church of the Holy Sepulchre or the Latin Patriarch conferred the title of Knight of the Holy Sepulchre on pilgrims whom he deemed worthy of that signal honor. Among these privileged pilgrims was the Viscount François René de Châteaubriand, who described the ceremony in his *Travels to Jerusalem and the Holy Land:*

> I had seen every thing at Jerusalem; I was acquainted with the interior and exterior of that city, and better acquainted with them than with the interior of Paris and its vicinity: I began, therefore, to think of my departure. The Fathers of the Holy Land determined to confer on me an honour which I had neither solicited nor deserved. In consideration of the feeble services which,

as they said, I had rendered to religion, they requested me to accept the Order of the Holy Sepulchre. This Order, of high antiquity in Christendom, though its origin may not date so far back as the time of St. Helena, was formerly very common in Europe. At present it is scarcely ever met with except in Spain and Poland: the superior of the Latin convent, as guardian of the Holy Sepulchre, has alone the right to confer it.

We left the convent at one o'clock and repaired to the Church of the Holy Sepulchre. We went into the chapel belonging to the Latin Fathers; the doors were carefully shut, lest the Turks should perceive the arms, which might cost the religious their lives. The superior put on his pontifical habits; the lamps and tapers were lighted; all the brethren present formed a circle round me, with their hands folded upon their breasts. While they sung the *Veni Creator* in a low voice, the superior stepped up to the altar, and I fell on my knees at his feet. The spurs and sword of Godfrey de Bouillon were taken out of the treasury of the Holy Sepulchre: two of the religious, standing one on each side of me, held the venerable relics. The superior recited the accustomed prayers and asked me the usual questions: he then put the spurs on my heels and struck me thrice over the shoulders with the sword, on which the religious began to sing the *Te Deum,* while the superior pronounced this prayer over my head: "Lord God Almighty, bestow thy grace and blessing on this thy servant," etc.

All this is but a shadow of the days that are past. But if it be considered that I was at Jerusalem, in the church of Calvary, within a dozen of paces of the tomb of Jesus Christ, and thirty from that of Godfrey de Bouillon; that I was equipped with the spurs of the Deliverer of the Holy Sepulchre; and had touched that sword, both long and large, which so noble and so valiant an arm had once wielded; if the reader bear in mind these circumstances, my life of adventure, my peregrinations by land and sea, he will easily believe that I could not remain unmoved. Neither was this ceremony in other respects without effect. I am a Frenchman; Godfrey de Bouillon was a Frenchman; and his ancient arms, in touching me, communicated an increased ardour for glory and for the honour of my country.

My certificate, signed by the guardian and sealed with the seal of the convent, was delivered to me. With this brilliant diploma of Knighthood, I received my humble passport of a pilgrim. I preserve them as a record of my visit to the land of the ancient traveller, Jacob.[34]

A more detailed description of the ceremony was recorded by a pilgrim who was in Jerusalem in 1734. Charles Thomson, a man of wealth, whose itinerary, *The Travels of the Late Charles Thomson,* has been regarded as a classic work, describes the ceremony in all its particulars:

The next Day an *Italian* Gentleman, of a good Family and Fortune, was created a Knight of the *Holy Sepulchre* by the Father-Guardian of the Convent, the Price of which Honour is about twenty Pounds Sterling. Most Writers who mention this Order carry its Institution as far back as the Time of the Apostle St. *James,* Bishop of *Jerusalem,* or at least to that of *Constantine the Great;* pretending that *Godfrey* of *Bouillon* and his Successor *Baldwin* were only the Restorers thereof. But this Antiquity is chimerical; nor is it certain, that this Order was even founded so early as the Time of the two last-mention'd Princes. . . .

The Guardian and most of the Friars, with a great many Pilgrims (in which Number we include ourselves), attended the *Italian* to the Church of the Holy Sepulchre, where Mass was celebrated on this Occasion: After which the Candidate for Knighthood had the usual Oath administer'd to him, which is to the following Effect. The Knights swear to be present at Mass every Day, if they have an Opportunity; to serve in Person in the *Holy Land,* whenever War is commenced against the Infidels, or to send others in their stead; to oppose the Persecutors and Enemies of the Church; to avoid unjust Wars, dishonest Gain, and private Duels; to endeavour to reconcile Dissensions, to advance the common Good, and particularly to defend the Widow and the Orphan; to refrain from Swearing, Perjury, Blasphemy, Rapine, Usury, Sacrilege, Murder, and Drunkenness; to live chastly, to shun the Company of imfamous Persons, and both in their Words and Actions, through the whole Course of their Lives, to shew themselves worthy of the Honour to which they are advanced. The *Italian* having taken this Oath, the Guardian caused him to kneel down before the Entrance of the Sepulchre; and laying his Hand upon his head, exhorted him to be loyal, valiant, virtuous, and an undaunted Soldier of *Jesus Christ.* Then giving him a Pair of Spurs, which he put upon his Heels, and after that a Sword (the same, they say, that was *Godfrey* of *Bouillon's),* he commanded him to use it in Defense of the Church and himself, and to the Confusion of Infidels. He then sheath'd it, and girded it to his Side; after which going close to the Sepulchre, and leaning his Head upon the Stone, the Guardian created him a Knight by giving him three Strokes on the Shoulder, and as often repeating these Words: *I ordain thee a Knight of the Holy Sepulchre of our Lord Jesus Christ, in the Name of the Father, and of the Son, and of the Holy Ghost.* This done, the Father kiss'd him, and put about his Neck a Chain of Gold, to which hung a Cross of the same Metal. Then the new created Knight arose, kiss'd the Sepulchre, restor'd the above-mention'd *Insignia* to the Guardian, and so the Ceremony was concluded.[35]

The Knights of the Holy Sepulchre have nothing in common with the Knights Templars or any of the military orders which flourished in Jerusalem during the days of the Crusader Kingdom of Jerusalem. This is so despite the prevailing tradition that the order was founded by Godfrey of Bouillon. No evidence supports this tradition.

From the fifteenth to the mid-nineteenth century the grand master of the order was the superior of the Franciscan monastery in Jerusalem. He was generally called the Guardian of the Church of the Holy Sepulchre, and it was he who bestowed the knighthoods on the Catholic pilgrims he deemed worthy of the honor. In 1847 Pope Pius IX transferred the title to the Patriarch of Jerusalem. Today this title is held by one of the cardinals at the Vatican. Since 1868, women have been admitted to the order.

The insignia of the Knights of the Holy Sepulchre is a white cape with a red cross of Jerusalem.

"Red" and "White" Russian Churches

One of the anomalies of Jerusalem's holy places is that some of the Russian holy shrines belong to the "Red" Russian Church in Moscow and others belong to the "White" Russian Church, whose headquarters is in New York. Why, people ask, does the Chapel of St. Alexander Nevsky near the Church of the Holy Sepulchre with its important excavations belong to the White Russian Church, whereas the Cathedral in the Russian Compound belongs to the Red Russian Church? Why does the Convent of the Ascension on the top of the Mount of Olives and the Convent of St. Mary Magdelena of Gethsemane belong to the White Russian Church, whereas the Russian Convent of Ein Karem, which is the traditional birthplace of St. John the Baptist, belong to the Red Russian Church?

To solve this riddle, one must start with the fact that all the Russian holy places were originally the property of the Tsarist Russian Government. After the Russian Revolution, the so-called White Russian Church with headquarters in New York and the so-called Red Russian Church with headquarters in Moscow laid claim to and still claim to be the rightful successors to the pre-revolution Tsarist Orthodox Church, and each has laid claim to all the Russian churches and holy places in the Holy Land. The British government which ruled the Holy Land after the fall of the Tsarist regime decided the issue in favor of the White Church in exile. All the Russian church properties in the Holy Land thus came under the jurisdiction of the Russian émigré church in New York. This decision was in force during the thirty years of British rule. But a radical change took place after the Israel-Arab war of 1948–1949. In that war Russia was Israel's ally. The strategic interests of Moscow required that Great Britain be driven out of the Middle East. During those early years of Russian friendship, Israel recognized the Soviet Union's claim to the tsarist properties in the Holy Land. The Soviet Union thus became the legal owner of all tsarist Russian properties within the boundaries of the State of Israel, and the Russian holy places came under the jurisdiction of the Red Russian Church. But Israel's jurisdiction included only the new city of Jerusalem and Mount Zion. The Old City and the Mount of Olives were annexed by the Hashemite Kingdom of Jordan. There a different logic prevailed. Since the Soviet Union helped Israel, it was *ipso facto* the enemy of the Arabs. Since there was an anti-Soviet Russian church with headquarters in New York, the Jordanian government continued the British policy and recognized the White Russian Church as the rightful successors to the tsarist church properties.

After the Six-Day War, Jerusalem was reunited and all the Russian holy places in Jerusalem were within the domain of Israel. In accordance with the law of the *Status Quo,* no changes could be made in the status of holy places. Once a holy place was declared to be under the jurisdiction of a religious organization, it was permanently to remain so. Also, Russia was no longer Israel's ally. Hence there are in Jerusalem Red Russian holy places and White Russian holy places.

The rivalry between the two Russian ecclesiastical missions in Jerusalem is bitter. *Christian News from Israel,* in a news item dated 1972, reported:

> Archimandrite Anthony Grable, Head of the Ecclesiastical Mission of the Russian Church Outside Russia, proclaimed a "week of sorrow" during the visit of the representatives of the Moscow Patriarchate, regarded by him and his church as non-canonical tools in the hands of the atheistic Soviet regime.

Needless to say that the Red Russian hierarchy regards the White Russian Church with equal animosity and contempt.

Logically all the Russian holy places in Jerusalem should be under one jurisdiction. But logic is not always a decisive factor in determining human affairs. Tradition and geo-political considerations often supersede logic, especially in critical issues of national and international dimensions. This is also the case in the realm of religious affairs—as in the disposition of the holy places in Jerusalem.

The Chapel Named "The Lord Wept"

About halfway up the western incline of the Mount of Olives there is an exquisite Christian shrine called the Chapel of the Lord Wept, or, more correctly, *Dominus Flevit.* This tiny chapel accommodates only thirteen people. However, it is admired by all visitors and has often been called the "jewel" of the shrines erected by Antonio Barluzzi. This architectural pearl stands on the spot where, according to Christian tradition, Jesus wept over the impending destruction of Jerusalem.

The tear-shaped chapel has a large window above the altar looking out over the Holy City. Some people have questioned the authenticity of the spot on which the chapel was erected. They say that the slope is too steep at this point for a procession of the kind described in the New Testament account. But, say the defenders of the tradition, no other spot has ever been associated with this event. Besides, this spot is particularly suited for pilgrims to view the whole city and to be reminded of the tears that Jesus shed over the impending doom that awaited the Holy City (Luke 19:37, 41–44).

Christian pilgrims seldom fail to visit the Chapel of the Lord Wept. All tourists should make the effort both to visit an architectural jewel and to view the Holy City from this excellent vantage point. The enchanting view will surely be the high point of their tour, to be remembered when everything else is forgotten.

"Hunting the Devil" in a Church

The Ethiopian Orthodox Church has retained some of its primitive rituals. Consequently, its services appear strange and exotic to the Western observer. To non-Ethiopians in Jerusalem, the Ethiopian procession and ritual on the eve of the Feast of the Resurrection are especially popular. Estelle Blyth, in her book *When We Lived in Jerusalem,* describes this strange but meaningful ceremony, which she calls "Hunting the Devil." Her description, too, is not free from misconceptions. She writes:

> [The ritual] takes place in their church outside the [Old] City, which is circular in form, a large sanctuary in the centre absorbing nearly all the space. One priest takes the part of the Evil One, and is stationed inside the church, the doors of which are locked by him. The Abbot and his clergy, choir, and acolytes, all full-robed, walk in procession to the doors of the church, upon which the Abbot beats with his staff, crying aloud, "Lift up your heads, O ye gates, and be ye lift up, ye everlasting doors, and the King of Glory shall come in!" (Ps. 24:7). The priest from within calls back in mocking tones, "Who is the King of Glory?" The Abbot and choir chant in reply, "It is the Lord of Hosts, He is the King of Glory!" This is repeated thrice; then the priest inside unlocks the doors and the procession surges into the church and gives chase to him. When he has been caught and chastised, the service is continued in the church . . . .

They are a strange people, the Abyssinians; they are proud and fanatical in their beliefs, and are probably the oldest Christian nation in the world, their conversion having taken place in the fourth century A.D., and they have never changed their faith. They allow polygamy, but not the eating of swine's flesh; Pilate is one of their saints because he said, "I am innocent of the Blood of this Just Man." Their artists portray all their saints as black and all their devils as white, which, when you come to think of it, is entirely reasonable. Their ecclesiastical robes are old and curious; they wear high crowns of velvet overlaid with gold and silver; they use the ancient Egyptian sistra in their services; and their midnight procession upon the roof of the Church of the Holy Sepulchre at Easter takes place under large velvet umbrellas.[36]

Actually, the ritual represents a search for the body of Jesus; and the hymns which follow celebrate the Resurrection with joy. This exotic ritual is a reaffirmation of their faith in the central aspect of the Christian theology.

It should also be noted that Estelle Blyth erred in her statement that the Ethiopians represent their saints as black. Actually, their convention is to paint saints white and devils black. The Ethiopians believe that the people of Africa were originally white, but they slowly adapted to their environment. Moreover, the Ethiopians are not entirely a black people. There is a considerable admixture of whites in their racial make-up. According to a prevailing tradition, the Ethiopian royal family descended from King Solomon and the Queen of Sheba. King Solomon was obviously not black.

FIVE

The Moslems and
Their Holy Places

The Exquisite Moslem Shrine
on the Temple Mount

The Temple Mount was a holy place even in the days of Abraham. Four thousand years ago on this hill Abraham built an altar for the intended sacrifice of his son Isaac. Over the sacred rock on this holy mount were erected the Temples of Solomon, Zerubabel, and Herod.[1] On this spot the Romans built their pagan temple, and the Moslems built the Dome of the Rock. During the Crusaders' Kingdom of Jerusalem, the Knights Templars worshiped in the Dome of the Rock, which they had converted into a church.

The Talmud says that "he who has not seen the Temple [of Herod] has not seen beauty in his life." In a similar vein does Estelle Blyth quote M. Edouard Naville as saying that "in all his travels he had seen only two utterly perfect buildings, the Taj Mahal and the Mosque of Omar (Dome of the Rock), and he knew not which to place first."[2]

When the Caliph Omar conquered Jerusalem in 638, he asked to be shown the place where Solomon's Temple stood. The Christians hesitated because they had used that place as a garbage dump. That was their way of showing contempt for the Jews. When Omar was finally shown the Jewish holy place, he cleaned it and restored it to its normal state. Now there is a magnificent structure on that spot, generally called the Mosque of Omar.

But this world-famous shrine neither is a mosque nor does it have any connection with the Caliph Omar. Knowledgeable people call it the Dome of the Rock. It is not a mosque, because a mosque is a house of public prayer, and public prayer is never conducted in this building. Nor did the Caliph Omar build it. He did erect a small mosque on the Temple Mount, but that mosque was located farther south where the El Aksa Mosque now stands.

This marvelous structure was erected in 691 by the Caliph Abd el-Malik. According to some scholars, his motivation was to divert the Moslem pilgrims from going to Mecca, because the people of Mecca and Medinah had rebelled against him. Most scholars, however, are inclined to believe that the Caliph's motivation was to establish the superiority of Islam over Christianity by building a shrine in Jerusalem more glorious than any of the Christian churches. The Christian shrine which was built over the Holy Sepulchre by Constantine consisted of two structures—the Anastasis, which was a round structure over the Tomb of Jesus, and the Martyrium, a cathedral or house of worship. The Moslem counterparts were the Dome of the Rock and the El Aska Mosque. The Dome of the Rock, although it is octagonal, has the same dimensions as the circular church, the Anastasis, and it enshrines the holy rock. The El Aska Mosque corresponds to the Martyrium and it is the Moslem house of prayer.[3]

Be that as it may, the Caliph Abd el-Malik devoted a sum equal to seven years of the total revenue of Egypt to the building of this shrine. According to an inscription which runs around the outer colonnade within the dome, it took seven years to complete the structure. Dean Stanley of Westminster visited the Holy City as a pilgrim in 1853. In his itinerary, *Sinai and Palestine,* he writes:

> From whatever point that graceful dome with its beautiful precinct emerges to view, it at once dignifies the whole city. And when from Olivet, or from the Governor's house, or from the north-east wall, you see the platform on which it stands, it is a scene hardly to be surpassed. A dome graceful as that of St. Peter's, though of course on a far smaller scale, rising from an elaborately finished circular edifice—this edifice raised on a square marble platform rising on the highest ridge of a green slope, which descends from it north, south and east to the walls surrounding the whole enclosure—platform and enclosure diversified by lesser domes and fountains, by cypresses, and olives, and planes, and palms—the whole as secluded and quiet as the interior of some college or cathedral garden, only enlivened by the white figures of veiled women stealing like ghosts up and down the green slope, or by the turbaned heads bowed low in the various niches for prayer—

The Dome of the Rock. (Courtesy of Central Zionist Archives, Jerusalem.)

this is the Mosque of Omar: the Haram es-Sherif, "the noble sanctuary," the second most sacred spot in the Mahometan world, — that is the next after Mecca; the second most beautiful mosque, — that is the next after Cordova.[4]

A visitor entering the Dome of the Rock is blinded by the sudden change from the dazzling sunlight outside the shrine to the subdued light within. But no sooner is the visitor's vision adjusted than he or she is overwhelmed by the magnificence of the interior. The splendid columns of granite and porphyry with their gilded capitals, the graceful mosaics, and the exquisite geometric designs and decorative inscriptions in gold are breathtaking. The visitor marvels at the slabs of veined marble, which are so placed edge to edge as to form lovely patterns. Especially intriguing are the four huge monoliths of native limestone which are closest to the rough stone outcropping in the center. But most impressive are the lights and shadows that are cast by the unique windows. These windows are not, as many think, of stained glass. They are mosaics, consisting of tiny pieces of colored glass, each piece separately framed, fitted together, and arranged skillfully so that their varied colors harmonize and produce the desired light. Outside these windows there are perforated screens which tone down the colored light so that the total effect is truly enchanting. The noted archaeologist, Charles W. Wilson, in his book *Jerusalem, the Holy City,* describes these marvelous windows:

> The windows of the external wall and clerestory are remarkable for the beauty of their tracery, no less than for the brilliancy of their colouring and for the admirable way in which the different colours are blended, producing perfect harmony in the whole. To be seen to advantage they should have the full blaze of a Syrian sun streaming through them. One window near the western door is of special beauty. The light is admitted through three mediums. First, there is on the outside a thick perforated framework of cement covered with faience; this allows the light to pass to a second window of stone with white glass, and thence to the inner window, which gives the design and colouring. In this inner window the small pieces of coloured glass are inserted obliquely, and not vertically, so as to overhang and meet the eye of the spectator at right angles. Nothing can equal the exquisite taste with which the pieces of glass are arranged or the charming brightness of the colouring; and the combined effect is certainly not surpassed by that of any windows in Europe. Some of the windows bear the name of Suleiman, and the date 935 (1528 A.D.), the same period to which the finest specimens of the porcelain tiles are assigned.[5]

The eight walls of the structure are topped by the great dome, which is ninety-six feet from the floor and measures seventy-five feet in diameter. The center of the shrine is occupied by the most sacred object on the Temple Mount, the holy rock for which the beautiful building and the dome were erected.

Visitors in Jerusalem, be they pilgrims or tourists, should visit this magnificent shrine repeatedly, for no one can possibly assimilate the charm and beauty of this noble sanctuary in one visit.

The Forgery in the Dome of the Rock

The perfect crime hardly ever comes off. The criminal usually overlooks a detail which gives him away. This is what happened with a forgery in the Dome of the Rock. In this shrine on the Temple Mount there is an exquisite inscription written in gold letters. It reads:

In the name of God, the Merciful, the Compassionate! The servant of God, Abdallah, the Imam el Mamun, Commander of the Faithful, built this dome in the year 72 (A.D. 691). May God accept it at his hands, and be content with him. Amen! There is no god but God alone; He hath no partner. Say He is the one God, the Eternal; He neither begetteth nor is begotten, and there is no one like Him. Mohammed is the Apostle of God; pray God for him. There is no god but God alone; to Him be praise, who taketh not unto Himself a son, and to whom none can be a partner in His kingdom, and whose patron no lower creature can be; magnify ye Him. Oh! Ye who have received the Scriptures, exceed not the bounds in your religion, and speak not aught but truth concerning God. God is but One. There is no god but He, the Mighty, the Wise.[6]

For centuries people credited the Caliph el-Mamun with the erection of this remarkable shrine until it was noted that there was a discrepancy between the time of the Caliph el-Mamun's reign and the date of the inscription. The Caliph Abdullah el-Mamun ruled from 813 to 833, about a century and a half after the date 691 which is recorded in the inscription. A little scholarly detective work unraveled the mystery. It was simply a case of a clever forgery in which one name was erased and another cleverly substituted. The forger, however, neglected to change the date which gives the forgery away.

The Dome of the Rock was built by the Caliph Abd el-Malik, who reigned in 691. About a century and a half later, the Caliph Abdullah el-Mamun repaired the building. It was then that the forgery was committed. Today people smile at the forger's slip-up, but they nonetheless admire the exquisite decorative script of both the original artist and of the forger.

The Marvelous Rock Within the Dome

Near the center of the Temple Mount there is a stone outcropping over which was erected the famous Dome of the Rock. For the Moslems this rock is very holy. Its holiness is exceeded only by the Black Rock in Mecca. For the Jews it is the holiest spot on earth. In ancient times Solomon's Temple stood on this spot, and it is claimed that the altar of burnt offerings stood on this rock.[7]

The history of the rock goes back to the days of Abraham, four thousand years ago, when the Patriarch, in obedience to God's bidding, took his son Isaac to Mount Moriah to be offered up as a sacrifice. Moslem tradition preserves a variant of that biblical story. According to them, it was not Isaac but Ishmael, the ancestor of the Arabs, who was the intended victim, and it was not to Mount Moriah where the sacred Rock of Jerusalem is located, but to the Black Rock of Mecca that Abraham took his son. But the rock on Mount Moriah is also very holy in Islam

The holy rock within the Dome of the Rock.

because it was from that rock that Mohammed ascended to heaven. According to Moslem tradition, a single prayer in this holy place is better than a thousand prayers elsewhere.

Herbert Rix, who visited Jerusalem in 1906, writes about the strange ecstasy that overpowered him when he visited the Dome of the Rock. It was not the exquisite beauty of the Moslem shrine that touched his heart, but the crude, rough limestone outcropping that roused his imagination. He writes half-apologetically:

> To some it seems childish and irrational to feel interest in that which is associated with historical events by mere locality or physical contact: it seems akin to the passion of the Oriental for sacred trees and sacred hills and the sacred ground which the body of a saint has touched. Yet I confess that it was with deep emotion that I approached this venerable rock. By no other relic in this holy city had I been impressed and thrilled as I was by this one. When I came to myself and found my mouth parched with the absorbing interest of the moment, I began to get an inkling of what the Prophet [Mohammed] meant by his "night-journey to heaven" when he knelt upon this rock.

> This fascination was due to my firm conviction (and subsequent study has not shaken it) that this was the actual spot upon which stood the altar of burnt-offering in the Temple of Solomon, in the Temple of Zerubabel, and in the Temple of Herod.[8]

The rock is a mass of limestone, fifty-seven feet long and forty-three feet wide, jutting up above the shrine's marble floor. It resembles a rocky reef rising above the surface of a calm sea; it projects six and a half feet above the pavement.

At the top of the rock there is a bore which leads into a cave beneath. It is believed that the hole was the channel that led to the cesspool beneath the altar. A canal from the cave permitted the blood of the sacrifices and the water of the priestly ablutions to drain off into the Kidron Valley.

The Rock's height was decreased by the Crusaders, who leveled it in order to erect upon it a high altar for the services in their *Templum Domini*. Yet the Rock's sanctity was not diminished. Indeed, the Crusaders' chisel marks became, in the Moslem tradition, the finger grooves left by the angel Gabriel, who held on to the rock and prevented it from following Mohammed to heaven.

There is also a depression in the southwestern corner of the rock, which the Moslems say is Mohammed's footprint—for the Prophet rose to heaven from this very spot. And a gilt urn hangs directly above this footprint. The urn is said to contain two hairs from Mohammed's beard.

Among the rock's additional distinctions is the Jewish tradition that it is the center of the world and that God created Adam from the dust of this rock. In short, the rock is a very holy place. For the Jews it is the holiest of all holy places because of its association with their Holy Temple. For the Moslems it is second in holiness only to the black rock in Mecca. For the Christians it is holy because of its association with Jesus, who worshiped and taught in the Temple.

One would expect a rough rock to be an eyesore and a disfigurement to any carefully designed structure erected over it. Yet we read in Mrs. A. Goodrich-Freer's *Inner Jerusalem* a moving description of the unbelievable harmony between the rock and the incomparably beautiful structure above it. The rock fits into its magnificent surroundings as a well-cut diamond fits into a well-fashioned gold ring. Mrs. Goodrich-Freer writes:

> Perhaps the strongest impression which one carries away is not that of the marvelous, the perhaps unrivaled, richness and harmony of colouring, the dignified repose of form—a repose so absorbing in its grace of unity that one is deprived of the power of attention to detail—but rather a sense of the extraordinary contrast between the perfection of the work of art and the simplicity of the work of nature; the glory of light and colour, of rich material, the pride of invention, the triumph of painter and craftsman, the liberality of the rich, the praise of the mighty dead, mellowed by centuries of waiting, sanctified by generations of worshipers, baptized by the blood of thousands, expressive of the hopes, aspirations, prayers of millions of our fellow-creatures, and all for what?—a piece of bare brown rock, rudely cropping out of the ground, sacred alike to Moslem, Jew and Christian, to the readers of the Koran, of the Old Testament and of the New. Description here would be even more futile than elsewhere; for magnificent and impressive as is the Dome of the Rock even from the point of view of art, it is to this shock of contrast that one is largely indebted for the emotion it cannot fail to inspire in any soul sensitive to beauty, alive with imagination, responsive to the suggestion of memory.

> Here is no treasure encased in shrine of marble like the Holy Sepulchre, hung with silken tapestry like the Cave at Bethlehem, making difficult appeal to faith like the footstep on the Mount of Ascension, enclosed in gold and precious stones like a dozen relics at a dozen altars in the churches of the Holy City, but the bare bosom of our mother earth, prototype of all that is most sacred, all which most cries aloud for reverence in the common things of daily life.[9]

The Sacred Cave Under the Holy Rock

Under the sacred outcropping in the Dome of the Rock there is a cavern which is also a very holy place for the Moslems. According to the Moslem tradition, some of the greatest prophets have prayed in this cavern. Among them were Abraham, King David, King Solomon, Elijah, and Mohammed himself. In the center of the floor there is a slab which the Arab guides usually strike, calling the visitors' attention to the peculiar ring or echo. Evidently there is a hollow, which the Arabs call a *bir,* that is, a well or a shaft. The guides explain that this is the *Bir Aruakh,* the Well of Souls. The guides also assure the visitors that the well leads to purgatory. To get out of that place of suffering, one must get through this narrow hole. Obviously, one cannot negotiate this passage without assistance. So Mohammed stands near that hole and gets hold of the poor wretch's hair and pulls him out. That is why it used to be the custom for Moslems when shaving their heads to leave a lock of hair at the top of their scalp. Otherwise how could the Prophet lift the poor fellows out of the house of affliction?

William Prime visited this holy cave under the sacred rock and recorded his guide's explanation of the miraculous nature of the cave's roof, which is a natural vault:

> This is a curious chamber underneath the great rock itself, surrounded and inclosed by stone walls, reaching from the floor to the under side of the rock. Let it be distinctly marked, Sheik Mohammed Dunnuf assured me solemnly, again and again, that the rock hangs in the air seven feet above the ground, of its own power or the power of God, and is not supported by this wall, even to the amount of a half ounce. The wall is built up only to prevent the rock falling, in case the power should for any cause be withdrawn, and, as some unlucky Moslem might be underneath at that moment, the result would be disastrous if the wall were not there. . . .

> [When Mohammed ascended to heaven] the rock followed him, lifting itself into the air; but he commanded it to pause, and it paused just there, and there hangs in the air; and he is a vile skeptic who believes that those stone walls built under it have any thing to do to keep it there, and may the curse of God and the Prophet be on him if he persists in his infidelity.[10]

The holy cave is never visited by Moslem women. This is not because of discrimination against the feminine sex. It is purely a preventive measure to safeguard the well-being of everyone, including the women. In former days both men and women would enter the holy cavern and pray as befits the faithful. But once a woman entered for prayer and during her visit prattled all the gossip she knew and she knew all the gossip worth knowing. Since there is in the sacred cave an opening to the netherworld, all the gossip was passed on to the dwellers below. To make sure that it never happens again, Moslem women have been barred from entering the holy cave.

The minaret of Omar, next to the Church of the Holy Sepulchre.

The Authentic Mosque of Omar

Near the Church of the Holy Sepulchre there is a mosque which the Arabs call El Omariveh, the place of Omar. Moslem tradition relates that the Caliph Omar visited the Church of the Holy Sepulchre immediately after capturing Jerusalem. While he was inspecting the Christian holy places he heard the Muezzin's call to prayer. Instead of performing the ritual on the spot, as Moslems are required to do, Omar walked out of the Church and there performed the prescribed rites. When asked why he did not pray on the spot where he heard the Muezzin's call, he replied that had he done so, his followers would have seized the Church and turned it into a mosque. To prevent this from happening, he left the Church and prayed outside. The mosque south of the Church of the Holy Sepulchre was erected on the spot where Omar prayed. This mosque is the official memorial to Omar, and not the Dome of the Rock, which is popularly called the Mosque of Omar.

> The minaret [of the mosque], writes Rev. J. E. Hanauer, was built in 1465–6. . . . Christians were greatly annoyed because it overtopped the Church of the Sepulchre, and they offered a great sum of money to the builder, Sheikh Barhan ed din bin Ghanem, to induce him to abandon his design. He, however, refused, and then, as Moslems say, Mohammed appeared in a dream to a man whom he directed to salute Ibn Ghanem in his name, and assure him of his intercession at the Day of Judgment as a reward for his having built this minaret above the heads of the infidels.[11]

Herman Melville, in his lengthy poem *Clarel,* writes concerning the Caliph Omar's magnanimous deed:

> The story's known: how Omar there . . .
> Clad in his clouts of camel's hair,
> And with the Patriarch robed and fine
> Walking beneath the dome divine,
> When came the Islam hour for prayer
> Declined to use the carpet good
> Spread for him in the church, but stood
> Without, even yonder where is set
> The monumental minaret.[12]

The Columns of Ordeal in the El Aksa Mosque

After visiting the Dome of the Rock, the visitor usually makes his way to the El Aksa Mosque, wherein he is shown on the right side of the pulpit

The El Aksa Mosque on the Temple Mount. (Courtesy of Zionist Archives and Photo Service of the Jewish Agency, Jerusalem.)

Interior of the El Aksa Mosque. (Courtesy of Central Zionist Archives, Jerusalem.)

two columns close to each other. They are so near one another that an ordinary person can get through them with difficulty. Moslems say that only persons who can squeeze through these columns are admitted to paradise. In the year 1881, a rather stout Arab decided to enter paradise despite his corpulence, and he died in the process. People wondered whether this stout Moslem had gained his reward. He surely tried hard. Ever since that mishap the passage between the columns has been blocked and no Moslem is able to test his chance of obtaining eternal bliss.

Leslie Farmer tells of guiding a group of soldiers on the Temple Mount:

> The men with me were very interested in two pillars, quite close together, but worn away by generations of men who had squeezed between them. The theory is, I explained, that nobody can enter heaven who cannot pass between those pillars. Moslems allow that a rich man can enter, provided that he is not also a fat man. Because, however, in 1881 a stout gentleman died between the pillars as he strove frantically to pass between them, a bar was placed there to prevent further tragedies. That has now been removed, and visitors can once more try the "columns of ordeal." One of the men insisted upon stepping through, which he did easily, only to find the immam standing at the other side smilingly holding out his hand for *baksheesh*. [13]

Not only do fat men have no prospect of sharing in the heavenly bliss, but their lot in this world, too, is rather bleak. Albert Rhodes, an American consul in Jerusalem, does not mention the other-worldly significance of these columns. His account deals with the more immediate impact of the ordeal on fat men and women. Modern weight-watchers will surely be delighted with Rhodes's account:

> There are two marble pillars in the mosque which afford considerable amusement to the Frank [Western] travellers. They stand just far enough apart to allow an ordinary-sized person to squeeze through sideways. The tradition is, that all who can pass through in this way are to be blessed with happy marriages, and those who cannot, to unhappy ones. Of course, all who are fat are doomed to matrimonial misery.
>
> I remarked to the sheikh, who was inclined to portliness, that he must be very unfortunate in his conjugal relations.
>
> "Oh," said he, "*inshallah* [God willing]. I took care to get married before I became fat."
>
> "Were your wives also able to pass the ordeal of the pillars?"
>
> "*Inshallah,* yes. One of them with much difficulty; but by the blessing of the Prophet, and much fasting, she managed finally to squeeze through. Thus I

am the husband of two turtle-doves, and the father of sons who are like unto young lions."

"Do all the Frank ladies who visit the mosque try the pillar-test?"

"They all laugh at it very much, yet they all try it; and although the fat ones pretend to laugh so heartily, I think they often seriously regret they cannot manage it."

I easily slipped through the columns. "*Taib!*" ejaculated the sheikh. I was assured of matrimonial happiness.

"I hope she may be as beautiful as she will be happy," observed the sheikh.

"*Taib!*" said I, as a sort of *inshallah.*[14]

The longing to learn their fate after death is not limited to the Moslems. People of all faiths seek and often find mystic signs which inform them of their future in the afterworld. It is not surprising to find in Jerusalem a Christian tradition whereby one can ascertain his or her future in the hereafter. An eighteenth-century traveler reported what he called "a strange superstition," that prevailed among the Greek Orthodox and the Armenians:

> On a stone lying on the rock, in which the holy sepulchre is hewn, are four small holes, placed in the form of a cross, said to be impressions made by St. George's fingers. . . .

> The Greeks and Armenians are possessed of a strange superstition, with regard to these holes, and even try their spiritual state by them, which is done in the following manner: They kiss the stone very devoutly, shut their eyes and endeavour to put their four fingers into them. If by accident they succeed, they are firmly persuaded that they have certainly acquired a seat in heaven.[15]

The Mosque That Honors Mohammed's Steed

At the southern end of the Western (Wailing) Wall there is a ramp leading to the Temple Mount. The gate is named in Arabic *Bab el-Magharibeh.* Ascending to that gate and entering the Temple area, one is near a winding staircase which is located a little south of the gate. This staircase leads down to a subterranean chamber which is called the Mosque of el Borak. This mosque is a very holy place, because Mohammed's miraculous steed, El Borak, was quartered in it. To prove the great sanctity of the place, the visitor is shown the iron ring to which the steed was tethered. El Borak, it should be noted, was not an ordinary creature. El Borak had a human head and a pair of wings. On this miraculous steed Mohammed made his journey from Mecca to Jerusalem in one night.

Since the Mosque of El Borak adjoins the inside of the Western (Wailing) Wall, Arabs have laid claim to the whole Western Wall of the Temple Mount. This wall is thus holy for the Moslems and for the Jews — for the Jews on its external facade and for the Moslems on its internal. This double sanctity played a tragic role in the riots of the 1920s and 1930s. Physical combat and bloodshed were the earmarks of those unfortunate disturbances. While the Jews were satisfied with the right to worship near the external side of the wall, the Arabs claimed the whole wall and would not tolerate Jewish worship on the outer side of the holy place. Historians, however, claim that the real motives of these holy battles were political. They were part of the Arab-Israel war, which is still taking its toll in human blood.

Moslems at Prayer

One of the memorable experiences of a Western visitor in Jerusalem is the sight of an Arab at prayer. The ritual of Moslem worship is very different in content and expression from that of the Jewish or Christian tradition. It

A Moslem at prayer.

*A Moslem making his ablutions before entering the Dome of the Rock (1967).
(Courtesy of Israel Government Press Office.)*

contains few words and no hymns, but many genuflections and prostra-
tions. But the Moslem's sincerity at worship is not inferior to that of the
Jew or Christian. Horatius Bonar, a Christian minister, described a
Moslem at prayer:

> While standing here I noticed a Mohammendan going through his prayers.
> . . . Amid all the noise and confusion, the man commenced his devotions,

just as if no one were near. Lifting up his open hands on each side of his head, he cries out, *Alah-hu-Akbar,* "God is great." He then folds his hands in front of his body, muttering sentences from the Koran. Then he stoops forward, putting his hands on his knees, as if making a low bow, and cries again, "God is great." Then he raises himself, and, standing bolt upright, utters the same cry. Then, still muttering verses from the Koran, he drops down upon his knees, making his nose to touch the ground, with his open palms on the ground on each side of his head. In a minute or two he raises his head and body, still muttering his Arabic; then bringing himself into a sitting or squatting posture, with his body resting on his heels, and his hands on his knees, he concludes the first *Rekah* of devotion. . . . I was told that these gestures and postures, required by the prophet for prayer, are very difficult to learn, being much more minute and intricate than they appear. The performance of these is a part of the education of children. And no one can excel a Mohammedan at these devotional mechanics.[16]

Moslems hear the Muezzin's call for prayer five times a day and respond where they happen to hear it, be it indoors or outdoors. They pray at the mosque only on Fridays, and the worship at the mosque is essentially the same as private prayer, except that on Friday a sermon is preached by the Imam. This prolongs the service considerably.

The Moslem service at the mosque has always been decorous. Even in the Middle Ages when church and synagogue services were lacking in decorum, the Moslem worship was orderly. With no ushers to direct them to their proper places, the Moslems line up quietly in straight rows, facing a niche in the wall that indicates the direction of prayer, toward Mecca, and they participate in the rituals without ever speaking to the people next to them. Among the reasons for this perfect quiet at services, Moslems tell a tale worth repeating. It is a legend confirmed by a slab on the outside of the southern wall of the Dome of the Rock. The story of this slab is widely known. It goes back to the days of King Solomon, the wisest of all mortals. Solomon was once praying near the holy rock. Close by, two magpies were making a fearful din with their incessant chattering. Solomon—who spoke the language of all animals—told them that they were disturbing his prayers and asked them to keep quiet. But the magpies kept chattering. Solomon turned them into stone, and the stone was incorporated in the Dome of the Rock. To this day, one can see the two magpies in the above-mentioned slab drinking from a vase between them. They no longer disturb the faithful at prayer.

In the Middle Ages, when Christian and Jewish worship was marked by disorder, many a Christian and Jew envied the Moslems' reverent behavior in the mosque. Felix Fabri, a fifteenth-century Dominican monk, was particularly impressed by this decorous attitude of the Moslems. He writes in his *Book of Wanderings:*

> O human brother, would that thou couldst see at Jerusalem how devoutly the worshipers enter therein [in the mosque], how gravely they bear themselves in praying, how modestly the women show themselves there, with their faces always veiled, and how the men pray in silence apart from them! Couldst thou see this, thou wouldst be deeply shocked and grievously wroth with the neglect and irreverence shown by the faithful in our own churches. [17]

Similarly did the thirteenth-century Jewish scholar, Rabbi Abraham ben Maimon, son of the famous Moses Maimonides, attempt to emulate the Moslems by introducing in the synagogue not only decorum but also some of the expressive gestures which he admired in the Moslem worship. He lost out. Tradition is stronger than logic.

Decorum is now an essential trait of Occidental worship, but Western visitors in Jerusalem are still intrigued by the intricate Moslem rituals at prayer.

Moslem Festivals and Holy Days

Western tourists and pilgrims in Jerusalem are perplexed by the seeming mystery of the Moslem festivals and holy days. They read in the local press about the Ramadan, the Haj, the *Id al-Fitr,* or the *Id Al-Adha.* These esoteric words mystify the uninitiated. Most tourists make peace with their ignorance and continue on their planned schedules. Some visitors, however, seek to penetrate the mystery of the Moslem feasts and fasts. They want to know the meaning of the strange observances of the Moslem community.

It happens that unveiling these mysteries is an easy task, because the Moslem religious feasts and fasts are relatively simple both in terms of their theological foundations and in the manner of their observance. The Moslems have only two important festivals—the *Id al-Fitr* (Feast of the Breaking of the Fast), which comes at the end of the Ramadan Fast, and the *Id al-Adha* (Feast of the Sacrifice), which comes at the end of the Haj or the annual pilgrimage season when Moslems visit Mecca—a requirement they must fulfill at least once during their lifetime. To be sure, there are many local holidays in the widespread lands of Islam, and there are many feasts in honor of local saints. But these are secondary to the two central Islamic holidays observed by all Moslems.

The importance of the *Id al-Fitr* and the *Id al-Adha* derives from their connection with two of the "Five Pillars of Islam," which constitute the five basic duties of a Moslem. The Five Pillars are:

1. Faith in the one God and in His Prophet Mohammed.
2. Five daily prayers to be performed when the Muezzin's call to worship is heard.
3. Giving alms to the poor.
4. Fasting during the month of Ramadan, which commemorates the descent of the Koran from heaven.
5. Making at least one pilgrimage to Mecca during one's lifetime.

As noted above, the *Id al-Fitr* follows the month-long fast of the Ramadan during which Moslems do not eat, drink, or smoke daily from sunrise to sunset. When the fast of the Ramadan is finished, the Moslem is in a happy mood and celebrates the festival of the *Id al-Fitr* for three or four days.

The *Id al-Adha* follows the pilgrimage season. This feast, too, lasts three or four days, and it commemorates the near sacrifice of Abraham's son. According to the biblical account (Gen. 22), Abraham took his son Isaac to Mount Moriah for the intended offering. According to the Koran, Ishmael was the intended victim and Mecca was the designated place of the sacrifice. In commemoration of that event, there is the Haj to Mecca, which reenacts Abraham's journey, and the *Id al-Adha* (the Feast of the Sacrifice) when every Moslem participates in a family sacrifice. A lamb, sheep, or camel is slaughtered; part of the victim is given to the poor; and the rest is consumed by the family.

The two festivals are not mentioned in the Koran. They are merely appendages to the Ramadan and the Haj. And the nature of their observance is simple. In addition to the family feast, Moslems participate in a public service at which they hear a sermon by the Imam. The prayers on these festivals do not differ basically from the daily prayers, except that they are held in the open and the sermon is delivered after the prayers. During these festivals the giving of charity is especially meritorious. Many beggars line up along the path to the mosque, and Moslems make sure to distribute alms to as many of the poor as they can.

There is no obligation to rest from work on these festivals. A Moslem is required to suspend work only during the time of the public service. However, most Moslems do refrain from working during these festivals. They dress in their best garments and partake in the festive meals. Some also visit the graves of their relatives and make pilgrimages to the tombs of saints.

The Month-Long Fast of the Ramadan

To observe a fast of no eating, no drinking, and no smoking for a whole day is debilitating and trying. Moslems, however, fast for thirty consecutive days. This annual month-long fast, called the Ramadan, is one curious event a visitor may encounter in Jerusalem.

When Mohammed founded his new religion, he instituted a twenty-four-hour fast on the tenth day of the first month. This corresponded to the Jewish fast of the Day of Atonement [*Yom Kippur*], which falls on the tenth day of the first month of the Hebrew calendar. When Mohammed failed to win over the Jewish tribes of the Arabian Peninsula, he turned against the Jews. Among his anti-Jewish enactments was the cancellation of that fast day. In its place he established the month-long fast of the Ramadan.

The reader need not feel too sorry for the poor Moslems who are obliged to fast a whole month. To begin with, the daily fast is only from sunrise to sunset. The Moslems rise early and eat and drink enough to last them a full day. At sunset, when the ceremonial cannon is fired, they partake of lavish meals which they enjoy all the more because of the day's abstention from food, drink, and smoking. Only when the Ramadan falls during the summer months does the fast become an ordeal. The days are long and hot, and abstention from drink becomes a gnawing torment.

The effect of the fast on the Moslems is described by the archaeologist Charles Warren, who observed its impact on Arabs he employed during his archaeological researches in Jerusalem:

> Ramadan commenced this year on the 26th December, when for a whole moon the Moslems neither eat, drink, nor smoke between daylight and darkness; this fast retrogrades close upon eleven days each year, and in the present year, 1876, it commenced on 20th September. It was fortunate for our work that it then took place at the time of year when the days are shortest, for when it occurs during the summer time the unhappy victims become so exhausted that they are unable to work: it is really a cruel sight to see the children, even those at the breast, kept from any nourishment during the weary hours of the day. This long fast is one of the many symptoms that the Moslem religion belongs to the tropical zone, where the days and nights are nearly the same length. It is possible to live without food during days of twelve or fifteen hours, but how is it possible to live during Ramadan in summer, say in the latitude of Aberdeen, where during the middle of summer there is practically no night? Ramadan in such a latitude would be out of the question; for the rule by which the Moslem knows when he may eat, is when it becomes so dark that he cannot distinguish a black thread

from a white one; and he must fast again when they are distinguishable. At Midsummer in Aberdeen he might distinguish the white thread from the black one all the night through and never find his eating hour come round.

The richer Moslems, during this month, sleep all day and carouse by night, and thus get rid of much of its weariness, but they heartily dread it, and try to shirk it; however, the spies are too numerous, and the man who breaks his fast gets into great trouble.

Several stories I heard regarding the way in which a neglect of this rule is punished; it is looked upon as an offence against the law of the land. Many men told me that they would break it if they dared, but they were afraid of spies even in their own household. [18]

Today the Ramadan is no longer universally observed. Some Arabs surreptitiously break the fast. Still there are many Moslems who observe the fast as punctiliously as in former days. And the Jordanian law forbidding Moslems to eat, drink, or smoke during the Ramadan fast is still in force in the areas occupied by Israel during the Six-Day War. Thus it was reported in *The Jerusalem Post* of July 22, 1980, that the Military Government arrested seven Arabs in Ramallah for violating the Ramadan fast and imposed a fine of ten Jordanian dinars ($25) on each offender. Even so, the universal gloom is no longer as evident, and business in the bazaar is "as usual." Some of the merchants are ill-humored and in a state of fatigue. But visitors will hardly notice it. They get all the smiles due to a customer.

At the end of the Ramadan there are three days of festive celebration, the *Id el-Fitr*, the "festival of the breaking of the fast." It is celebrated with great rejoicing. No Moslem works during these days. In Israel, "the holiday is causing near paralysis at many enterprises." Since many Arabs are employed in the building trades, construction sites are at a standstill. Hotels have difficulties, because many Arabs are employed as waiters and kitchen help. When the Ramadan fast and the *Id el-Fitr* festivities are over, life in Jerusalem returns to its normal pace, and everyone is the happier for it.

The Rise and Fall of the Nebi Moussa Festival

There was a time when the Arabs of Jerusalem celebrated an annual festival which they called the Festival of *Nebi Moussa* (the Prophet Moses). The central feature of this observance was a pilgrimage to the tomb of the prophet Moses. It was a grand procession which started in Jerusalem and culminated at the "tomb of Moses." The Arabs located this tomb in the wilderness southwest of Jericho. According to the Bible, Moses "was buried in the valley in the land of Moab over against Beth-Peor; and no man knoweth of his sepulchre unto this day" (Deut. 34:6). But the promoters of this curious festival found a grave, not far from Jericho, and designated it as the burial place of the prophet Moses.[19] The political purpose of the mass pilgrimage was to attract Moslem crowds to Jerusalem during the Greek Easter season to offset the crowds of Christians who gathered annually in Jerusalem for the Holy Week. The memory of the Crusaders still worried the Moslems. They feared lest the Christians stage a revolt during one of the Easter celebrations and take possession of Jerusalem. The Moslem crowds gathering in Jerusalem for the *Nebi Moussa* pilgrimage would intimidate the Christians and discourage them from attempting a coup. This accounts for the strange date of the festival which was scheduled according to the Christian calendar so that it always coincided with the Greek Easter celebrations.

The Moslem pilgrims would arrive in Jerusalem with their distinctive flags and bands of music, mainly drums and cymbals. The flag bearers, the music bands, and the pilgrims gathered in the Haram (Temple Mount), and after prayers in the El Aksa Mosque, the notables, including the pasha, joined in the procession.

The holy flag, followed by the pasha and the Grand Mufti of Jerusalem, headed the procession. The pilgrims with their bands followed in accordance with established traditional order. Crowds of spectators lined the road, and Turkish soldiers kept the road open. At the Lions (St. Stephen's) Gate a cannon was fired as a salute to the pilgrims, and the women spectators responded with a loud ululation. At Bethany, the mayor of Jerusalem received the Mufti and the other notables in the procession. Coffee was served, the Mufti offered a prayer, and a salute of seven cannon shots was fired. The procession now continued on its way to the grave of the Prophet Moses. The wealthy rode in carriages; others rode on donkeys, mules, or camels; the poor walked. From the time of the pilgrims' arrival in Jerusalem up to the Bethany ceremonial send-off, dervishes and entertainers performed for the amusement or edification of the spectators. Some dervishes twirled round and round in religious frenzy and performed religious dances and "miracles." Snake charmers performed their rituals while others ate live coals. The Reverend J. A. Wylie, a

Scottish pilgrim in 1883, gave an eyewitness account of the festival in his book, *Over the Holy Land:*

All Jerusalem turned out to witness the departure of the pilgrims. The old Saracenic [Lions or St. Stephen's] gate poured out, for two or three hours on end, a continuous stream of human beings, till the vast slope running down the Kedron was covered with a dense mass of Turks, Arabs, Copts, Armenians, Russians, Greeks, and Franks; for in no city of the world are so many diverse nationalities to be seen at once as in Jerusalem at the time of Easter. A row of spectators looked down from the city wall, and in the valley beneath a vast circle of people wound round Mount Olivet, and waited on the Bethany road to see the hawadjees [pilgrims] as they passed. The affair, in sooth, was but a vast assemblage of ragamuffins, and yet perhaps it was the most striking and gorgeous spectacle of the sort of all we have chanced to see in many lands. No country but the East, and no city but Jerusalem, and Jerusalem at this season, could have exhibited such a gathering.

The effect it produced was owing entirely to the vast variety of brilliant colours and novel and striking costumes here brought under the eye. . . .

Two small brass cannon, mounted on a little hillock among the Mohammedan graves, just outside the St. Stephen's Gate, now began firing. Their tiny discharge rolled in feeble echoes across the Kedron valley, and died away on the Mount of Olives. A second and a third salute, and a ground swell shook the sea of turbans and kufiyehs around us, and the crowd put itself into an attitude of expectancy as deep and reverent as if the prophet himself had been approaching. . . .

At last the procession was seen issuing from the gate of St. Stephen. It was headed by a small body of Turkish infantry. It were hard to say what was the colour of their uniform. Originally it had been a dark blue, trimmed with red; but now, vexed with long wear and engrained with mud and dust, it had come to be of no colour in particular, unless it were, as we heard an English artist call it, the colour of dirt. They trotted away down the narrow path kept clear for the procession in the crowd. Next was heard the sound of sackbut, timbrel and flute. The instruments seemed afflicted with a hoarseness, for their strains were rough and sad. Then came a forest of flags of all colours; some green, showing a white crescent and a star sparkling in its bosom. . . . Other flags were red, or blue, or yellow, with the crescent emblazoned in gold, or the Moslem creed in Arabic letters. There followed a second body of infantry, each soldier marched as suited him, but it must be confessed that the path was rough. Dwarfish in figure, ill-clad, ill-drilled, had a Scottish Highlander seen these Ottoman warriors, he would, we suspect, have pronounced them "a set of *shaughlin bodies.*" There followed some dozen or so of officials, wearing, of course, their insignia of office. And now came the Pasha on a white Arab steed: he looked comparatively young; he had a pale and thoughtful face, and was simply dressed, forming a striking contrast to the gorgeous figures around him. He wore a red caftan, with a black silk tassel, and a blue-frock coat with red edgings. By his side walked, on the one hand, the Governor of the city, and on the other the Mufti of Jerusalem. The Mufti was a stout, heavy man, in green turban — it is the prophet's colour — and long blue robe, forming the most conspicuous figure in the procession.

The Pasha and his suite rode down the slope to where the pilgrims to the tomb of Moses, marshalled in line, with banners and flags, waited for him in the bottom of the Kedron valley. We do not doubt that the address of the pasha awakened a becoming enthusiasm, and gave the pilgrims a good start, though we were too far away to hear even an echo of it, and there is no newspaper in Jerusalem in which we could read it next morning. The pilgrims, moving forward, soon disappeared round the flank of Mount Olivet, and the crowd began to pour back again into the city. In an hour thereafter nothing was to be seen in the valley of Jehoshaphat but the white tombstones of the Moslem dead on the one side, and the yet greater array of Jewish graves on the other, with a few lepers sitting with their tin box at the turnings of the path, and here and there a shepherd stretched on the thin grass beside his little flock of goats.[20]

The shrine at the reputed *Nebi Moussa* grave is a rectangular building with about one hundred rooms. During the *Nebi Moussa* feast the pilgrims were housed and fed in this building. In the center of the inner court there is a cenotaph covered with a green cloth. Pilgrims who could not find accommodations within the building pitched tents on the surrounding

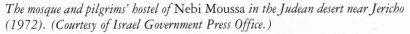

The mosque and pilgrims' hostel of Nebi Moussa *in the Judean desert near Jericho (1972). (Courtesy of Israel Government Press Office.)*

hills. The flags were placed in the mosque, and the pilgrims settled down for six days—from Friday to Thursday—during which they performed semireligious exercises and indulged themselves in feasting in honor of the Prophet Moses.

The return to Jerusalem lacked the spectacular enthusiasm of the start of the pilgrimage. Three of the flags—those of Moses, David, and Mohammed—were deposited in the Dome of the Rock. The local flags were taken back to their respective towns and villages and deposited in the local mosques.

The *Nebi Moussa* pilgrimage had all the earmarks of a national festival and an annual folk celebration. But it disappeared almost mysteriously. Most Jerusalemites are uninformed as to how the *Nebi Moussa* festival vanished. The explanation, however, is simple. Just as the celebration's birth was politically motivated, so was its sudden end. After the rise of Zionism, the *Nebi Moussa* festival became an annual nationalist demonstration, and it was increasingly exploited as an anti-Jewish uprising. In time these demonstrations became annual pogroms, and led to the organization of Jewish self-defense units. As long as the fighting involved only Jews and Arabs, the British were not overly concerned. However, in 1936 the Arabs became bold enough to revolt against the British, while at the same time terrorizing the Jewish population. The British ceased to be "neutral," and enforced "law and order." One of the first steps taken was to forbid the *Nebi Moussa* festival. In 1948, the war with the Jews began. The time was not suitable for such a celebration. Thereafter, the Jordanian authorities who ruled the Old City did not find it politically wise to revive the festival. Thus the *Nebi Moussa* festival and pilgrimage became just a memory of an exciting and colorful folk celebration.

But institutions die hard. After fifty years of dormancy, the pilgrimage to the "grave" of the prophet Moses was suddenly revived. In 1987, the Jewish Passover and the Christian Easter coincided, and many Jewish and Christian pilgrims were anticipated. The Supreme Moslem Council had completed the renovation of the complex of buildings at the Tomb of Moses. The Waqf (Islamic Religious Trust, with headquarters on the Temple Mount) issued a call for Moslems to revive the pilgrimage to Nebi Moussa. Over 50,000 pilgrims are said to have responded. The political character of the week-long celebrations was also revived. Inflammatory speeches were delivered, but the government did not interfere. The Israeli authorities could, of course, proscribe the pilgrimage if it ever gets out of hand as did the British Mandatory Government in 1936 and the Jordanian Government in 1949.

Dervishes and Their Curious Performances

At the *Nebi Moussa* procession from Jerusalem to the "grave of Moses" the Arab pilgrims used to be entertained with music and dances. Chief among the attractions were the frenzied twirling and other strange performances of the dervishes. Henry A. Harper, the noted nineteenth-century landscape painter, described one of these acts which he observed during a *Nebi Moussa* celebration:

> Close to the flags stood a dervish, a very holy man. He was dressed in slight clothing, with bare arms and bare legs; but in his waist-belt was a perfect armoury of skewers and daggers. The music grew more vigorous, and the dervish began to dance. The procession moved on. Soon the holy man took a large skewer and thrust it through his cheek shrill cries from the women hailing the deed. The operator moved on. His actions grew wilder, the cries became louder; another skewer, and then a dagger, were thrust through the fleshy part of his arm. From every balcony came cries of joy. We traversed the city, and when outside St. Stephen's Gate, leaving the ranks of the pilgrims and pushing in front, we saw the holy man stuck as full of skewers and daggers as a pincushion is of pins. But, strange to relate, there was not a drop of blood to be seen from his face or figure! Whatever the explanation, there were the facts.[21]

Similar descriptions of the strange performances of the dervishes are common in travel literature. Bertha Spafford Vester, the charismatic leader of the American Colony, reports:

> They [the dervishes] came to Jerusalem especially for the Prophet's feast and procession. Some ate live coals, other forced spikes through their cheeks.[22]

And Elizabeth Anne Finn describes the dervishes:

> After writhing about in an extraordinary manner, by way of dancing, and waving a naked sword, one of the conjurers, to my horror, suddenly stabbed himself in various places, but did not hurt himself. Then they pretended to eat fire, and licked red-hot iron in a manner that looked terrible.[23]

Was King David a Moslem?

This is an odd question. But for some Arabs in Jerusalem the question is not so strange, for King David was indeed a Moslem. The fact that King David lived more than a millenium and a half before Mohammed was born was no problem for the members of the Dahudi family, hereditary keepers of the holy shrine of King David's Tomb on Mount Zion. The family name of the clan is derived from its presumed royal ancestor. Since the Dahudi family has always been Moslem, it follows that their ancestor, King David, was a Moslem. How can it be otherwise? Is it conceivable that so holy a man was not one of the faithful?

Fannie Fern Andrews, in her well-researched work, *The Holy Land Under Mandate,* records this fact quite simply:

> So fully has local Islam adopted David and his tomb that the clan of impoverished Moslem Arabs dwelling in this district has taken the name — the Dahudi family. They claim that they are David's royal descendants; and, with a typically Oriental view of history, say that King David was a follower of Mohammed.[24]

Not only was the Prophet David a Moslem, but according to Arab folklore, Jesus, too, was one of the faithful and he observed the Ramadan fast. Ermete Pierotti, who lived in Jerusalem in the mid-nineteenth century, tells in his work, *Customs and Traditions of Palestine,* the following Arab tradition:

> To the north of Neby Musa [the tomb of the Prophet Moses] and the west of Jericho, is a mountain called Kuruntul, i.e., of the Quarantine, being so called by the Christians and Mohammedans in remembrance of the fast kept there by our Saviour, or the prophet Isa, as the latter call him. I relate the Arab story. "To this wild spot the great prophet Isa retired with his disciples to keep the holy month of the Ramadhan, afar from the tumults of the world. As the view westward was obstructed by the mountains of Jerusalem, and consequently the sunset [when the fast ends daily] could not be seen, he made, by the permission of God, an image in clay representing a winged creature, and after invoking the aid of the Eternal, breathed upon it; immediately it flapped its large wings and fled into one of the dark caverns in the mountain. This creature was the *Khofash* (bat), which lies hid so long as the sun shines upon the world, and comes forth from its retreat when it sets. Every night at . . . the moment of breaking the fast, this bat fluttered around Isa, who then prepared himself with his disciples for prayer. As soon as they had performed this sacred duty, the Merciful caused to descend from heaven a silver table, covered with a cloth whose brilliancy illuminated the darkness, on which were placed a large roasted fish, five loaves, salt, vinegar, oil, pomegranates, dates, and fresh salad, gathered in the gardens of heaven. On these the prophet supped, and the angels of heaven ministered at table."[25]

It is thus an established fact that both King David and the Prophet Isa (Jesus) were devout Moslems.

The Golden Gate, with Moslem Cemetery in front. (Courtesy of Israel Government Press Office.)

Moslem Precautions Against the Coming of the Jewish Messiah and the Second Coming of Jesus

Pilgrims and tourists are intrigued by the Golden Gate. They admire its arches, but they cannot enter the precincts of the Temple Mount through this gate because it is walled up and is blocked by many Moslem tombstones. Jews venerate this gate because it led to the holy Temple, and

Christians pay homage to the Golden Gate because Jesus passed through this gate on the day of his triumphal entry into Jerusalem. In later years, the Emperor Heraclius, when he brought back the True Cross from its captivity in Persia, also entered Jerusalem, bearing his precious trophy, through the Golden Gate. In commemoration of these events, the Crusaders used to open the Golden Gate annually on two occasions—on Palm Sunday and on the Day of the Exaltation of the Cross, which commemorates Heraclius's entry with the Cross.

The reasons for the permanent closing of the Golden Gate are found in folklore rather than history. The Moslems, we are informed, believe that through this gate will enter the Jewish Messiah, and he will restore the Holy City to the Jews. Another version of this tradition is that Jesus, when he returns, will enter the city through this gate as he did prior to his crucifixion, and he will restore the city to the Christians. The prospect of such a calamity, be it Jewish or Christian, demanded that a foolproof strategy be formulated and executed. That strategy consisted of walling up the gate. An additional precaution was taken by blocking the path to the gate with a cemetery. Jews and their Messiah will be effectively blocked, because Jews become ritually defiled on entering a cemetery. This will preclude their entry into the Temple precincts through the Golden Gate. There is another version of the Moslem strategy. They claim that the prophet Elijah, the forerunner of the Jewish Messiah, is a *Kohen,* that is, of priestly descent. Since a *Kohen* is prohibited from entering a cemetery, Elijah will be unable to enter Jerusalem to announce the coming of the Messiah. And the Messiah will surely not come unannounced.

As to the Christian threat, Jesus and his followers will be prevented from entering the Holy City because the Golden Gate is firmly walled up. F. R. Oliphant, in his book *Notes of a Pilgrimage to Jerusalem,* remarks:

> There is a tradition, especially strong among Mohammedans, who fear that it may be true, that a Messiah will revisit the earth who will have no respect for the Prophet at all, and drive his followers out of the city to re-establish the Christian rule. He will enter Jerusalem through the Golden Gate, it is said, so the Mussulman authorities have taken the commendable precaution of walling it up to prevent his getting through. Certainly, a Messiah who could not get through a closed-up gate, would not be likely to set even the Jordan on fire.[26]

In the Six-Day War, the Jews did not wait for the Messiah. They conquered the Old City by storming the Lions (St. Stephen's) Gate. Though the entry of the Israeli army was not through the Golden Gate, it was just as effective. Will the Jewish Messiah, when he finally arrives — or Jesus, when he finally returns — insist on entering through the Golden Gate? This is a question for theologians to ponder.

Equal Contempt for All Infidels

In the Old City one finds a mosque and a tall minaret near every important church and synagogue. Close to the Church of the Holy Sepulchre is the Mosque of Omar, its tall minaret overtopping the prominent domes of the Church. And close to the ruins of what was once the central Jewish house of worship, the Hurvah synagogue, is a small mosque with a tall minaret which used to rise above the synagogue's dome. These mosques were deliberately built near the infidel houses of worship to demonstrate the superiority of Islam to Judaism and Christianity. Sarah Barclay Johnson, in her *Hadji in Syria*, writes:

> Determined not to be outdone by the Christians, and with the special intention of annoying them, the Mohammedans have erected two tall minarets — one in front and the other in the rear of the Church of the Holy Sepulchre — from the tops of which the five citations of the muezzin are daily wafted over the Christian domes. [27]

The Moslems also added injury to insult. They located a tannery next to the Church of the Holy Sepulchre so that the stench of the tanning is certain to penetrate the Christian nostrils during their worship. To this day Arabs call Palmers Street, which leads to the courtyard of the Church of the Holy Sepulchre, "Street of the Tannery." And so as not to show any partiality, the Arabs located a filthy, foul-smelling slaughterhouse which attracted many stray dogs and countless creeping things next to the central synagogue.

The Arabs also expressed their contempt for the Church of the Holy Sepulchre by calling it *El-Kamamah,* the church of the dunghill. This designation derives from the Greek Orthodox name of the Church — *El Kiamah,* [the Church of] the Resurrection, which the Arabs prefer to pronounce *El-Kamamah,* "the Dunghill."

Nachum T. Gidal, in his superb work *Eternal Jerusalem*, demonstrates the Turkish contempt for the infidels, both Jewish and Christian. He writes:

> As late as 1850, for instance, the official form of permission to bury the dead, which had to be given by the Moslem Turkish authorities, was

worded, in the case of a Greek Orthodox person: "To the priest of the people of Rum: You whose garment is as black as Satan's, despicable monk, fat, dirty fraudulent priest . . . take notice that you have permission to dig a hole and throw into it the repellent and evil-smelling carcass of the unbeliever. . . ." Similar was the wording in the case of a deceased Jew, Armenian, or Roman Catholic.[28]

Today both the tannery and the butchery are only bothersome memories. After the Crimean War, the influence of the European powers began to predominate in the Middle East, and the Turks saw fit to remove the nuisances, as well as the irritating insults. Palmers Street is no longer ill-smelling. It is now among the most attractive streets in the Old City. Only the mosques with their tall minarets next to the churches and synagogues have remained. Arabs still see in them a sign of Islam's superiority over Judaism and Christianity.

Why Allah Chose Jerusalem

A famous second-century rabbi, Rabbi Simeon ben Yohai, is quoted as having delivered a discourse based on the biblical text: "He rose and measured the earth" (Hab. 3:6). "The Holy One, blessed be He, considered all cities and found no city wherein the Temple might be built, other than Jerusalem."[29] But Rabbi Simeon did not tell us on what grounds the Almighty made this choice. Jewish tradition provides a number of suitable reasons, but none is as charming and edifying as a legend often repeated and erroneously attributed to Jewish sources. In the process of frequent retelling, various alterations and additions were made, so that versions of the legend multiplied. The central message, however, remained unchanged. None could possibly improve on its lofty moral. According to the story, God chose Jerusalem because a touching drama of genuine brotherly love took place there on the very hill where the Holy Temple was erected. The original tale was recorded by Alphonse de Lamartine in his classic travelogue, *Recollections of the East*. Lamartine's account follows:

> [This] recalls to my mind one of the most delightful traditions invented, transmitted, or preserved among the Arabs. The following is what they relate concerning Solomon's choice of the site now occupied by the mosque:
>
> "Jerusalem was a cultivated field; two brothers possessed that part of the ground where now the temple stands; one of the brothers was married and

had several children; the other was single; they cultivated in common the field they had inherited from their mother; when harvest time was come, the two brothers bound up their sheaves, and made two equal heaps of them, which they left upon the field. During the night, the unmarried brother had a good thought; he said to himself, 'My brother has a wife and children to keep; it is not right that my share should be as large as his; come, I will take some sheaves out of my heap and add them secretly to his; he will not perceive it, and so he will not be able to refuse them.' And he did as he had thought. The same night, the other brother awoke and said to his wife, 'My brother is young; he lives single and without company; he has nobody to assist him in his labour or to console him in his weariness; it is not right that we should take as many sheaves from our common field as he. Let us get up, and go and carry secretly to his heap a certain number of sheaves; he will not perceive it, and so he cannot refuse them.' And they did as they had thought. The next day, each of the brothers went to the field, and was very much surprised to see that the two heaps were still equal; neither one nor the other could account to himself for this prodigy. They did the same for several successive nights, but as each had carried to his brother's heap the same number of sheaves, the heaps still remained equal; until one night both stood sentinels to search out the reason of this miracle, and they met one another carrying the sheaves they had mutually designed for each other.

"Now the place where so good a thought came at the same time and recurred so continually to two men, must be a spot pleasing to the Deity; and men blessed it, and chose it to build on it a house for God."[30]

What a delightful tradition! How does it breathe the innocent goodness of patriarchal manners! How simple, natural, and primitive is the inspiration that induces mankind to dedicate to God a post where virtue has germinated on the earth!

SIX

Pilgrims, Tourists, Missionaries, and Cranks

The Behavior of Pilgrims at Their First Sight of the Holy City

Many pilgrims have described their emotions when they first caught sight of Jerusalem. They write that their experience was so overwhelming that they could not control their tears. When the pilgrims reached the crest of the Mount of Olives and Jerusalem suddenly burst on their gaze, they usually halted, flung themselves on their knees, and spent a few minutes in ecstatic prayer. They then stood up and gazed at the Holy City surrounded by its majestic walls and towers. The first sight of the Holy City usually remained imprinted indelibly on their minds. They remembered how they stood on the Mount of Olives and gazed intently not only on the Holy City with its embattled walls but also on much of the biblical landscape. To the left they saw the land of Moab, known today as the Hashemite Kingdom of Jordan. They saw distinctly the Jordan River and the Dead Sea. Close by on the Mount of Olives they saw the many Christian holy places and the ancient Jewish cemetery. Below they saw the Kidron Valley and the eastern wall of Jerusalem rising above the dry wadi.

The French scholar, Felix Bovet, came on a pilgrimage to Jerusalem in 1858. The account of his first glance at Jerusalem is typical:

> All of a sudden, however, at about four o'clock . . . after passing over a little dip in the ground, I catch sight, at not more than ten minutes' distance at

most, of the embattled walls and cupolas of Jerusalem; my emotion conquers my fatigue. The impression made upon me surpasses all that I had imagined. My eyes fill with tears. My first feeling was a kind of softening of the heart, that indescribable mixture of admiration and of pathos which is inspired by the sight of that which one loves. Here, then, lies before me that poor little town which has felt itself greater than all the greatest things of the earth, and has recognized itself as the principal city of the world! . . .

At a few steps in front of me I see a group of men and horses; they are the Austrian pilgrims, who, at sight of the Holy City, have dismounted to pray. I also dismount and kneel down with indescribable emotion, "For my brethren and companions' sakes, I will wish thee prosperity, O Jerusalem" (Ps. 122:8). [1]

In a similar vein did Horatius Bonar, a Scottish missionary, describe his emotions on spotting the Holy City from the distance:

"What place is that?" I asked. "That place? It is Jerusalem!"—Jerusalem! What a thrill went through the heart! Jerusalem! Is it so? And have we seen Jerusalem at last?

We ceased to speak; smitten dumb by a feeling, of which I had never known the like, nor ever expect to know again.

Wonder, solemnity, joy, sadness, were all mingled together. Yet above these, or at least *with* these, there rose up *affection;* affection as tender and profound as that with which one regards the city of their birth, their father's resting-place, and their children's home. British nationality seemed for a moment lost in something greater than itself.

A man's first look at Jerusalem is not a thing which calls up exclamations, or which gets vent in words; and so we mused in silence, not asking any questions, nor turning round to adjoining objects, nor doing anything that would break the new spell that had in a moment bound us, or interfere with the one thought that filled us, — "this is Jerusalem." [2]

If the Christian pilgrims were overawed by the sacred associations which the first sight of Jerusalem aroused in them, the Jewish pilgrims were overpowered by the memories of their glorious past and the awareness of their deplorable present. The first sight of the Holy City called to their minds the ancient days when God's Presence dwelled in their midst, and they contrasted those days with the humiliations and persecutions during their long exile. Jewish pilgrims would usually rend their clothing as a sign of mourning over the destruction of the Holy City and the Holy Temple. Rabbi Meshullam ben Rabbi Menahem came to Jerusalem in

1481. In his itinerary he described his emotions at seeing the city for the first time:

> On Wednesday, the 29th July, we reached the Holy City of Jerusalem, and when I saw its ruins I rent my garments a hand breadth, and in the bitterness of my heart recited the appropriate prayer which I had in a small book.[3]

Similarly does Rabbi Obadiah da Bertinoro, a distinguished scholar who arrived in Jerusalem six years later, write in one of his long letters:

> About three-quarters of a mile from Jerusalem, at a place where the mountain is ascended by steps, we beheld the famous city of our delight, and here we rent our garments, as was our duty. A little farther on, the sanctuary, the desolate house of our splendour, became visible, and at the sight of it we again made rents in our garments.[4]

Rending one's clothes is a traditional Jewish sign of mourning and is still practiced at funerals. The immediate family of the deceased cut the lapel or some other visible part of their clothes during the funeral service. Sighting Jerusalem was the beginning of an ongoing state of mourning. Reading dirges at the Western (Wailing) Wall accompanied by weeping was a continuation of that process.

The different reactions of Jews and Christians at their first sight of the Holy City reflect their respective traditions. For the Christians, Jerusalem was the place where their faith was born and in which are the holy places of Christendom. They come as pilgrims to visit these holy places and to pray near them. For the Jewish pilgrims Jerusalem is the glorious City of David, the center of their nation and their faith. They come to Jerusalem to live there and to be buried in its soil. The Christian pilgrim greeted the sight of the Holy City with ecstasy and exaltation; the Jewish pilgrim greeted the Holy City with tears and longing.

The Russian Pilgrims

In 1859, the first Russian Imperial pilgrim, the Grand Duke Constantine Nikolaevitch, arrived in Jerusalem. He was also an envoy of the Russian Court to investigate the formulation of Russian policy involving pilgrims in Palestine. On the basis of the Grand Duke's recommendations, the Imperial Treasury allocated half a million roubles and an additional 600,000 roubles were donated by the people. Ten acres of land were

Russian pilgrims, buying candles for use in the Church of the Holy Sepulchre.

acquired outside the city walls, not far from the Jaffa Gate. In 1864 the Trinity Cathedral and a series of hostelries were dedicated. There was room in these hostels for 800 pilgrims and additional accommodations for monks and priests. A hospital and a consulate were also erected. This complex is now situated in the center of the New City and is still called the Russian Compound.

In 1881 a second Imperial pilgrim came to Jerusalem, the Grand Duke Sergey Alexandrovitch. He founded the Imperial Palestine Society, which served the Russian pilgrims with dedication and efficiency. In 1889 the Society erected additional accommodations, especially for pilgrims of means. The accommodations were available at ordinary hotel rates. The society also built a refectory and a bathhouse, installed ventilation in the old buildings, and built stoves for heating the rooms. It is difficult for a modern person to imagine what the conditions were prior to 1889 when none of these essential installations existed. Pilgrims suffered stifling heat in the summer and tormenting cold in the winter. There were no water and no drains, let alone bathing facilities. Some pilgrims died from so simple a cause as suffocation when they sought the warmth of burning charcoal or gas stoves in unventilated rooms.

The Russian pilgrims were imbued with deep faith and abundant piety. Many of them were utterly poor. They entrusted their fate to Providence, walking thousands of miles from their distant hamlets to Odessa, where they boarded wretched pilgrim ships and sailed for the Holy Land. They endured misery and suffering on their journey. Yet they sang sweetly as they walked from Jaffa to Jerusalem, rejoicing in their good fortune to be privileged to reach the Holy City and to pray at the holy places. From the Holy City, these pilgrims walked to the Jordan River and immersed themselves in its water, wearing their shrouds. This was a stirring sight.

Claude R. Conder, the famous archaeologist, reported:

[At Easter] the town swarms with Russian men and women. The strength and endurance of these peasants is wonderful: old women of sixty or seventy trudge on foot from Jaffa to Jerusalem, a distance of thirty-five miles by road; they undergo the fatigues of the crowded Easter ceremonies, and then walk down again to the coast. The savings of a whole life are sometimes expended on such a pilgrimage, and the only reward is the bunch of wax candles which, together perhaps with a coarse lithograph of some saint, the pilgrim brings back to his native village, where he enjoys henceforth the reputation which the pilgrimage ensures.

The scene in the Russian cathedral at Easter time, is striking and instructive. . . . The men [are] unkempt and uncombed, their furrowed features peering out from shaggy locks and long beards, their clothes of dull colours and thickly padded, their feet and legs cased in huge knee-boots. The women wear the same neutral tints, and knee-boots; they have heavy shawls over their heads. The priests are also bearded, with hair down to their shoulders—truly a barbarous priesthood, with a barbarous congregation. The Saviour is represented in Russian pictures with a similar beard and hair.

The religious ecstasy of the congregation was always intense. They took no part in the service, but continued to cross themselves, and knelt at intervals to kiss the floor, many knocking their heads so hard against it as to be heard at the other end of the church. Small tapers were burnt on the great silver candlesticks, and those who stood near the door passed the taper to those in front, each person bowing to the one who handed it, until those near the screen received it; it was then lighted, and when half burnt was put out, and left for its owner to claim.

The ritual was impressive. . . . I have attended many religious services, Christian, Jewish, and Moslem, but none more remarkable for barbaric grandeur and pomp. The songs of Latin monks, the shrill nasal clamour of the Armenians, the Jewish gesticulation, are all far less dignified than the solemn chants of the Russian cathedral. The fanaticism of the pilgrims, drawn from the lowest and most ignorant peasant class, surpasses anything in Christendom, and is only equaled by that of the Moslems.[5]

Before leaving Jerusalem, the Russian pilgrims provided themselves with icons, crosses, beads, five-fold Jerusalem crosses, pictures of the holy places, and mementos carved from olive wood or mother of pearl. These trinkets kept alive their vision of the Holy City.

Many of the Russian pilgrims never reached Jerusalem. Of those who did, many did not survive the long return trek to their native hamlets. Those who died in the Holy Land were envied, because they had the good fortune of being buried in holy soil. And fortunate indeed were those laid to rest in the Holy City itself.

Those pilgrims who reached Jerusalem and returned home safely were treated by their neighbors almost as saints. The Russian peasants were sure that some of the sanctity of the Holy City and its holy places rubbed off on the pilgrims.

The number of Russian pilgrims kept growing. In the years before the First World War, the annual number of Russian pilgrims was almost ten thousand, and accommodations were again inadequate. But no new Russian imperial pilgrim arrived in Jerusalem to initiate the building of additional accommodations. Then came the Communist Revolution in 1917. The Communist regime had no interest in pilgrimages. Like all religious activities, pilgrimages were regarded as antirevolutionary. The Russian Compound ceased to function; the Cathedral was closed; and eventually the whole compound, except the Cathedral, was sold to the Israeli government. The buildings were turned into government offices, courtrooms, and police headquarters.

Interior of Russian Cathedral in Jerusalem (1949). (Courtesy of the Central Zionist Archives, Jerusalem.)

Since the Russian pilgrims ceased to come, the holiday season in Jerusalem has not been the same. A meaningful and colorful element of the Easter celebration is gone seemingly forever.

A Modern "Crusader"

Of all the pilgrims who came to Jerusalem during the nineteenth century none attracted as much interest and none left as deep an impression on the

Holy City as Kaiser Wilhelm II. The Kaiser came to Jerusalem in 1898 to consecrate the Lutheran church which was built in the Muristan. This historic site, near the Church of the Holy Sepulchre, was originally presented by the Sultan to the King of Prussia, who later became Kaiser Wilhelm I. In those days the plot was an eight hundred-year-old rubbish heap with a majestic gateway now embodied in the new Lutheran church.

As the coming of the Kaiser was approaching, anticipatory excitement rose to a high pitch. He was coming, said the Kaiser, as a "Crusader." The Turks were determined that the Kaiser's visit should be an impressive event. The city was cleaned; the city's stray dogs were poisoned; new roads were built and old ones repaired; the troops stationed in Jerusalem were issued new uniforms; and the military band practiced German melodies day and night.

The great day arrived. The Kaiser's party landed in Haifa on a

Emperor Wilhelm II, entering Jerusalem in 1898. (From J. Boudet, Jerusalem: A History. New York, G.P. Putnam's Sons, 1967, p. 262.)

specially built landing that ran out from the German Colony. The Kaiser had it published that he landed "on German soil." The road from Haifa to Jerusalem had been widened and historic sites had been demolished for the Kaiser and his entourage to travel in comfort. It was a very hot day. Regardless, the horses were driven in haste; and forty horses dropped dead in harness and were left along the road.

Then came the Kaiser's triumphal entry into the Holy City. Unlike the Crusaders of eight centuries ago, the new "Crusader" insisted on entering the Holy City on horseback. There is a tradition that only a conqueror may enter the city gates on horseback. But no one dared deny any whim of the new "Crusader." So the Turks fell back on a clever strategem. They breached the wall near the Jaffa Gate and filled in the protective moat. Thus the Kaiser entered on horseback and the Kaiserin and her ladies drove into the city in open carriages, but not through a city gate. The breach is still there. The current City Plan, however, provides for the closing of that breach and restoring the city wall to its original state.

The Kaiser was liberal in bestowing iron crosses and other marks of honor on Turkish officials. He was equally liberal in his hints of things he liked to possess. This strategy of acquiring treasure by admiring and hinting paid off. The Kaiser acquired a number of priceless parcels of land on which German institutions soon began to rise. One of these institutions was the Stiftung Kaiserin Augusta Victoria on the Mount of Olives.

The Stiftung on the Mount of Olives had its origin in a hint by the Kaiserin. One hot day the Kaiserin drove up the Mount of Olives. Relieved by the breeze on the crest of the sacred hill, she remarked, "I wish I could build here a house for the poor missionaries to rest in during the hot summers!" Her wish was duly relayed to the Sultan, and he presented her with a large tract reaching across the crest of the hill on both slopes. The complex of buildings erected on that tract included a hospice and a church. It was generally believed that the building had military and strategic objectives. It commanded Jerusalem and the countryside, and it was equipped with a tower and a powerful searchlight which could be seen far out at sea as well as across the Jordan. It was also rumored that cannon emplacements were built into the walls. All this for the poor, tired missionaries.

Another German institution that had its beginning during the Kaiser's visit was the Dormition Abbey on Mount Zion. Its strategic and

The Church of the Dormition on Mount Zion (1963). (Courtesy of Israel Government Press Office.)

military value was recognized by the Israeli military staff, who used the roof of the Dormition Abbey as a military look-out throughout the nineteen years the Jordanians occupied the Old City.

The Kaiser had more on his mind than being a "Crusader." The Kaiser was preparing for the "great day," which, as we know, fell on August 1, 1914.

The German Emperor's Contribution to the Holy City

G. K. Chesterton was not known for his admiration of the Kaiser or the German national ambitions. The tragedy of the First World War he blamed on the German passion to dominate the world. Hence, one cannot regard Chesterton's reaction to the Kaiser's pompous entry into Jerusalem as thoroughly objective. It is, however, like all of Chesterton's writing, imaginative and thought provoking. In his book *The New Jerusalem,* written immediately after the First World War, Chesterton reacts to the gaping breach in Jerusalem's wall, near the Jaffa Gate:

Immediately at the side of one of these humble and human gateways [the Jaffa Gate] there is a great gap in the wall, with a wide road running through it. There is something of unreason in the sight which affects the eye as well as the reason. It recalls some crazy tale about the great works of the Wise Men of Gotham. It suggests the old joke about the man who made a small hole for the kitten as well as a large hole for the cat. Everybody has read about it by this time; but the immediate impression of it is not merely an effect of reading or even of reasoning. It looks lop-sided; like something done by a one-eyed giant. But it was done by the last prince of the great Prussian imperial system, in what was probably the proudest moment in all his life of pride.

What is true has a way of sounding trite; and what is trite has a way of sounding false. We shall now probably weary the world with calling the Germans barbaric, just as we very recently wearied the world with calling them cultured and progressive and scientific. But the thing is true though we say it a thousand times. And any one who wishes to understand the sense in which it is true has only to contemplate that fantasy and fallacy in stone; a gate with an open road beside it. The quality I mean, however, is not merely in that particular contrast; as of a front door standing by itself in an open field. It is also in the origin, the occasion and the whole story of the thing. There is above all this supreme stamp of the barbarian; the sacrifice of the permanent to the temporary. When the walls of the Holy City were over-thrown for the glory of the German Emperor, it was hardly even for that everlasting glory which has been the vision and the temptation of great men. It was for the glory of a single day. It was something rather in the nature of a holiday than anything that could be even in the most vainglorious sense a heritage. It did not in the ordinary sense make a monument, or even a trophy. It destroyed a monument to make a procession. We might almost say that it destroyed a trophy to make a triumph. There is the true barbaric touch in this oblivion of what Jerusalem would look like a century after, or a year after, or even the day after. It is this which distinguishes the savage tribe on the march after a victory from the civilised army establishing a government, even if it be a tyranny. Hence the very effect of it, like the effect of the whole Prussian adventure in history, remains something negative and even nihilistic. The Christians made the Church of the Holy Sepulchre and the Moslems made the Mosque of Omar; but this is what the most scientific culture made at the end of the great century of science. It made an enormous hole.[6]

The Souvenirs That Christian Pilgrims Acquired in Jerusalem

The vendors in Jerusalem's bazaars are always doing a lively business selling souvenirs to the many visitors in the city. The tourists pack away their purchases in their overloaded satchels, and at home they distribute them among their friends as mementos from the Holy City. During Holy Week the customers are of a different character. They are not as affluent as the tourists, but in a way, they are better customers because they do not haggle. Most of these customers are Greek Orthodox pilgrims. They concentrate their purchases on religious objects, such as crosses, beads, icons, holy pictures, and bottles with water from the Jordan River or the Siloam Pool. These items are only the raw materials which the pilgrims turn into precious holy things. Proceeding to the Church of the Holy Sepulchre, they place their souvenirs on the Stone of Unction and then on the Holy Sepulchre itself. The Greek Orthodox priest sitting near the Holy Sepulchre is accommodating. He sprinkles holy water on the souvenirs. Some pilgrims also dip their purchases in the Jordan River. After these sanctifications the souvenirs are really precious. They are expected to protect their owners from disease and accident and to bring blessings to their business transactions. They will enable the childless woman to bear children and the mother of several daughters to bear a son.

Some pilgrims concentrate on matters of eternity. They bring their shrouds to the Holy City, spreading them on the Stone of Unction and on the Holy Sepulchre, then washing them in the Jordan River. The expectation of burial in such shrouds is a blessed prospect indeed. A pilgrim with such a precious possession is the envy of his neighbors.

Among the odd souvenirs that pilgrims are reported to have acquired in Jerusalem, some were not purchased, but gathered from holy places. Sarah Barclay Johnson says that no real pilgrim would leave the vicinity of the St. Stephen's (Lions) Gate without "finding a flesh-colored limestone, penetrated by veins of reddish hue; for these, they say, were once common limestones, but no sooner was the proto-martyr stoned to death than they assumed this veiny form in sympathy."[7] And S. D. Phelps reports that during his visit in the Garden of Gethsemane he was "kindly permitted to take a few flowers, rose-leaves, an olive branch, and a little box of earth from the Garden."[8] Horatius Bonar, a Scottish missionary, reports that "leaving this house of Lazarus I struck upwards through some fields, or rather orchards, where I gathered a few olive leaves and almond blossoms to preserve, in after years, the memory of the scene."[9]

Some tourists want enduring mementos not only to last throughout their lives, but to become part of their mortal remains. Thackeray in his itinerary reports that in the courtyard of the Church of the Holy Sepulchre there are:

> Some worthies who drive a good trade by tattooing pilgrims with the five crosses, the arms of Jerusalem; under which the name of the city is punctured in Hebrew, with the auspicious year of the Hadji's visit. Several of our fellow-travellers submitted themselves to this queer operation and will carry to their grave this relic of their journey.[10]

The most curious souvenir from Jerusalem is reported by Alexander A. Boddy in his *Days in Galilee and Scenes in Judaea:*

> Cold weather and neuralgia unfortunately necessitated a number of visits to a German dentist who had recently commenced practice at Jerusalem. . . .
>
> In broken English he told me of an American lady who had rushed in upon him suddenly a little time before.
>
> "Doctor, I reckon I want a tooth stopped," she said.
>
> "Kindly take a seat, Madam," he replied.
>
> She sat in the dentist's chair and opened her mouth. The dentist carefully looked in and after a time said, "Which tooth, Madam?"
>
> "Oh, that makes no matter—any tooth," she replied.
>
> "But," remonstrated the dentist, "I don't see any tooth which requires stopping."
>
> "I'm going to have a tooth stopped in Jerusalem, anyhow," she replied. "If you put in ever so little gold it will do, but I must have a memento of this city, whatever I pay for it."
>
> To satisfy this enthusiastic lady he managed to make a hole and put in some gold, for which he was rewarded handsomely.
>
> A strange way of remembering Jerusalem![11]

And Stephen Olin reports:

> I heard of an American clergyman, a visitor to Jerusalem some three or four
> years ago, who consecrated his clerical robe and bands by placing them in
> contact with the traditionary tomb of the Savior. [12]

A summary of Jerusalem souvenir gathering was written by Edwin
Sherman Wallace, the American consul in Jerusalem in the late nineteenth century:

> Every day during the tourist and pilgrim season rosaries and crucifixes are
> brought [into the Chapel of the Holy Sepulchre] and laid for consecration
> upon the marble slab. The attending priest pronounces his blessing upon
> them and they become specially holy. Thousands upon thousands of rosaries
> and crosses are thus treated every year and find their way to countries and
> homes most remote from the Holy City. In April of 1894 a Catholic priest
> from one of the large inland cities of Ohio, purchased fifteen hundred
> rosaries, had them all blessed in this way—one for every member of his
> congregation; he was a wise pastor in thus showing no favoritism. Every year,
> also, thousands of cards, having on them pressed flowers of the Holy Land,
> are treated in the same way. The superscription on many of these cards
> announces that they bear flowers from the Garden of Gethsemane, but the
> statement cannot be always true, for this little garden spot does not grow
> flowers enough to supply the demand. The only way to know positively that
> you have flowers from Gethsemane is to go yourself and pluck them; and this
> is not an easy matter, for the priestly custodians guard their charge with
> jealous care. Nor have articles, which are supposed to have been laid on the
> tomb and blessed, been always so honored. And what does it matter whether
> they have or not? If contact with any particular place makes more holy, it
> should suffice that the thing has been in sacred Jerusalem. But as residence in
> the city does not have any such effect upon persons, it is not probable that it
> has any holier action upon cards or rosaries. [13]

The Vandalization of Holy Shrines

How can pious pilgrims vandalize their holy shrines? But they do. Not all
pilgrims, but some have done it throughout history. The holier the shrine,
the more it has been vandalized by the very people who revere it.

Felix Fabri, a German monk, was in Jerusalem near the end of the
fifteenth century. His description of how the pilgrims vandalize the holy
shrines is enlightening. He writes that he saw pilgrims walking—

> round about the church with iron tools hidden in their clothes, and when
> they came to the holy places scratched and picked at the sacred stones,

chipping and knocking pieces off them to carry home with them for relics. . . . Through this silly breaking off pieces of stones we were brought into great peril, not once only, but more than once. Once, after the pilgrims had gone home, we stayed all night in the Church of the Anastasis, and in the morning it was discovered that pieces had been broken off the rock of Calvary, the slab of the sepulchre, and the stone of the Lord's unction. When the other Eastern Christians saw this, they cried out in the church against us, calling us thieves and robbers; a dangerous riot was stirred up against us, and they threatened us that they would complain of us to the Moorish and Saracen lords. Hearing this, the Father Guardian was afraid, thinking that a great danger was hanging over us. He called us all together, into the chapel of the blessed Virgin, and by his apostolic authority excommunicated those who had broken the stones, nor would he let them go out of the church until the broken pieces were given up to him. So there we stood in confusion and disgrace, and all men raged against us for the sacrilege which we had done. . . .

Men do not break these pieces off out of devotion, but some avaricious knights, who are patrons of some churches or altars, do this to the end that by these things they may stir up crowds of people to visit their churches, and thereby get gain, and so it is greed which eggs them on to try to do this.[14]

Felix Fabri also related how he came into possession of a "good-sized piece" of a most holy Christian relic, the stone which was rolled to the mouth of the Holy Sepulchre. The Armenians possess this holy stone and have used it as a table for the altar of the house of Caiaphas which is in their compound. Fabri relates that he and his party—

kissed this sacred stone, and viewed it narrowly. Meanwhile the priests of the church watched us carefully, that none of us should break pieces off the stone with any iron tool, for they greatly reverence that stone. . . .

During my first pilgrimage a good-sized piece of this stone came into my hands. It was bought by a knight for two ducats from an Armenian priest, who entered the church with the knight by stealth, lest the other Armenians should see them, and broke off a piece of the stone. This same knight died at sea, and I inherited this piece of stone from him, and brought it with me to Ulm.[15]

H. Rider Haggard, an early twentieth-century pilgrim in Jerusalem, quotes Baedeker in connection with the authenticity of the seat in which the Empress Helena sat while the original cross was unearthed. He writes:

There is an underground chapel called that of St. Helena, where the Cross was found. Near the altar, too, is a seat in which the Empress Helena sat while the Cross was unearthed. Unfortunately for the genuineness of this relic, as the cold-blooded Baedeker points out, an Armenian patriarch of the seventeenth century, complained in his day that he had frequently been obliged to renew this seat because the piety of pilgrims led them to bear it away piecemeal.[16]

We also read in a recent article from *The Christian Century:*

One of the explanations of the vandalism by pious pilgrims is that they have an overpowering urge to take something of Jerusalem's holiness home. It is said that in past centuries pilgrims who knelt to kiss the original cross would bite off wooden splinters and hide them in their mouths. The old wooden cross is gone from Jerusalem, perhaps eaten away by the faithful.[17]

To be sure, the overwhelming majority of pilgrims come to Jerusalem only to see, touch, and pray at the holy relics of Christendom. Some pilgrims, however, become obsessed with an irresistible urge, similar to that experienced by some collectors. They yield to that *force majeure* and help themselves to a piece of the shrine. Being upright men and women, they rationalize their pious thefts by the presumption that their noble ends justify their ignoble deeds. Chipping off a small piece from the Holy Sepulchre will not be missed by anyone. But think of the good this chip will do for thousands who will come to worship in the church where the pilgrim will place it! This small piece of the holy shrine will now be treasured and revered by thousands. The small chip will do so much good for the faithful who cannot come to Jerusalem. So some self-righteous people go on vandalizing holy shrines and historic monuments. The vandals return to their homes with pride, and they are rewarded with praise for enriching the spiritual life of their fellow citizens.

Experience has taught the guardians of the shrines not to trust the pilgrims. Not only are the Holy Sepulchre and the Stone of Unction protected by slabs of marble, but a Greek Orthodox priest is always on duty inside the chapel of the Holy Sepulchre to watch over the shrine. Another priest sits on Mount Calvary and carefully eyes every visitor. The guardians of the holy shrines have learned not to rely on the piety of the pilgrims.

More on Vandalism of Holy Shrines

The first of the pious vandals who injured Jerusalem's holy places was none other than the Emperor Constantine himself. It was he who removed the *Scala Sancta,* or holy staircase, down which Jesus went from Pontius Pilate's Judgment Hall to the Basilica of St. John Latern at Rome. There are now in the wall, near the traditional Judgment Hall where the holy staircase was, only two old arches, now filled up.

Equally shocking is the vandalism of the Crusaders, who, upon capturing Jerusalem, turned the Dome of the Rock into a church which they named the *Templum Domini.* They hewed down the crown of the sacred rock in order to fit on it their high altar. This act of vandalism was not performed in ignorance, for the Crusaders sold the chippings for their weight in gold.[18]

The Garden of Gethsemane has also suffered much from pious pilgrims. Two of the venerable ancient trees died about half a century ago. Father Joseph, the acting superior, has blamed their death on souvenir hunters who arrived in large numbers after the British conquest of Jerusalem. So many branches were clipped from these two sacred olive trees, that no amount of care could save them. Two new ones were planted in their place, but they do not carry the sanctity of their predecessors, which reputedly dated from the days of Jesus.

J. L. Stephens, whose travel book was published in *The Universal Library,* tells of his visit in the Gethsemane Garden. He notes that "one of the largest [of the ancient trees is] barked and scarified by the knives of pilgrims."[19]

People who perform acts of vandalism are always secretive. They are evidently conscious of doing something not only forbidden but also shocking. However, there are some who boast of their successes. One of these boastful vandals was a prominent leader of the Masonic brotherhood. He recorded his noble achievement in his book *Freemasonry in the Holy Land.* Robert Morris writes:

> Long before reaching this city, I had resolved, at all hazards, to place the Masonic mark of the Square and Compass conspicuously upon some one of the huge ashlars that make up the wall of the old Temple area on its eastern side. The task was by no means a pleasant one, nor altogether safe.

> Across the valley of Jehoshaphat, in plain view, is the village of Silwan (Siloam), whose inhabitants are among the most fanatical people in the vicinity. Close by, on the north, is a large Moslem graveyard, often crowded with Mohammedan women, who would scarcely permit a Christian to walk so near their cherished tombs, much less commit the profanity of cutting into the Temple-wall with a chisel. Add to this, one of the principal roads around the city runs within thirty steps of the ashlar I had selected for my operations, so that I was liable to interruption at any moment—and the reader will appreciate the difficulties of the task. However, I was not easily deterred; and placing an assistant in the road below, with instructions to keep a vigilant lookout, I marked out my figure, and began. Perhaps the real

danger of this attempt, after all, lay in the military lookouts upon the works one hundred feet above my head. Had they witnessed my operations, it was like them to pitch a donick or two over the wall, or even to fire their pieces down upon me; and this, according to the usages of that sanctuary, would have been justifiable in them. But I made my mark deep and bold, as future travellers will not fail to see. It is cut in the fifth stone of the second tier of blocks, counting from the southeast corner of the old Temple-wall to the north. The block is a large one, though not the largest in that part of the structure.[20]

In more recent years a royal vandal caused an irreparable loss to one of Jerusalem's shrines. In the Dome of the Rock there was a screen around the rock which was "a perfect example of twelfth century wrought-iron work." The screen was installed by the Crusaders. This relic of the crusading period no longer exists. It was removed and destroyed by King Hussein of Jordan. The reason for this act of vandalism has not been ascertained.

The above are a few examples of the innumerable acts of vandalism that have been inflicted on the sacred and historic relics of the Holy City. Of course, Jerusalem is not the only victim of this human weakness. Every holy place, every historic site, and every repository of precious things suffer from this destructive urge which deprives many otherwise honest people of a share in their heritage.

Cranks and Fanatics

Bertha Spafford Vester writes: "Religious fanatics and cranks of different degrees of mental derangement seemed drawn as by a magnet to the Holy City."[21] Most of these eccentrics believed themselves to have been chosen by God for a grand purpose. They usually regarded themselves the reincarnations of biblical personalities sent to perform a divine mission. They each came to Jerusalem with a particular *idée fixe* and spent their lives pursuing their obsessions. They were absorbed in their compelling goals with singular dedication and admirable piety. They usually harmed no one and often performed deeds of kindness with selflessness and generosity. Ronald Storrs, the governor of Jerusalem during the British Mandate, remarked:

> Visionaries of [Chinese] Gordon's high uplifted phantasy were sadly outnumbered by sheer cranks: acquiring or developing their crankdom in an air which seems to render the strangest ideas, not only interesting but almost probable.[22]

Among them were "prophets" and "apostles," "kings" and "messiahs." Among the Jews, the Prophet Elijah, the forerunner of the Messiah, predominated. Among the Christians, John the Baptist was among the most frequent arrival. Among them, too—albeit, less frequently—were inventors of perpetual motion machines.

The Scottish missionaries, Bonar and M'Cheyne, met with one of these cranks in Jerusalem:

> Mr. Johnson, from Scotland, was a peculiar individual. He has lived in Jerusalem like a hermit for over two decades, waiting for the coming of Jesus. He tried to be both Christian and Jew. He wore a beard and side curls, dressed like a Jew, and obeyed the commandments of the Torah. Yet he awaited the coming of Jesus. He applied to the rabbis to be received as a proselyte and met all the requirements of conversion, but he would not renounce Jesus. So he has remained in isolation, spending his solitary hours in meditation and prayer, no less than an observing Jew, yet outside the community of Israel. He is "waiting upon the Lord," just like Moses who was commanded to spend forty years in Horeb, doing nothing till the Lord informed him of his mission.[23]

Estelle Blyth states that Jerusalem had an excessive share of the world's cranks. As an illustration, she described one:

> Without doubt, we had our full share of cranks as well as critics. In moments of melancholy, we often felt that we had more than our fair share, and we would wonder, with patient resignation, what there could be in the air of Palestine which drew to it cranks of all sorts, but especially religious cranks, with such a fatal fascination? To such odd characters, however, we owed much of the salt and humour wherewith our daily bread was seasoned. Not long before my Father went out, the natives had been much exercised in mind over the strange appearance of a solitary man who had drifted out to Jerusalem, no one knew how or whence. Like other good people with a little mental twist, he felt an urgent call to reform the Holy City. Wherever he went, he dragged with him a large and heavy wooden cross, and he preached to whomever he could induce to stop and listen to him. Odd people are safe in Palestine, for the people regard them with a sort of reverence as having been touched by the Hand of God; and this poor cross-bearer was safe enough, but no one would listen to his message or follow him, which was not very wonderful, as he knew no language but his own. He strove without success, then fell ill, and died, and the wooden cross was set up over his grave. Another independent evangelist used to wander through the streets of Jerusalem, shouting, "Woe, woe, woe to the inhabitants of Jerusalem!"[24]

Jerusalem's cranks had missions and great expectations. They had supernatural revelations; usually arriving in answer to a divine call. These eccentrics were essentially harmless. Some, however, became a public nuisance. The Arabs regarded these somewhat deranged people as "holy men." Jews and Christians regarded them as poor demented souls whom they pitied and tolerated. These eccentrics, each with his own idiosyncrasy, have been as much a part of Jerusalem as the holy places and the holy shrines.

The Christian Missionaries

The Christian missionaries in Jerusalem were intent on bringing salvation to the "lost sheep of Israel." The missionaries were convinced that their activities were humane and altruistic. They were engaged in the sacred work of opening the eyes of the Jews to the true faith and thus saving their souls from perdition. What could be nobler? But they were blind to the pain and anguish that they inflicted on their intended beneficiaries. They frequently kindled fires of fear, hate, and strife among a people who had lived peacefully and bothered no one—least of all their Christian neighbors.

The Jews reacted to missionary activities with bitterness. To be sure, there were some Jews who tried rational argument, as we read in *The Jewish Chronicle* of London, dated August 30, 1901:

> When Christian missionaries seek to decoy Jews from the fold in which they were born, we meet them with the argument that they would do well to restrict their efforts to the members of their own flock. Instead of making bad Jews into worse Christians, let them labor, we urge, to make bad Christians into better Christians.

But rational arguments were of no avail. The missionaries were so convinced of the benevolence of their activities that nothing could dissuade them from their "sacred work." They pursued their "calling" with dedication and vigor. The Jews, however, failed to see the missionaries as saviors. Instead they felt imperiled and resorted to desperate measures to avert the threat of their spiritual annihilation.

The battle against the Christian missionaries was one of the most heart-rending chapters in the history of the Jews of Jerusalem. It is reminiscent of the war of the Maccabees against the Syrian Greeks for which the Jews thank God annually for giving victory "to the weak over the strong and to the few over the many."

The missionaries, failing to make converts by the usual methods, resorted to indirect action. They gave the Jews the kind of services which the Jews could not resist. These benign benefits were intended to lure the Jews to the mission where Christian influence could be brought to bear upon them. These tempting benefits were: (1) A hospital where treatment of the sick was free and efficient; (2) schools for children where clothing and other needs were provided free of charge; (3) trade schools for the indigent and unemployed; (4) direct assistance of food and clothing to the poor; and (5) distribution of Bibles in which the New Testament was included.

The strategy also called for the employment of converted Jews as missionaries. This was especially offensive to the Jewish community, which regarded these missionaries as renegades and hated them intensely. The Jewish missionaries were shunned with disgust and contempt.

Typically, the missionary headquarters was outwardly Jewish in appearance. There were no crosses, the food was *kosher,* and the language spoken was usually Hebrew. These outward trappings did not deceive the Jews, but they made it easier for the needy to compromise with their conscience and to rationalize their acceptance of the assistance being proffered.

The Jews saw in the missionaries a mortal enemy seeking to trap the poor and to lead them to eternal perdition. The Jewish leaders tried hard to save the victims from what they regarded as spiritual death. They did not counterattack, because Judaism has ceased to be a missionary religion ever since Christianity became dominant in the fourth century. They had learned from bitter experience that missionary work was very risky. Many a Jewish community paid in blood for daring to accept a Christian convert. Even if a Christian came of his own volition and asked to be converted to Judaism, the Jews were fearful of the consequences. They hesitated, or refused entirely to receive him. The Jews therefore waged only a defensive war against the aggressive missionary activities. In that defensive war the imposition of the *Herem* or excommunication on those who yielded to the temptations of the missionaries was the most effective. The *Herem* meant expulsion from the Jewish community, and it resulted in social ostracism, refusal of pecuniary assistance, and denial of burial in the Jewish cemetery. Thus it happened that a woman who went to the missionary hospital and died there was refused burial in the Jewish cemetery. The missionaries appealed to the pasha, but the rabbis refused to lift the excommunication. The corpse was finally buried outside the Jewish cemetery enclosure.

The Jewish community had another weapon. Since most of the Jews in Jerusalem were poor, many of them were dependent on the small stipends that the community distributed weekly. The moment it became known that anyone was in touch with the missionaries he was deprived of his stipend. But this weapon was ineffective because the missionaries reimbursed those who were thus penalized. Indeed, it became an attractive inducement for dissemblers whose "conversion" was profitable.

Notwithstanding the strenuous and sophisticated efforts of the missionaries their success was limited. Many knowledgeable people have declared the missions a failure. Their activities gained only few converts, and these converts were seldom a credit to the church. There are many reports by reliable witnesses that verify the missionary failure. One of these witnesses was William Makepeace Thackeray, who visited Jerusalem in 1845. He writes in his *Notes of a Journey from Cornhill to Grand Cairo:*

> I don't believe the Episcopal apparatus—the chaplains, and the colleges, and the beadles—have succeeded in converting a dozen of them; and a sort of martyrdom is in store for the luckless Hebrew at Jerusalem who shall secede from his faith. Their old community spurn them with horror.[25]

Similarly does Herman Melville write in his *Journal:*

> A great deal of money has been spent by the English Mission in Jerusalem. . . . The present Bishop (Gobat, a Swiss by birth) seems a very sincere man, and doubtless does his best. But the work over which he presides in Jerusalem is a failure—palpably. One of the missionaries under Gobat confessed to Mrs. Saunders that out of all the Jew converts, but one he believes to be a true Christian.[26]

And Bayard Taylor, in his work *The Lands of the Saracen,* notes:

> It is estimated that each member of the community has cost the Mission about £4,500: a sum which would have Christianized tenfold the number of English heathen. The Mission, however, is kept up by its patrons as a sort of religious luxury.[27]

By the turn of the century the missionaries no longer could compete with Jewish institutions superior to their own. Mrs. A. Goodrich-Freer describes this new situation in her book *Inner Jerusalem:*

> In former times, when the rich Jews did but little for the small number of their race then living in Jerusalem, the notion of bribing them to Christianity with medicine and lesson books might conceivably be less unpractical

than now, when we can give them nothing except the religion they reject, with which they are not at least as well, often far better, provided on their own account. They have, except the Germans, the finest hospital, the only proper disinfecting laboratory, the only wholly isolated wards for the reception of diphtheria and small-pox patients, the only poor-house, the only mad-house, the only Hospital for Incurables, the only School of Art, the only effective Technical Schools, the only Weaving School, the only Public Library, and the only newspaper in Jerusalem. They have the only Girls' School under English Government inspection and properly trained certificated teachers (the Evelina de Rothschild School), the only Cookery School for girls, the only place where young women are taught gardening, domestic economy, laundry work and first aid to the injured. Their needlework excels even that of the convents, which is saying a great deal, and their Kindergarten, of some 250 children, is directed by a teacher trained at the Froebel School in Dresden; while the headmistress, a highly educated Englishwoman, is a Queen's scholar holding first-class Government diplomas, and of considerable experience in both primary and secondary schools. . . .

What chance has the best-intentioned institution of the London Jews' Society against such work as this?[28]

The missionaries are still in Jerusalem, but their activities are generally subdued. They engage in persuasion, and they accept converts who come voluntarily. But they refrain from "buying" converts. Indeed, Israeli law forbids the offering of material benefits to prospective proselytes. It also forbids the acceptance of such benefits. It seems that the time is not too distant when neighborly co-existence will characterize the Jewish-Christian relationship in Jerusalem.

The Story of Warder Cresson, the "First American Consul in Jerusalem"

Among the numerous cranks and eccentrics Jerusalem has attracted were Jews who sought to bring the Messiah and Christians who tried to hasten the Second Coming of Jesus. These cranks usually distinguished themselves by their overwhelming zeal. Some people have referred to them as "madmen with a divine spark in their eyes." One of these cranks was an American named Warder Cresson.

In its April 1971 issue, the *Pennsylvania Magazine of History and Biography* published a well-documented article entitled "Quaker, Shaker, Rabbi Warder Cresson, the story of a Philadelphia Mystic." That Warder Cresson was a Quaker, Shaker, and mystic is an established fact; that he was a rabbi is questionable. It is even doubtful whether Cresson was really the first American consul at Jerusalem as is often claimed, for his credentials were revoked a month after they were issued. The baffling story of the Philadelphia Quaker who ended up as a pious Jerusalem Jew is one of the many curiosities of the Holy City.

Frank Fox, author of the above-mentioned article, started his fascinating story with a quotation from an appendix in one of Warder Cresson's books, *The Key of David,* in which the author summarized the "Lunacy Case or the Great Lawsuit for Becoming a Jew." At the outset of this appendix, Cresson states briefly what he considered to have been the chief reason for the lunacy case against him:

> My object, as I said before, was "the pursuit of Truth," and with truth, I desired *Strength* and *Rest.* I remained in Jerusalem in my former faith until the 28th day of March, 1848, when I became fully satisfied that I never could obtain *Strength* and *Rest* but by doing as *Ruth did,* and saying to her *Mother-in-law,* or *Naomi,* (the Jewish Church,) "Entreat me not to leave thee, or to return from following after thee; for whither thou goest, I will go; and where thou lodgest, I will lodge: thy *people* shall be *my* people, and thy God my God. Where thou diest, will I die; and there will I be buried: the Lord do so to me, and more also if AUGHT BUT DEATH PART THEE AND ME" (Ruth 1:16-17).
>
> In short, upon the 28th day of September, 1848, I was circumcised, entered the Holy Covenant, and became a Jew. . . .
>
> Soon after my return home to my family, which I did upon the 20th day of September, 1848, I found that there was a growing OPPOSITION and ENMITY towards the course that I had taken, which were daily more and more manifested against me. I tried every way I could to convince my Wife and Family, whom I most *sincerely* and *most ardently loved,* and to conciliate my views with theirs, but this I found to be impossible, unless I would *abjure* or perjure myself, and deny the very foundation and greatest principle of my faith, which is the *Unity* of God.
>
> My Wife, Elizabeth T. Cresson, was born and educated a Friend, or Quaker, as I was; but, about the time I went to Jerusalem, or a little while before, she had been baptized, and became, during my absence, a rigid Episcopalian, and believer in "One God being Three," and in "Three *being one;*" that is, in a *Trinity.*
>
> I soon found, upon conversation with her, that she could not explain to me how it was possible for *only one Indivisible God* to be *divided* into *Three,* and then for these *three divided parts* to be thrown back again into that which they say is *Indivisible;* all the satisfaction I could get was, "that it was a *Great*

Mystery," (see Rev. 17:5,) "That it was *Inexplicable,"* and that it was, in short, to receive all this mass of *inconsistent stuff* with *"implicit faith,"* without inquiring *why* or *wherefore,* and hence throwing away my reason, *"Heaven's best gift,"* as completely as I would have to do were I to become a follower of "Brahma," "Juggernaut," or the "Grand Lama."

Here was the point, and the one great point, upon which first commenced all our *after difficulties,* she maintaining that "three was one, and that one was three;" that is, she supported a "TRINITY," and I maintaining that ONE was ONLY ONE, and never was nor never could be three; that is, I supported the "UNITY" of God.[29]

Warder Cresson was born on July 13, 1794, into a prominent Quaker family. In 1821 he married Elizabeth Townsend, and in 1824 he purchased a farm and became a successful farmer. In 1827 Cresson published his first religious tract entitled "An Humble and Affectionate Address to the Select Members of the Abington Quarterly Meeting." In this message to the Quaker community, Cresson criticized his fellow Quakers, who adhered to outward form instead of inward religion. Shortly thereafter Cresson was accused of having joined a religious society known as the Shakers. However, he was not expelled from the Quaker community.

In 1830 Cresson published another tract entitled "Babylon the Great Is Falling." In it he attacked the prevailing corruption which, he claimed, was due to the accumulation of wealth in the hands of the few and the widespread rapacity of government officials. He forecast the disintegration of American society unless it reformed its ways in line with the teachings of Christianity.

The decade of the 1830s was a time of religious ferment in America. Those were the years of frontier evangelism, when many Christians were preoccupied with millennial speculations. The Second Coming of Jesus was anticipated by many Christians, and according to some, the Jews were to play an important role in these eschatological events. A number of new and flourishing Christian sects had their beginnings in those days.

Warder Cresson immersed himself in the religious speculations of the day. In his search for the truth he came into contact with two prominent Jews who apparently impressed him greatly. One of these was Rabbi Isaac Leeser, whose writings Cresson studied and found in them similarities with his own theological views. The second was Mordecai M. Noah, who tried to establish a Jewish state on Grand Island in the Niagara River near Buffalo. Mordecai M. Noah's influence became apparent in Cresson's activities during the last years of his life.

In 1844 Cresson went to Washington and applied for the post of American consul in Jerusalem. He wished to serve as a volunteer without compensation. On May 17, Cresson was officially notified of his appointment. But one month later his commission was revoked because Secretary of State John C. Calhoun had heard of Cresson's "passion for religious controversy." "No doubt," the secretary was informed, "Cresson expects to convert Jews and Mohammedans in the East." But Cresson had already left for Jerusalem, unaware that he was no longer the American consul in Jerusalem.

During the four years of Cresson's stay in Jerusalem, he acted as American consul, quarreled with the "soul-snatching" missionaries whom he accused of selfishness and ostentation, and corresponded frequently with Rabbi Isaac Leeser. He became deeply interested in Judaism, and in his book *The Key of David,* he questioned some basic Christian dogmas and denied the divinity of Jesus. As stated, Cresson converted to Judaism on March 28, 1848, and he assumed the name Michael Boaz Israel.

Six months after his conversion Cresson returned to Philadelphia and soon became involved in a lawsuit with his wife and other members of the family who accused him of lunacy. Before Cresson left for Jerusalem, he had given his wife power of attorney, and she sold his farm and his personal effects. Upon his return, his wife and other members of the family charged him with lunacy and claimed title to his property. The case was tried before a sheriff's jury, and a verdict of insanity was issued. A legal contest now began in the Philadelphia Court of Common Pleas, which involved not merely the issue of Cresson's sanity, but also a basic principle of American democracy, that of the freedom of religion. The case aroused wide interest and has been called "one of the strangest in legal history." The outcome of this "bizarre trial" was Cresson's vindication.[30]

Upon his return to Jerusalem, Cresson began to promote a program aimed at reforming the social and economic structure of the Jewish community in the Holy Land. He planned to set up a model farm in the Valley of Rephaim, and to teach the Jews modern farming methods. His aim was to make the Jews self-supporting and thus do away with the institution of *Halukah,* which collected money in the diaspora and distributed weekly stipends to the poor. His plan went beyond the economic transformation of Jewish life in the Holy Land. He was, in a sense, a forerunner of the Zionist movement.[31] But Cresson's Zionism was premature. It took several more decades and several tragic events to awaken the

Jews from their medieval torpor and to render them responsive to the call of modern Zionism.

Robert Walter Stewart, a Scottish minister, visited Jerusalem in 1854. In his itinerary he comments on the conversion of Warder Cresson:

> Among the living curiosities of Jerusalem I must not omit to mention an American who had once been a Christian, but had afterwards apostatized to Judaism, and on the principle of doing in Jerusalem as the Jews do, had divorced his Christian wife and married a young Jewess. It is the only instance I ever heard of such retrogradation, and naturally leads to the speculation whether he is to be classed in the category of knave or fool. His intention, when first announced, must have taken the rabbis exceedingly by surprise, as creating a new era in the history of modern Judaism, and it is not therefore to be wondered at that they should wear him as a feather in their caps.[32]

Cresson spent his last years in Jerusalem in obscurity. He married a Jerusalemite woman, Rachel Moleano, and had two children, David ben Zion and Abigail Ruth. "It was a strange household," wrote a contemporary who knew Cresson. "Husband and wife knew not one word of each other's language and had to converse entirely by signs."[33] Herman Melville met Cresson during his visit to Jerusalem and was impressed by his views and example. In Melville's long narrative poem, *Clarel: A Poem and Pilgrimage in the Holy Land,* the character Nathan, a Christian turned Jew, is obviously patterned after Cresson.

Warder Cresson died on October 27, 1860, and was buried on the Mount of Olives. His children did not survive him for long. David ben Zion died in 1863, and Abigail Ruth died in 1865. Cresson's life was an adventure in the world of mysticism. He was guided by rules of rectitude and the "pursuit of truth," and he followed his convictions with stubborn consistency. Despite his mystic inclinations, Cresson was a practical and efficient farmer in his youth, and in his last years, he became one of the precursors of "practical" Zionism. In the Holy City Cresson found his spiritual home, and there he ended his stormy life, fully anticipating Israel's vindication and his own salvation.

A Recent "King of Jerusalem"

Jerusalem has had many kings. Among the best known were King David, King Solomon, and King Herod. There were also several European monarchs who prided themselves on possessing the honorary title of King of Jerusalem, and they inscribed on the coins they minted *Rex Hier*[*oso-lyma*]. Some of these pretentious but hollow titles appeared on coins as late as the nineteenth century. But the most curious of Jerusalem's kings was a recent arrival in the Holy City named Denis Michael Rohan.

Among the Christian cranks Jerusalem has attracted, the "divine" mission they espoused was usually connected with the awaited Second Coming of Jesus. According to these eccentrics, Jesus was waiting for the appropriate conditions to make his second coming. So they came to Jerusalem to prepare the proper setting for the millennium.

Denis Michael Rohan, an Australian, aged 28, arrived in Jerusalem in the summer of 1969. His mission was to prepare for the Second Coming of Jesus, which, according to his calculations, was to occur after the rebuilding of Solomon's Temple on Mount Moriah. To facilitate his grandiose enterprise, he had to clear the ground on the holy mount for the erection of the Temple. This meant the demolition of the El Aksa Mosque, which, according to Rohan, occupied that sacred spot. On August 21, 1969, Rohan set fire to the El Aksa Mosque, Islam's third holiest shrine. The mosque itself was not seriously damaged, but one of Jerusalem's precious art treasures, the pulpit of the mosque, was totally destroyed. This cedar wood pulpit with its canopy and its exquisite cabinet work was admired and described by many visitors. An Arabic inscription which ran along the railing recorded that the pulpit was the work of an artist from Aleppo. It was made in the twelfth century and brought to Jerusalem by order of Saladin. Besant and Palmer, in their work *Jerusalem, the City of Herod and Saladin*, say that this pulpit was "one of the most exquisite pieces of carved woodwork in the world."[34] A late-nineteenth-century writer, James Smith, described this pulpit as a "magnificent example of the finest arabesque work in wood":

> It was brought to Jerusalem by the renowned Saladin (A.D. 1189), after the reconquest of Palestine by the Moslem armies, and it is an object of the highest admiration by visitors, as well as of great veneration by Moslems. Only one who has seen this rich and graceful structure can believe how exquisite is its fine carving, all fitted together without a nail being driven into it, and how charming in their elegant variety are the carved and raised panels profusely inlaid with ivory and mother-of-pearl.[35]

A curious aspect of the carving on this pulpit is that the Arabs worshiping in the El Aksa Mosque never noticed that the Christian carver of their splendid pulpit "played his Mohammedan masters the trick of introducing in his designs the hated sign of the cross, a fact which apparently escaped their notice to this day."[36]

This work of art is no longer in existence. Its demolition was the first step in the realization of Denis Michael Rohan's grandiose plan.

The arson in the El Aksa Mosque stirred up a violent reaction among the Moslems in the Holy Land and in the adjacent Arab states. Protests were also heard from distant Moslem countries. The situation in Jerusalem was calmed when the perpetrator was arrested. The neighboring Arab countries, however, continued their anti-Israel agitation, claiming that the arson in their holy mosque was part of an Israeli plot to occupy the holy Mount Moriah and to rebuild Solomon's Temple.

At the trial before the Jerusalem District Court, Rohan stated that his mind had never been as well balanced as it was then. He referred to himself as the "king of Jerusalem" and claimed that his purpose in setting fire to the El Aksa Mosque was to fulfill his destiny, which was to rebuild God's Temple and thus prepare the necessary condition for Jesus' return to rule the world from Jerusalem. By burning down the El Aksa Mosque, he was destroying one of Satan's temples and demolishing Satan's power to torment God. He "planned with a thinking mind" this incendiary act in accordance with God's revelations to him.

At the trial it was also disclosed that Rohan had been treated in a mental hospital in Australia for "acute schizophrenia reactions." Court-appointed psychiatrists testified that Rohan was suffering from paranoiac schizophrenia and that the motives for his criminal conduct should be sought in delusions of grandeur. In short, Rohan was not criminally liable for his actions by reason of insanity. The court ruled that Rohan be confined in a mental hospital.

Shortly after the trial, Denis Michael Rohan was deported to his native country and, to use a biblical idiom, "the land had rest" from the turmoil created by the modern "king of Jerusalem."

The Strange Phenomenon of the American Colony

Who has not heard of the American Colony in Jerusalem? It is a fascinating chapter in the annals of Jerusalem, more intriguing than any tale created by a gifted storyteller. The story begins with a tragedy and ends with the remarkable courage of a family which rose above personal suffering and became a blessing to its community.

The central personalities of this story are Mr. Horatio G. Spafford, a successful lawyer in Chicago, and his wife Anna, whose parents had immigrated to America when Anna was four years old. The couple met in a Sunday school class where Horatio was the teacher and Anna Lawson was a student. They married in 1861.

The Spaffords lived happily in a suburban home from which Mr. Spafford commuted daily to his office in Chicago. Then came the great Chicago fire of 1871. That fire demolished the city and reached the suburban neighborhood of the Spaffords. The family fled with four small children, barely saving their lives. Somehow their house survived the fire. It was nothing less than a miracle. However, through the fire's destruction of property, Mr. Spafford was ruined financially.

Two years later, Mr. and Mrs. Spafford decided on a grand vacation in Europe. The whole family, father, mother, and the four little girls— booked passage on the luxurious ship, the *S.S. Ville du Havre*. A pressing business matter made it necessary for Mr. Spafford to stay behind. He planned to join the family later. Mrs. Spafford and the children sailed for Europe in 1873 with happy anticipations.

The *Ville du Havre* sailed on November 21, 1873, on a calm Atlantic. That night, while everyone was asleep, two loud noises awakened the passengers. An English ship, the *Lochearn,* had rammed the *Ville du Havre.* Among the passengers of the *Ville du Havre* all was soon confusion and panic. People in nightdresses crowded into lifeboats, some of which refused to budge. They had been freshly painted, and were firmly stuck. As the hysteria and panic grew, the ship suddenly shuddered and began to sink. Mrs. Spafford and her four children went down together along with all those who had been unable to leave the ship in the lifeboats. Only twelve minutes after the ship was struck it went down with its human cargo. Against all odds, Mrs. Spafford was saved. She remembered only how she found herself lying in a boat, bruised and sick. Two hundred twenty-six lives were lost, among them the four little Spafford girls. Only fifty-seven passengers were saved.

Mrs. Spafford came to believe that this unbearable tragedy had deep meaning. She must have been "spared for a purpose." She became convinced that she "had work to do."

One need not dwell on the agony suffered by Mr. Spafford. When he received the wireless telegram from his wife, saying, "Saved alone," his thoughts turned to a search of meaning. Within two years, two disasters had struck: the Chicago fire when he lost his possessions and the shipwreck of the *Ville du Havre* with the loss of his four children. He wrestled with doubt and unanswerable questions. He, too, reached the conclusion that his work was not finished. Instead of indulging in their sorrow, the Spaffords threw themselves into philanthropic and evangelistic tasks. They found comfort in their work for the destitute and hopeless people in Chicago. They also found consolation in the new family they were building on the wreck of the old. Two children were born, a boy and a girl. The girl, named Bertha, survived; but scarlet fever carried off the little boy. This new tragedy took place in February 1880.

It was after the loss of their fifth child that the Spaffords began to think seriously of going to the Holy City. Meanwhile, another child was born. They named her Grace. But the final blow that made their vague thoughts about Jerusalem an urgent reality was the shock of being expelled from their church because of their "heresies." The Spaffords became convinced that God could not be the harsh, punishing deity of their church. They questioned such dogmas as hell and eternal punishment. They came to believe that, on the contrary, God's love precludes such tenets.

The Spaffords disposed of their home and practically everything in it and departed with their two little girls for Jerusalem, where they hoped to start life anew. The news of the Spaffords' plan to leave for Jerusalem spread, and some people joined them. But wild rumors began to spread. It was said that the Spaffords started a new religious sect called the Overcomers. Some zealots resorted to persecution.

The Spaffords and a band of pilgrims left Chicago on August 17, 1881. Their children were three and a half years old and seven months old. The Chicago pilgrims arrived in Jerusalem without plans. For six weeks they stayed in a hotel. Then they purchased a house in the Old City within the Damascus Gate, overlooking the entrance to Solomon's Quarry. The Chicago group, twenty-five in all, settled down in this house. They lived a simple life, taking their meals together, and jointly participating in religious devotions. Instead of preaching, they occupied themselves with nursing the sick, feeding the hungry, and caring for the orphaned. Because of their concern for others, they found peace and harmony among themselves, and they gained the esteem of many Jerusalemites. Mr. Spafford started Bible study classes which proved popular, and Mrs. Spafford organized a mothers' group which was well attended. The Americans, or the "Family," as they called themselves, soon won the trust and friendship of their neighbors. Their reputation as honest, friendly, and helpful spread throughout the community.

When the Chicago group arrived in Jerusalem, local residents called them the "Americans." Later, they began to call them "the American Colony." For some Christians in Jerusalem these Americans were an enigma. As it is often the case with unorthodox benefactors, the people at the American Colony were mistrusted and persecuted by the established Christian groups, especially the missionaries. Rumors began to spread, and suspicions began to multiply. Some suspected these Americans of un-Christian conduct and heretical beliefs.[37] The British missionaries resented their passive approach in their missionary work. They also resented the Americans doing missionary work in the British sphere of action. In addition, these Americans taught Christianity primarily as an ethical way of life. The resentments turned to slander and persecution.

The principal persecutors of the American Colony were, strange to say, the American consuls in Jerusalem, the Reverend Edwin Sherman Wallace and his successor Dr. Selah Merrill. They accused the members of the colony of living an immoral life. In 1897 a statement was issued, entitled "Spaffordism: A Conclusive Expos of the Spaffordite Fraud in Jerusalem." It was signed by sixteen American citizens, and it accused the colony of immoral practices.

In 1895 Mrs. Spafford and several members of the colony visited Chicago. They were approached by a group of about thirty simple, pious Swedish fundamentalists who wanted to join the American Colony in Jerusalem. When Mrs. Spafford and her co-workers returned, the colony grew to seventy-seven souls, of whom twenty-five were children. Their quarters in the Old City were too small to house them. So they looked for and found new accommodations in the Sheikh Jarah Quarter, in the Arab section north of the Old City. They rented the large home of a wealthy Arab family and moved into it. Later they purchased it, and that property is known to this day as the American Colony. They had hardly settled down in 1896 when another Swedish group of thirty-eight—eighteen of whom were children—joined the colony. These newcomers were related to the American Swedes, but they came directly from Sweden. Thus the colony grew to 130, of whom forty were children. Their financial situation became precarious. The income from nursing and teaching was not enough to feed so large a community. The pressure of urgent needs led to greater effort and finally to success. Several industries were started. Among these were weaving—table linen, furniture coverings, and tweed for suits; and knitting—utilizing a machine which produced woolen and cotton underwear, sweaters, and jerseys. A herd of cows was acquired; a bakery was started and cakes and pies were sold; jams and preserves were sold. The confectionery was popular and profitable; shoemaking, tailoring, and dressmaking were begun. They engaged in farming; and their photographic endeavors made an important contribution to the history of the Holy City. The colony's large collection of photographs and stereopticon slides is now in the Library of Congress in Washington. The American Colony ceased to be a poor, struggling group; it became a complex of profitable enterprises. Some cynics have said of the colony, "they came to do good and ended up doing well."

In 1900 the Swedish writer, Selma Lagerlof, visited Jerusalem. Hearing of the "ill repute" of the life at the American Colony and learning of the presence of Swedes in that group, she decided to visit the colony to see for herself. She visited frequently and was impressed with the people and their industries. She then wrote her Nobel Prize–winning novel, *Jerusalem*.

Finally, the American Colony was vindicated in a court case, and the false rumors of immoral conduct ceased. The persecutions had lasted for twenty-five years.[38]

Horatio Spafford and his wife are buried in the Protestant cemetery on the southern declivity of Mount Zion. The American Colony which they founded continued its work under the able leadership of Bertha Spafford Vester, whom the Spaffords had brought to Jerusalem at the age of three and a half. Today, nothing is left of the American Colony except for a profitable hotel named the American Colony Hotel. The American Colony has indeed been one of Jerusalem's phenomena, worthy of remembrance and gratitude.

On September 22, 1981, twenty foreign descendants of the founders of the American Colony gathered at the American Colony Hotel in East Jerusalem to celebrate the hundredth anniversary of its founding. Israel's President Yitzchak Navon joined the celebration, which marked the arrival in Jerusalem of Horatio and Anna Spafford in 1881. These religious pioneers deserve to be honored not only by their descendants but also by all Jerusalemites.

The Tragic Story of the German Colony

Most people have heard of the Knights Templars. They were a religious order of fighting monks who flourished during the time of the Crusader

Kingdom of Jerusalem. They achieved fame and wealth but ended in disgrace. They were finally disbanded by papal order. Not many people, however, have heard of the modern Templers, a German religious sect that established itself in the Holy Land in the nineteenth century. The history of the German Templers is also a success story with a tragic ending.

The founder of the Temple Society was a German professor, Christoph Hoffmann. He established a college near Stuttgart in which he taught and agitated for reform in the Lutheran Church. Like many Christians of that time, he came to believe that the Second Coming of Jesus was at hand. But Jesus could not come unless there was a Christian Church that was ready to receive him, that is, a church the membership of which lived by the teachings of the Bible. In 1858 Hoffmann and his followers were expelled from the Lutheran Church. They therefore organized themselves into an independent community. In 1867 some of Hoffmann's followers met and decided to establish their new church in the Holy Land. The Templers, as the new sect came to be called, migrated to Palestine, where they established seven colonies, the largest of which was at the foot of Mount Carmel near Haifa. Another of their agricultural colonies was in Sarona near Jaffa, which is now in the very center of Tel Aviv. Still another Templer settlement was established in the Emek Rephaim district in Jerusalem. The Templers engaged in agriculture, commerce, and trade; and according to Claude R. Conder, who did his archaeological work in Palestine at the time of the Templars' settlement in the land, they were "hard-working, sober, honest, and sturdy; and however mystic their religious notions may be, they are essentially shrewd and practical in their dealings with the world."[39] By 1875 there were 750 Templers in the Jerusalem Colony.

At first the Templers suffered poverty and disease, but they persevered, and in time they overcame all hardships and prospered. When the population of Jerusalem experienced a shortage of currency, the Templers coined their own money, which was widely circulated in the country. The neatness of the Templer settlements, their honesty, and their industry had a beneficial influence on the surrounding population. They were regarded as a blessing to the country and were highly respected by the native population.

These honest and industrious German settlers who expected to establish Christian communities fit to receive Jesus at his Second Coming met a tragic end. Instead of Jesus, it was Adolph Hitler who arrived, and the grandchildren of the pious Templers became ardent Nazis, founding an active Nazi party in Palestine. Four hundred young men of Templer origin enlisted in the German army, and the rest of the Germans in Palestine maintained their loyalty to Hitler till the end. The British government interned all the Germans in Palestine. Most of them were deported to Australia, and the rest were exchanged for British prisoners in Germany.

In 1948 the property of the Templers was taken over by the Israeli government and was finally acquired through the Reparations Agreement with the German Federal Republic.

Today there are no known descendants of the Templers in Jerusalem, but the district where the Templers dwelled is still called the German Colony. The area has been officially declared a historic zone and the unique architectural character of the German Colony will thus be preserved. Numismatists prize the rare Templer coins. But many of the residents, not knowing the history of their neighborhood, wonder why their neighborhood is called the German Colony, seeing that no Germans dwell in their locale.

The Makuya Pilgrims

One of the most colorful and joyous events in Jerusalem is the annual pilgrimage of the Christian Japanese sect known as the Makuya. The Makuya, or Tabernacle movement, was founded by the late Professor Ikuro Teshima, who wrote in the preface to his work *Original Gospel Faith:*

> Christianity is a . . . universal religion born through the Hebrew spirit, and can only be understood by Hebrew and the Hebrew-minded, just as Bushido (the way of samurai) is a Japanese way, and can only be understood by Japanese-minded. Hence it is the aim of the Makuya to create a Christianity which is Japanese in character free of Western Christian influences.[40]

The Makuya regard the unification of Jerusalem after the Six-Day War as a modern miracle, a fulfillment of biblical prophecy and the heralding of the Messiah's Second Coming. Accordingly, the Makuya have presented one hundred thousand Israeli lira toward a memorial on Ammunition Hill where the most desperate battle for the capture of the Old City was fought during the Six-Day War.

Ikuro Teshima, founder of the movement, has made it a basic principle of the faith to "return to the original Gospel." Since the primitive Christian Church shared the same root with Judaism, "Christians must pay proper respect to the Jewish people and the Land of Israel."[41] These principles have led the Makuya to foster programs and to perform deeds that promote a loving relationship toward Israel, its people, and its culture. A number of Japanese of the Makuya sect have come to Hebrew University to study the Bible in its original tongue and to live in Israel for extended periods. But the most impressive act of the loving association with the Jewish people and the Land of Israel has been the sect's annual pilgrimage to Jerusalem. In 1973, 375 members of the Makuya sect came to Jerusalem to pay homage to Israel on the occasion of the twenty-fifth anniversary of the establishment of the State. This pilgrimage was headed by Professor Ikuro Teshima himself. The group prayed at the Western (Wailing) Wall and then marched through the streets of Jerusalem, dancing and singing Hebrew songs.

This has become an annual ritual, attracting crowds of Israelis who admire the colorful Japanese garments worn by the pilgrims and marvel at the spectacle of their distant friends who come annually in increasing numbers to bring love and friendship to the city and its dwellers. Some see in this Japanese pilgrimage the fulfillment of the prophetic words: "To thee shall the nations come from the ends of the earth" (Jer. 16:19).

The Eternal Pilgrim

There is a pilgrim who comes to Jerusalem twice each century. He makes his way to the Church of the Holy Sepulchre, but he gets only as far as the courtyard in front of the church entrance, never entering the church. That pilgrim is none other than the legendary Wandering Jew, who, according to Christian tradition, reaches the church entrance only to have the doors close at his approach. He begs for admission, but he hears only a voice that bids him to pursue his endless wanderings as a punishment for the fateful sin which he committed at the time of Jesus' crucifixion.

According to the Christian tradition—recorded in numerous chronicles, poems, and miracle plays—a certain Jew, named Ahasuerus, witnessed Jesus carrying his cross and, instead of pitying the suffering martyr, drove him along saying, "Go, go, thou tempter and seducer, to receive your due." Jesus is said to have replied, "I go, and you will wait till I come back." So that sinful Jew has been wandering all over the world all these centuries. Subsequently the Jew repented and converted to Christianity, but his sin has not been forgiven. He has been begging for death, but death always eludes him. He has sought release from the curse of unending life by means of battle, flood, and fire, but he always fails. Every jubilee he makes a pilgrimage in order to pray at the Holy Sepulchre, where he hopes to achieve release from the curse of his endless life of wandering. But the doors of the church and penitence are permanently closed to him.

This strange tradition has persisted throughout the Christian world. It has been used both to exhort Christians to greater piety and to propagate anti-Semitism.

The most intriguing account of the Wandering Jew's semi-centennial pilgrimage to the Church of the Holy Sepulchre is related by Mark Twain in *The Innocents Abroad:*

> And so we came at last to another wonder, of deep and abiding interest—the veritable house where the unhappy wretch once lived who has been celebrated in song and story for more than eighteen hundred years as the Wandering Jew. On the memorable day of the Crucifixion he stood in this old doorway with his arms akimbo, looking out upon the struggling mob that was approaching, and when the weary Saviour would have sat down and rested him a moment, pushed him rudely away and said, "Move on!" The Lord said, "Move on, thou, likewise," and the command has never been revoked from that day to this. All men know how that the miscreant upon whose head that just curse fell has roamed up and down the wide world, for ages and ages, seeking rest and never finding it—courting death but always in vain—longing to stop, in city, in wilderness, in desert solitudes, yet hearing always that relentless warning to march—march on! They say—do these hoary traditions—that when Titus sacked Jerusalem and slaughtered eleven hundred thousand Jews in her streets and byways, the Wandering Jew was seen always in the thickest of the fight, and that when battle-axes gleamed in the air, he bowed his head beneath them; when swords flashed their deadly lightnings, he sprang in their way; he bared his breast to whizzing javelins, to hissing arrows, to any and to every weapon that promised death and forgetfulness and rest. But it was useless—he walked forth out of the carnage without a wound. And it is said that five hundred years afterward he followed Mohammed when he carried destruction to the cities of Arabia, and then turned against him, hoping in this way to win the death of a traitor. His calculations were wrong again. No quarter was given to any living creature but one, and that was the only one of all the host that did not want it. He sought death five hundred years later, in the wars of the Crusades, and offered himself to famine and pestilence at Ascalon. He escaped again—he could not die. These repeated annoyances could have at last but one effect—they shook his confidence. Since then the Wandering Jew has carried on a kind of desultory toying with the most promising of the aids and implements of destruction, but with small hope, as a general thing. He has speculated some in cholera and railroads, and has taken almost a lively interest in infernal machines and patent medicines. He is old, now, and grave, as becomes an age like his; he indulges in no light amusements save that he goes sometimes to executions, and is fond of funerals.

There is one thing he cannot avoid; go where he will about the world, he must never fail to report in Jerusalem every fiftieth year. Only a year or two ago he was here for the thirty-seventh time since Jesus was crucified on Calvary. They say that many old people, who are here now, saw him then, and had seen him before. He looks always the same—old, and withered, and hollow-eyed, and listless, save that there is about him something which seems to suggest that he is looking for some one, expecting some one—the friends of his youth, perhaps. But the most of them are dead, now. He always pokes about the old streets looking lonesome, making his mark on a wall here and there, and eyeing the oldest buildings with a sort of friendly half-interest; and he sheds a few tears at the threshold of his ancient dwelling, and bitter, bitter tears they are. Then he collects his rent and leaves again. He has been seen standing near the Church of the Holy Sepulcher on many a starlight night, for he has cherished an idea for many centuries that if he could only enter there, he could rest. But when he approaches, the doors slam to with a crash, the earth trembles, and all·the lights in Jerusalem burn a ghastly blue! He does this every fifty years, just the same. It is hopeless, but then it is hard to break habits one has been eighteen hundred years accustomed to. The old tourist is far away on his wanderings, now. How he must smile to see a pack of blockheads like us, galloping about the world, and looking wise, and imagining we are finding out a good deal about it! He must have a consuming contempt for the ignorant, complacent asses that go scurrying about the world in these railroading days and call it traveling.

When the guide pointed out where the Wandering Jew had left his familiar mark upon a wall, I was filled with astonishment. It read: S.T. — 1860 — X.

All I have revealed about the Wandering Jew can be amply proven by reference to our guide.[42]

The Wandering Jew has often personified the Jewish people as a nation that had no homeland for almost two thousand years. In a recent novel, *The Second Scroll* by the Canadian Jewish author, Abraham Klein, the Wandering Jew makes his last journey from the European Holocaust to the reborn Jewish State of Israel. Thus ends his eternal curse.[43]

"Little Harlem"

Every American city has at least one section inhabited almost exclusively by blacks. The largest concentration of blacks is said to be in a section of New York City known as Harlem. Jerusalem, too, has a black community which some people have called Little Harlem. Unlike the American black municipal districts, Jerusalem's black neighborhood is minuscule in area; its inhabitants are few in number; and its essential character and history are altogether unique. The community consists of less than two hundred families and lives mainly within the walls of two abandoned Turkish prisons in the Moslem Quarter of the Old City. Their origin, too, is not traceable to ancestral enslavement, but rather to poverty and piety.

The history of Jerusalem's black community began during the British conquest of Palestine in the First World War. Before General Allenby set out on his expedition across the Sinai Desert, he recruited a contingent of African laborers to lay railroad tracks and a water pipe across the Sinai Desert. The British Army advanced only as fast as the Africans progressed with their engineering tasks. When the black laborers returned to their homes in central Africa, they told their families and friends of the wonders they beheld and experienced in the Holy City. For them Jerusalem was truly a metropolis. They spoke with fascination of the *Sakhra* (Temple Mount), the Dome over the Holy Rock from which the Prophet ascended to heaven, and the holy El Aksa Mosque in which they were privileged to worship. These marvelous accounts kindled in the hearts of many of their co-religionists fervent yearnings to visit that marvelous city and at the same time make the Haj. In the thirties, a few black Moslems began to arrive in Jerusalem. Some of them literally walked from their distant hamlets. They crossed deserts, suffered hunger and thirst, were robbed by highwaymen, and were decimated by disease. The survivors who reached the Holy City settled near the *Sakhra* in a street named Ala Uddin or, in English, Alladin Street. This street is only one block long, but it is important, because it leads to one of the Temple Mount gates and also to the headquarters of the Moslem religious trust, known as the Waqf. In this street stand two abandoned Turkish prisons erected as long ago as the thirteenth century when the Egyptian Mamelukes ruled the city. It was the practice of the Mamelukes to exile dignitaries who were suspected of malpractice to the faraway provincial town of Jerusalem. These exiled notables built themselves palatial homes and erected and endowed Moslem religious academies known as *medrassas*. Two of these academy buildings were erected on Ala Uddin Street. When the Turks conquered Jerusalem in the fifteenth century, they converted these *Medrassa* buildings into prisons. The one on the north side of the street came to be known as Blood Prison because in it were incarcerated prisoners who were condemned to death. On the opposite side was the prison for less serious criminals. The neighboring gate to the Temple Mount came to be known as the Prison Gate. When the British Mandatory Government abandoned these prisons, the homeless Africans moved into the cells and converted them into living quarters. Some of the more enterprising built themselves two-room huts in the prison courtyards, which now resemble tiny villages with small alleys running the length and width of the courtyard settlements. They also converted a section of the Blood Prison into a mosque, thus establishing themselves as an autonomous Moslem community. In recent years the Jerusalem municipality installed running water and electricity in the blacks' improvised homes and built public toilets and a community bathhouse. Thus another distinct, well-defined community was added to the multinational and multireligious city of Jerusalem.

Today a second generation of black Jerusalemites has grown up. They know little of the tribal tongues spoken by their elders; they are employed in various trades; and they work in every part of the city. The process of assimilation, however, has begun to agitate the older generation. Some of the young people are moving out of the community quarters; some have intermarried. The survival of the community is thus endangered.

The tiny black community is only one of the many small sectarian and racial groups of the city. But its disappearance would be a loss, for this relatively new settlement of honest, peaceful, hard-working, religious souls constitutes part of the multifaceted character of the Holy City. The disappearance of even a tiny community diminishes the city's essential destiny, which, according to the Prophet, is to become a "house of prayer for all peoples" (Isa. 56:7).

SEVEN

The British in Jerusalem

What Led the British Government to Issue the Balfour Declaration?

Most people assume that the British concern with the Jews of Palestine dates from 1917, when the British government issued the Balfour Declaration. British involvement in the Zionist aspirations, say these people, was motivated by the exigencies of the First World War. Britain was exploiting every source of support in its struggle with the Central Powers. This motive, though rational, is far from being the only, or even the main, consideration.

The official British concern with the Jews of the Holy Land goes back to 1839, when Great Britain officially accepted the Jews in Palestine as its protégés and expressed its official concern for them.

James Finn, British consul in Jerusalem from 1845 to 1862, states in his memoirs:

> The institution of consulates in the Holy City proved a blessing to non-Turkish subjects of all religions, but especially to the poor oppressed Israelites.

> In 1839, Lord Palmerston's direction to his first Consul in Jerusalem was "to afford protection to the Jews generally." The words were simply those, broad and liberal as under the circumstances they ought to be, leaving after events to work out their own modifications. The instruction, however, seemed to bear on its face a recognition that the Jews are a nation by themselves.[1]

Mrs. Finn, the consul's wife, in her *Reminiscences,* summarizes the history of this special relationship and the role that her husband played in the implementation of that policy. She writes:

> Lord Palmerston in the year '39 instructed the British Consul, Mr. Young, to exert friendly protection on behalf of all Jews generally, whether British subjects or not. This he followed up in '41 by a circular note, after the Turks had been restored in possession of the Holy Land, in which he said that the Porte had promised to attend to any representation made to it by the Embassy of any act of oppression against Jews, and that therefore the Consul was to "enquire diligently" and to report any such case, and that although he could not interfere actively officially, excepting for British subjects, he was in every case of oppression to let the authorities know that the British Government felt an interest in the welfare of Jews in general and were anxious that they should be protected from oppression. He was to tell the authorities that the Porte had offered to attend to any representation made by the British Ambassador. . . .
>
> The above orders of the British Foreign Office were followed by another, ordering that if any Jew of foreign nationality happened to be repudiated by his own Consul, Mr. Finn should enquire into the case and protect him, unless the repudiating Consul could furnish a strong and sufficient reason against him. This again was followed in '49 by the British Government accepting the care of all Russian Jews in Palestine, the Russian Government being anxious to discard them.[2]

The British motivations for issuing the Balfour Declaration may have been political, but only partially so. Religious considerations were also important elements in the British involvement. This was publicly confirmed by Lloyd George, who was Prime Minister when the Balfour Declaration was issued. His revealing statement was made in 1925 after listening to a lecture by Philip Guedalla on "Napoleon and Palestine." The lecture dealt with Napoleon's strange declaration, which was a sort of forerunner of the Balfour Declaration.[3] Lloyd George stated that the British "motives were mixed." They were partly ideological and partly political. The Balfour Declaration, said Lloyd George —

> was undoubtedly inspired by natural sympathy, admiration, and also by the fact that, as you must remember, we had been trained even more in Hebrew history than in the history of our own country. I was brought up in a school where I was taught far more about the history of the Jews than about the history of my own land. I could tell you all the kings of Israel. But I doubt whether I could have named half a dozen of the kings of Wales. So that you must remember that was very largely the basis of our teaching. On five days a

week in the day school, and on Sunday in our Sunday schools, we were thoroughly versed in the history of the Hebrews. We used to recite great passages from the prophets and the Psalms. We were thoroughly imbued with the history of your race in the days of its greatest glory, when it founded that great literature which will echo to the very last days of this old world, influencing, moulding, fashioning human character, inspiring and sustaining human motive, for not only Jews, but Gentiles as well. We absorbed it and made it part of the best in the Gentile character. So that, therefore, when the question was put to us, we were not like Napoleon, who had never been in a Sunday school and had probably read very little of that literature. We had all that in our minds, so that the appeal came to sympathetic and educated — and, on that question, intelligent — hearts. But I am not going to pretend there was not a certain element of interest in it, too. You call yourselves a small nation. I belong to a small nation, and I am proud of the fact. It is an ancient race, not as old as yours, and although I am very proud of it, I am not going to compare it with yours. One day it may become great; it will perhaps be chosen for great things. But all I know is that up to the present it is small races that have been chosen for great things. And there we were, confronted with your people in every country of the world, very powerful. You may say you have been oppressed and persecuted — that has been your power! You have been hammered into very fine steel, and that is why you can never be broken. Hammered for centuries into the finest steel of any race in the world! And therefore we wanted your help. We thought it would be very useful. I am putting the other side quite frankly. We had had already very great help. I personally owe a deep debt of gratitude to Dr. Weizmann, and I am his proselyte. In the Ministry of Munitions, I was confronted with one of the most serious crises with which I was ever beset. It was one of those unexpected things that come upon you like a cavalry charge coming up against a chasm. And I found such a chasm. As I marched from gun to gun, from shell to shell, I suddenly found that we had not got one of the great motive powers to make cordite — wood alcohol. I turned to Dr. Weizmann. Alcohol had to be made out of wood, and he trained little animals — I don't know through how many generations — to eat sugar, and the alcohol was made out of maize, and then there was plenty of "corn in Egypt," and we were saved. I felt a deep debt of gratitude, and so did all the Allies, to the brilliant scientific genius of Dr. Weizmann. When we talked to him and asked him, "What can we do for you in the way of any honour?" he replied: "All I care for is an opportunity to do something for my people." It was worth anything to us in honour, or in coin of the realm, but all he asked for was to be allowed to present his case for the restoration of his people to the old country which they had made famous throughout the world. Acetone converted me to Zionism. So the case was put before us, and when the War Cabinet began to consider the case for the Declaration, it was quite unanimously in favour. I think we secured the co-operation of the French at that time, and the famous Balfour Declaration was made. But there is no man with a greater part in the conversion of the Gentiles running the war than my friend Dr. Weizmann. I am glad of it, both on the ground of sympathy and of interest. I was a very strong advocate of the conquest of Palestine. Some day I shall be able to tell the story of how near a thing that was, when we organised all our forces, took all our guns and munitions for the final attack with the idea of capturing Jerusalem, but the danger on the Western front very nearly forced us to take the troops away. If that had happened, I think Palestine would still have been in the hands of the Turk. Because it is idle to say that in the terms of peace you could have insisted on clearing Palestine. The Turk has not retired from any country from which he was not driven before the armistice. He has a way with him of signing documents. Say to him: "Give up Palestine," he simply says: "Where shall I sign?" Say to him: "You must give up Constantinople," and his pen is ready. The Turk will sign any document you can present to him and he will never honour one of them. The Turk signed everything after the armistice, but he has never retired from a single yard of territory from which we had not driven him at the point of the bayonet.[4]

The Comedy of Jerusalem's Surrender

Field-Marshal Viscount Wavell states in his biography of General Allenby that "the capture of Jerusalem stirred the imagination of the whole world." This is not surprising. But the manner in which the Holy City surrendered to the British was a source of universal amusement. General Wavell describes that event and so do several other writers, among them one who witnessed the "comic opera." Major Vivian Gilbert, in his book *The Romance of the Last Crusade,* relates this curious event:

[Private Murch, the army cook,] was both hot and tired. He sat down on a large stone and mopped his face with the oily rag he had removed from the muzzle of his rifle and placed in his pocket before leaving camp; then, removing the cigarette stump from behind his ear, he lit it and took one or two satisfying puffs before casting it aside and taking a further look at the surrounding country. . . .

"'Ello! What was that?"

The end of the road, previously deserted, was now covered by a large crowd advancing from the shelter of the houses. It was still some distance away, but a carriage drawn by a pair of horses could be seen leading the procession. As it got nearer two men on horseback could be distinguished carrying white banners on long poles and riding a little in rear of the dilapidated vehicle.

Murch got up and strolled towards them. He was quite mystified as to the meaning of this strange performance. He could see that many of the people,

The surrender of Jerusalem to the British in 1917. (Courtesy of The American Colony, Jerusalem.)

there were women and children amongst them, carried white flags and handkerchiefs, and these they continually waved before them; perhaps it was a native funeral, thought the army cook.

At length they espied him, and, with loud cries and clapping of hands, crowded round, all talking at once.

They were in a wild state of excitement, and for a moment, Private Murch thought of flight. Then he decided he would hold his ground; after all, he was a British soldier, whereas these villagers were only a lot of "blawsted natives"; there was nothing to fear.

His arms were seized and frantically pulled up and down; he was patted all over, and almost deafened with piercing shrieks of joy uttered by the women. They seemed particularly pleased with his uniform and general appearance, and the greatest interest was shown in his brass buttons and his rifle.

In spite of these rather embarrassing attentions, he could not help feeling highly gratified with the obvious admiration he was causing. It was the first time since he had been a soldier that his "turn out" had excited any marks of approval from anyone. That this should happen at a time when he honestly felt he was not looking his best, was truly remarkable.

At the height of all this excitement, a coloured gentleman in a white night shirt shouted loudly, "Allah Akbar," and seizing the cook in both arms endeavoured to kiss him. Our hero was luckily able to frustrate this design by wrenching one arm free and assuming a threatening attitude, but only just in time.

The noise now died down, and a little man in a black frock coat with a tarbush on his head and looking very much like a Turk, could be heard speaking from the carriage.

"You are British soldier, are not you?" he asked in a high falsetto voice.

"I should say so," replied Private Murch.

"Where is General Allah Nebi?" now enquired the man in the red fez.

"'Anged if I know, mister," answered the private.

"I want to surrender the city please. 'Ere are ze keys; it is yours!" went on the stranger, producing a large bunch of keys and waving them before the bewildered Britisher, who now began to think he had fallen amongst lunatics.

"I don't want yer city. I want some heggs for my hofficers!" yelled the disgusted cook.

*   *   *   *

Whilst all these things were happening the major was awaiting anxiously the return of the cook with his breakfast. The other officers also were beginning to feel hungry; as for the colonel, he made a few caustic remarks with reference to brilliant ideas in general and sent for his own servant to take the cook's place.

I happened to be at battalion headquarters when Private Murch, hot and out of breath, arrived.

"Where have you been for the last four hours?" demanded the colonel in a freezing tone.

The perspiring private proceeded to relate his amazing adventures in a rich cockney dialect.

In spite of his rambling and at times incoherent recitation, it dawned on us at last that one of the greatest events in the history of the world, for which thousands had given their lives and for which millions of pounds of English money had been poured out, had just taken place.

When the man came to the end of his story, the colonel turned to us and said quietly, "Gentlemen, Jerusalem has fallen!"

Then he seized a field telephone, rang up the brigadier, and acquainted him with the startling news.

Brigadier-General Watson was wildly excited—he was the nearest general to the Holy City and to him would fall the honour of accepting the surrender: his name would be flashed to every corner of the globe.

"Where's my horse?" he shouted. "Saddle him up immediately and tell the groom to follow me," and he hurried to his tent for his best red cap and fly whisk.

In a few minutes he was galloping madly up the Jaffa-Jerusalem road followed by an orderly on a mule.

He met the mayor in his carriage outside the Jaffa Gate. The road was now black with people, for everyone in the city was at last aware the Turks had left for good.

Together the mayor of Jerusalem and the English brigadier rode through the streets of Jerusalem until they came to the El Kala citadel. On the steps at the base of the Tower of David the mayor surrendered the Holy City and handed over the keys. General Watson accepted in the name of the Allies, and was loudly cheered by the inhabitants as he rode back to brigade headquarters.

In the meantime, however, directly the brigadier had left the British lines, the brigade major rang up the divisional commander and informed him of what was taking place. Major-General Shea got on the field telephone and said, "Stop the brigadier, I will *myself* take the surrender of Jerusalem!"

It was, of course, too late to stop the brigadier then: he was already in Jerusalem. So when he got back, flushed with success, the brigade major told him what the divisional general had said. Brigadier-General Watson decided the only thing to do was to ride back to the city and hand the keys back to the mayor, who was informed that Major-General Shea was now on his way to see him.

General Allenby, walking into Jerusalem. (Courtesy of the National and University Library, Jerusalem.)

Fresh cheering in the streets announced the ceremonial arrival of the divisional commander in his car, accompanied by a glittering staff. The mayor came out, made another little speech, surrendered Jerusalem again, and handed over the keys which had been handed back to him a short time before by the brigadier. Major-General Shea made a tactful speech that was loudly cheered by the crowds in the streets; and then, amidst the clapping of hands and welcoming cries of the populace, motored back to his headquarters on the Mount of Grapes.

His first duty on returning was to send a telegram to the commander-in-chief, through the 20th Corps, worded as follows:

"I have the honor to report that I have this day accepted the surrender of Jerusalem."

By return came the message:

"General Allenby will himself accept the surrender of Jerusalem on the 11th inst.; make all arrangements."

On December 11th General Allenby, followed by representatives of the Allies, made his formal entry into Jerusalem.

The historic Jaffa Gate was opened after years of disuse enabling him to pass into the Holy City without making use of the gap in the wall through which the kaiser entered in 1898.

Allenby entered on foot and left on foot, and throughout the ceremony no Allied flag was flown, whilst naturally no enemy flags were visible. The mayor came out on to the steps of the Tower of David, surrendered the city and handed over to the commander-in-chief the keys which had been returned to him by the divisional general the previous afternoon.[5]

In December 1978 Alec Wilsom, a former private in General Allenby's Expeditionary Force, visited Jerusalem. According to Mr. Wilsom, it was his commander, Major W. J. Beck, who was the first British officer that met Jerusalem's Mayor al-Husseini and negotiated the city's surrender. Major Beck was killed a few months later in the battle for Amman and was buried in the British military cemetery on Mount Scopus.

General Allenby's Proclamation
"To the Inhabitants of Jerusalem the Blessed"

There are many reports of General Allenby's entry into Jerusalem on December 11, 1917. Most of these reports contrast Allenby's reverent entry on foot as a pilgrim with the pompous entry of Kaiser Wilhelm II in 1898, who insisted on entering Jerusalem on horseback. One first-hand description of Allenby's entry into Jerusalem was provided by Joseph F. Broadhurst, the policeman in charge. In his book *From Vine Street to Jerusalem,* he writes:

On the 11th December, two days after our entry, General Allenby was due to arrive. I hastily did what was necessary for his safety, by having every house searched on the line of route. This was to see if any Turkish officer or men were still in hiding. I also posted men on the roofs of houses as an added precaution. Allenby entered on foot through the massive Jaffa Gate, followed by his staff, both British and foreign. The whole of Jerusalem watched him go by with silent yet eloquent expressions. Our own troops, in battered helmets and war-stained uniforms, lined the route, presenting arms for the first time in months. Not an allied flag, indeed, not a flag of any kind flew over the city. No sound of firing came from the Turks beyond the Mount of Olives. There was not a vestige of flamboyancy about this strangely moving ceremony, the most unforgettable I have ever seen; just the slow, muffled footfalls on the dusty roadway from the booted feet of a body of solemn-eyed staff officers in worn Service dress. Perhaps it was the look on the soldier who led them which charged the atmosphere. It was widely stated that the crowd was much larger than when the Kaiser had entered in 1898.[6]

Upon entering the city, Allenby ascended the steps of the Citadel and, standing under the shadow of the Tower of David, he read his proclamation, which was later posted in the strategic places of the city. The proclamation was addressed "To the Inhabitants of Jerusalem the Blessed" and was issued in seven languages—English, French, Arabic, Hebrew, Greek, Russian, and Italian. He signed the proclamation by his full name—Edmund Henry Hyman Allenby, General. In his proclamation, he stated that the principle of the *Status Quo* for religious institutions and holy places would continue to be in force and that law and order would be maintained. The proclamation read as follows:

To the inhabitants of Jerusalem the Blessed and the people dwelling in the vicinity. The defeat inflicted upon the Turks by the troops under my command has resulted in the occupation of your city by my forces. I therefore here and now proclaim it to be under martial law, under which form of administration it will remain so long as military considerations make it necessary. However, lest anyone of you be alarmed by reason of your experience at the hands of the enemy who has retired, I hereby inform you that it

Entry to Tower of David, from where General Allenby read his proclamation (1917). (Courtesy of Central Zionist Archives, Jerusalem.)

is my desire that every person should pursue his lawful business without fear of interruption.

Furthermore, since your City is regarded with affection by the adherents of three of the great religions of mankind, and its soil has been consecrated by the prayers and pilgrimages of multitudes of devout people of these three religions for many centuries, therefore do I make known to you that every sacred building, monument, holy spot, shrine, traditional site, endowment, pious bequest, or customary place of prayer, of whatsoever form of the three religions, will be maintained and protected according to the existing customs and beliefs of those to whose faiths they are sacred.

The Commonwealth War Cemeteries in Jerusalem

According to popular etymology, the Hebrew name of Jerusalem (*Yeru-Shalem*) means the City of Peace. Actually the name Jerusalem derives from a synthesis of two Canaanite words which allude to the city's pre-Hebraic role as the center of worship of a local deity named Shalem. Jerusalem literally means "The City of the god Shalem." When the Hebrews conquered the city, they assumed that *Shalem* was identical with the Hebrew word for peace, *Shalom*. Thus Jerusalem came to mean the City of Peace, and Isaiah's prophecy of universal peace when the nations "will beat their swords into ploughshares and their spears into pruning hooks" (Isa. 2:4) became associated with Jerusalem. The city's exalted role is also noted in the Christian Bible, where *Shalem* is defined as peace (Hebrews 7:12). It is paradoxical, therefore, that Jerusalem should contain within its city limits extensive war cemeteries in which are buried thousands of warriors who fell in the battles for Jerusalem. The city's destiny of peace has hardly been substantiated by its history. Indeed, Jerusalem has served time and again as one of the bloodiest battlefields in the world.

What may be Jerusalem's most impressive—though far from its largest—military burial ground is the Jerusalem War Cemetery on Mount Scopus in which were interred British and Commonwealth casualties of the First World War. In ancient times Mount Scopus was the staging ground for the Roman army's final assault on the fortifications of Jerusalem during the war of 67–70 c.e. Today this hill is occupied by Hebrew University and the Hadassah Hospital. Next to the hospital lies the graceful and well-kept Commonwealth War Cemetery in which are buried 2,474 soldiers who fell in this theater of the First World War.

As one approaches the cemetery he or she notes an inscription on the impressive gateway which proclaims that

> the land on which this cemetery stands is the free gift of the people of Palestine for the perpetual resting place of those of the Allied armies who fell in the war of 1914–1918 and are honored here.

This inscription is repeated on either side of the gateway in Hebrew and Arabic translations.

Facing the entrance outside the cemetery is a stately memorial with an epitaph which reads:

1915–1918

> To the glory of God and in memory of the part played by the Australian Imperial Forces in Sinai, Palestine, and Syria. This memorial has been erected by the Commonwealth of Australia.

On entering the cemetery one sees a vast array of simple grave markers symmetrically arranged; and, in the center, is a lofty cross that towers over the whole necropolis. The headstones are of equal size, two feet eight inches in height. On each slab is engraved the service or regimental badge, followed by the rank, name, unit, date of death, and age of the interred. Then comes a large cross and in many cases also an inscription chosen by relatives. Some of these epitaphs are touching, as for example: "The widow's only son." "You are not forgotten, dear brother. Sister J." "Soldier of St. John's College, Cambridge. Beloved by All." About a hundred of the headstones bear a simple, melancholy inscription: "A soldier of the Great War," the religious emblem, and "Known to God." These memorialize unidentified corpses.

Notwithstanding the tall cross in the center, not all the interred are Christians. In the northern section of the cemetery there are twenty-four slabs on which is engraved in place of a cross the Jewish emblem of the six-pointed star, commonly known as the *Magen David* (Shield of David). Inside the emblem are engraved five Hebrew letters, the initials of the traditional Jewish prayer for the dead: "May his soul be wrapped up in God's treasure of eternal life." These headstones mark the graves of Jewish soldiers who fell in the battles for the Holy Land.

The most pathetic memorial is an extensive wall in the rear of the cemetery, flanking a chapel erected by

> the officers, non-commissioned officers, and men of the Egyptian Expeditionary Force to the honored memory of their comrades who fell in the Palestine campaign 1914–1918.

On this wall are engraved the names of 3,359 officers and men "who have no graves." These were casualties hurriedly buried in or near the battlefields where they fell. Their graves remained unmarked; their whereabouts unrecorded.

Allenby's army also contained a contingent of Indian soldiers, composed of both Hindus and Moslems. The casualties of these warriors required a burial place of their own, because their burial customs are radically different from those of Christians and Jews. The Moslems bury their war casualties in mass graves, and the Hindus cremate the corpses and then bury the ashes. A separate cemetery was therefore established in a quiet area, removed from the built-up sections of the city. Today, however, the cemetery is surrounded by apartment houses and busy streets in the Talpiot neighborhood. The cemetery is fenced in. But, since there are no tombstones in it, the children used to climb over the fence to play football and other games. Now there is a Hebrew sign posted on the fence stating that "78 Indian soldiers are buried here" and that "all kinds of games are absolutely prohibited."

At the entrance there is a more conventional sign which reads:

Jerusalem Indian Cemetery

The keys to this cemetery may be obtained from the British Consulate General, Tower House, Station Road, Jerusalem, where the register of the graves may also be consulted.

On entering the cemetery one notes that in place of the usual individual gravestones, there are two large monuments facing each other from opposite ends of the cemetery. One of them memorializes the mass grave of the Moslem soldiers, and the other commemorates the Hindu soldiers. The former bears an inscription which notes that "31 Musulman soldiers of the Indian army are buried here" followed by an Arabic quotation from the Koran. The latter notes that "47 soldiers of the Indian army are honoured here" followed by an epitaph in Sanskrit. No names are engraved on these monuments.

General Allenby's conquest of Palestine was a victory of historic proportions. In its day it was compared with the Crusader capture of Jerusalem in 1099. It marked the end of four hundred years of Turkish rule and inspired the hopeful anticipation of a new era of peace and progress in the Holy Land. These hopes, however, were not substantiated. In place of peace, there has been unending strife among the local inhabitants and between them and the Mandatory Government. This strife escalated and reached its climax in the Arab uprisings beginning in 1936. These disturbances came to an end in 1939, when the Second World War erupted and the British finally put a quick end to the Arab rioting. During the three decades of the Mandatory Government, the British casualties—soldiers and policemen—were buried in a nonmilitary cemetery, the Mount Zion Protestant Cemetery.

The presence of war cemeteries in Jerusalem clearly indicates that the psalmist's prayer "for the peace of Jerusalem" (Ps. 122:6) has not yet been answered. It remains a messianic hope.

A Strange "Incident" at the Wailing Wall

British rule in Palestine was marked by civilized polish and concern for the Holy City's religious and historic monuments. But government policy was always subordinate to imperial interests. This becomes clear from the strange British behavior during the so-called incidents at the Western (Wailing) Wall beginning with the first outbreak in 1920.

Everyone visiting the plaza in front of the Western (Wailing) Wall notes the Jewish worshipers perpetually at prayer. Today, these worshipers are neither disturbed nor do they disturb anyone. This peaceful situation has not always been so. During the British Mandate from 1918 to 1948, there were so-called incidents which were often pitched battles. These conflicts now seem like bad dreams. But, in their days, they were real and tragic. There were bloodshed and casualties. One of these "incidents" occurred in the year 1920.

The story is weird and unbelievable. The incident occurred on the Day of Atonement, which fell that year on September 24. The Jews set up a screen at the wall to separate the men from the women. This was normal practice. But this time the Jews fastened the screen to the pavement. The officials of the Arab Waqf protested this unprecedented act. They also objected to the portable ark for the scrolls of the Torah, which, they said, was larger than in previous years. The Arabs also objected to some additional seats which were set up. The British deputy district commander visited the place and ordered the removal of the screen before the morning service. The service of the Day of Atonement had begun at sunset and—no work being allowed on this most holy of holy days—the beadles refused to remove the screen. One beadle did promise to remove the screen, but intended to do so at the end of the holy day, not in the morning.

Jews crowded at a worship service near the Western (Wailing) Wall during the British Mandate. (Courtesy of Central Zionist Archives, Jerusalem.)

On the morning of the Day of Atonement, the deputy district commissioner sent a police officer to check whether the screen had been removed. Should the screen still be there he ordered the police officer to remove it by force.

The congregation knew nothing of the government's orders nor even of the beadle's undertaking to remove the screen. When the officer arrived during the morning services and tried to remove the screen, the congregation resisted. With the help of additional police and after a physical struggle, the screen was removed.

The Jews were outraged. So were many Englishmen. The editorial in *The Palestine Weekly* of September 28, 1928, protested vigorously:

> The proceedings, from beginning to end, bear the stamp of abysmal ignorance of Jewish beliefs and ritual, aggravated by a total disregard of the grave and far-reaching consequences. It is really astounding that a superior government official, who has been living in Palestine continuously for the past ten years, who has held several important government appointments and who has had ample opportunity of learning what is mere honored custom, what is holy ritual and what is considered as holy of holies, should trample under foot the most sacred observances of the Jews. . . . It must be noted that if there was an infringement, it had been done regularly for the past four hundred years ever since Sultan Selim I gave the Jews certain rights over the Wailing Wall. The official reply given by the Acting High Commissioner to the protest of the Jewish Agency and Palestine Jewry is as inadequate as it is misleading. In the first place, there is no definite 'status quo' beyond an undertaking on the part of the Jews not to encumber the space in front of the Wall with heavy pieces of furniture not easily movable. This has always been strictly adhered to. . . . In view of the foregoing a mere expression of regret at what happened cannot be considered as adequate.[7]

Several weeks later, on November 1, 1928, the General Moslem Conference reacted to the "incident" with a set of resolutions which included a threat:

> (a) To strongly protest against any action or attempt which aims at the establishment of any right to the Jews in the Holy Burak area and to deprecate any such action or attempt. The Conference further protest against leniency, disregard or vacillation which the Government may show in this respect.
>
> (b) To ask the Government immediately and perpetually to prevent the Jews from placing under any circumstances whether temporary or permanent any objects in the area, such as seats, lamps, objects of worship or reading, and to

prevent them also from raising their voices or making any speeches, in such a manner as would not compel the Moslems to take such measures themselves, in order to defend at any cost this holy Moslem place and to safeguard their established rights therein which they have exercised for the last thirteen centuries.

(c) To hold Government responsible for any consequences of any measures which the Moslems may adopt for the purpose of defending the Holy Burak themselves in the event of the failure of the Government which are entrusted with the maintenance of public security and the safeguarding of the Moslem Holy Places to prevent any such intrusion on the part of the Jews.[8]

The British officials' insensitivity toward the Jewish populace and partiality toward the Arab population were later evidenced in official British policy. The White Paper of 1939 and the Bevin blockade of the shores of Palestine against the illegal immigrants from the Nazi extermination camps were logical extensions of the incident on that Day of Atonement and the many similar incidents which occurred on subsequent occasions.

A "Jewish" Y.M.C.A.

The Jerusalem Y.M.C.A. was founded in 1878, but its new monumental buildings on King David Street, opposite the King David Hotel, did not open their doors to the public until 1933. During the century of its existence, Jerusalem has undergone many radical changes. The population has grown from less than twenty-five thousand inhabitants to almost half a million. Over thirty thousand tourists visit the Y.M.C.A. annually, and its program includes more than sixty assorted cultural and sporting activities.

The splendid facilities of the Jerusalem Y.M.C.A. were made possible by a donation of one million dollars made by James Newbiggin Jarvie of Montclair, New Jersey, and by additional gifts from many individuals in America and England. The neo-Byzantine edifice was designed by Arthur Loomis Harman, a prominent architect from New York, whose firm designed the world-famous Empire State Building. The cornerstone was laid in 1928 by the then High Commissioner, Lord Plumer; and the building was officially opened in 1933 by Lord Allenby.

Among the characteristics of the Jerusalem Y.M.C.A. building is its superabundance of symbols. Every part of the structure is symbolic of the institution's central principles, and every inscription proclaims a basic tenet of the Y.M.C.A.'s message to the community. Thus the majestic central tower flanked by the auditorium on one side and the physical education building on the other represents the institution's motto—the development of body, mind, and spirit. The approach to the entrance is bordered by twelve cypresses, and the auditorium has twelve windows symbolic of the twelve Hebrew tribes, the twelve disciples of Jesus, and the twelve followers of Mohammed. In front of the impressive stairway leading up to the entrance of the building is a plaque on which is inscribed a quotation from General Allenby's dedication address. The

The Jerusalem Y.M.C.A.

inscription is in Hebrew, English, and Arabic. It reads:

> Here is a place whose atmosphere is peace, where political and religious jealousies can be forgotten, and international unity be fostered and developed.

And on the central facade there are three inscriptions in Hebrew, Aramaic, and Arabic, quotations from the Jewish, Christian, and Moslem holy scriptures. The inscriptions proclaim:

"The Lord our God is One."

"I am the way."

"There is no God but Allah."

But the most impressive message of the institution is to be seen in a bold graphic representation in which a six-pointed star of David, a crescent, a cross, and the Y.M.C.A.'s emblematic triangle are integrated in one harmonious design.

Leslie Farmer, a Second World War chaplain in the British army, was stationed in Jerusalem. In his book *We Saw the Holy City,* he described the Jerusalem Y.M.C.A.:

> The finest building in New Jerusalem, dominating the city with the highest tower in it, is the famous Jerusalem home of the Young Men's Christian Association. . . . All that was best in the social life of the Holy City, not only for men in uniform, but amongst young Arabs and Jews, centred in that pinnacle of white stone with adjacent buildings clustering at its foot. It seemed to possess everything a young man could want: a library with thousands of volumes, many of them in Arabic and Hebrew, as well organized as any borough library in England, with a huge section devoted to devotional and theological subjects; the only swimming-pool for hundreds of miles; a gymnasium with rooms for boxing, wrestling, squash courts, all under an immense dome; a large concert auditorium; hostel bedrooms and public restaurant; an Army canteen and billiard rooms; a soda fountain; tennis courts; a football ground; and a multitude of other amenities of that kind. It stands on a hilltop outside the west wall of the Old City. . . .

> We ascended by lift to the observation gallery above the carillon high in the tower. There are thirty-five bells in the carillon, the largest weighing 1 1/2 tons. Often on Sunday evenings we listened to the hymn-tunes, many of them Evangelical favourites of England and America, ringing across Old Jerusalem and New. . . .

The auditorium—the Golden Hall of Friendship—has an elaborate stage and orchestra pit and a four-manual organ with nearly 3,000 pipes. A man can pass through the largest pipe; the smallest is the size of a lead pencil.[9]

The Jerusalem Y.M.C.A. also houses a museum of antiquities known as the Herbert E. Clark Collection of Near Eastern Antiquities. This museum is not a competitor of the Rockefeller Museum or of the several other archaeological museums in the city, but it is decidedly worth visiting.

Prior to the establishment of the State of Israel, the membership of the Jerusalem Y.M.C.A. was mostly Christian. Only a small fraction of its membership was Jewish and Moslem. After the Jewish-Arab war of 1948–1949, the city was divided and the Y.M.C.A. found itself in the Israel section of the city, hermetically sealed off from much of its Christian constituency. But the Y.M.C.A. continued to function, and its ranks were gradually filled with Jews who were welcomed in accordance with the institution's liberal policies. By now the membership, which is over three thousand, is said to be ninety-five per cent Jewish, three per cent Christian, and two per cent Moslem; and the dominant language in the Y.M.C.A. corridors is Hebrew. More striking is the fact that many of the Y.M.C.A. members come from the Orthodox Jewish neighborhoods. They are attracted to the Y.M.C.A. by the separate bathing schedules for men and women. The institution is closed, except to residents, on the Day of Atonement; and the chairman of the board is a prominent Jewish lawyer, Mr. Pinhas Rabinovitch. It was in 1974 that Mr. Rabinovitch was asked to serve on the Y.M.C.A.'s board. But he could not accept the honor conferred on him, because a clause in the Y.M.C.A.'s constitution limited membership on the board to Christians. In 1975 a new constitution was drafted in which it was stated that "The Y.M.C.A. shall maintain a strictly non-political policy, and shall make no distinction of race, nationality, sex or faith either in its administration and managerial operations or in its institutional activities." Mr. Pinhas Rabinovitch could now in good conscience accede to the invitation to join the board and then to become its chairman. It should be added, however, that both Mr. Rabinovitch and the director of the Y.M.C.A., Mr. James Rhoads, maintain that the institution, by adopting the principle of universality, has become more truly a Christian institution. Notwithstanding this official interpretation of the institution's character, there are some who insist that the Jerusalem Y.M.C.A., by virtue of its overwhelming Jewish membership and the other aspects of "its administration and managerial operations" and "its institutional activities," is virtually a "Jewish" Y.M.C.A.

How the British Left Jerusalem

Terence Prittie calls the British Mandate in Palestine a fiasco. Among the reasons for the fiasco, he lists the British failure to grasp "the deep and fervent Jewish belief in the sanctity of Jerusalem and its place in the Covenant."[10] And the manner of the British withdrawal from Palestine was "inglorious." Terence Prittie writes:

> The last British High Commissioner, Sir Alan Cunningham, folded up the Union Jack and left silently, almost as a thief in the night, for Haifa and his passage home. That, possibly, was the most miserable episode of all in an experiment in colonial rule which had promised so well.[11]

Terence Prittie continues his account, giving the reasons that led up to this "miserable episode":

> The British fell between two stools and the manner of their falling was inglorious. . . . Why did the British fail quite as badly as they did? The Balfour Declaration and its implicit contradictions was only one contributory cause. The anti-Semitism of the British Foreign Secretary, Ernest Bevin, was perhaps another. More important was the British habit of equating one warring faction with another, and not trying to sort out a solution on the basis of justice and common sense. Important, too, was the British failure to understand the deep and fervent Jewish belief in the sanctity of Jerusalem and its place in the Covenant. Britons were apt to remark that Jerusalem was equally holy to the Jewish and Muslim worlds. It was not; technically, it was the third city of the Muslim world, whereas it was wholly unique in Jewish tradition and religous belief.[12]

That Jerusalem is only third in the hierarchy of Moslem holy cities is stated categorically by a Moslem traveler, Nasir-I-Khusran, who visited Jerusalem in the eleventh century. In his diary he states that a prayer in Mecca is equal to one hundred thousand prayers elsewhere; a prayer in Medina is equal to fifty thousand prayers elsewhere; and a prayer in Jerusalem is equal to twenty-five thousand prayers elsewhere.[13] Jerusalem is clearly not of equal sanctity in Judaism and Islam.

Sir Alan Cunningham, the last British high commissioner, left Haifa on board a British destroyer without handing over his stewardship in an orderly manner befitting a responsible government. Anarchy and the rapid dispossession of the Jewish community were hopefully anticipated by the British Foreign Secretary Ernest Bevin. Six well-equipped Arab armies converged on the land, and a quick Arab victory seemed assured. This, he thought, will teach these obstinate Zionists a lesson. But the fortunes of war are unpredictable. The small, relatively unarmed contingents of the Jewish underground, now turned army, successfully resisted and then defeated the armies of the invading Arab states. This, said many a Jew, was obviously "the finger of God." Messianic times must be at hand.

EIGHT

Jerusalem Divided and Reunited

The Miracle of Jerusalem's Development During the Past Century

In the middle of the nineteenth century there were practically no human habitations outside the city walls of Jerusalem. Beyond the city gates there were only brown and stony hills, deep valleys, scattered ancient sepulchres, and cemeteries. The desert literally came up to the walls of the city. A person approaching the city saw only the empty hills, the necropolis, and the city's stately walls. Only when the visitor entered one of the city's gates did he or she discover a living town.

In the course of the past century and a half, suburbs of considerable size have grown up all around the city walls. On the west a new city has grown up—a metropolis with all the attributes of modernity. But, unlike other cities, one does not find in Jerusalem the typical urban sprawl. The desert has receded from the walls of the Old City, and it now ends at the last line of residences of the New City.

Prior to the development of Jerusalem's suburbs the Jews lived in the overcrowded, overpriced, and disease-ridden huts and hovels of the Jewish Quarter within the city walls. To venture out of the city walls at night, let alone to live there, was unthinkable. But the overcrowding became unbearable, and some brave souls began to talk of building homes outside the safety of the city's fortifications. A number of small settlements sprung up, not without paying the price in blood. These small settle-

*View of the New City of Jerusalem, with Independence Park in the foreground
(1951). (Courtesy of Israel Government Press Office.)*

ments of several families each grew and became suburbs. Eventually these
suburbs merged and became the New City. But each of the original
settlements has retained its character as a *Sh'khunah,* a neighborhood.
Each neighborhood had its own history, its founders, its heroes, and its
victims. This is a unique aspect of Jerusalem's New City.

On a chart posted in the small park in front of Jerusalem's modest city
hall there are some surprising population figures. According to that chart,
there were in 1870 only 22,000 residents in Jerusalem, of whom 11,000
were Jews, 6,500 Moslems, and 4,500 Christian. In 1977, Jerusalem's
population was 357,000, of whom 260,000 were Jews, 85,000 Moslems,
and 12,000 Christians.

In 1981 Jerusalem became the largest city in Israel. Its population
was 407,000. Tel-Aviv and Haifa, which had been larger than Jerusalem,
now ranked as second and third respectively. Tel-Aviv without its substantial suburbs had a population of 335,000, and Haifa had 230,000
residents. But Greater Tel-Aviv, that is, Tel-Aviv together with its immediate suburbs is still by far the largest city in Israel with a population of
almost a million.

Jerusalem's rapid growth and unique development during the last
century and a half are truly one of the miracles of the Holy City.

What Saved Jerusalem from the Arab Bombardment?

During the Israel-Arab war of 1948–1949, the Arabs repeatedly shelled the Jewish section of the city. The houses, however, withstood the bombardment. Robert St. John was in Jerusalem in 1948 and was an eyewitness to the struggle for Israel's independence. In his book *Shalom Means Peace,* he tells the intriguing story of how the New City resisted the Arab bombardment. He writes:

> It was one day in Tel-Aviv, after the New City had had nearly two weeks of day-and-night shelling from Arab guns in the Old City. Then, when the second truce or the so-called permanent peace went into effect, two natives of Jerusalem were having an argument at the next table in a Tel-Aviv cafe. One of them insisted that it was American canned goods that had saved the city. He said:

> "Every shop in town had rows of dusty cans on the top shelves, mostly American-style foodstuff which had never especially appealed to our people. But when the siege of the New City began and food got scarce, they remembered the top shelves, and it was those dusty cans that kept us alive."

> The other man had a different theory. He said it was an irony of history that Jerusalem would have fallen to the Arab Legion, which was staffed, trained, and equipped by the British, if it had not been for Ronald Storrs, one-time British governor of the city. He argued it this way:

> "We cursed Storrs for many years because of what we called his pro-Arab bias. But when the mortar shells began to come over we sang praises to his name. At night we'd lie in bed listening to the cannonading. It was a fearful sound. Sometimes it would go on for hours. We'd lie there thinking that surely most of the New City had been destroyed. But in the morning, after it was all over, we'd go out and be astonished at what we saw. The shells the Arabs used weren't able to penetrate those great blocks of stone. Had our homes been built of lesser material they would have been destroyed and thousands of people would have been killed. But the shells just seemed to bounce off that Storrs stone. And so maybe your canned goods had something to do with it, too, but it was the Storrs Plan that saved the New City from being destroyed."[1]

Ronald Storrs, when he became the military governor of Jerusalem in 1918, issued an edict requiring the use of local stone for the building of houses. Tradition and elegance were the principal aims of the decree. Yet, it was the local stone used as construction material that withstood the Arab shells.

The city wall, seen through the barbed wire dividing the Jewish and Arab sections of Jerusalem (1948). (Courtesy of Central Zionist Archives, Jerusalem.)

The Divided City

For nineteen years, from 1948 to 1967, Jerusalem was divided into an Arab city and a Jewish city. The Arab section consisted of the Old City, the Mount of Olives, and the adjacent Arab suburb to the north. The Jewish part consisted of the western section, often called the New City, and Mount Zion. The Arab section of the city was governed by the Hashemite Kingdom of Jordan; the Jewish section was the capital of the State of Israel.

The division of the city was practically absolute. Only rare exceptions were made in the case of some privileged individuals. Otherwise there was no communication whatever between the two sections. Barbed wire, concrete walls, and a no-man's-land effectively sealed off the respective populations from contact with each other. It was said that even the cats in East Jerusalem when they were out calling never crossed over to the Israeli section of the city. The same was no doubt true of Israeli cats.

The border between the two sections of the city ran through some buildings, and even some rooms, so that one part of these buildings was in Israel and the other part was in Jordan. One such building was the Notre Dame de France, which housed a hospital. It was claimed that some patients had their heads in Israel and their feet in Jordan or vice versa.

There were no Jews in the Old City. During the war of 1948–1949, the Arabs expelled the Jewish inhabitants from the Old City. This brought an end to the centuries-old Jewish Quarter. But the Jewish holy places with the exception of the Tomb of David were all in the Old City and on the Mount of Olives. The Armistice Agreement between Israel and Jordan provided that the Jews were to be given free access to the Western (Wailing) Wall and to the Jewish Cemetery on the Mount of Olives. However, the Jordanian government reneged on that pledge. The Jews were thus in the New City, and most of their holy places were in the Jordanian Old City. The artificial nature of the divided city is described by John Gray in his *History of Jerusalem:*

> The unhappy division of Jerusalem through the Arab-Jewish conflict also separated communities not directly interested in the conflict. Thus for instance the noble Anglican Cathedral of St. George was in Jordan and the Scots Memorial Church and Hospice of St. Andrews, the dignified war memorial to Scottish soldiers who fell in Palestine in the First World War, looked over the derelict no-man's-land from Israel to the south-west hill and the Jaffa, or Hebron, Gate. The free fellowship of scholars was also hindered. Objects from the rich archaeological fields of Palestine were distributed between the Rockefeller Museum in Jordan and new museums in Israel, while the various learned institutions were similarly separated. The Monastery of St. Stephen with its world-famous *École Biblique,* the home of the learned Dominicans, whom Sir Ronald Storrs called justly 'the intellectual aristocracy of Jerusalem,' and the German Archaeological Institute were in Jordan, while the progressive Jesuit Pontifical Biblical Institute and the tremendous intellectual power-house of the Hebrew University were isolated in the Jewish part of the city.[2]

And the human element of the artificial division of the city is poignantly described by a young American Jew, Hillel Halkin, now living in Haifa:

> It is difficult to describe the particular combination of resignation, longing, and unreasonable hope with which one looked out in those years from the Israeli side at the impenetrable Ottoman rooftops of the Old City, or clambered up strange rooftops in pursuit of a glimpse of the golden mosque

or the paving stones of the Temple Mount. . . . And because one knew, or imagined, that on the other side there were Arabs looking back with a similar mixture of emotions at houses they had once lived in and neighborhoods that had been their own, the entire city seemed to shrivel into one concentrated symbol of loss, as though it were not space at all that was dividing it from itself, but something more cruel and final—time, perhaps, or eternity.[3]

For nineteen years Jordanian soldiers stood guard on the ramparts of the Western Wall of the Old City, while Israeli soldiers were stationed on the roof of the Church of the Dormition on Mount Zion. The guardians of the Arab and Jewish sections of Jerusalem faced each other as perpetual enemies. This artificial division of Jerusalem lasted till the Six-Day War in 1967, when the Israeli army captured the Old City. The concrete walls and the barbed wire were removed, and the city was restored to normalcy. Jerusalem once more became a "city which is bound firmly together" (Ps. 122:3). The populations of the Old City and the New City immediately began to mingle, and prosperity has favored the residents of the united city.

Two Memorials of Jordanian Rule

When the psalmist proclaimed that Jerusalem was "the perfection of beauty, the joy of the whole earth," he must have stood on the crest of the Mount of Olives and viewed the marvelous panorama of the Holy City. No one can view Jerusalem from that vantage point and fail to be fascinated by that wondrous scene. Many thoughts and emotions are evoked by this noble vista. One of these is the striking contrast between two memorials left by the Jordanians after their nineteen years of rule in the Old City.

From the Mount of Olives one sees the magnificent dome of the Mosque of Omar (Dome of the Rock) which shines in Jerusalem's brilliant sunshine. King Hussein strengthened the foundations of the walls and the ceiling, repaired the windows and the outer tiles, and covered the dome with anodized aluminum. The enterprise took ten years and was completed in 1965. It is a splendid memorial to King Hussein's nineteen-year reign in the Holy City.

From the same vantage point one's eyes inevitably are drawn to the incline of the Mount of Olives and the ancient Jewish cemetery. Some forty thousand tombstones were desecrated. By now some of the slabs have been restored to their former places, and the scattered bones have been

Tombstones from the desecrated Jewish cemetery on the Mount of Olives, used as a pathway in the Azaria Arab Legion Camp on the Jerusalem-Jericho Road (1967). (Courtesy of Israel Government Press Office.)

gathered and reinterred in a common grave. But enough of the devastation is still there to remind the observer of the nineteen years of King Hussein's rule in the Holy City, when almost all the synagogues, talmudic academies, and philanthropic institutions were systematically destroyed and the holiest Jewish burial place was plundered and desecrated.

Eliezer Whartman, a correspondent for the North American Newspaper Alliance, wrote in one of his syndicated articles:

> I was a member of a press tour that visited the liberated area of Jerusalem shortly after the Six-Day War. The sights we saw will remain engraved on my memory forever.
>
> We were witness to a monstrous deed: the wanton destruction of all but one of the 52 Jewish houses of worship that, until the Jordanians seized East Jerusalem in 1948, had graced the Old City, some of them for centuries; and the unspeakably callous profanation of the Jewish cemetery on the Mount of Olives, which left that ancient and historic burial place a sacrilegious shambles.
>
> It was the story of hundreds of Scrolls of the Law, reverently preserved for generations, plundered and burned to ashes. . . . Of tens of thousands of tombstones torn up, broken into pieces or used as flagstones, steps and building materials; of large areas of the cemetery leveled and converted into parking lots and a filling station; of graves ripped open and skeletal bones scattered to the four winds and an asphalt road cut through the pitiful remains to provide a short cut to a new hotel built incongruously upon the Mount of Olives. . . . Of the 50,000 tombstones in the cemetery, 38,000 were removed or damaged. The stones were used, among other things, for the construction of a Jordanian army camp at Bethany, three kilometres from the cemetery. . . .
>
> There were stories and rumours during the 19 years of the Jordanian occupation of East Jerusalem of what was happening there to Jewish holy places. But the picture that unfolded before our horrified gaze in June, 1967, was far more gruesome, the depredation far more widespread, than anything that could have been imagined.

Thus, two memorials—the shining Dome on the Temple Mount and the desecrated cemetery on the Mount of Olives—speak clearly and sadly of the Jordanian presence in Jerusalem from 1948 to 1967.

Restoring Jerusalem's Ancient Monuments

The Turks ruled Jerusalem for four hundred years. These were centuries of neglect which resulted in the deterioration and, in some cases, the total destruction of precious historic and religious monuments. When the

British drove the Turks out of the city in 1917, a new era of preservation and restoration of Jerusalem's antiquities began. Two men, endowed with a deep love of Jerusalem, have left their mark on the Holy City, and their names will forever be associated with the preservation and restoration of Jerusalem's sacred and historic places. One is Sir Ronald Storrs, British governor of Jerusalem from 1917 to 1926. The other is Mr. Teddy Kollek, mayor of Jerusalem since 1965. Both men channeled their activities through organizations that they founded. Sir Ronald Storrs founded the Pro-Jerusalem Society; Mr. Teddy Kollek founded the Jerusalem Foundation.

Sir Ronald Storrs was a man of culture who appreciated the historic and religious character of Jerusalem. He tried to be "even-handed" in the administration of the city's affairs. However, his prejudices could not be fully concealed. The Jews regarded him as anti-Semitic. Sir Ronald Storrs emphatically denied this accusation. He admitted, however, to being anti-Zionist, which the Jews regarded as being pro-Arab. But in regard to Jerusalem even his opponents agreed that he was an ardent lover of the Holy City. After nine years of service in Jerusalem, he was appointed governor of Cyprus. It is related that someone congratulated him on his promotion. Sir Ronald Storrs responded, "After Jerusalem there is no promotion." Among his outstanding accomplishments was the founding of the Pro-Jerusalem Society, composed of representatives of the Jewish, Christian, and Moslem communities, who, despite their religious and political antagonisms, joined in a common effort to restore the remnants of Jerusalem's antiquities. In the governing council of the Pro-Jerusalem Society, the representatives of the communities met and cooperated amicably in the work of preserving and restoring Jerusalem's monuments. They discussed the problems on their agenda and shared in the society's decisions. Under Sir Ronald Storrs's guidance, the society achieved some of its goals. Sir Ronald Storrs wrote that he learned how to be "an expert schnorer," because he was constantly in search of funds to finance the society's projects. In his memoirs, he described the founding of the intercommunal body and the achievements under its auspices:

> The Psalms of David and a cloud of unseen witnesses seemed to inspire our work. "Built ye the walls of Jerusalem." We put back the fallen stones, the finials, the pinnacles and the battlements, and we restored and freed from numberless encroachments the mediaeval Ramparts, so that it was possible to "Walk about Zion and go round about her: and tell the towers thereof: mark well her bulwarks, set up her houses" [Ps. 48:12-13]. Of the interest and variety of these three sacred miles I never grew weary.[4]

Teddy Kollek, a colorful personality, endowed with energy, charm, and vision, emulated Sir Ronald Storrs and invested his seemingly boundless resourcefulness in the execution of the original objectives of the Pro-Jerusalem Society as well as the creation of a beautiful modern city. Teddy Kollek skillfully guided the city's development. To finance his vast and varied program, he established the Jerusalem Foundation, which helped raise the necessary funds. And in order to restore the city's historic and authentic patterns, he organized the Jerusalem Committee in 1969. This committee originally contained seventy internationally famous architects, town planners, artists, and scholars. By 1978 the committee had grown to 120 members. Although the function of the Jerusalem Committee was only advisory, its guidance and criticism had a beneficial impact on the work of the Jerusalem Foundation.

Among the remarkable achievements of the Jerusalem Foundation and the Jerusalem Committee are the restoration of the Jewish Quarter in the Old City, the creation of the National Park around the city walls, the restoration of many neglected monuments, and the building of many new public institutions. Most important was the development of the new City Plan, according to which some old neighborhoods were to be restored and preserved as historic areas, while some decrepit sections of the city were to be rebuilt as attractive residential neighborhoods. Jerusalem will in all probability become not only one of the most beautiful cities to live in, but also one of the most inspiring cities to visit as pilgrims or tourists. All this is, of course, subject to political developments which are currently casting dark shadows on the luminous Holy City.

"The Temple Mount Is in Our Hands"

In the Six-Day War, General Mordecai Gur commanded the Reserve Paratroop Brigade which captured the Old City. He kept a log, which was published by the Defense Ministry Publishing House under the title *The Temple Mount Is in Our Hands*. The book is largely a first-hand account of the battle of Jerusalem. The following excerpts are Mordecai Gur's log entries of June 7, 1967, the day the Temple Mount and the Western (Wailing) Wall fell into the hands of the Israeli army.

> 10:00—OPPOSITE US is the Dome of the Rock. We proceed along a well-tended path. Greenery and trees on either side. We're here. We're inside. We're inside the Old City! We're on the Temple Mount! To our right—the stairs, the wide stairs—the columns and arches.

"Stop, Ben-Zur (Gur's driver), stop!" The door is already open and the men are jumping out of the halftrack and the other vehicles. We go up the magnificent wide stairs. We're in the court. Opposite—right before our eyes—within reach—is the Dome of the Rock.

No shooting here. This is a holy place.

I ask for the walkie-talkie. Senderowitz comes over. I take the microphone: "Stop—stop—all forces: stop!" A few seconds later—again: "All Pupil (*Talmid*) stations: this is Pupil—all forces, stop! Over!"

Israeli soldier near the Western (Wailing) Wall (June 1967). (Courtesy of Israel Government Press Office.)

Israeli soldiers overcome by emotion while standing in front of the Western (Wailing) Wall (June 7, 1967). (Courtesy of Israel Government Press Office.)

We're in the Temple Mount compound. We run to the centre of the compound—right next to the Dome of the Rock.

Again I take the walkie-talkie: "The Temple Mount is in our hands. This is Pupil. The Temple Mount is in our hands. Over!" . . .

10:05—THE WESTERN WALL. Everybody is in a hurry to get there. . . .

As far as I'm concerned, I've attained my objective. The Temple Mount is in our hands. The Temple Mount is also the Wall. And when I'm in the forechamber, I'm not drawn to the exterior walls.

I feel at home here. The object of all the yearnings. The Temple Mount! Mount Moriah. Abraham and Isaac. The Temple. The Zealots, the Maccabees, Bar-Kochba, Romans and Greeks. A confusion of thoughts. But there is one feeling that is firmer and deeper than everything. We're on the Temple Mount! The Temple Mount is ours! . . .

AT 12:11 THE WALL compound was packed with people and they began a *Minhah* (Afternoon) Service. . . .

I walked toward the praying soldiers. They noticed me and made way for me. I thanked them but stayed in the rear.

In all that throng I wanted to feel privately. I didn't pay attention to the praying. I felt it, and that was enough for me. I looked up at the stones. I looked at the praying Paratroopers: some wearing helmets, others in skullcaps. The buildings surrounding us on three sides gave the Wall compound such an intimate character.

I recalled our family visits to the Wall 25 years earlier, walking through the narrow lanes and markets. I didn't remember any details. I was a youngster then. But the impression of the people praying at the Wall has always stayed with me. Or is it the pictures I saw in later years? Jews in *kapotas* and *shtreimels,* long white beards—they and the Wall had merged into one. . . .

IN THE RIGHT corner, somewhat apart from the soldiers, stood a man. No, he wasn't standing, he was as though glued to the stones. He was part of the Wall. One of its stones. Wearing a long, brown *kapota.* A black hat on his head. Long hair protruding from under it. Nothing stirred. Neither head nor hair. Neither body nor legs. Both hands bent at the elbows, their outstretched palms affixed to the stones as though desiring to penetrate them.

I "tuned in" on him like Radar and I couldn't take my eyes off him. I "clung" to him from afar as he clung to the Wall from close up. Through him I felt the Wall. Through his as-it-were-paralysed body I felt the beats of the Jewish heart throbbing in the stone.

Thus we stood there linked for a few minutes—he, I, the Wall.

I turned away and went back to the Temple Mount compound.

I asked Amos to round up the battalion commanders for orders.

We are in Jerusalem to stay.[5]

In a recent issue of *The Jerusalem Post* one of its contributors described an incident that took place on the eve of the Ninth of Av in 1946 when eleven kibbutzim were established and settled overnight in the Negev "in the teeth of British opposition." This memoir reflects what the Western Wall and the Temple Mount have meant to the Jews throughout the centuries:

> A group of local and foreign journalists went to the Negev to see the new settlements. Leaving before sunrise, we were back in Jerusalem late in the afternoon. On the way back the Jews among us decided to go to the Western Wall that night, as it was the eve of Tisha B'Av, the anniversary of the destruction of the Temple, first by the Babylonians and then later by the Romans. . . . We felt it our duty to go to the Wall because there was a curfew, and hardly anyone else could go there. . . .

> Several British police officers and constables at the Wall looked at us with surprise, but did not ask to see our curfew passes. We walked with assurance and did not look like the crowds who normally come to pray at the Wall. Our small group—there were fewer than 15 of us—went there as a demonstration: you cannot keep all the Jews away from the Western Wall of the Temple. It was our moral and national duty to make the traditional Ninth of Av pilgrimage when most others were prevented. . . .

> There was none of the customary loud chanting, and wailing on that night. Some 30 men sat in a circle, a candle on the ground in front of each forming an inner circle of soft light in the windless night. A bearded Jew was reading from the Scriptures in a high sing-song.

> Those of our group who knew how to pray sat down on the ground and began praying without further ado. I looked in amazement at colleagues who had suddenly turned into traditional mourners, keening and swaying in rhythm with their chanted prayers. The ageless pain and sorrow flowed from their lips as naturally as if they had never done anything but pray and mourn.

> One of the senior newspapermen, the editor of a socialist daily, pulled a skullcap from his pocket, took off his shoes, and seated himself cross-legged on the ground, one of the candle-lit circle of men. I thought: "His soul has taken off his working clothes. This is the real man—not the one who sits at a desk, surrounded by telephones and secretaries." There he was, rocking back and forth and singing prayers just as Jews have been doing for nearly 2000 years. . . .

> Why is it that this purely symbolic relic means so much to millions of people all over the world? To hundreds of generations of those millions? Because it is a wound. A wound that never heals. . . .

> We walked back with heavy hearts. The mist had dispersed and the moon shone brightly. The streets were eerily empty. In earlier years, crowds would

have been cramming the narrow streets and lanes advancing at snail's pace, taking several hours to reach the Wall and return. The compact mass of bodies carried you on, and there was no turning back until you reached the Wall.

This time it took us barely 20 minutes to cover the distance between Zion Square in the centre of New Jerusalem and the Western Wall. One of our newspapermen said:

"This night will go down in history, and history repeats itself. We were conquered by Persians, Babylonians, Greeks, Romans, and Turks, and we were ruled by them. Ruled but never broken. Now we are ruled by the British, who did not conquer us but rule us, and are trying to break us but cannot. Nor will anyone. Who are they to succeed where all the others failed? We are a very ancient people and more stubborn than any other people on earth. We are the Stiff-Necked People."

We applauded, grateful to him for formulating our thoughts so aptly.

The elderly newspaperman from Tel-Aviv who had lost himself in prayer at the Wall was Zalman Rubashov, editor-in-chief of the Labour Party daily, *Davar,* later to be Zalman Shazar, president of the State of Israel.[6]

Why Hebrew University Has Two Campuses

The northwestern ridge of the Mount of Olives is known as Mount Scopus. On this ridge are the impressive new buildings of Hebrew University. Another large campus of the university is situated on the other side of the city, on a hill called Givat Ram. Why, it has been asked, does Hebrew University need two campuses which require students to commute by bus from one campus to the other? Was it poor planning? Or was it an unforeseen growth of the student body and lack of building space that made it necessary to build a second campus? Neither of these assumptions is valid. It is rather the checkered history of modern Jerusalem that accounts for this strange development.

The original plan called for the erection of all the university buildings on one campus, and that campus was to have been on Mount Scopus. Mount Scopus was chosen because of its historical associations. Military commanders throughout the city's history chose to launch their assaults on Jerusalem from Mount Scopus. In the first century Titus directed his siege of Jerusalem from this hill. In 1099 the Crusaders advanced on the city from this hill. And in 1914 the British, who entered the country from Egypt southwest of Jerusalem, planned to attack the city from the direction of Mount Scopus.

At the first Hebrew University convocation on the Mount Scopus campus after the
Six-Day War, an honorary doctorate was conferred on Yitz'hak Rabin. (Courtesy
of the Zionist Archives and Photo Service of the Jewish Agency, Jerusalem.)

When Hebrew University was officially opened in April 1925, the
people who gathered on Mount Scopus were deeply moved by the spectacular view. To the west they saw Nebi Samwil on the historic hill called
Ramah, where the Prophet Samuel's traditional tomb is located. To the
east they saw the Dead Sea gleaming in the sunshine. And to the south
they saw Jerusalem spread out like a huge map. The psalmist's words,
"beautiful of elevation, the joy of all the earth," must have been uttered by
many of those present.

The university on Mount Scopus consisted of only a few modest
buildings, but imaginative plans were made for expansion. Then came
Israel's War of Independence in 1948–1949. At the end of the war the city
was divided. The Old City came under Jordanian domination and the
New City became part of the State of Israel. Ironically, Mount Scopus

remained Israeli territory—an Israeli enclave within Jordanian territory—completely cut off from the New City. According to the Armistice agreement, Jordan was obligated to permit free access to Mount Scopus so that Hebrew University might continue to function. But the Jordanians reneged on their treaty and blocked the road to Mount Scopus, permitting only a bi-weekly convoy of Israeli guards to relieve the guards who had been on duty during the preceding fortnight. The Jewish institutions on Mount Scopus, consisting of Hebrew University and Hadassah Hospital, had to find new quarters. Thus came into existence the new campus on Givat Ram and the new Hadassah Hospital in Ein Karem, both in the New City.

In the 1967 Six-Day War the Jordanians were driven out of Jerusalem and the city was reunited. Mount Scopus was little more than a desolate hill. The buildings of Hebrew University and Hadassah Hospital were in a sad, dilapidated state. The authorities decided to rebuild the campus and the Hadassah Hospital on Mount Scopus without abandoning the "old" campus on Givat Ram and the "old" hospital in Ein Karem. The campus on Mount Scopus was to concentrate on the humanities, and the Givat Ram campus was to serve the sciences. Today two bus lines connect the

Three French clergymen studying at the Hebrew University in Jerusalem (1963). (Courtesy of Israel Government Press Office.)

campuses, and the buses are always crowded with students shuttling between the Mount Scopus and the Givat Ram campuses. The two campuses are here to stay.

The Holy City Under Jewish, Christian, and Moslem Rule

In ancient times Jerusalem was the capital of Israel, and today Jerusalem is once more the capital of the State of Israel. For the Christians, too, Jerusalem ranked as the most important city in the Holy Land. When the Crusaders conquered the city, they made it the capital of their kingdom; and when the British drove the Turks out of Palestine in 1917, they made Jerusalem the capital of the land. But during the twelve hundred years of Moslem rule the land was governed from Acre, Safed, Damascus, and other cities. Jerusalem was then treated as a mere provincial town. When Jerusalem came under Jordanian rule in 1948, it was relegated to a secondary position. Amman was the capital, and Jerusalem was again a provincial town of the realm. Only once during the twelve hundred years of Moslem rule was Jerusalem briefly the seat of a caliph. That was during the reign of Abdul Malik, the caliph who built the Dome of the Rock, and that was when a rival caliph controlled Mecca.

The Turks occupied the seat of power for exactly four centuries. The Sultan Selim conquered the city in 1517, and General Allenby drove the Turks out of Jerusalem in 1917. This is the longest period of a single dynasty's rule in the history of Jerusalem with the possible exception of the Davidic dynasty, which ruled from 1050 B.C.E. to 586 B.C.E. During the four centuries of Turkish rule there was an interlude of nine years, between 1831 and 1840, when the Egyptian Ibrahim Pasha ruled Jerusalem. His rule was relatively equitable and enlightened. But it was too short to have a lasting effect. With the help of Great Britain, the Turks returned, and corruption and neglect again became the earmarks of the pashas' rule in Jerusalem.

At the turn of the century Jerusalem was still a medieval city. So reported Mr. Edwin Sherman Wallace, the American consul in Jerusalem from 1893 to 1898. He blamed the Turkish government for Jerusalem's backwardness: "As long as they retain [control of the city], Jerusalem will be medieval in appearance." His report is enlightening and amusing:

> The spirit of modern progress has not touched the city yet. It has come from the west, swept across the Mediterranean, left its impress on Alexandria and

Cairo, but has passed through the Suez Canal and on to the Far East. Jerusalem has been passed by and, were it not for its popularity as a stopping-place for tourists from Europe and America, would be as Oriental as any one could wish. These visitors are leaving some of their customs and costumes. Some of the rising generation of natives affect the European dress. The combination of the man and the habit is not a success; each detracts from the other. . . .

Some of the letters of inquiry from our enterprising American firms which are sent to the consulate are laughable in the light of present conditions. Electric engineers and manufacturers of electric goods want to know all about the system of street railway now employed and what is the likelihood of introducing their special improved appliances for rapid transit. If they could only see what system is in use! To go from one part of the city within the walls to another, one must walk or mount a donkey. A line of carriages runs from the Jaffa Gate a mile west along the road. But such carriages! He who enters some of them does so at the expense of comfort and safety.

Street illumination is still in its infancy. In the entire city there are twenty-eight small oil lamps stuck up here and there on the sides of the houses. They are uncared for and on a dark night do nothing more than indicate that they are lighted. To believe that they do anything in the way of lessening the gloom is a freak of imagination. American companies wish to put in electric lights if the way is clear. But it is not; several insurmountable barriers intervene. In the first place the Turkish authorities do not desire so much light; it would reveal too much. They would not permit the introduction of electricity for illuminating purposes if some company should agree to furnish it gratis. . . . Another reason is that the Turk fears electricity in any form. He only admits the telegraph because he is compelled to. . . .

There are no telephones and not likely soon to be any. An American missionary who had charge of some schools several miles away and with which it was necessary for him to have frequent converse had a telephone sent to him. When he proceeded to put it in condition for service a Turkish officer was sent to make inquiries. The affair and the benefit of it was explained to him and he went away and reported it to his superiors. Word soon came to the progressive missionary that he must desist in its operations. Such an innovation could not be allowed unless he had an order from the sultan. He had no such order and was in no mood to pay the sum necessary to obtain it. The telephone has been lying unused for several years.

This is the kind of people who have control of the city. As long as they retain it Jerusalem will be mediaeval in appearance. The native and Jewish inhabitants do not care; the visitor prefers to see a city untouched by the hand of modern improvement. The former are indifferent in the matter; the latter have a sentiment. The one will not be roused from their indifference so long as the Turk is governor; the other is in no danger of having his sentiment destroyed.[7]

In 1917 the British captured Jerusalem. They did much to eradicate corruption in government, but the essential character of daily life remained almost unchanged. Thus Pierre van Paassen describes the filthiness of Jerusalem's bazaar as he saw it shortly before the outbreak of the Second World War:

> Of cleanliness there is not a trace: the blood of slaughtered animals gushes into the streets; a million flies zoom over the heaps of refuse and offal into which little brown children dig for overripe figs or cucumbers. Here is a donkey taking advantage of a traffic jam to relieve itself. The urine spatters over a row of crackling flat loaves of bread that a baker's assistant has spread out on the edge of the roadway to cool off. The baker, viewing the scene from his cellar through an opening just level with the street, emits a stream of vile names addressed at the mother of the donkey's owner. This gentleman, until then calmly sucking a pomegranate, suddenly purses his lips, spits out the pips, and hits the baker smack in the eye. A gale of laughter greets this performance. Business is suspended. There are explanations to passers-by who have missed the show. A policeman elbows his way through the crowd and traffic begins to move again.[8]

It was only after the Six-Day War in 1967, when the Old City was captured by the Israeli army, that reasonable cleanliness arrived in Jerusalem. A modern sewage system was installed, and street cleaning was instituted on a daily basis. Butchers were required to install electric refrigeration in their shops, and dogs ceased to roam the streets in search of carcasses and other edible garbage. Visitors in Jerusalem need no longer hold their nostrils as they wander about and enjoy the religious and historic sights of the Old City.

Equally important has been the ecumenical attitude adopted by the government of Israel in regard to the various religious sects in Jerusalem. On June 22, 1967, the Knesset passed the following law:

> 1. The Holy Places shall be protected from desecration and any other violation and from anything likely to violate the freedom of access of the members of the various religions to those places.
>
> 2. (a) Whoever desecrates or otherwise violates a Holy Place shall be liable to imprisonment for a term of seven years.
>
> (b) Whoever does anything that is likely to violate the freedom of access of the members of the various religions to the places sacred to them or their feelings with regard to those places shall be liable to imprisonment for a term of five years.
>
> 3. This law shall add to and not derogate from any other law.

4. The Minister of Religious Affairs is charged with the implementation of this law and he may, after consultation with or upon the proposal of representatives of the religions concerned, and with the consent of the Minister of Justice, make regulations as to any matter relating to such implementation.

5. This law shall come into force on the date of its adoption by the Knesset.

Five days later, the prime minister, Levi Eshkol, invited the heads of the religious communities in Jerusalem and addressed them:

All Holy Places and places of worship in Jerusalem are now freely accessible to all who wish to worship there, to members of all faiths without discrimination. The Government has made it a cardinal principle of its policy to safeguard the Holy Places, ensure their religious and universal character and provide free access to them. This policy will be maintained scrupulously, through regular consultations with you or your designated representatives. . . . It is our intention to place the internal administration and arrangements in the Holy Places in the hands of the religious leaders to whose community they belong.

To be sure, political unrest has continued to plague the inhabitants of the city. But corruption and religious discrimination are things of the past. Nor are the city and its holy places neglected. Jerusalem is a modern city with a rich religious and historical heritage.

Forecasting Jerusalem's Future

Armed with hindsight, one can read some of the dismal forecasts concerning the destiny of the Jewish people and of Jerusalem as intriguing curiosities. Thus the name of the Jewish people has been erased from the roster of nations on a number of occasions. It is a curious fact that the first time the name Israel appears in the annals of history is an announcement of its total annihilation. Pharaoh Merneptah inscribed on the column of victory in his Temple of the Dead: "Israel's . . . seed exists no more." This is Israel's introduction on the stage of history. And the psalmist pleads with God against Israel's enemies who "lay crafty plans" against them. "They say, 'Come let us wipe them out as a nation; let the name of Israel be remembered no more!'" (Ps. 83:5). Edward Gibbon regarded the hope of ever establishing a state of Israel with Jerusalem as its capital as a mere dream. In his classic work, *The Decline and Fall of the Roman Empire,* Gibbon writes in connection with the Crusaders' attack on the walls of the

Holy City: "The Jews, their nation, and worship were forever banished."[9]

These gloomy prophecies concerning the Jews and Jerusalem are also to be found in the travel literature of the nineteenth and early twentieth centuries. Thus the famous writer, Matilde Serao, wrote in her book, *In the Country of Jesus:*

> There is little hope that we shall ever be able to form a *people* in Jerusalem. Neither will the Jews ever form a people here; for they are no longer a nation, but a mere assemblage of persons come from the farthest parts of the earth and quite incapable of organisation and re-annexation. . . .

> It is a curious fact, but Jerusalem seems doomed never to have a distinct people of its own like any other city. The Arabs from the plains, the handsome Bedouins from the desert of Jericho and even from Arabia Petraea, will never form the people of Jerusalem, since they only come here to buy and sell.

> Possibly Jerusalem will never again have a people of her own.[10]

We also read in Henry Van Dyke's excellent work *Out-of-Doors in the Holy Land:*

> Jerusalem is no longer, and never again will be, the capital of an earthly kingdom. But she is still one of the high places of the world, exalted in the imagination and the memory of Jews and Christians and Mohammedans, a metropolis of infinite human hopes and longings and devotions.[11]

And a similar report appeared in a 1911 publication of the London Society for Promoting Christianity Amongst the Jews. "The prospects of Zionism ever succeeding are absolutely nil. The facts," says the writer, "speak for themselves":

> Multitudes [of Jews] come to Palestine anticipating that to reach that country is the end of all their troubles, but, coming, find a land whose climatic conditions (largely due to preventable causes) are unsuited to their health, in which they can find no kind of employment, and where, in all too many cases, they deteriorate physically and morally. The young, progressive, and enlightened, whether immigrants or born in the land, emigrate to more progressive countries—specially to North and South America and the British Colonies—and the sickly and weakly, the mentally deficient and the indigent, remain behind. This exodus of the best has received a renewed stimulus through the new law that Jews must serve in the Turkish army; the Jews have no wish to fight for the religion of Mahommed. The result of all this is that Jerusalem is crowded out of all proportion with chronic invalids—consumptives, blind and partially blind, the anaemic and the paralysed—and with virtual mendicants.

Today the State of Israel is an established fact, and Jerusalem is its capital. Needless to add that Jerusalem is still "one of the high places of the world" and will, in all probability, remain "exalted in the imagination and the memory of Jews and Christians and Mohammedans."

When people speak of Jerusalem's future, they usually concentrate on the political and social aspects of the city's life. Will the city remain united? Will it continue to be the capital of Israel? Will the ethnic and religious communities live in harmony? Since spiritual considerations are not pressing, they are usually relegated to future deliberations. There are visionaries, however, who dare to disregard the pressing problems of the moment and to dream of Jerusalem's spiritual destiny. One of those dreamers was Sir Ronald Storrs, who was Jerusalem's governor under the British Mandate. In a public address in London in 1921, Sir Ronald Storrs said:

> From Jerusalem has gone forth at sundry times and in divers tones a God-gifted organ-voice, which has thrilled and dominated mankind. I do not dare to prophesy, for the East is a university in which the scholar never takes his degree; but I do dare to believe that what has happened before may happen again, and that if we can succeed in fulfilling, with justice, the task that has been imposed upon us by the will of the nations, and if we can reconcile or unite at the source the chiefs and the followers of those three mighty religions, there may sound once more for the healing of the nations a voice out of Zion. [12]

Although Sir Ronald Storrs professed a hope that "a voice out of Zion" will yet come forth for the healing of our troubled world, the celebrated Rabbi Abraham Isaac Kook, who was chief rabbi of Jerusalem during Sir Ronald Storrs's administration, spoke of Jerusalem's role with certainty. He read a new meaning into the words of Isaiah (2:3): "For out of Zion will come forth the Torah and the word of the Lord from Jerusalem." The saintly Rabbi Kook said: "The word of God, which will go forth from Jerusalem, will infuse new life into the Torah which will come forth from Zion." [13]

NINE
Miscellaneous Oddities

The Longest Beard in the World

Here is a riddle: Who was the man with the longest beard in the world? Jerusalem has the answer. That distinguished person was a Jerusalemite— a hermit named Onuphrius. He lived alone in the desert for seventy years until he was found by an abbot named Paphnutius. That was in the fifth century. According to the Christian tradition, the abbot prayed all night with Onuphrius. In the morning Onuphrius died. In passing, it may be noted that the Christian name Humphrey is derived from the hermit's name.

This hermit, Onuphrius, reputedly had an extraordinary beard. It was so long that it reached the ground. Onuphrius would have tripped over it had he not made it a practice to tuck the end of the beard in his girdle.

If the reader doubts the authenticity of this tradition, he is advised to visit the cave where this man with the fabulous beard lived. The cave is located on the hill called Abu Tor, which faces Mount Zion across the Valley of Hinnom. Perched on the eastern tip of Abu Tor is a Greek Orthodox monastery named after St. Onuphrius. It is unfortunate that this monastery is rarely included in the itinerary of the Western pilgrim or tourist. Tradition has it that the saintly monk lived in the spacious cave which is now the shrine of the monastery. The cave is full of primitive paintings, one of which represents the hermit and his remarkable beard which touches the ground.

Traditional portrait of St. Onuphrius.

Some Jerusalemites claim that there once lived a Jew in the Old City whose beard might have been as long as or longer than that of St. Onuphrius. There is a tradition that one of the residents of the Jewish Quarter was very impressed with the saintliness and scholarship of Rabbi Hayim ben Attar, whose commentary on the bible, entitled *Or Ha-Hayim* (A Guide for the Living), is widely studied. The admirer of the saintly scholar took it upon himself daily to sweep the prayer room where Rabbi Hayim ben Attar worshiped. He did so not with a broom but with his lengthy beard. How long was that beard? Regrettably, the tradition does not say. There is little doubt that the beard was of adequate length to be regarded as one of the longest on record. But St. Onuphrius's beard still holds the official record and deserves to be listed in *The Guinness Book of World Records*.

The Russian Duchess Who Is Buried on the Mount of Olives

Christian princes of state are often buried in cathedrals. In 1920 a Russian princess was privileged to be interred in a church which is holier than all the cathedrals of Europe. That church is situated on the Mount of Olives. The story of how a member of the Russian nobility came to be buried outside Russia is brief and tragic.

Next to Gethsemane on the Mount of Olives stands the beautiful Russian church built in memory of the Tsarina Marie Alexandrowna, the wife of Tsar Alexander II. The church was erected in the 1880s by her royal son and his brothers. Its imperial splendor is reflected by its onion-shaped domes overlaid with sheets of beaten gold. In 1888 the church was consecrated by the Grand Duke Sergius and the Grand Duchess and was named the Church of Magdalene. Little did the grand duchess suspect that she would be privileged to be interred in the magnificent church she was consecrating.

Thirty years passed and the Russian Revolution broke out. The Russian royal family came to an ignoble end when they were thrown down a mineshaft and stoned to death. Among the royal victims was the Grand Duchess Sergius. In 1920 her remains were brought to Jerusalem and buried in the church she had consecrated thirty-two years earlier.

The Burial Place of One of the Signers of the Magna Carta

One of the surprising curiosities in Jerusalem is a tombstone at the entrance to the Church of the Holy Sepulchre which marks the burial place of Sir Philip D'Aubigny, one of the signers of the Magna Carta. Sir Philip D'Aubigny came to the Holy City as a Crusader in 1222 and died

Russian Church of Magdalene (1898). (Courtesy of Zionist Archives.)

in 1236. There is no record of the fourteen years of his residence in Jerusalem except the slab between the two entrances to the Church of the Holy Sepulchre. Rev. J. E. Hanauer researched this historic monument and describes it in his book *Walks In and Around Jerusalem:*

> Stretched in front of the cluster of columns, between the two great portals of the Church of the Sepulchre, is a marble slab, bearing the epitaph of Philip D'Aubeny, and a Norman shield with his armorial bearings. In 1887, by reference to several ancient records, I succeeded in proving that this is the tombstone of Sir Philip D'Aubeny, tutor of Henry III of Winchester, who, crowned when only a child of eight years of age, was entrusted to his care during the protectorship of the able Earl of Pembroke. Before the accession of Henry III, however, and during the reign of King John, we find the name of Sir Philip D'Aubeny amongst the barons who signed the Magna Carta. Sir Philip D'Aubeny left England for the holy wars in Palestine in 1222. He resided in the country for fourteen years, dying in 1236.

> The identity of the personage buried here has been incontestably proved by the armorial bearings, as well as by historical references, with the family of D'Aubeny, still existing in England, the chief seat of which appears to have been the manor of South Petherton, Somersetshire.[1]

In all probability the Crusader, Sir Philip D'Aubigny, strove for a burial inside the Church of the Holy Sepulchre. Two fellow Crusaders, Godfrey of Bouillon and Baldwin I, were interred inside the church. But Sir Philip D'Aubigny got only as far as the entrance. The only consolation that he can be offered, with the help of hindsight, is that the coffins of his fellow Crusaders soon became empty sarcophagi. In 1243 the Mongol horde, called the Kharezmians, captured Jerusalem. During the short period that they tarried in the Holy City they dismantled Godfrey's and Baldwin's tombs in search of spoil and scattered the bones of these first rulers of the Kingdom of Jerusalem. The bones were not gathered for reinterment and the tombs remained empty. Later, as a result of the disastrous fire in the Church of the Holy Sepulchre in 1808, the Crusader tombs were completely destroyed.

The last episode of this curious burial in front of the entrance to the Church of the Holy Sepulchre was published in *The Jerusalem Post* of November 2, 1977, in a news item entitled "Family Reunion in Jerusalem After 700 Years." The article, by Judy Siegel, is reproduced in full:

> An Englishwoman was reunited over the weekend with her 13th-century Crusader forebear at the Church of the Holy Sepulchre in Jerusalem's Old City, through the assistance of Mayor Teddy Kollek.

Alisa Rushbrook had written to the mayor that one of her ancestors was Philip D'Aubigny, who took part in the Crusaders' exploits in the Holy land some 700 years ago. This fact, she wrote, was authenticated in 1925 by Sir Ronald Storrs, the military governor of Jerusalem, in an article he wrote for "The Times" of London. Archaeological excavations at the time uncovered Philip's bones and tablets describing his family tree in the church where, according to most Christian traditions, Jesus was buried.

The Englishwoman had been to Jerusalem several times before in an attempt to uncover the tablets in the grave and take photographs, but she had never been successful. Clergy of three of the sects in charge of the church—Greek Orthodox, Catholic and Armenian—have been involved in a disagreement and would not grant approval to uncover the rubble.

The mayor, who "has an excellent relationship with leaders of the various churches," proceeded to mediate among the clergymen, and Mrs. Rushbrook was invited to the church. Arriving with her husband, she found the tablets and took pictures to record the Latin script.

The tomb of Sir Philip D'Aubigny in front of the double entrance to the Church of the Holy Sepulchre is now covered with well-worn planks to protect it from vandalism and from further deterioration due to the incessant footsteps of the throngs of visitors at the church.

An Underground Masonic Hall

Recently there was a press report on "the third Masonic pilgrimage to Israel." More than three hundred Freemasons from fifteen countries participated. The journalist reporting this event in *The Jerusalem Post* posed a rhetorical query: "Why are Freemasons making pilgrimages to Israel?" His answer was:

> Because Jerusalem is the historical and legendary cradle of Freemasonry. They will visit the holy sites connected to the building of Solomon's Temple under the supervision of master mason Hiram, with one of the highlights being a visit to the reputed site of King Solomon's quarry in Jerusalem.

Edwin Sherman Wallace, the American consul in Jerusalem in the 1890s, in his book *Jerusalem the Holy,* described Solomon's quarry near the Damascus Gate, and he added:

> This cavern is of special interest to the Masonic Order. Small and large parties of this fraternity visit the city every year and seem to find their chief delight in the gloomy recesses where they hold, many of them, that Masonry

was instituted by King Solomon himself. Many a bit of the white stone, large enough to be worked into an emblem of the Order, finds its way into the trunks of the brethren and is carefully guarded till it takes its place among the sacred relics of the home lodge. Several large blocks have been shipped to various cities in America, destined to be worked into some Masonic Temple.[2]

But the most curious masonic event connected with Solomon's quarry was its exploration by the nineteenth-century Masonic leader and historian Robert Morris. In his book *Freemasonry in the Holy Land,* he related how he founded the first Masonic lodge in Jerusalem. He describes the curious ceremony that took place inside Solomon's quarry:

Entering [Solomon's Quarry] with a good supply of candles, we pushed southward as far into the quarry as we could penetrate, and found a chamber happily adapted to a Masonic purpose. It was a pit in the ancient cuttings, about eighteen feet square. On the east and west, convenient shelves had been left by the original workmen, which answered for seats. An upright stone in the centre, long used by guides to set their candles upon, served us for an Altar. About ten feet above the master's station there was an immense opening in the wall, which led, for aught I know, to the original site of the Temple of Solomon. We were perfectly tyled by silence, secrecy, and darkness, and in the awful depths of that quarry, nearly a quarter of a mile from its opening, we felt, as we never had before, how impressive is a place which none but the All-seeing Eye can penetrate.

Laying my pocket Bible open on the central stone, three burning candles throwing their lustre upon it, and the trowel, square, etc., resting near by, a few opening remarks were made by myself, to the effect that never, so far as I knew, had a Freemasons' lodge been formed in Jerusalem since the departure of the Crusading hosts more than seven hundred years ago; that an effort was now making to introduce Freemasonry into this, the mother-country of its birth; that a few of us, brethren, providentially thrown together, desired to seal our friendship by the associations peculiar to a Masonic lodge; that for this purpose, and to break the long stillness of these ancient quarries by Masonic utterances, we had now assembled, and would proceed to open a Moot Lodge, under the title of Reclamation Lodge of Jerusalem. This we now proceeded to do, in a systematic manner. A prayer was offered, echoing strangely from that stony rock that had heard no such sounds for centuries, and the other ceremonies proceeded. . . .

The vast quarry thus consecrated by Masonic forms, shows at every point the marks of the chisel as well defined as the day the workmen left it. Slabs of stone partially dressed are lying upon the floor; other, partly cut out of the wall stand where a few more blows would detach them. Many emblems of crosses, Hebrew characters, etc., remain, and the next visitor will see amongst them the Square and Compass, as cut by our hand.[3]

In Jerusalem there is also a "Masonic Hall," which is a subterranean chamber near the Western (Wailing) Wall. In the excavations along the Western (Wailing) Wall, northward near Wilson's Arch, several underground vaulted halls were discovered. Among these halls was one that was probably part of the Hellenistic gymnasium for athletic games. Being so very old, the hall came to have mystic meaning for the Masons. They associated it with mysterious rituals in Solomon's Temple. The Masons therefore used this room for their own rituals and called it Masonic Hall. The Masons of Jerusalem no longer meet in that mysterious underground hall. However, it is a matter of interest that in Jerusalem a Masonic Hall exists. It does not compare with the splendors of Masonic halls in America. But its rituals were performed closer to the site of King Solomon's Temple.[4]

A Hoard of Human Bones

Many tourists visit the Sinai Peninsula because in it is the traditional holy mount on which God revealed Himself to the Israelites and gave them the Ten Commandments. The high point of their visit is not Mount Sinai, however, but the pyramid of skulls at the St. Catherine Monastery at the foot of the holy mountain. These stacked-up skulls of departed monks impress tourists no end. So much so that they forget the original purpose of their trip, and when they return home they talk of the marvelous pyramid of skulls that they saw in the monastery. Mount Sinai is hardly ever mentioned.

In Jerusalem, too, there is a hoard of human skeletons—skulls, arms, legs, and all the other bones of departed monks, hermits, and pious Christian pilgrims. This hoard is not arranged neatly into a pyramid but is more ghastly than the skulls in St. Catherine's Monastery. Yet, few ever talk about these bones because few ever see them. In Jerusalem there are more important historic and sacred places to visit. Besides, the approach to that heap of human bones is difficult and even risky. Why trouble the tourists with perilous adventures when there are so many more important and more exciting sights than a hoard of human skeletons?

Jerusalem's heap of human bones is housed in an ancient charnel house known as Aceldama, the "field of blood." It is the field reputedly purchased with the thirty pieces of silver that Judas received for betraying Jesus to the Romans. In the Christian Bible it is related that Judas repented of his betrayal of Jesus and threw down the money in the

Temple. The priests refused to accept the money for the Temple treasury because it was "the price of blood." So they used the money to purchase the Potter's Field for the burial of strangers. That is why that field came to be known as the field of blood, or Aceldama (Matt. 27; Acts 1:19). Today there is a Greek Orthodox monastery in the southern part of Aceldama, named St. Onuphrius, and on the hill above the monastery is the medieval charnel house erected by the Crusaders for the burial of pilgrims who died in the Holy City. The dead were lowered into Aceldama, where the corpses disintegrated, leaving the skeletons as their permanent mortal legacy to the Holy Land. These skeletons accumulated from century to century. The poor pilgrims, monks, and hermits whose bodies were lowered into Aceldama were not mourned, not only because they had no relatives in the land to bewail their loss, but also because they were envied. It was widely believed that those who were buried in Aceldama would not undergo the dreaded judgment that awaited all other human beings. It was also believed that the bodies lowered into Aceldama decayed quickly without unpleasant smells. Aceldama is situated on the hill across from Mount Zion. In it there is a vast accumulation of human skeletons, far more than the number of skulls at St. Catherine's Monastery. The sight of this hoard of human bones is ghastly. The city fathers did not choose to make of that charnel house a tourist attraction, and they should be credited with the sensitivity that persuaded them to let the bones of the medieval Christian pilgrims lie undisturbed in their humble burial place.

A Strange Export

In the course of its long history, Jerusalem has exported a strange variety of merchandise. The most important of its exports were spiritual in nature. Prophets, psalmists, and saints produced these intangible articles which were later incorporated in the Jewish and Christian Bibles. These spiritual treasures were translated into scores of languages and were disseminated to the four corners of the earth. The impact of these spiritual products resulted in the development of Judaism and the establishment of the first Christian Church in Jerusalem. When the Jews were scattered throughout the world, they carried their "Teaching" with them. And when Christianity became dominant among the Gentiles, the church of Jerusalem was transferred to Rome, to Constantinople, and to other centers of Christendom.

In the Middle Ages and in the centuries which followed, Jerusalem's exports were reduced to religious trinkets—crosses, crucifixes, and bottles of Jordan water. In recent years Jordan water was exported not just in bottles, but in barrels, as we read in the *Christian News from Israel:*

> On June 11th, twelve barrels, sent from the U.S.A. . . . were taken to the Jordan and filled with water from the river. They were subsequently shipped back in the same boat. . . . The water is to be used for a big baptismal ceremony in the Griffith Stadium in Washington in September.

> A small expedition, composed of an American Methodist, Dr. Howard Mead, of Greensborough, N.C., Dr. Herbert Torrance, Director of the Scottish Mission Hospital in Tiberias, Mr. Sipper of the Ministry of Religious Affairs, and several members of the nearby Jewish communal settlement, Degania, watched the water from the biblical stream flow into the huge containers. Dr. Torrance signed a certificate to the effect that the barrels contained pure Jordan water.[5]

But Jerusalem's most curious export was soil which reputedly had the mysterious quality of consuming corpses in record time. And, incredible as it sounds, there was an international market for this remarkable soil, because the cemeteries in a number of European cities could not accommodate all the corpses, especially those of the poor. Why not bury these corpses in a soil which rapidly consumes the bodies? The graves could then be used over and over again.

Southeast of Jerusalem there is a hill called the Hill of Evil Counsel. On that hill there is a gloomy arched building, most of which is underground. This building is on the field known as Aceldama, described previously. The underground building assumed the name of the field. This building came to be used as a burial place for Christian pilgrims who died in Jerusalem. The corpses of these strangers were lowered into this charnel house and left to decompose. Rumor had it that the soil of the tomb and of the adjacent field consumed bodies within twenty-four hours. How else can it be explained that corpses have been lowered into that pit for centuries and the pit was never full?

That the soil of Aceldama had the mysterious quality of consuming corpses expeditiously has been noted by many writers. The nineteenth-century archaeologist B. C. Schick, in his report in *The Palestine Exploration Fund,* quotes "Prof. Krafft of Bonn who says in his Topography in Jerusalem (now 46 years ago), that it was proved by a dead dog, which was cast down [into Aceldama], drying quickly and giving no bad smell."[6]

William Lithgow, who was in Jerusalem in 1612, mentioned this tomb in his *Totall Discourse.* He wrote:

> As I looked downe, I beheld a great number of dead corpses; some whereof had white winding sheets, and newly dead, lying one above another in a lumpe; yeelded a pestilent smell, by reason they were not covered with earth, save only the architecture of a high vault. [7]

Similarly does William Makepeace Thackeray, who was in Jerusalem in 1844, refer to this voracious tomb. In his *Notes of a Journey* he wrote:

> An enormous charnel-house stands on the hill where the bodies of dead pilgrims used to be thrown; and common belief has fixed upon this spot as the Aceldama, which Judas purchased with the price of his treason. [8]

Another prominent American contemporary of Thackeray, Stephen Olin, a distinguished Methodist clergyman who was president of Wesleyan University in Middletown, Connecticut, visited the Holy City as a pilgrim in 1840. In the account of his travels he compares Aceldama with similar charnel houses in Rome and Naples. He wrote:

> It is not unlike the public cemeteries which I visited near Rome and Naples, into which the humble dead are promiscuously thrown in immense numbers, and with circumstances of indecency, and even brutality, painful and shocking to the feelings. This structure is twenty-four paces in length by twelve in width. It was, for centuries, the burying-place for Christian pilgrims. [9]

The fame of Aceldama's unique dirt spread and, strange to report, there were customers for that marvelous soil. So Jerusalem began to export shiploads of dirt. The eighteenth-century traveler Richard Pococke reported in his classic work: "They talk much of a vertue in this earth to consume dead bodies, and, it is said, that several shiploads of it were carried to what they called the Campo Santo in Pisa." [10]

But Jerusalem was never a success in such mundane enterprises, and this commercial venture did not prosper. The Aceldama soil did not perform to the satisfaction of the city fathers in Pisa. The bodies buried in the imported dirt were not consumed as quickly as anticipated, and the customers ceased to import it.

Why was the soil from Aceldama not efficacious in Italy? One theory has it that the Italian cities imported the soil without the field mice. If so, this was a regrettable oversight.

An Eighteenth-Century Insurance Policy Against Property Loss

Moslem religious doctrines and beliefs were derived mostly from Judaism and Christianity. When the Arabs conquered the Holy Land, they appropriated many Jewish and Christian holy places. They occupied Mount Moriah and erected on it the Dome of the Rock. They also took possession of David's tomb on Mount Zion because King David had been accepted as one of Islam's prophets. Similarly did they seize the Church of the Ascension on the Mount of Olives because Jesus also became one of their prophets. But they never took possession of the Church of the Holy Sepulchre and the many Christian holy places associated with the Crucifixion because Islam denies the Crucifixion, burial, and resurrection of Jesus. The Moslems claim that Jesus never died. He was taken directly to heaven. Although the Church of the Holy Sepulchre was safe from seizure by the Moslem hierarchy, it was not secure against damage or demolition by Moslem mobs. A minor dispute between an Arab and a Christian could easily develop into a communal conflict and might result in the devastation of the Church of the Holy Sepulchre and its cluster of chapels and holy places. In such a circumstance little help could be expected from the pasha and his troops. How then could the Christians protect their most sacred church against mob violence? How could they ensure the safety of the Holy Sepulchre when insurance companies were still unknown in Jerusalem? A Dutch diplomat, the Honorable J. Aegidius van Egmont, "Envoy Extraordinary from the United Provinces to the Court of Naples, and a fellow Dutchman, John Heyman, Professor of the Oriental Languages in the University of Leyden" reveal the secret of how the Christians obtained insurance against mob violence in the mid-eighteenth century. The distinguished writers, in their two-volume work on their travels in the Holy Land and its adjacent regions, state:

> The father procurator of the convent [Church of the Holy Sepulchre] is known to take up money at a very high interest. . . . This has . . . been considered only as a refined piece of policy, such sums being borrowed only from Turks of considerable wealth and power, in order to attach them to the interest of the convent; for should the house be destroyed, and the monks driven from their abode, there would be at once an end of both principal and interest.[11]

It was by virtue of this cunning device that the Church of the Holy Sepulchre was saved from repeated destructions. To be sure, the Church was devastated on several occasions by invading hordes, fanatic Moslem rulers, and fire, but never by local mob action.

The Great Forger

One of the worshipers at Christ Church in Jerusalem was a converted Jew, M. W. Schapiro. He was a knowledgeable antiquarian and a well-known dealer in antiquities. He once sold an ancient Hebrew manuscript from Yemen to the British Museum. His acquisition of that manuscript, however, is murky. He had gone to Yemen in search of antiquities. Posing as a rabbi, he won the confidence of the Yemenite Jews who showed him their precious treasure, the Temanite Scroll. Schapiro offered to buy it, but the Yemenite Jews would not sell it. With the help of the Turkish governor, Schapiro removed the Temanite Scroll by force and sold it to the British Museum.

In 1886, Schapiro offered the British Museum another manuscript. This manuscript was much older and by far more precious. It was written by none other than Eleazar, a grandson of Aaron, Moses' brother, and the writing was in the ancient Hebrew script which is to be found on ancient Jewish coins and on some ancient monuments. Schapiro said he found this rarest of ancient manuscripts in a cave in the mountains of Moab. Scholars and learned people everywhere were in a state of excitement. Was this manuscript authentic? If so, it is one of the most precious finds, and its value was beyond calculation. After examining the manuscript, some scholars published articles in learned periodicals. Schapiro asked a million pounds sterling, and the British Museum was ready to pay the required sum.

A French scholar, who had been the French consul in Jerusalem, M. Clermont-Ganneau, recalled an incident involving Schapiro. It was in the year 1860 when the Prussian Crown Prince Frederick, who later became Emperor Frederick II of Germany, came to Jerusalem on a pilgrimage. The Turkish government gave the prince a valuable gift, a plot of land in the heart of the Old City, near the Church of the Holy Sepulchre, on which the Germans built the Lutheran Church of the Redeemer. Schapiro, too, gave the prince a precious gift, some Canaanite pottery idols which, Schapiro claimed, were found in the mountains of Moab. These idols were presumably the *Teraphim* or household gods of the ancients who lived in that area (see Gen. 31:19, 30–35). The prince was pleased with the gift and bestowed a decoration on the donor.

A servant of Schapiro's, who had quarreled with his master, confessed to M. Clermont-Ganneau his complicity in the forgery of these idols. When M. Clermont-Ganneau arrived in London, he recalled that episode and decided to examine the precious manuscript which Schapiro was selling to the British Museum. His examination was more thorough than that of the other scholars. He compared this manuscript with the Temanite Scroll which Schapiro had sold to the British Museum, and he discovered that the parchment of the manuscript was part of the Temanite Scroll and the ancient Hebrew script was a forgery.

When the fraud was exposed, Schapiro fled to Rotterdam, where he committed suicide. Schapiro's gifted daughter, Myriam Harry, in her book, *La Petite Fille de Jerusalem,* gives another version of that episode. But her version is highly subjective.

What happened to the Schapiro manuscript? The British Museum sold it at auction for eighteen pounds sterling, and the purchaser resold it for twenty-five pounds sterling. The scrolls have not been heard from again. They can surely fetch a much higher price today, but hardly a million pounds sterling, even after the steep devaluation of the British pound.

A Christian Gains Entry to the Tomb of David

"No place about Jerusalem, not even the *Haram* (Temple Mount), is guarded with such jealousy" as the Tomb of David on Mount Zion. So said J. L. Porter, the author of *The Giant Cities of Bashan.* For centuries, the Tomb of David had been closed to all infidels, that is, to Jews and Christians. As might be expected, the more closely the tomb was guarded by the Moslems, the keener was the curiosity of both Jews and Christians and the greater was their temptation to gain entry to the tomb and see the forbidden shrine. In the nineteenth century there were several "infidels" who risked their lives to gain admittance. In those days bakshish opened all doors, but not the door of this holy tomb. Not even all Moslems were privileged to gain admittance. It was watched over by hereditary guardians who admitted only those Moslems who had the proper connections. There was only one way for an "infidel" to fulfill his curiosity, and that was to pose as a Moslem of rank and to seek admittance with the help of the most convincing of all arguments, a respectable bakshish. In the nineteenth-century travel literature there are several captivating stories of such risky adventures. One of these is by Dr. J. T. Barclay, an American medical missionary. The account describes the risks and intrigues that were required of anyone not a Moslem inclined to enter upon such an adventure:

> No spot about the Holy City is half so jealously guarded as this sanctum sanctorum of the Moslems, so confidently believed by Jew and Christian as well as Mussulman to contain the dust of the "Sweet Singer of Israel." Hence the superstitious awe with which it is venerated by Mussulmans, is only equaled by the itching curiosity of Jews and Christians to explore the hidden area of its mysterious recesses. Many have been the attempts by foul means and by fair, by lavish buckshishes as well as by furtive efforts, to gain admittance; but all efforts have proved entirely abortive, until quite recently,

Sarcophagus of King David's Tomb on Mount Zion. (Courtesy of Israel Government Press Office.)

when my daughter had the good fortune to be admitted, without money, without price, and without intrigue—simply through the strong attachment of a Moslem lady. Many have succeeded to their heart's content in bribing the body guard of the royal prophet; indeed a few hundred dollars will readily compass such a feat. But then the good old sheikh has rather a curious way of fulfilling the terms and conditions of his covenant, by palming off a tumulus of richly canopied stone and mortar on the floor of an *upper room,* which, however, he is willing to swear by the beard of Mohammed is the veritable tomb of King David, Solomon, Hezekiah, Uzziah, etc., etc., etc. Indeed, I was myself victimized "on that wise." . . .

My daughter, however, was far more fortunate than any of us, as will be perceived on reading the following extract from her journal. It was just at that critical juncture of Ottoman affairs attendant upon the breaking out of the war between Russia and Turkey when the Sultan had sent an imperative firman to the Holy City, enjoining all the faithful, under penalty of "five hundred sticks," to repair to the Haram every Friday at twelve o'clock, to pray for the success of the war against the infidels; of course, all the "faithful" were conscientiously bound to be there at the specified time! It fortunately so happened, too, that my daughter's hands being well tattooed with henna at the time, she was in possession of a most desirable—indeed, indispensable passport. Circumstances seemed to be so propitious in every respect, and the contingency of danger so remote and improbable, that, after holding a brief family council, we could but agree that she should accept the pressing invitation of the generous lady, who, by-the-bye, being a relative of the old Neby Daud effendi, and intimately acquainted with all the premises as well as the keepers and domestics, was the best possible cicerone—considerations certainly of no small moment in such an adventure, especially in the event of exigency.

Extract—"Early one morning, during the great Mohammedan feast of Rhamadan, I was called to the 'parley' room to see my friend Moosa. This little fellow having become rather a frequent visiter, I was at first inclined to excuse myself; but remembering he had lately hinted at the possibility of my gaining an entrance into the Tomb of David, and in consideration, too, of the fact, that being their fasting season, the everlasting finjan of coffee and douceur of sweetmeats—those otherwise indispensable marks of Turkish civility—might now be dispensed with, I concluded to make my appearance. On entering the room my pleasing suspicions were confirmed, by seeing him close the door and mysteriously place his forefinger on his lips, in token of profound secrecy. He laid his ponderous turban on the divan beside him, doffed his slippers, crossed his legs, and then disclosed the nature of his errand. In short, I was informed that his sister was ready for an adventure; and, as I was too, we were not long in reaching 'Turfendah,' (his sister), who immediately commenced operations. My hair was taken down and braided in scores of little plaits. A red cloth cap, with a blue silk tassel, was placed on my head, and around it a gauze turban, with gold tassels and embroidery.

My robe and trowsers were of the finest Damascus silk, my girdle of cashmere, and tunic of light blue stuff, embroidered in silver flowers. My hands were already dyed with 'henna,' having undergone this process on the occasion of a former adventure in the Mosque of Omar, and still retained the deep yellow hue; my skin was pretty deeply tanned, too, from a residence of several years under a burning Syrian sun, which was quite an addition to my Turkish appearance. The sheet, veil, and slippers came in due order; and having secreted my pencil and sketch-book in the folds of my girdle, we sallied forth, accompanied by Turfendah's favorite slave.

"The reputed Tomb of David is just outside of Zion Gate, hard by the Coenaculum and American cemetery. It is surrounded by an irregular pile of buildings, and surmounted by a dome and minaret. In the interior are some of the most grotesque architectural embellishments imaginable, on the capitals of some remains of the Crusaders' architecture. Just think of the frightful owl occupying the place of the classic acanthus and the mythic lotus! We passed the several halls and corridors, evidently of the style of the Quixotic era of the Crusaders' domination, before reaching the consecrated apartment, whose entrance is guarded by double iron doors. We found here an old derwish prostrate in prayer, on the cold stone floor. Not being privileged, as we, to enter the sacred precincts, he was content with gazing at the Tomb through the iron bars; for it is a rare thing for even a Mussulman ecclesiastic to gain admittance—my companion and her family only enjoying this privilege, because they are very near relatives of the curator of the tomb. Our slave was despatched for the key, which she had no difficulty in obtaining, on the plea that her mistress wished to pray on the holy spot. But what was my consternation on seeing another slave return with her! I confess that I trembled, and was thinking I had best leave my awkward slippers behind, in case of retreat, as they would greatly impede my progress, and might thereby cause me to lose my head! She peered under my veil, asked who I was, and seemed satisfied with the careless reply of Turfendah, that I was merely a friend of hers from Stamboul! She invited us up stairs to see the old keeper's hareem; and Dahudeah (Moosa's little wife) who is always glad to exchange the purgatory of a residence with her lord and master, for a visit of a few days here; for I can testify from personal observation, that the young effendi lords it over her in true Oriental conjugal style! Turfendah regretted she could not accept her kind invitation, and, as she was so much exhausted from fasting, she would prefer deferring it to another time! The slave then left, to our mutual relief, and, having dismissed the old derwish, the doors were closed and doubly locked. The room is insignificant in its dimensions, but is furnished very gorgeously. The tomb is apparently an immense sarcophagus of rough stone, and is covered by green satin tapestry, richly embroidered with gold. To this a piece of black velvet is attached, with a few inscriptions from the Koran, embroidered also in gold. A satin canopy of red, blue, green, and yellow stripes, hangs over the tomb; and another piece of black velvet tapestry, embroidered in silver, covers a door in one end of the room, which they said, leads to a cave underneath. Two tall silver candlesticks stand before this door, and a little lamp hangs in a window near it, which is kept constantly burning, and whose wick, though saturated with oil—and, I dare say, a most nauseous dose—my devotional companion eagerly swallowed, muttering to herself a prayer with many a genuflection. She then, in addition to their usual forms of prayer, prostrated herself before the tomb, raised the covering, pressed her forehead to the stone, and then kissed it many times. The ceiling of the room is vaulted, and the walls covered with blue porcelain, in floral figures. Having remained here an hour or more, and completed my sketch, we left; and great was my rejoicing when I found myself once more at home, out of danger, and still better, out of my awkward costume."[12]

In the 1948–1949 war between the Jews and the Arabs, Mount Zion was captured by the Jewish soldiers. The Arab guardians of the Tomb of David fled; the shrine was opened to all; and it has remained open to this day.

Model of the three Herodian towers—Hippicus, Phasael, and Miriamne—in the citadel of ancient Jerusalem, reconstructed on the grounds of the Holyland Hotel. (Courtesy of Israel Government Press Office.)

Interior Courtyard of the Second Temple, as reconstructed on the grounds of the Holyland Hotel in Jerusalem (1967). (Courtesy of Israel Government Press Office.)

A Journey of Two Thousand Years into the Past

Tourists travel to distant lands to see the world. If they wish to see the world of yesterday they visit museums where relics of the past are on display, or they go to archaeological sites where ancient monuments have been dug up and preserved. But visitors in Jerusalem can see not only the city of today and the relics of ancient and medieval times, but the whole city of Jerusalem of two thousand years ago.

The archaeologist Michael Avi-Yonah was the architect of a detailed model of ancient Jerusalem built on a scale of 1:50. The model, which is located on the grounds of the Holyland Hotel in the New City, was made in 1969 and has been periodically altered to accord with new archaeological findings. As the visitor walks around this huge model, he or she leisurely sees the Jerusalem of King Herod's day. One can examine the famous "Second Wall" of the city's northern fortifications. This wall has been the center of much controversy because on its exact location depends the authenticity of the traditional Calvary and the Holy Sepulchre. The visitor can also see the three towers that King Herod built near what is now the Jaffa Gate. Part of one of these towers has been preserved to this day. It is known as the Tower of David and is part of the Jerusalem Citadel. The visitor can also see King Herod's palace and, above all, the Temple which Herod built on Mount Moriah. Of equal interest are the palaces of the rich and the huts of the poor, the market and amusement places, the streets and alleys, and many other aspects of ancient Jerusalem. Walking around this grand model, one has the feeling of being a tourist in ancient Jerusalem. One takes a trip not merely in space—from hometown to modern Jerusalem—but also a trip in time—from the twentieth century to the first century B.C.E. —a journey of two thousand years into the past.

Six Religious Calendars

Before embarking on a trip to the Holy Land the tourist is usually supplied with some basic information about the land, the people, and the customs that he or she is apt to meet in that strange meeting place of so many peoples and faiths. The prospective visitor in Jerusalem is usually informed that there are three Sabbaths in the Holy City—Friday for the Moslems, Saturday for the Jews, and Sunday for the Christians. Jerusalem also has three Christmas celebrations, each of which is observed with abundant ceremony and pageantry. The Latin and Protestant Christmas comes first. Then comes that of the Greek Orthodox, which is also observed by the Copts, Ethiopians, and Syrian Orthodox. And finally there is the Armenian Christmas. But the prospective tourists are hardly aware of the many calendars that play a decisive role in the religious life of the residents. These calendars regulate the religious feasts, fasts, and holy days.

The Latins and Protestants follow the familiar Gregorian calendar, which was introduced by Pope Gregory XIII in 1582 and is dominant in the Western world. The Greek Orthodox Church, however, uses the

Julian calendar, which was introduced in Rome by Julius Caesar in 46 B.C.E. The dates of the Julian calendar are behind those of the Gregorian calendar by about thirteen days. This accounts for the duplicate Christian holy days in Jerusalem. This situation exists wherever Eastern and Western Christian communities co-exist. [13]

There are two additional Christian communities in Jerusalem, the Copts and Ethiopians, who order their religious life by calendars which originated in Egypt instead of Rome. The Copts, who are now a minority people in Egypt, are the authentic descendants of the ancient Egyptians, and their calendar is based on the ancient Egyptian calendar. In that calendar, the year consisted of twelve months of thirty days each plus a thirteenth short month of five days. Since the astronomical year consists of approximately 365 1/4 days, every fifth year was a day short of the astronomical year. Emperor Augustus imposed on the Egyptians in 30 B.C.E. the Julian calendar, which made every fifth year into a leap year of 366 days.

The Coptic calendar does not start counting the years from the traditional date on which Jesus was born, but from the year 284 C.E. when the Roman Emperor Diacletian ascended the throne. Thus the year 1980 corresponds to the year 1696 in the Coptic calendar. Why this strange discrepancy? The explanation is to be found in a historic event which left a deep scar on the Coptic national memory, comparable to that of the Turkish massacre of the Armenians and the Nazi Holocaust of the Jews. The Roman Emperor Diacletian ruled for twenty years from 284 to 304. He proclaimed himself to be a divine person and enforced emperor worship with untold cruelty. Tertullian, a contemporary, says: "If the martyrs throughout the world were to be put in one side of the scales and the Coptic martyrs alone were to be put in the other, the latter would outweigh the former." These persecutions made a deep impression upon the mind of the Copts, and they "have ever since reckoned time from what they call the Era of Martyrdom, using the first year of the hated Diocletian as the starting-point." [14]

Another distinctive aspect of the Coptic calendar is that the New Year does not start in mid-winter but in the fall, as does the Jewish New Year. It falls generally on a date which corresponds to September 11 of the Julian calendar. All the Coptic religious observances except New Year coincide with those of the Greek Orthodox Church. Thus the Coptic Christmas is celebrated on a date in the Coptic calendar which corresponds to December 25 of the Julian calendar.

The Ethiopian calendar is similar to that of the Copts, except that the years are calculated from the date of the birth of Jesus. But, according to the Ethiopian computation, Jesus was born seven years earlier than the date listed in the Western and Eastern calendars. The year 1980 is therefore listed in the Ethiopian calendar as 1973. The division of the year into months is the same as in the Coptic calendar, and their religious observances likewise coincide with those of the Greek Orthodox Church, except for New Year's Day, which is observed in the fall.

Another important calendar in Jerusalem is that of the Jews, who are the oldest and largest of the Holy City's communities. The Jewish calendar counts the years from the creation of the world according to the biblical account, so that the year 1980 of the Western calendar was 5740, and the weekly holy day is the biblical Sabbath. The Jewish year consists of twelve lunar months of twenty-nine or thirty days each. This lunar year is converted into a solar year by means of the Metonic cycle, which consists of nineteen years, seven of which contain thirteen lunar months—the twelve other years consisting of twelve lunar months each. Needless to add, the holy days of the Jewish calendar have no relationship to those of the Christians.

Still another calendar which is widely used in Jerusalem is that of the Moslems, who constitute the second largest community in the Holy City. This calendar counts the years from the date of Mohammed's flight from Mecca to Medina. This took place in the year 622 of the Western calendar. The Moslem year consists of twelve lunar months, and the calendar does not compensate the deficiency in the solar year by periodically intercalating an additional month. The Moslem religious holidays and fast days therefore move back from season to season. Thus the Ramadan fast recedes every year by about ten days, and with the passage of time it falls in different seasons of the year.

The Franciscan Press in Jerusalem publishes annually a calendar for use by the members of its own order and by everyone else who has dealings with the different religious communities. A page from that calendar is herewith reproduced. It will be noted that the calendar is in Italian because the Order's headquarters is in Italy. The dates are listed in the following order: Gregorian, Julian, Coptic, Moslem, and Jewish. According to the page herewith reproduced, the date, January 3, 1980, of the Gregorian calendar was December 21, 1979, in the Julian calendar; the 24th of the month Kihak, 1696, of the Coptic calendar; the 15th day of the month Safar, 1400, in the Moslem calendar; and the 14th day of the month Tebet, 5740, of the Jewish calendar. The many calendars are somewhat confusing. But Jerusalemites manage to co-exist and to enjoy the many colorful observances in their multireligious community. And the government, too, takes note of the many calendars and respects them. According to Israeli law, parliamentary sessions may not take place on Fridays, Saturdays, or Sundays, the religious rest days of Islam, Judaism, and Christianity.

The Jerusalem Chamber in Westminster Abbey

In the fourteenth century a room was added to Westminster Abbey. It was named after the Holy City. Among the room's attractive furnishings are a number of old tapestries illustrating biblical scenes, such as the Return of Sarah from the Egyptians, the Circumcision of Isaac, and Rebecca at the Well.

The Jerusalem Chamber is known for several noteworthy events which took place in it. The best known of these events is the death of King Henry IV, which took place at the room's fireplace. The king was planning to go to the Holy Land in 1413. While praying at St. Edward's Shrine, he was taken ill and was brought to the Jerusalem Chamber and placed by the fire. He recovered consciousness and asked where he was. He was told, "Jerusalem." The king then realized that his life had come to an end because it had been prophesied that he would die in Jerusalem.

Many historical meetings have been held in the Jerusalem Chamber, among them the committees engaged in producing the Authorized Version of the Bible in 1611, the Revised Version in 1870, and again the New English translation of the Bible in 1961. The bodies of many famous people, among them Joseph Addison and Sir Isaac Newton, have lain in this room before their burial in the Abbey.

The Jerusalem Chamber is one of the private rooms of the Deanery and is now used for meetings of the dean and the chapter as well as other gatherings and receptions arranged or permitted by the dean.

A Christian Commemoration of the Destruction of the Temple

That the Jews mourn the destruction of Jerusalem and the burning of the Temple on the anniversary of that catastrophe is understandable and well known. On the ninth day of the Hebrew month Av the Jews fast and recite

The Rockefeller Museum in Jerusalem, opened in 1938. (From Neftali Arbel, Jerusalem: Past and Present. Tel Aviv, S. Friedman Publishing House, 1969, p. 203, with permission.)

many dirges, including the Book of Lamentations. What is strange is that they are not alone in commemorating that event. The Greek Orthodox Church also marks the fall of Jerusalem. But instead of doing so on the Ninth of Av, which generally falls in August, they do so in the fall, on the fourth of November. This discrepancy of dates can be partially explained by the fact that the Hebrew month Av is the ninth month in the Hebrew calendar, and November is the ninth month in the Julian calendar. But the discrepancy between the ninth day and fourth day of the month is a problem for scholars to solve.

There is another discrepancy. Whereas the liturgy of the Jews provides for the reading of the Book of Lamentations, that of the Orthodox Church provides for the reading of a selection from the Apocryphal book, The Rest of the Words of Baruch. This dissimilarity, however, can be explained. The prophet Jeremiah was a Jew, and the author of The Rest of the Words of Baruch was, according to some scholars, a Judeo-Christian.[15] Why read from the book of Lamentations written by a Jewish prophet if one can read a relevant biblical text written by a Christian?

Mr. John D. Rockefeller's "Unusual Question"

The Rockefeller Museum in Jerusalem was opened in 1938 and was named the Palestine Archaeological Museum. Ten years later the museum was confiscated by the Jordanian government. After the Six-Day War the building and its contents became the property of the Israeli government. It was then that the name of the museum was changed to the Rockefeller Museum in gratitude to John D. Rockefeller, Jr., who had donated one million dollars. The management of the museum was transferred to the Israel Museum.

The Rockefeller Museum is situated on a hill facing the northeast corner of the Old City wall. It was from there that the Crusaders under the leadership of Godfrey de Bouillon scaled the wall of the city in 1099. It was also from that site that the Israelis launched their successful attack on the Old City in 1967.

The museum is a spacious structure built around a central court, occupying an area of ten acres. The building is full of archaeological specimens of great value to scholars.

Mrs. Bertha Spafford Vester related the story of the founding of the museum and an "unusual question" asked by the museum's benefactor:

> In March of 1929 Mr. and Mrs. John D. Rockefeller and their son David visited Jerusalem with Dr. Breasted, the great Egyptologist, and they stopped at the American Colony. Mr. Rockefeller had offered the Egyptian Government several million dollars to build a suitable museum to preserve the precious antiquities when the inundation of the Nile made the greater part of Cairo damp. Pressure was brought upon the Egyptian authorities over the management and disposition of funds, and they rejected Mr. Rockefeller's munificent offer.
>
> Dr. Breasted influenced Mr. Rockefeller to supply Jerusalem with a fitting museum. True, many of the valuable antiquities discovered under the Turkish regime were now housed in the museum at Istanbul. These objects form a valuable list; the Siloam Inscription; the Temple Stone, known to have belonged to the Temple; the bilingual stone from Gezer, one of the boundary marks; the Holy Sepulchre inscription in Kufic. The "Orpheus Mosaic" found at the Damascus Gate; the remains from excavations at Gezer, Bethshean, ancient Jericho, and Samaria; the Sarcophagus attributed to have

held the remains of Alexander the Great and another sarcophagus in Jerusalem holding the body of Queen Helena, from the Tomb of the Kings, are now in the Louvre. Under the British mandate, with a Department of Antiquities to safeguard antiquities and retain finds in the land of discovery, the gift from Mr. Rockefeller was gladly accepted.

During their visit we went for a walk. Mrs. Rockefeller and Dr. Breasted were ahead and I was with Mr. Rockefeller. We were on our way to the old museum temporarily located in an old Arab rented house when Mr. Rockefeller asked me an unusual question—unusual, because so few people could ask such a question. He asked, "Do you remember, Mrs. Vester, whether it was one or two million dollars I donated towards the Jerusalem museum?"[16]

The Pilgrim with the Holy Toothpick

Every city has its peculiarities and curiosities. But not every city can boast of a holy toothpick. Estelle Blyth, whose father was the Anglican bishop in Jerusalem from 1887 to 1914, relates in her book *When We Lived in Jerusalem:*

> One day, passing through the hall, [Bishop Blyth] was greeted by an Abyssinian pilgrim, wrinkled and very old, who had brought with him a most precious gift for the English Bishop. It was an ancient toothpick, which for many years had been the special property of the holy abbots of some monastery in Abyssinia; each had used it in turn, and it was of a surpassing sanctity in consequence. Proudly he held it out, a weird-looking instrument with an ivory handle yellow and cracked with age and a long metal hook, whose bent and rusty appearance entirely bore out his claim of long life and much use. My Father thanked him very much, but said that he could not think of depriving him of so great a treasure; and presently the dear old man hobbled off, made happy by a little bakshish, and with the holy toothpick still in his possession.[17]

NOTES

Foreword

1. Van Dyke, Henry, *Out-of-Doors in the Holy Land,* London, 1908, pp. 47–18.
2. Storrs, Ronald, "Introduction" to *Our Jerusalem,* by Bertha Spafford Vester, London, 1951, p. 5.
3. Bellow, Saul, *To Jerusalem and Back,* New York, 1976. p. 93.
4. Adinopulos, Thomas A., "Jerusalem the Blessed: The Shrine of Three Faiths," in, *The Christian Century,* April 12, 1978.
5. Toynbee, Arnold, *Cities of Destiny,* New York, 1967, p. 28.

Preface

1. Finn, Elizabeth Anne, *Home in the Holy Land,* London, 1866, p. v.
2. Warren, Charles, *Underground Jerusalem,* London, 1876, pp. 83–84.

Introduction

1. Clarke, Edward D., *Travels in Various Countries of Europe, Asia, and Africa,* Vol. 2, London, 1812, pp. 523–524.
2. Hutton, Laurence, *Literary Landmarks of Jerusalem,* New York, 1895, pp. 16–19.
3. Smith, George Adam, *Jerusalem,* Vol. 1, London, 1907, p. 5.
4. *Massekhet Derekh Eretz,* edited and translated by Michael Higger, New York, 1935, p. 56. See also *Yomah* 54b. For references in the Apocrypha, see the Book of Enoch 26:1 and the Book of Jubilees 8:19.
5. Ashbee, C. R., *A Palestine Notebook,* London, 1923, p. 20.
6. Chesterton, G. K., *The New Jerusalem,* London, 1920, p. 113.
7. Stampfer, Judah, *Jerusalem Has Many Faces,* New York, 1950, p. 13.

Chapter One

1. Wilson, Charles, *Jerusalem the Holy City,* London, 1888, p. 4.
2. Bellow, Saul, *To Jerusalem and Back,* New York, 1976, p. 10.
3. Vester, Bertha Spafford, *Our Jerusalem,* London, 1951, pp. 100–102.
4. Oliphant, Laurence, *Haifa or Life in Modern Palestine,* New York, 1887, pp. 317–318.
5. Haas, N., "Anthropological Observations on the Skeletal Remains from Giv'at ha-Mivtar," *Israel Exploration Journal,* Vol. 20 (1970), pp. 38–59.
6. Finley, John, *A Pilgrim in Palestine,* New York, 1919, p. ix.

7. Fabri, Felix, *The Book of Wanderings of Brother Felix Fabri,* translated from the Latin by Aubrey Stewart, in *Palestine Pilgrims' Text Society,* London, 1896, Vol. 9, p. 262.

8. Thackeray, William Makepeace, *Notes of a Journey from Cornhill to Grand Cairo,* London, 1846, p. 157.

9. Besant, Walter, and E. H. Palmer, *Jerusalem, The City of Herod and Saladin,* London, 1889, pp. 207–209.

10. Rix, Herbert, *Tent and Testament,* New York, 1907, p. 233.

11. Mackenzie, Agnes Mure, *Robert Bruce, King of Scots,* Edinburgh, 1956, pp. 358–359.

12. Scottish Pilgrims to the Holy Land" in *The Innis Review,* Vol. 20 (1904), Glasgow, pp. 104–105.

13. Martens, A., D. F. M., *Who Was a Christian in the Holy Land,* Jerusalem, 1924, p. 342.

14. Finley, John, *A Pilgrimage in Palestine,* New York, 1919, p. 99.

15. Stewart, Robert Walter, *The Tent and the Khan,* Edinburgh, 1857, p. 315.

16. Finn, James, *Stirring Times,* London, 1878, Vol. 1, pp. 175–176.

17. Haggard, A. Rider, *A Winter Pilgrimage,* London, 1908, pp. 297–298. For an account of Jerusalem's water problem, see pp. 67–71.

18. Jowett, William, *Christian Researches in Syria and the Holy Land,* London, 1826, pp. 232–234.

19. Pierotti, Ermete, *Customs and Traditions of Palestine,* London, 1864, pp. 88–90.

20. Baron, Salo W., *A Social and Religious History of the Jews,* New York, 1952, Vol. 2, p. 329. For theories regarding Napoleon's motivations in regard to his declaration see *Napoleon and the Jews* by Franz Kobler, New York, 1976. Also *Napoleon and Palestine* by Philip Guedalla, London, 1925.

21. Guedalla, Philip, *Napoleon and Palestine,* London, 1925, p. 31.

22. Finn, Elizabeth Anne, *Reminiscences of Mrs. Finn,* London, 1929, p. 50.

23. Gillman, Henry, *Hassan: A Fellah,* Boston, 1898, p. 214.

24. Nugent, Lord, *Lands, Classical and Sacred,* London, 1845, pp. 127–128.

25. Spencer, J. A., *The East: Sketches of Travels in Egypt and the Holy Land,* London, 1850, pp. 269–270.

26. Taylor, Bayard, *The Lands of the Saracen,* New York, 1859, pp. 77–78.

27. Harper, Henry A., *An Artist's Walks in Bible Lands,* London, 1901, p. 27.

28. Patai, Raphael (ed.), *The Complete Diaries of Theodor Herzl,* London, 1960, Vol. 2, p. 746.

29. Paassen, Pierre van, *Days of Our Years,* New York, 1940, p. 355.

Chapter Two

1. These synagogues are no longer in existence. They were demolished by the Arabs during the nineteen years (1948–1967) when the Old City was under Jordanian occupation.

2. Saulcy, F. de, *Narrative of a Journey Round the Dead Sea and in the Bible Lands,* London, 1854, Vol. 2, p. 218.

3. Schaff, Philip, *Through Bible Lands,* London, 1878, p. 271.

4. *Midrash Tanhuma, Kedoshim*

5. Quoted in *Walks In and Around Jerusalem* by J. E. Hanauer, London, 1926, p. 108.

6. Smith, George Adam, *The Historical Geography of the Holy Land,* London, 1931, pp. 318–319.

7. Halsted, Rev. Thomas D., *Our Mission,* London, 1866, p. 160.

8. Curtis, George William, *The Howadji in Syria,* New York, 1852, p. 156.

9. *Midrash Rabbah, Naso*

10. Dixon, William Hepworth, *The Holy Land,* Leipzig, 1865, Vol. 2, p. 3.

11. Twain, Mark, *The Innocents Abroad,* New York, 1869, p. 298.

12. Blyth, Estelle, *When We Lived in Jerusalem,* London, 1927, p. 39.

13. Warren, Charles, *Underground Jerusalem,* London, 1876, p. 522.

14. Holmes, John Haynes, *Palestine Today and Tomorrow,* New York, 1929, pp. 12–13.

15. Sumner, Mary Elizabeth, *Our Holiday in the East,* London, 1882, p. 144.

16. Farmer, Leslie, *We Saw the Holy City,* London, 1944, p. 85.

17. Barclay, J. T., *The City of the Great King,* Philadelphia, 1857, pp. 482–483.

18. Vester, Bertha Spafford, *Our Jerusalem,* London, 1951, p. 86.

19. Bellow, Saul, *To Jerusalem and Back,* New York, 1976, p. 39.

20. Patai, Raphael, *The Complete Diaries of Theodor Herzl,* London, 1960, Vol. 2, p. 753.

21. Josephus, *The Jewish War,* VII, 1:1.

22. Whaley, Thomas, *Buck Whaley's Memoirs,* London, 1906, p. 212.

23. See pp. 17–20.

24. Robinson, Edward and E. Smith, *Biblical Research in Palestine, Mount Sinai and Arabia Petraea,* London, 1841, Vol. 1, pp. 506–507.

25. Wilson, Charles and Claude R. Conder, *The Survey of Western Palestine: Jerusalem,* London, 1884, p. 336.

26. Andrews, Fannie Fern, *The Holy Land Under Mandate,* Boston, 1931, Vol. 1, p. 17.

27. *Canon Pietro Casila's Pilgrimage to Jerusalem in 1494,* translated by M. Margaret Newett, Manchester, 1907, p. 248.

28. Excavations of the site of Bethesda have yielded no trace of the five stoas mentioned in the Bible. Some archaeologists identify the Bethesda Pool with a cave east of the traditional site. "Water of a small stream collects in this cave, and because of its reddish hue was considered to have healing powers."

29. Finley, John, *A Pilgrim in Palestine,* New York, 1919, pp. 227–228.

30. Goodrich-Freer, A., *Inner Jerusalem,* London, 1904, pp. 365–366.

31. Thomson, Andrew, *In the Holy Land,* London, 1886, pp. 114–115.

32. Porter, J. L., *The Giant Cities of Bashan and Syria's Holy Places,* London, 1868, pp. 145–146.

33. Barclay, J. T., *The City of the Great King,* Philadelphia, 1857, p. 455.

34. Twain, Mark, *The Innocents Abroad,* New York, 1869, pp. 298–299.

35. Curtis, George William, *The Howadji in Syria,* New York, 1852, pp. 166–167.

36. Hanauer, J. E., *Walks In and About Jerusalem,* London, 1926, pp. 147–148.

37. Lynch, W. F., *Narrative of the United States Expedition to the River Jordan and the Dead Sea,* Philadelphia, 1849, pp. 404–405.

38. Wylie, Rev. J. A., *Over the Holy Land,* London, 1883, p. 97.

39. Blyth, Estelle, *When We Lived in Jerusalem,* London, 1927, pp. 210–211.

40. Bellow, Saul, *To Jerusalem and Back,* New York, 1976, p. 10.

41. Twain, Mark, *The Innocents Abroad,* New York, 1869, p. 297.

42. Scholem, Gershom, *From Berlin to Jerusalem,* New York, 1980, p. 167.

43. Warren, Charles, *Underground Jerusalem,* London, 1876, pp. 44–45.

44. See also "Sir Ronald Storr's Legacy to Jerusalem" on the matter of the mandatory use of stone as building material of houses, p. 48.

45. Smith, George Adam, *Jerusalem,* London, 1907, Vol. 1, p. 24.

46. Twain, Mark, *The Innocents Abroad*, New York, 1869, p. 298.

47. *Tosefta, Sanhedrin* 13:2.

48. *Yad, Teshuvah* 3:5.

49. *Christian News from Israel*, Vol. 25 (1975), No. 2 p. 100.

50. *Ibid.*, pp. 100–101.

51. Wallace, Edwin Sherman, *Jerusalem the Holy*, London, 1898, pp. 77–78.

52. Paassen, Pierre van, *Days of Our Years*, New York, 1940, pp. 355–356.

53. Finley, John, *A Pilgrim in Palestine*, New York, 1919, p. 50.

54. Holmes, John Haynes, *Palestine Today and Tomorrow*, New York, 1929, pp. 55–56.

55. Bonar, Horatius, *Days and Nights in the East*, London, 1866, p. 234.

56. Josephus, *Jewish Antiquities*, London, 1963, Book XV, 122f.

57. Vester, Bertha Spafford, *Our Jerusalem*, London, 1951, p. 323.

Chapter Three

1. Baedeker, Karl, *Handbook for Travellers: Jerusalem and Its Surroundings*, London, 1876, p. 68.

2. Black, Archibald Pollak, *A Hundred Days in the East*, London, 1865, p. 133.

3. This evil was eliminated by Moses Montefiore who had the Wall built up to a level higher than the platform above that made it difficult to throw things down on the heads of the worshipers.

4. After the Jordanians annexed the Old City of Jerusalem and the territory west of the Jordan River, the name Transjordan was changed to Jordan.

5. *Christian News from Israel*, Vol. 20 (1967), Nos. 3–4, pp. 16–17.

6. Marshall, Eric, and Stuart Hample, *Children's Letters to God*, New York, 1966.

7. Ashworth, John, *Walks in Canaan*, Manchester, 1869, p. 72.

8. Warren, Charles, *Underground Jerusalem*, London, 1876, pp. 367–368.

9. *Christian News from Israel*, Vol. 25 (1975), No. 2, p. 107.

10. Warren, Charles, *Underground Jerusalem*, London, 1876, pp. 374–377.

11. Clarke, Edward D., *Travels in Various Countries of Europe, Asia, and Africa*, London, 1812, Vol. 2, p. 591.

12. See pp. 102–103.

13. Bovet, Felix, *Egypt, Palestine, and Phoenicia: A Visit to Sacred Lands*, Trans. from the French by W.H. Lyttelton, London, 1882, pp. 227–228.

14. For the story of that strange village see pp. 71–73.

15. *Midrash Rabbah, Numbers* 15:13.

16. For a discussion of the Temple vessels see: "The Vessels and Furniture of the Temple of Jerusalem" in *Walks In and Around Jerusalem*, by J. E. Hanauer, London, 1926, pp. 400–407.

17. Johnson, Sarah Barclay, *Hadji in Syria*, London, 1858, pp. 98–100.

18. Thomson, W. M., *The Land and the Book*, London, 1905, p. 638.

19. *Ibid.*, p. 100.

20. Wallace, Edwin Sherman, *Jerusalem the Holy*, London, 1898, p. 228.

21. Pierotti, Ermete, *Customs and Traditions of Palestine*, London, 1864, pp. 76–77.

22. Finn, James, *Stirring Times*, London, 1878, Vol. 1, pp. 117–118.

23. Beaumont, William, *Diary of a Journey to the East*, London, 1856, Vol. 1, p. 198.

24. Wilhelm, Kurt, *Roads to Zion,* New York, 1948, pp. 76–77.

25. Finn, James, *Stirring Times,* London, 1878, Vol. 2, pp. 462–464.

26. The above history of the Hurvah is based on the excellent account in Shimon Ben-Eliezer's *Destruction and Renewal: The Synagogues of the Jewish Quarter,* Jerusalem, 1973, pp. 20–27.

27. Readers interested in a brief yet authoritative exposition of the esoteric subject of the Kabbalah should read the classic article on "Cabala" by Louis Ginzberg in *The Jewish Encyclopedia,* Vol. 3, pp. 459–479.

28. Ben-Eliezer, Shimon, *Destruction and Renewal: The Synagogues of the Jewish Quarter,* Jerusalem, 1973, pp. 28–29.

29. *Ibid.,* pp. 29–30.

30. Hanauer, J. E., *Walks In and About Jerusalem,* London, 1926, pp. 36–37.

31. Pausanias, *Description of Greece* (trans. by W. H. S. Jones), Cambridge, Mass., 1939, Vol. 3, Book 8, pp. 427, 429.

32. Macleod, Norman, *Eastward,* London, 1866, pp. 184–185.

33. Oesterreicher, John M. and Anne Sinai, *Jerusalem,* New York, 1974, p. 251.

34. *Aliyah* means, literally, "going up." Traveling to or settling in the Holy Land is termed "going up" by the Jews. Inside Israel, traveling to or settling in Jerusalem is also considered "making *aliyah.*"

35. Finn, James, *Stirring Times,* London, 1878, Vol. 2, p. 527.

36. Olin, Stephen, *Travels in Egypt, Arabia Petraea and the Holy Land,* New York, 1844, Vol. 2, p. 147.

37. Châteaubriand, François René de, *Travels to Jerusalem and the Holy Land,* London, Vol. 2, part 4, p. 161.

Chapter Four

1. By the grace of the Greek Orthodox Church, the Anglican Church holds services in the chapel of Adam, which is below the Chapel of Calvary.

2. Ashbee, Charles Robert, *A Palestine Notebook, 1918–1923,* London, 1923, pp. 2–3.

3. Madden, R. R., *Travels in Turkey, Egypt, and Palestine,* Vol. 2, London, 1829, pp. 342–343.

4. Skinner, Thomas, *Adventures During a Journey Overland to India by Way of Egypt, Syria, and the Holy Land,* London, 1837, pp. 230–231.

5. Curzon, Robert, *Visits to Monasteries in the Levant,* London, 1849, pp. 209–219, 223.

6. Wilde, W. R., *Narrative of a Voyage,* Dublin, 1840, Vol. II, p. 214.

7. Goodrich-Freer, A., *Inner Jerusalem,* London, 1904, p. 152.

8. Finn, Elizabeth Anne, *Reminiscences of Mrs. Finn,* London, 1929, p. 57.

9. Prime, William C., *Tent Life in the Holy Land,* New York, 1857, pp. 145–147.

10. Robinson, Edward, and E. Smith, *Biblical Researches in Palestine, Mount Sinai and Arabia Petraea,* London, 1841, Vol. 2, p. 80.

11. Schaff, Philip, *Through Bible Lands,* London, 1878, pp. 268–269.

12. Bonar, Horatius, *Days and Nights in the East,* London, 1886, pp. 234–235.

13. Kenyon, Kathleen M., *Jerusalem: Excavating 3000 Years of History,* London, 1967, p. 154.

14. Farmer, Leslie, *We Saw the Holy City,* London, 1944, p. 147.

15. Conder, Col. C. R., *The City of Jerusalem,* London, 1909, p. 8.

16. Oliphant, Laurence, *Haifa or Life in Modern Palestine,* New York, 1887, pp. 313–314.

17. Ashbee, Charles Robert, *A Palestine Notebook, 1918–1923,* London, 1923, pp. 1, 3.

18. Fosdick, Harry Emerson, *A Pilgrimage to Palestine,* New York, 1927, p. 266.

19. Finn, James, *Stirring Times,* Vol. 2, London, 1878, p. 458.

20. Madden, R. R., *Travels in Turkey, Egypt and Palestine,* Vol. 2, London, 1829, pp. 329, 331–332.

21. Finley, John, *A Pilgrim in Palestine,* New York, 1919, pp. 244–245.

22. Thomson, W. M., *The Land and the Book,* London, 1905, pp. 663–664.

23. Finley, John, *A Pilgrim in Palestine,* New York, 1919, p. 56.

24. Van Dyke, Henry, *Out-of-Doors in the Holy Land,* London, 1908, pp. 76, 78.

25. Rhodes, Albert, *Jerusalem as It Is,* London, 1865, pp. 206–209.

26. Thomson, W. M., *The Land and the Book,* London, 1905, p. 663.

27. *Ibid.*

28. Burton, Isabel, *The Inner Life of Syria, Palestine, and the Holy Land,* Vol. 2, London, 1876, p. 111.

29. *Christian News from Israel,* Vol. 27 (1980), No. 3, p. 137.

30. *Ibid.*

31. Many embassies have subsequently returned.

32. The wretched existence of the Ethiopians in Jerusalem during the mid-nineteenth century is described by James Finn in his *Stirring Times,* Vol. 2, London, 1878, pp. 272–281.

33. See Ezek. 1:15.

34. Châteaubriand, François René de, *Travels to Jerusalem and the Holy Land,* Vol. 2, London, 1835, pp. 156–157.

35. Thomson, Charles, *The Travels of the Late Charles Thomson,* Vol. 3, London, 1744, pp. 182, 183–184.

36. Blyth, Estelle, *When We Lived in Jerusalem,* London, 1927, pp. 317–318.

Chapter Five

1. Some archaeologists claim that Solomon's Temple and its successors were built on the spot where now stands the small cupola that Moslems call the Dome of the Tablets, which stands about 330 feet to the northwest of the Dome of the Rock. For a well-documented presentation of this thesis, see "Where the Ancient Temple of Jerusalem Stood," by Asher S. Kaufman in *Biblical Archaeology Review,* Vol. 9, No. 2 (March-April 1983), pp. 41–59.

2. Blyth, Estelle, *When We Lived in Jerusalem,* London, 1927, p. 40.

3. One may add that many inscriptions in the Dome of the Rock are anti-Christian. See pp. 29–30.

4. Stanley, Arthur Penrhyn, *Sinai and Palestine,* London, 1857, pp. 168–169.

5. Wilson, Charles W., *Jerusalem, the Holy City,* London, 1888, p. 60.

6. *Ibid.,* pp. 56–57.

7. See note in this chapter.

8. Rix, Herbert, *Tent and Testament,* New York, 1907, p. 230.

9. Goodrich-Freer, A., *Inner Jerusalem,* London, 1904, pp. 224–225.

10. Prime, William C., *Tent Life in the Holy Land,* New York, 1857, pp. 184–185.

11. Hanauer, J. E., *Walks In and Around Jerusalem,* London, 1926, p. 236.

12. Melville, Herman, *Clarel,* Vol. 1, New York, 1876, p. 96.

13. Farmer, Leslie, *We Saw the Holy City,* London, 1944, pp. 99–100.

14. Rhodes, Albert, *Jerusalem as It Is,* London, 1865, pp. 236–237.

15. Egmont, J. Aegidius Van, *Travels Through Part of Europe, Asia Minor, etc.,* Vol. 1, London, 1759, p. 308.

16. Bonar, Horatius, *Days and Nights in the East,* London, 1866, pp. 22–23.

17. Fabri, Felix, *The Book of Wanderings of Brother Felix Fabri,* trans. from the Latin by Aubrey Stewart in *Palestine Pilgrims' Text Society,* Vol. 9, London, 1896, pp. 259–260.

18. Warren, Charles, *Underground Jerusalem,* London, 1876, pp. 347–348.

19. J. Aegidius Van Egmont in his *Travels* (Vol. 1, London, 1759, p. 345) states that "others, with more probability, derive it [the grave of *Nebi Moussa*] from a Turkish saint of that name, who resided near the Dead Sea."

20. Wiley, J. R., *Over the Holy Land,* London, 1883, pp. 370–375.

21. Harper, Henry A., *Walks in Palestine,* London, 1888, pp. 30–31.

22. Vester, Bertha Spafford, *Our Jerusalem,* London, 1951, p. 121.

23. Finn, Elizabeth Anne, *A Third Year in Jerusalem,* London, 1869, p. 24.

24. Andrews, Fannie Fern, *The Holy Land Under Mandate,* Vol. 1, Boston and New York, 1931, p. 165.

25. Pierotti, Ermete, *Customs and Traditions of Palestine,* Cambridge, 1864, pp. 70–72.

26. Oliphant, F. R., *Notes of a Pilgrimage to Jerusalem and the Holy Land,* London, 1891, p. 51.

27. Johnson, Sarah Barclay, *Hadji in Syria,* London, 1858, pp. 71–72.

28. Gidal, Nachum, T., *Eternal Jerusalem, 1840–1917,* Jerusalem, unpaginated.

29. *Vayikra Rabbah,* 13:2.

30. Lamartine, Alphonse de, *Recollections of the East,* translated from the French by Thomas Phipson, London, n.d., pp. 333–334.

Chapter Six

1. Bovet, Felix, *Egypt, Palestine, and Phoenicia: A Visit to Sacred Lands,* London, 1882, p. 113.

2. Bonar, Horatius, *Days and Nights in the East,* London, 1866, pp. 181–182.

3. Quoted in *Jewish Travellers,* by Elkan N. Adler, London, 1930, p. 189.

4. *Ibid.,* p. 234.

5. Conder, Claude R., *Tent Work in Palestine,* Vol. 2, London, 1878, pp. 297–300.

6. Chesterton, G. K., *The New Jerusalem,* London, 1920, pp. 56–58.

7. Johnson, Sarah Barclay, *Hadji in Syria,* London, 1858, p. 59.

8. Phelps, S. D., *Holy Land with Glimpses of Europe and Egypt,* New York, 1877, p. 312.

9. Bonar, Horatius, *Days and Nights in the East,* London, 1864, p. 264.

10. Thackeray, William Makepeace, *From Cornhill to Grand Cairo,* London, 1869, pp. 465–466.

11. Boddy, Alexander A., *Days in Galilee and Scenes in Judaea,* London, 1900, pp. 326–327.

12. Olin, Stephen, *Travels in Egypt, Arabia Petraea and the Holy Land,* Vol. 2, New York, 1844, p. 302.

13. Wallace, Edwin Sherman, *Jerusalem the Holy,* London, 1898, p. 192.

14. Fabri, Felix, *Palestine Pilgrims' Text Society,* Vol. 9, "The Wanderings of Felix Fabri," Vol. 2 (Part 1), London, 1897, pp. 90–91.

15. *Ibid.,* Vol. 1 (Part 1), p. 319.

16. Haggard, H. Rider, *A Winter Pilgrimage,* London, 1908, p. 347.

17. Indinopulos, Thomas A., "Jerusalem the Blessed: The Shrine of Three Faiths," in *The Christian Century,* April 12, 1978.

18. See Besant, Walter, and Palmer, E. H., *Jerusalem: The City of Herod and Saladin,* London, 1880, p. 434.

19. Stephens, J. L., *Incidents of Travel in Egypt, Arabia Petraea, and the Holy Land,* in *The Universal Library: Voyages and Travel,* London, 1853, p. 377.

20. Morris, Robert, *Freemasonry in the Holy Land,* New York, 1872, pp. 373–374.

21. Vester, Bertha Spafford, *Our Jerusalem,* London, 1951, p. 130.

22. Storrs, Ronald, "Introduction" to *Our Jerusalem, Ibid.,* p. 6.

23. Bonar, Andrew, and M'Cheyne, R. M., *Narrative of a Mission of Inquiry to the Jews from the Church of Scotland,* London, 1845, pp. 146–147.

24. Blyth, Estelle, *When We Lived in Jerusalem,* London, 1927, pp. 230–231.

25. Thackeray, William Makepeace, *Notes of a Journey from Cornhill to Grand Cairo,* London, 1846, p. 151.

26. Melville, Herman, *Journal of a Visit to Europe and the Levant — Oct. 11, 1856–May 6, 1857,* Princeton, 1955, pp. 155–156.

27. Taylor, Bayard, *The Lands of the Saracen,* New York, 1859, p. 78.

28. Goodrich-Freer, A., *Inner Jerusalem,* London, 1904, pp. 68–70.

29. Cresson, Warder, *David the True Messiah,* Philadelphia, 1952, pp. 204–206.

30. For a concise summary of the "trial for lunacy," see *Pennsylvania Magazine of History and Biography,* April 1, 1971, pp. 174–182.

31. See Karp, Abraham, J., "The Zionism of Warder Cresson," in *Early Zionism in America,* edited by Isidore S. Meyer, New York, 1958, pp. 1–20.

32. Stewart, Robert Walter, *The Tent and the Khan,* Edinburgh, 1857, p. 306.

33. Monk, H. Wentworth, *A Simple Interpretation of Revelation,* London, 1859, p. 189.

34. Besant, Walter, and Palmer, E. H., *Jerusalem, the City of Herod and Saladin,* London, 1908, p. 434.

35. Smith, James, *A Pilgrimage to Palestine,* Aberdeen, 1895, p. 85.

36. Oliphant, F. R., *Notes of a Pilgrimage to Jerusalem and the Holy Land,* London, 1891, p. 55.

37. A good account of the American Colony's religious commitments and activities is found in *Inner Jerusalem,* by A. Goodrich-Freer, London, 1904, pp. 42–45.

38. For an account of the persecutions and the vindication of the American Colony, see *Our Jerusalem* by Bertha Spafford Vester, London, 1951, pp. 212–223.

39. Conder, Claude R., *Tent Work in Palestine,* Vol. 2, London, 1878, p. 309.

40. Teshima, Ikuro, *Original Gospel Faith,* Tokyo, 1970, p. 158.

41. For a brief but meticulous statement on the Makuya, their history, theology, and religious activities, see "Makuya: Christian Zionists from the Land of the Rising Sun," by Sylvia L. Mehlman, in *Christian News from Israel,* Vol. 27 (1982), No. 4, pp. 158–161.

42. Twain, Mark, *The Innocents Abroad,* Vol. 2, New York, 1869, pp. 319–322.

43. For a scholarly and insightful discussion of the saga of the Wandering Jew, see *Curious Myths of the Middle Ages,* by Sabine Baring-Gould, New York, 1978, pp. 1–25.

Chapter Seven

1. Finn, James, *Stirring Times,* Vol. 1, London, 1878, p. 106.

2. Finn, Elizabeth Anne, *Reminiscences of Mrs. Finn,* London, 1929, pp. 246–248.

3. See pp. 42–43.

4. "Afterword" by Lloyd George to Philip Guedalla's lecture on "Napoleon and Palestine," London, 1925, pp. 47–51.

5. Gilbert, Vivian, *The Romance of the Last Crusade: With Allenby to Jerusalem,* New York, 1927, pp. 163–170. See also *With Allenby in the Holy Land,* by Lowell Thomas, London, 1938, pp. 122–125.

6. Broadhurst, Joseph F., *From Vine Street to Jerusalem,* London, 1936, pp. 138–139.

7. Quoted by Fannie Fern Andrews in *The Holy Land Under Mandate,* Vol. 2, Boston, 1931, p. 229.

8. *Ibid.,* p. 239.

9. Farmer, Leslie, *We Saw the Holy City,* London, 1944, pp. 218, 221.

10. Prittie, Terence, "Jerusalem Under the Mandate," in *Jerusalem,* edited by John M. Oesterreicher and Anne Sinai, New York, 1974, p. 60.

11. *Ibid.*

12. *Ibid.*

13. Nasir-I-Khusrau, *Diary of a Journey Through Syria and Palestine,* translated from the Persian by Guy Le Strange, in *Palestine Pilgrim's Text Society,* Vol. 4, London, 1893, p. 48.

Chapter Eight

1. St. John, Robert, *Shalom Means Peace,* New York, 1949, pp. 81–82.

2. Gray, John, *A History of Jerusalem,* London, 1969, pp. 310–311.

3. Halkin, Hillel, "Building Jerusalem," in *Commentary,* September 1971, p. 61.

4. Storrs, Ronald, *Memoirs of Sir Ronald Storrs,* New York, 1937, p. 329.

5. Gur, Mordecai, "The Temple Mount Is in Our Hands," in *The Jerusalem Post Magazine,* Translated from the Hebrew by Moshe Kohn, April 19, 1974.

6. Raymist, Malka, "Pilgrimage Under Curfew," in *The Jerusalem Post,* August 3, 1984, p. 13.

7. Wallace, Edwin Sherman, *Jerusalem the Holy,* London, 1898, pp. 84–85.

8. Paassen, Pierre van, *Days of Our Years,* New York, 1940, p. 355.

9. Gibbon, Edward, *The Decline and Fall of the Roman Empire,* Vol. 2, Chicago, 1952, p. 400.

10. Serao, Matilde, *In the Country of Jesus,* translated from the Italian by Richard Davey, London, 1905, pp. 75, 77.

11. Van Dyke, Henry, *Out-of-Doors in the Holy Land,* London, 1908, pp. 49–50.

12. Storrs, Ronald, *Orientations,* London, 1937, p. 454.

13. Kook, Abraham Isaac, "The Banner of Jerusalem," Jerusalem, n.d., p. 5.

Chapter Nine

1. Hanauer, J. E., *Walks In and Around Jerusalem,* London, 1926, pp. 78–79. References to the tomb of Sir Philip D'Aubigny are also to be found in Herbert Ham's *My Pilgrimage to Jerusalem in December, 1899,* London, 1961, pp. 30–31, and in Fannie Fern Andrews's *The Holy Land Under Mandate,* Vol. 1, Boston, 1931, pp. 166–167.

2. Wallace, Edwin Sherman, *Jerusalem the Holy,* London, 1898, p. 228.

3. Morris, Robert, *Freemasonry in the Holy Land,* New York, 1872, pp. 463, 465.

4. For a fuller description of Jerusalem's Masonic Hall see *The Mountain of the Lord,* by Benjamin Mazar, New York, 1975, pp. 219–220.

5. *Christian News from Israel,* Vol. 1 (1959), No. 7, p. 5.

6. Schick, B. C., "Aceldama," in *Palestine Exploration Fund,* London, 1892, p. 288.

7. Lithgow, William, *The Totall Discourse of the Rare Adventures and Painfull Peregrinations of William Lithgow,* Glasgow, 1906, p. 250.

8. Thackeray, William Makepeace, *Notes of a Journey from Cornhill to Grand Cairo,* London, 1846, p. 155.

9. Olin, Stephen, *Travels in Egypt, Arabia Petraea and the Holy Land,* Vol. 2, New York, 1844, p. 159.

10. Pococke, Richard, *A Description of the East and Some Other Countries,* Vol. 2, London, 1745, p. 25.

11. Egmont, J. Aegidius Van, *Travels, etc.,* Vol. 1, London, 1759, pp. 392–393.

12. Barclay, J. T., *The City of the Great King,* Philadelphia, 1856, pp. 208–212.

13. The Julian calendar is also followed by the Armenians, but their Christmas is observed on Epiphany, the traditional date of Jesus' baptism, which falls on January 6, corresponding to January 19 in the Gregorian calendar. This accounts for the third Christmas celebration in Jerusalem.

14. Leeder, S. H., *Modern Sons of the Pharaohs,* London, 1918, p. 66f.

15. See *The Rest of the Words of Baruch,* by J. Rendel Harris, London, 1889.

16. Vester, Bertha Spafford, *Our Jerusalem,* London, 1951, pp. 332–333.

17. Blyth, Estelle, *When We Lived in Jerusalem,* London, 1927, p. 21.

Index

Note: Page numbers followed by il denote illustrations.